Major Writers

of

Early American Literature

Everett Emerson

EDITOR

The University of Wisconsin Press

Published 1972
The University of Wisconsin Press
Box 1379, Madison, Wisconsin 53701

The University of Wisconsin Press, Ltd.
70 Great Russell Street, London

Printings 1972, 1973

Printed in the United States of America

ISBN 0-299-06190-6, LC 72-1378

Contents

*Major Writers of
Early American Literature*

Introduction

Major Writers of Early American Literature provides a fresh appraisal of the most important authors of seventeenth- and eighteenth-century America. Although knowledge of early American literature has been greatly widened and deepened in recent years, the standard study of this literature is nearly a hundred years old. It is time for a new study, which will take into account the modern reader as well as such recent findings as the discovery only a generation ago of America's best early poet.

The serious study of early American literature began with the work of Moses Coit Tyler, who in 1878 published his *History of American Literature, 1607–1765,* and in 1897 *The Literary History of the American Revolution.* These two classics, frequently reprinted, made such an immense advance in the scholarly appraisal of the period that they satisfied the needs of students of American literature for many years. The foremost student of early American literature since Tyler, Perry Miller (1905–63), was primarily an intellectual historian. His best books are brilliant studies of New England Puritanism. Significant contributions have been made by Louis B. Wright, Kenneth Murdock, and Howard Mumford Jones, the latter two being Miller's colleagues at Harvard. But only in the last few years has there been a conscious effort by a body of scholars to undertake a serious and continuing study of the first two centuries of American literature. One can even date this emergence: it was in 1966 that a journal, *Early American Literature,* was created to serve as a vehicle for the new studies. *Major Writers of Early American Literature* is among the first fruits of this new interest.

The writers examined in this volume are not the only significant early American authors, and doubtless some readers will miss a favorite writer here—Captain John Smith, perhaps, or Crèvecoeur, or Tom Paine. This study is based on the premise that a thorough investigation of a few undeniably important authors is more valuable than a survey that attempts to cope with the whole range of early American literature. The authors whose writings and intellectual concerns are analyzed here have been known to most readers at best as historical personages or as names represented in an anthology by a few pages from their writings. Except for Benjamin Franklin, Edward Taylor, and perhaps Jonathan Edwards, they are known even to advanced students of American literature in a casual way. Thus it has been possible for a person who would agree that a wide reading in Mark Twain's other writings is indispensable for an understanding of *Huckleberry Finn* to expound on the Puritan tradition with only the most limited knowledge of any Puritan writer. It would seem a truism that a discussion of Hawthorne's relationship with Puritanism ought to be undertaken only by one who knows a Puritan when he sees one, but a nodding acquaintance with our earliest literature has too often been all that students of American literature could claim.

The appeals of early American literature are to be found both in the works themselves and in the circumstances surrounding their creation. One can admire not only Franklin's *Autobiography*, the masterpiece of the period, but also the other works with which this book is concerned, strictly on their literary merits. The literature of early America has an appeal also because it is just that: the earliest literature in English produced in what is now the United States. Perhaps the most striking feature of the careers of our earliest writers is that they did not center on literature. Bradford was the leader of his little colony, Anne Bradstreet a housewife who stole hours from sleep for writing; Taylor, Mather, and Edwards were ministers, Franklin a printer until he decided to devote himself to public service; and Byrd was a businessman and colonial official. Charles Brockden Brown and Philip Freneau are the only writers considered here who can be said to have devoted themselves to *belles-lettres*, and the times made it impossible for them to have rewarding literary careers.

In addition, the America that produced this literature was a small area with a very small population, by modern standards at least. The whole of New England contained only about 106,000 people in 1700, with Virginia and Maryland having together a comparable population. The thirteen colonies had about half a million whites in 1700; more than twenty-five American cities each have as many people today. Virginia had no commercial centers, and Boston was the largest town in the colonies, with a total of some seven thousand people. But within this cluster of colonies were to be found both surprising variety and striking literary phenomena. In New England, where that complex attitude known as Puritanism was long dominant, an effective woman poet was to be found. (What other women poets, contemporary with Milton or earlier, come to mind from the riches of English literature?) A few years later, in a frontier town in western Massachusetts, a prolific metaphysical poet flourished, well after the metaphysical school had died in England. Not thirty miles away at the time of Edward Taylor's death, Jonathan Edwards was beginning a career that would bring him an international reputation and win him a permanent place in the history of Christian thought. In the middle colonies lived Edwards's contemporary Benjamin Franklin, one of the very greatest men of his day in the opinion of his fellows, both at home and in the salons of Paris. In Virginia was William Byrd, who had made friends with the most prominent English playwrights of his day some years before he wrote his witty and sophisticated account of his frontier adventures, perhaps for the eyes of his old London associates. The world of early American literature is both thoroughly provincial and quite cosmopolitan.

The quality of this literature that most deserves comment is its intellectualism. Although it is easy to make Cotton Mather out to have been a fool, to look at the extent of his correspondence is to recognize how intimately he identified himself with the learned world. He corresponded with Newton, Defoe, several Scottish ministers and educators (he held an honorary doctorate from Glasgow University), the Royal Society (of which he was a member), and German pietists. Despite Edward Taylor's location on the frontier, he too was an intellectual, as the learning and wit of his poetry shows. Nearly a hundred years later Charles Brockden Brown grew up in a family in which current ideas, especially political and social ones, were a great concern, and his books reveal a continuing interest in new radical and rationalist ideas. Philip Freneau steeped himself in contemporary French radical thought and did much to popularize it in America. Edwards's intellectualism is obvious, and even William Bradford, largely self-educated and the owner of only eighty books, was deeply devoted to learning.

This intellectualism is hardly to be expected. In a new land where practical skills were a necessity for survival, more predictable would have been the kind of society described in Mark Twain's *Roughing It.* Instead, there was a surprising preoccupation with books and learning. The number of books produced by New England divines is staggering: John Cotton wrote over thirty, Thomas Hooker twenty; Cotton Mather had over four hundred publications. The cultural richness of colonial Virginia and Maryland is only now beginning to be appreciated, with the rediscovery of poets such as Richard

Lewis and Colonel Robert Bolling. In fact, significant discoveries continue to be made, and even though another poet of Edward Taylor's stature is unlikely to emerge, it will nevertheless be many years before a comprehensive appraisal of early American poetry can be made.

Another quality of this early literature that should be noted is its originality. While the works of Freneau and Brown can be related easily to the English literature of the day, Brown put new wine into the slightly used bottles he found, and the earlier writers were strikingly innovative. Franklin began by imitating older writers, including Addison, but he soon discovered his own authentic voice. Taylor wrote in the metaphysical tradition, but his bold use of homely household imagery and the intensity of his Puritan passion make his verse unique. William Byrd may have been addressing a London audience in his account of the border survey between Virginia and North Carolina, but he was not simply an imitator of Augustan writers. Jonathan Edwards identified himself with the Calvinist tradition, but his use of the new psychology and his recognition of the role of the "heart" in the process of conversion make such works as his *Personal Narrative* and his treatise on the *Religious Affections* truly innovative. The uniqueness of Cotton Mather needs no arguing: among the baroque styles of the seventeeth century, the exoticism of the *Magnalia* is without precedent. The great bulk of early American literature is purposeful, not creative, for the creation of a rich literary culture requires more leisure than the colonists possessed. But here and there, in the Chesapeake Bay area in the mid-eighteenth century and in an occasional New England village, new and memorable voices were speaking.

Much early American literature is preoccupied with America, though the colonists read, in the main, English books. During the period 1783–1837 there was a conscious concern with the creation of a native American literature as the nation began its life of independence. But earlier American literature, though often provincial and countrified, is rarely colonial in the sense of being dependent on its mother country. From its beginnings the Massachusetts Bay colony asserted its independence and created radically new institutions in church and state, and the English Civil War and its aftermath made it difficult for New Englanders to regard England as home. After Massachusetts was granted a new charter in 1691, the first royal governor was a native son of New England, Sir William Phips, who is duly celebrated in Cotton Mather's epic *Mag-*

nalia. In the middle colonies the presence of such religious, national, and seminational groups as the Quakers, the Catholics, the Dutch, the Germans, the Welsh, and the Scotch-Irish made it difficult for the settlers to feel a strong sense of allegiance to England. Virginians have usually been considered the most colonial of the early Americans, but, as Daniel Boorstin has shown in *The Americans: The Colonial Experience* (1958), they were thoroughly preoccupied with their own local interests. They were not Americans or Englishmen; they were Virginians. Georgia of all the colonies best fits the concept of a *colony,* but neither Georgia nor the Carolinas made significant contributions to early American culture.

Interest in America, its landscape, its people (especially the Indians), and its developing traditions can be found as early as Captain John Smith's *True Relation* (1608). The concern with America is in Jefferson's *Notes on the State of Virginia* (1782), his only book; in Crèvecoeur's *Letters from an American Farmer* (1782); in the American Gothic novels of Brown; and in much of Freneau's poetry. It helps explain why there are so many early American historical works: Edward Johnson's *Wonder-working Providence of Sion's Saviour in America* (1654), Robert Beverley's *History and Present State of Virginia* (1705), Cadwallader Colden's *History of the Five Indian Nations* (1727), and of course Bradford's and Mather's massive histories. What bound Americans together so that they could fight together was their dissatisfaction with their dependent status and their unique experience with the new land.

Thus intellectualism, originality, and concern with America are themes that inevitably emerge from the essays that follow. David Levin, who has done so much to increase understanding of historical literature, in his essay on William Bradford in this volume asks the question: What good might it have done a historian to be a Puritan? Or, more specifically, what is Bradford's contribution to a comprehension of Puritanism? Though such distinguished historians as Samuel Eliot Morison and Peter Gay have devoted much study to Bradford, Levin goes beyond their findings. He considers sympathetically Bradford's portrayal of Puritan piety and uses Bradford's own piety as a key to his approach to history.

Ann Stanford's essay on Anne Bradstreet is a poet's analysis of a poet. Focusing on the difficulties of being a Puritan woman who wrote poetry in a colony just being established, she surveys Mrs. Bradstreet's literary development. She shows how our first dedicated poet used a variety of literary traditions for her own purposes in developing her own distinctively individual poetic technique. The analysis of technique and literary traditions is balanced by sensitive attention to Bradstreet's absorption with the human condition.

Donald E. Stanford's analysis of the poetry of Edward Taylor shares insights with the essays on Bradford and Bradstreet. He shows that, like Bradford, Taylor displays the nature of Puritan piety. Like Anne Bradstreet, Taylor had to face the problem of writing in a Puritan context, and, again like his Massachusetts predecessor, Taylor borrowed heavily from poetic traditions but adapted them to his own purposes. Stanford provides a thorough analysis of the large body of Taylor's verse and prose. Facing squarely the fact that Taylor's poetry requires the exercise of the historical imagination, he gives a discriminating appraisal of Taylor's achievement.

Cotton Mather, one of the strangest figures in the whole of American literature, is also the least understood. Sacvan Bercovitch locates clues to a comprehension of Mather and his writings in his commitment to the vanished Puritan theocracy, his ability to transform defeat into victory through the use of the imagination, and his strange identification with Jesus. Bercovitch investigates the whole range of Mather's extensive writings but focuses especially on his diaries, his *Wonders of the Invisible World, A Midnight Cry, Bonifacius, The Christian Philosopher,* and the *Magnalia Christi Americana.* His essay, the fullest yet written on Mather as a man of letters, includes a treatment of the effect of the Puritan imagination on later American literature.

The contribution of the South to the beginnings of American literature has been overshadowed by that of New England. This fact is largely a result of the inadequate knowledge of the literature of colonial Virginia and Maryland, which has received far less attention than that of New England. Richard Beale Davis, who has done much to correct this record, utilizes in the present study of William Byrd his extensive knowledge of this culture as he examines Byrd's extant writings. Since Byrd spent a good deal of his life in England, he was exceptionally conscious of what it meant to be an American, and Davis's study explores with care this aspect of Byrd's experience.

Jonathan Edwards and Benjamin Franklin suggest the variety of early American literature. Edwards has long been considered a crucial figure in American literature because of his adumbrations of nineteenth-century attitudes and themes. Daniel B. Shea's study of the writer, philosopher, and theologian does much to clarify this precession. Shea shows how Edwards's mind functioned and how he defined issues. While Edwards has been damned as a reactionary, Benjamin Franklin damaged his own reputation by creating a classic. His *Autobiography,* one of America's acknowledged great books, opens up for the reader only a limited view of the many-sided Franklin. As the excellent edition of his papers now being published makes its appearance one begins to see the greatness of the man. J. A. Leo Lemay's careful survey of Franklin's many genres is full of new information.

Unlike most of the American authors that preceded them, Philip Freneau and Charles Brockden Brown worked in imaginative literature. Freneau has attracted attention as the poet of the American Revolution and as a transitional figure whose manner is both neoclassical and romantic. But perhaps for these very reasons the nature of Freneau's achievement as poet has not been clear. In his essay Lewis Leary offers the solid critical evaluation that has been needed. Brown was the first significant American novelist, writing during the development of the novel as a form; he was the forerunner of Poe and Hawthorne, the father of American literary Gothicism. Thus he occupies a distinctive position in literary history. However flawed his novels, they continue to attract both readers and critics. Donald A. Ringe provides a concise analytical and evaluative criticism of Brown's major novels with particular attention to Brown's use of three fictional forms: the sentimental romance, the Gothic tale, and the novel of purpose.

The transplantation of Western culture to a new land opened up exciting possibilities. What kinds of creations was the new country to produce? What were the distinctive qualities of the American experience? The essays that follow supply answers to these questions. Knowledge of early American literature has often been limited to a few generalizations about the Puritan Mind, the American Enlightenment, and the development of literary nationalism. This volume provides a solid foundation for an intelligent appreciation of the beginnings of American literature.

1

William Bradford
The Value of Puritan Historiography

DAVID LEVIN

Famine once we had, wanting corn and bread,
But other things God gave us in the stead,
As fish and ground nuts, to supply our strait,
That we might learn on providence to wait;
And know by bread man lives not in his need,
But by each word that doth from God proceed.
But a while after plenty did come in,
From His hand only who doth pardon sin.
And all did flourish like the pleasant green,
Which in the joyful spring is to be seen.

. . . . .

Another cause of our declining here,
Is a mixt multitude, as doth appear.
Many for servants hither were brought,
Others came for gain, or worse ends they sought;
And of these, many grow loose and profane,
Though some are brought to know God and His name.
But thus it is, and hath been so of old,
As by the Scriptures we are plainly told . . . .
Bradford, "Some Observations of God's Merci-
ful Dealing with us in the Wilderness" (1654)

David Levin is Commonwealth Professor of English at the University of Virginia and a member of the university's Center for Advanced Studies. His books include *History as Romantic Art* (1959) and *In Defense of Historical Literature* (1967), and he is now preparing a critical biography of Cotton Mather. He has served as a fellow at the Center for Advanced Study in the Behavioral Sciences and as a

I

In the body of tradition that stands between modern readers and the best literary works of seventeenth-century New England, William Bradford holds an honorable place both as a political leader and as a writer. Three hundred and fifty years after the founding of Plymouth, we respect him as the faithful governor of Plymouth during the colony's first decades and as the writer whose unfinished history *Of Plymouth Plantation* helped to give the tradition literary form. It is in Bradford's history that we read of "pilgrims" who obey their calling to leave the known European world for a wilderness, seeking comfort in the Biblical reminder that heaven is their dearest country. It is Bradford's history that appeals to law as the true foundation of liberty, and to "the simplicity of the gospel, without the mixture of men's inventions," as the right model for worship. It is Bradford's history that unites religious, political, and aesthetic value by celebrating "the primitive order, liberty, and beauty" of the first Christian churches.*

Bradford's literary reputation rests entirely on the history that he began to write ten years after the founding of Plymouth. His awkward verses and his long, skillfully written dialogues defending Congregational church government against Roman Catholic, Episcopal, and Presbyterian theory and practice have not gained admission to our literary anthologies. It is his admirable prose style, his role as governor, and his representative quality as one of the mildest and most magnanimous of Puritan spokesmen that have won him his honored place in our literary history. Thousands of students who never see the entire volume *Of Plymouth Plantation* know Bradford as the writer, formerly a participant in the historical action, who "cannot but stay and make a pause" to reflect, in the most famous of all his passages, on "this poor people's . . . condition" during their first wintry days on Cape Cod; there "all things stand upon them with a weatherbeaten

senior fellow of the National Endowment for the Humanities, and has taught at Stanford University.

A portion of this chapter has previously appeared in *History and Theory* 7, no. 3 (1968): 385–93; it is reprinted here with the kind permission of Wesleyan University Press.

* Quotations from *Of Plymouth Plantation* in the text are from the Samuel Eliot Morison edition, used with his permission.

face," and "which way soever they turned their eyes (save upward to the heavens) they could have little solace or content in respect of any outward objects." The Bradford modern readers know best is the participant who writes that he respected some newcomers' conscientious refusal to work on Christmas Day—until he found them playing games. (He then told them that it was against his conscience for them to play while others worked.) The Bradford we all know best is the Old Founder who laments the dispersal of original church members and the decline of their original commitment to maintaining one loving, covenanted community.

Yet the distinction between Bradford the eminent colonial leader and Bradford the writer can too easily be blurred in a way that underestimates the achievement of Bradford the historian. The few commentators on Bradford's "conscious art" tend naturally to concentrate on his literary style rather than on his historical imagination.* Historians of history and literature, moreover, are inclined to emphasize changes, development, and differences in the ways of writing history, especially when they address a contemporary audience about seventeenth-century historians who had no great influence on the development of the art, the science, the profession. In explaining strange ways to modern students, it is only reasonable to concentrate on differences between the Puritans and ourselves, to show what was "puritan" about them. The very nature of the subject seems to impose a condescending perspective on the study of old histories. It is so important to notice predestination, Providence, and authorial piety that one has little chance to look for much complexity in the individual Puritan's work. And if one does write at some length about Bradford or Cotton Mather, one is tempted to concentrate on the historical facts and the author's remarkable character.

Students of literature need also to pay some attention to the substantive value of the histories they study. The question that has too rarely been asked about Bradford and others is not how Puritanism limited their histories but what *good* it might have done a historian to be a Puritan. What does Bradford the historian understand, interpret, portray in a way that no other historian has surpassed? Bradford was a Puritan not only when he committed narrow-minded errors but also when he acted meritoriously and wrote perceptively. His Puritan preconceptions gave him some special kinds of historical insight. The literary value of his book depends as much

* Since these remarks were written, Alan Howard, in an article cited in the bibliography to this chapter, has moved to avoid that distortion.

on the quality of his historical intelligence as on the virtues of his
style. As an interpreter of Puritan piety, for example, he seems to me
a better historian than George Langdon, Peter Gay, or John Demos,
all of whom have written more effectively than Bradford about other
qualities in Puritan life. Anyone who doubts Bradford's value as a
historian needs only to set *Of Plymouth Plantation* beside George
Langdon's recent history of the colony. Mr. Langdon's excellent book
repeatedly uses Bradford's information, and he often follows Bradford's interpretations, but he never treats Bradford as a fellow historian.

The mistake of much commentary—an error more damaging to
literary evaluation than to historical narrative—is to treat Bradford
only as an *example* of piety but not to stress the achievement of
Bradford the historian in *portraying* Puritan piety. Bradford's purpose in the first book of his history seems to be to represent the
Pilgrims' sufferings in a way that will show how frequently circumstances allowed them nothing else to rely on except their piety. In
a very early scene, for example, he dramatizes their predicament under
an English authority that refused to let them stay as they were, but
also refused to let them emigrate. To show the full range of Bradford's use of piety here, I shall have to quote at unusual length.

When the first boatload of emigrant men boarded a Dutch ship
near Hull for the voyage to Holland, the sudden appearance of hostile
English authorities forced the Dutch captain to "hoise sails, and
away." Bradford shows us the plight of both the separated groups
of Pilgrims from the point of view of the men being carried to sea

> in great distress for their wives and children which they saw thus
> to be taken, and . . . left destitute of their helps; and them-
> selves also, not having a cloth to shift them with, more than they
> had on their backs, and some scarce a penny about them, all they
> had being aboard the bark . . . and anything they had they
> would have given to have been ashore again; but all in vain, there
> was no remedy, they must thus sadly part. And afterward en-
> dured a fearful storm at sea, being fourteen days or more before
> they arrived at their port; in seven whereof they neither saw sun,
> moon nor stars, and were driven near the coast of Norway; the
> mariners themselves often despairing of life, and once with shrieks
> and cries gave over all, as if the ship had been foundered in the
> sea and they sinking without recovery. But when man's hope and
> help wholly failed, the Lord's power and mercy appeared in their
> recovery; for the ship rose again and gave the mariners courage
> again to manage her. And if modesty would suffer me, I might
> declare with what fervent prayers they cried unto the Lord in this

great distress (especially some of them) even without any great distraction. When the water ran into their mouths and ears and the mariners cried out, "We sink, we sink!" they cried (if not with miraculous, yet with a great height or degree of divine faith), "Yet Lord Thou canst save! Yet Lord Thou canst save!" with such other expressions as I will forbear. Upon which the ship did not only recover, but shortly after the violence of the storm began to abate, and the Lord filled their afflicted minds with such comforts as everyone cannot understand, and in the end brought them to their desired haven, where the people came flocking, admiring their deliverance; the storm having been so long and sore, in which much hurt had been done, as the master's friends related unto him in their congratulations.

But to return to the others where we left. The rest of the men that were in greatest danger made shift to escape away before the troop could surprise them, those only staying that best might be assistant unto the women. But pitiful it was to see the heavy case of these poor women in this distress; what weeping and crying on every side, some for their husbands that were carried away in the ship . . . ; others not knowing what should become of them and their little ones; others again melted in tears, seeing their poor little ones hanging about them, crying for fear and quaking with cold. Being thus apprehended, they were hurried from one place to another and from one justice to another, till in the end they [the authorities] knew not what to do with them; for to imprison so many women and innocent children for no other cause (many of them) but that they must go with their husbands, seemed to be unreasonable and all would cry out of them. And to send them home again was as difficult; for they alleged, as the truth was, they had no homes to go to, for they had either sold or otherwise disposed of their houses and livings. To be short, after they had been thus turmoiled a good while and conveyed from one constable to another, they [the authorities] were glad to be rid of them in the end upon any terms, for all were wearied and tired with them. Though in the meantime they (poor souls) endured misery enough; and thus in the end necessity forced a way for them. (pp. 13–14)

To avoid becoming tedious, Bradford says, he will omit "many other notable passages and troubles which they endured and underwent in these their wanderings," but he understands that he "may not omit the fruit that came hereby," and he saves it for the conclusion of his chapter:

. . . by these so public troubles in so many eminent places their cause became famous and occasioned many to look into the same, and their godly carriage and Christian behaviour was such as left a deep impression in the minds of many. And though some few shrunk at these first conflicts and sharp beginnings (as it was no marvel) yet many more came on with fresh courage and greatly animated others. And in the end, notwithstanding all these storms of opposition, they all gat over at length, some at one time and some at another, and some in one place and some in another, and met together again according to their desires, with no small rejoicing. (pp. 14–15)

This eloquent passage has been justly praised for its embodiment of the Pilgrim spirit in images of departure, peril, and arrival that foreshadow both the voyage across the Atlantic and the Christian's journey to heaven. The intervention of Providence draws as much modern notice, if less praise. What I wish to stress in addition is Bradford's attention to worldly as well as Providential cause. Bradford's refusal to see any conflict between Providential and natural causes has admirable as well as regrettable consequences. It requires him to look into the natural and human means through which Providential will usually works. In a North Sea storm the Lord may quiet the waves in answer to faithful prayers, but in narrating human events the Puritan historian must attend to the earthly causes by which "necessity forced a way" for the Lord's covenanted people. Bradford shows us the Pilgrims' misery, but also the logic of their emancipation (what else could be done with them?), the psychology of their victory (their cause became famous, and many more came on with fresh courage). Both examples of deliverance merit the "admiration" of the people, and it is Bradford's Puritan piety that obliges him to examine worldly causes and forbids him to "omit the fruit that came hereby."

Throughout the history, moreover, Bradford's piety functions not chiefly to attribute all causes to Providence but rather to motivate a full report and a strict inquiry into historical complexity. Commentators too often notice his partisanship and his early allusions to Providence, and then cite the doubts he later expressed as he lamented the decline of piety in the second decade after the founding of Plymouth. It is hard for us to believe that historians who portrayed God as their people's faithful shepherd would reveal much doubt in their study of His interventions in history, and we find it easy to emphasize such striking passages as the lament in which Bradford, troubled by the exposure of shocking enormities in 1642, guesses that the Devil may mount especially powerful assaults among God's covenanted people. In truth, the Puritan was expected to be always alert

for ambiguity in the historical revelation of God's will. From the opening pages of the history, Bradford depicts the saints in considerable
perplexity.

Before considering several examples, I must insist that Bradford's
portrayal of Puritan uncertainty is a historical interpretation of great
importance, an interpretation that follows from his own inquiry
into the significance of events. This valuable interpretation thus
follows from his piety, his special way of seeing, his interest in
discovering the Providential design in history. It will not suffice to
portray him occasionally as a writer whose puzzled comments *exempli-
fy* uncertainty about a particular phenomenon. We must recognize
that he himself *portrays* the Pilgrim community in its perplexity.
He recognizes the faithful search for God's will as the major quest
of the pilgrim's life.

At the very beginning of his history Bradford shows us his conviction that after Satan had failed to destroy the faithful with burn-
ings and open warfare "in the days of Queen Mary and before, he
then began another kind of war and went more closely to work
. . . to ruinate and destroy the kingdom of Christ by more secret
and subtle means, by kindling the flames of contention and sowing
the seeds of discord and bitter enmity amongst the professors and,
seeming reformed, themselves." In his account difficulties pursue
the Marian exiles to the continent; and the effort of Puritans to hold
firm against seductive pleas for retention of "divers harmless cere-
monies" is described as a lengthy battle continuing several
years until the poor people are enabled by "the continuance and increase of these troubles, and other means which the Lord raised up
in those days, to see further into things by the light of the Word
of God." It is only those believers who "saw the evil" in Anglican cere-
monies who, according to Bradford, at first shake off "this yoke of
antichristian bondage"; they join "as the Lord's free people" in a
church covenanted to walk not merely "in all His ways made known"
but also in all His ways later "to be made known unto them." Bradford reports that division occurred almost at once, and that one
of the two congregations fell afterwards "into some errors" in the
Netherlands and "there (for the most part) buried themselves and
their names."

Even though in doctrinal agreement, the covenanted remnant to
which Bradford devotes the rest of his history spends great quantities
of time and intelligence studying worldly evidence to find God's
will. Bradford the historian shows us that the Lord's free people
regarded their new covenant as a genuine liberation, and he is happy

to narrate the debates through which (they trusted) God's ways were later to be made known to them. It is respect for the difficulty of knowing that leads him to record the arguments for and against emigrating from Holland to America. Just as he sees it is no marvel that "some few shrunk" at the first conflicts in England, so his piety leads him to describe fully the objections to the great emigration and the fears of good men as the negotiations proceed after the crucial decision has been made. He knows that "in all businesses the acting part is most difficult, especially where the work of many agents must concur . . . ." It is no disgrace that good Pilgrims doubt the validity of the calling to emigrate or that the courage of faithful men like Robert Cushman fails for a while on the English side of the Atlantic. The Puritan's liberation frees him to struggle in the world for the glory of God. Some saints are braver than others. The doubts, fears, perplexities, and follies of good men can only add to the glory of the God that has brought the community through the dangers they feared.

This attitude allows Bradford to shape his narrative so that the most persuasive of worldly arguments *against* proceeding with the colonial adventure lead to a convincing restatement of his Providential theme. He can thus show conscientious men arriving at the conclusion that their best and only hope lies in reliance on Providence. His arrangement has a convincing tenor even for skeptical readers, because his representation of the contrary arguments is both generous and reasonable, and because it is informed with sound political knowledge. When King James tells the Pilgrims' agents that the Crown cannot officially grant them liberty to worship in their own way in America, but lets them know that he will "connive at them and not molest them" so long as they behave peaceably, many of the Pilgrims fear (Bradford says) that they should not risk their estates and their lives on such vague assurances. With extremely skillful use of indirect quotation, Bradford dramatizes the most forcible arguments on both sides in a way that leads us through intricate political understanding to dependence upon Providence:

> Yea it was thought they might better have presumed hereupon without making any suit at all than, having made it, to be thus rejected. But some of the chiefest thought otherwise and that they might well proceed hereupon, and that the King's Majesty was willing enough to suffer them without molestation, though for other reasons he would not confirm it by any public act. And furthermore, if there was no security in this promise intimated, there would be no great certainty in a further confirmation of the same;

for if afterwards there should be a purpose or desire to wrong
them, though they had a seal as broad as the house floor it would
not serve the turn; for there would be means enow found to
recall or reverse it. Seeing therefore the course was probable, they
must rest herein on God's providence as they had done in other
things. (pp. 30–31)

II

The great value of the Puritan historian, then, is that he can show us
piety functioning uncertainly but faithfully in the world, along with
other motives. In his portrayal of John Robinson and William Brewster,
Bradford achieves one of the best versions we have of the Congregational pastor's and elder's relation to their flock, and he deliberately
introduces his characterization of Robinson for its representative social
value. Sweetened by twenty years of nostalgic recollection, Bradford's
portrait begins with Robinson's "able ministry and prudent government" and with the

> mutual love and reciprocal respect that this worthy man had to
> his flock . . . . His love was great towards them, and his care
> was always bent for their best good, both for soul and body. For
> besides his singular abilities in divine things (wherein he ex-
> celled) he was also very able to give directions in civil affairs
> and to foresee dangers and inconveniences, by which means he was
> very helpful to their outward estates and so was every way as a
> common father unto them. And none did more offend him than
> those that were close and cleaving to themselves and retired from
> the common good; as also such as would be stiff and rigid in
> matters of outward order and inveigh against the evils of others,
> and yet be remiss in themselves, and not so careful to express a
> virtuous conversation. (p. 18)

The pastor teaches, so that his people grow "in knowledge and other
gifts and graces," and he governs, so that disagreements and offenses
are "ever so met with and nipped in the head betimes, or otherwise
so well composed as still [to preserve] love, peace, and communion."
Bradford thus helps us to enter a world in which there is no necessary
conflict between economic and pious motivation. Perhaps one reason
we find it difficult to enter such a world without the help of such a
historian is that our own view of religious motivation is narrower
than his.

Bradford, of course, wanted his narrative to record a valid model of Congregational church government (and to justify his generation) for an uncertain posterity, as well as to achieve an accurate, coherent history and to celebrate the glory of God. He frankly believed, and we ought gratefully to concede, that these different purposes are often served by the same methods. John Robinson's place as the admirable Congregational pastor would not be so effectively achieved in these pages if it depended solely or even primarily on the moving paragraph that I have just discussed. Even in 1630, about fifteen years before he actually wrote the bulk of his narrative, Bradford finishes that paragraph by foreshadowing Robinson's death: dearly as the people loved Robinson while he was alive, they "esteemed him . . . much more after his death, when they came to feel the want of his help and saw (by woeful experience) what a treasure they had lost . . . ." Robinson will figure throughout the rest of his life as a major character in the narrative, and much of the narrative that Bradford will later write as annual chapters dramatizes the congregation's painful failure "to find such another leader and feeder in all respects."

What brings to life the Robinson of Bradford's laudatory rhetoric is the abundant circumstantial evidence of his continuing influence in the rest of the history. Bradford shows Robinson debating with an Arminian professor in Leyden, preaching "a good part of the day very profitably" on the eve of the Pilgrims' departure from Leyden, falling down on his knees and tearfully commending his people to God as their ship prepares to sail. But the chief material of Bradford's historical success in this central characterization is the rich, incontrovertible supply of Robinson's letters. Bradford's judicious, extensive quotation reveals John Robinson as a forceful negotiator on economic and other issues and as an adviser on community government even after the congregation has emigrated to America. Robinson's moral power stands out most admirably in a letter to Bradford more than three years after the founding of Plymouth, when the pastor rebukes the colonists for having killed several Indians; Robinson understands at least some feelings of colonists and Indians alike, and the breadth of his understanding makes his rebuke and his prudential warning all the more persuasive:

> Oh, how happy a thing had it been, if you had converted some before you had killed any! Besides, where blood is once begun to be shed, it is seldom staunched of a long time after. You will say they deserved it. I grant it; but upon what provocations and invitements by those heathenish Christians [that is, not members of Plymouth Plantation or the congregation]? Besides, you being no

magistrates over them were to consider not what they deserved but
what you were by necessity constrained to inflict. (pp. 374–75)

Several of the long letters that Bradford copies into his text impress
the reader as footnotes to the narrative, and S. E. Morison, in the
best recent edition of the book, relegates many of the letters, including the one that I have just quoted, to an appendix. It seems to me
very important, however, to consider all the letters as part of Bradford's narrative. Although a few of them do serve chiefly as documen-
tation, many others deepen the characterization, build the larger
structure, and provide unique narrative details. Only through a letter
of Robinson's does Bradford let us see Captain Miles Standish's usual
humility and meekness as civil traits that probably issue "merely
from an humane spirit" rather than from Christian grace. Robinson's
fear that under provocation Standish may lack Christian "tenderness
of the life of man"—and his warning that "It is . . . a thing more
glorious, in men's eyes, than pleasing in God's or convenient for
Christians, to be a terror to poor barbarous people"—these help to
characterize both Robinson and Standish. Only through one of Robert
Cushman's many fine letters does Bradford first show us that the
treacherous preacher John Lyford was sent to the colony at the
insistence of several English stockholders, and that the two Pilgrim
agents in England reluctantly consented to this arrangement with
the express understanding that Lyford "knows he is no officer amongst
you." And it is one of Robinson's early letters that shows us the ideal
of the church covenant: "We are knit together as a body in a most
strict and sacred bond and covenant of the Lord, of the violation
whereof we make great conscience, and by virtue whereof we do
hold ourselves straitly tied to all care of each other's good and of
the whole, by every one and so mutually."
As the narrative develops, these apparently small matters grow in
significance. The letters of Robinson and Cushman show us the complexities of negotiations for the original voyage to Plymouth. They
also establish the pattern of governmental affairs for the first decades
of life in America. Instructions received in good faith must be loosely
interpreted or flatly disobeyed by agents under the immediate pres-
sure of unforeseen decisions—sometimes apparently dishonest and
evidently self-interested—made by the Englishmen who control the
money on which the whole enterprise depends. Bradford, who as a
participant had actually been with the colonists, uses the letters in his
history to show us a remarkably complete picture of all four groups:
the colonists, the agents, the investors (Adventurers), and (after the

founding of Plymouth) the prospective colonists who never did manage to leave the Netherlands. His choice and placement of the letters not only give us essential information but convey the genuine plight and the vivid feelings of men caught in their historical situation. Each of the main figures in this correspondence speaks in his own characteristic language, and Bradford's shrewd arrangement of the inconstant Adventurer Thomas Weston's letters among those of Robert Cushman, John Robinson, and Bradford himself demonstrates brilliantly that character and circumstance make up the essential substance of early colonial history. Weston's blustering accusations that the colonists have let him down appear in the record only after we have seen, through the death of half the colonists in the first winter, how utterly unjust those accusations are, and how desperately the colonists need the help that he has promised but has failed to deliver.

Throughout the first fifteen years of colonization, it is not only the content but the actual historical importance of slow communication that gives the letters their greatest value in Bradford's history. The letter of Weston to which I have just alluded was dated (as Bradford carefully notes) July 6, 1621, and addressed to Governor John Carver. By that time Carver had been dead for more than two months, and his successor William Bradford did not receive the letter until November 10. Letters arrive belatedly, and their contents show that correspondents on both sides of the Atlantic have contradictory expectations of one another. Letters prove to be important not only for what they say but because they were often the essential stuff of the colonists' experience. Eagerly awaited from England, they name new conditions imposed by the Adventurers or announce the French capture of a shipment of American furs from Plymouth. Intercepted by Governor Bradford on their way from Plymouth to England, the Reverend Mr. John Lyford's letters reveal his plans to destroy the Adventurers' confidence in the infant colony's religious and political government, and when he insists that he has been completely loyal to the colonists his own letters are suddenly produced in a grand confrontation to expose him. Letters about his scandalous conduct in Ireland arrive too late to serve as warning. It is letters, too, that bring chilling news of 50 percent interest rates in the early years, and even chillier news a decade later—when colonists awaiting supplies receive instead word that their ship has been sent on a disastrous fishing expedition, and when the Adventurers belatedly confess that for years they have kept no clear records of thousands of pounds of furs and other goods received in payment from the colony.

As evidence from the letters has already suggested, Bradford, in delineating the Pilgrims' struggle against adversity, gives close attention to the diversity of human character. He also displays abundant evidence that the Pilgrims found it difficult to *know* human character. The Puritan saints who act in this history believe that men are divided into the elect and the damned, but they know that they themselves are often unable to perceive the distinction. They know, too, that an elected Christian can behave incomprehensibly. They do not really understand the character of Robert Cushman, their own agent and friend, or that of Isaac Allerton and James Sherley, until it has been revealed through action, and even then their knowledge is inconclusive. Roger Williams remains a mystery to Bradford long after error has led Williams out of Plymouth and into trouble elsewhere; yet Bradford can thank God for Williams's teachings and can "hope he belongs to the Lord."

It is to Bradford's credit as a narrator that his consistent efforts to justify the Pilgrims and to dramatize their sufferings fill his pages with the bewildering actions of a succession of confidence men. Reading character is an essential quality in any successful colonizer and in Puritan religious life. Bradford's Puritan insistence on justifying his evaluation for the reader assures us of plentiful evidence from the letters of these men themselves, and his sympathy with the community that he portrays as their victim gives memorable power to the difficulties of all colonization. We can see in his account numerous practitioners of Simon Suggs's famous dictum: It is good to be shifty in a new country.

In portraying these confidence men, Bradford as narrator once again not only exemplifies but perceptively requires us to observe important qualities in seventeenth-century Puritanism; the passion for fairness and the liking for scenes of confrontation. The passion for justice (mixed though it often is with self-justification and even self-righteousness) flows powerfully through the letters about misunderstandings, and the combination of open rebuke with recapitulation of evidence sometimes makes the letters themselves serve as confrontations. A number of scenes in the history, moreover, represent Puritan leaders, armed with evidence or at least with the conviction that they must speak out for the truth, directly confronting their antagonists. In Leyden, John Robinson confutes an Arminian professor in public debate of theological issues. In New England, Pilgrims march to demand that Indian leaders verify or deny rumors of a plan to murder Squanto and attack the English settlements; and several of the rogues who figure so entertainingly in the narrative eventually appear in New England to face the indignation of their victims. The

most celebrated of these scenes is of course the attack on Thomas
Morton's "pagan" colony at Merrymount, but the most important is
the "trial" of John Lyford, the preacher who betrayed the colonists in
1624.

Lyford's story gains force through his pretentious hopes of replacing
John Robinson, whom Bradford has already characterized as the
ideal Congregational pastor. Bradford shows us how the actual scene
of the trial was prepared, through the interception of Lyford's letters
to England and the concealment of their discovery until they could
be revealed as a public denunciation of his claims to be the Pilgrims'
loving friend and pastor. (These letters, by the way, also disclose
that Lyford had been intercepting Bradford's letters.) The incident
would be impressive enough if Bradford had merely dramatized the
revelation, Lyford's confusion, and Lyford's confession and repentance. Bradford's account deserves especial praise because it shows
how lenient Puritan justice could often be and because it emphasizes
the political consequences. Even at this point, the Plymouth authorities and the congregation are willing to accept Lyford's repentance—
until he writes yet another secret letter against them. Then Lyford's
wife reveals that he has betrayed her, too, and belated reports from
London declare that his original departure from Ireland had been
precipitated by the discovery that he had seduced a young parishioner
who had sought his counsel before her wedding. Bradford, of course,
does not underplay this denouement, but the justification for his attention to the Lyford story has other, historically more significant
grounds: his next chapter argues that the banishment of John Lyford
provoked a majority of the original Company of Adventurers to break
off their relationship to the colony.

As a judge of the diverse characters who enliven his history, Bradford, though often magnanimous and often puzzled, is by no means
timid. He roundly condemns the behavior of Weston, Allerton, Lyford, Morton, Sir Christopher Gardiner, and others. But his high
standards do not stifle his interest in reading character, and the
variety itself supports two of his chief historical observations: (1) that
other colonies perished while the religious colony at Plymouth survived, and (2) that the growing proportion of nonreligious settlers
in the Plymouth colony reduced the original congregation's influence
and its commitment to unity.

III

The perplexity that Pilgrim leaders feel throughout Bradford's history as they struggle to understand character and circumstance seems to me more important than the persuasive theories of lament and decline with which several scholars have tried to explain Bradford's composition of the book. Bradford began writing the history in 1630, the year that the Massachusetts Bay colony was founded by a large group of influential English Puritans. Some scholars believe that the likelihood of Plymouth's being overshadowed by the populous new colony may have moved him to write the first fourth of his narrative in 1630, almost twenty-five years after the first specific event in which he had participated, and that the decline of the original congregation's exemplary unity may have prompted him to resume writing again and to compose the last three-fourths of the narrative in the years between 1645 and 1650. (By 1646 he had reached only the year 1621.)

My own view is that although Bradford does lament evidence of decline in the 1640s, and although these passages are among the most famous that he wrote, the pattern of his historical organization is perennially dialectical, cyclical, alternating, as in the early passage that I have quoted on the departure from England for the Netherlands. Success is followed by failure, safety by danger, disaster by fortunate escape and recovery. Financial tormentors among the colonial agents and Adventurers seem to succeed one another; Weston is followed by Allerton and Sherley in bitter correspondence with the colonists about the debt that seems to grow larger with each payment.

Difficulties exist from the beginning, then, and successes increase along with losses throughout the decades of the history. Insofar as there is a clear direction in the entire narrative, that too is ambiguous. It is a dual story of flourishing growth "from small beginnings" and of decline from original purity. That, in Bradford's view, is the pattern of all Christian narrative. The same historian might consistently see both threads in the pattern, but he might at different times concentrate on one or the other. Only with the millennium would the larger pattern be clear to human eyes. Bradford tells us in 1646 that when he began writing the history he did not see how near was the downfall of English bishops, and we can see for ourselves in the section composed in 1630 (and in the verses he wrote in 1654) that he felt as much encouraged as threatened by the friendly settlements in Massachusetts Bay.

It is in this context and with an eye toward the occasional pessimism of old age that we should consider Bradford's comments on the execution of young Thomas Granger (along with several animals) in 1642 for sodomy. Although apparently only the third capital sentence in twenty-two years, this gruesome episode leads Bradford to consider possible explanations for the recent growth of outrageous crimes in Plymouth. Rather than cite these passages as sufficient evidence of a controlling historical disappointment, we must notice the chronology of composition. Bradford did not write the last three-fourths of the history until *after* the events of 1642 and the death of his old friend William Brewster. Granger's execution had occurred several years *before* Bradford wrote optimistically of the perplexity into which the colonists had been thrown by news of John Robinson's death in 1626:

> . . . it could not but strike them with great perplexity, and to look humanly on the state of things as they presented themselves at this time. It is a marvel it did not wholly discourage them and sink them. But they gathered up their spirits, and the Lord so helped them, . . . as now when they were at [their] lowest they began to rise again, and being stripped in a manner of all human helps and hopes, He brought things about otherwise, in His divine providence as they were not only upheld and sustained, but their proceedings both honored and imitated by others. As by the sequel will more appear, if the Lord spare me life and time to declare the same. (p. 181)

Bradford and other Puritan historians recognized that belief in Providence raised as many difficulties for them as it solved. Indeed, there is one moment in which two sets of Congregationalists in *Of Plymouth Plantation* see Providence on opposite sides. In 1635–36, a group from Plymouth and a rival group from Massachusetts Bay enter conflicting declarations that Providence has entitled them to the same land on the Connecticut River. "Look," says one Congregational group to the other, "that you abuse not God's providence in such allegations." The Plymouth group agrees to negotiate only on condition that Thomas Hooker's invaders first grant Plymouth's right to the land, and then the sale is accepted. Where, then, a reader might ask, does the Providential choice finally rest? Plymouth's Providential title is acknowledged, but those who acknowledge it gain the Providential consolation of actual possession.

Knowing that Providence sometimes favored the saints by granting them prosperity did not blind Puritan historians to the wondrous ambiguity of even that blessing. Perhaps the best illustration of how Puritan beliefs encouraged rather than discouraged the study of historical evidence is Bradford's account of the prosperity that came from wampumpeag in 1628. His description of prosperity leads to a puzzle. The trade in wampum makes the Narragansetts and Pequots rich along with the English, and Bradford suggests that it may soon cease to be profitable.

> In the meantime [however], it makes the Indians of these parts rich and powerful and also proud thereby, and fills them with pieces, powder and shot, which no laws can restrain, by reason of the baseness of sundry unworthy persons, both English, Dutch and French, which may turn to the ruin of many. Hitherto the Indians of these parts had no pieces nor other arms but their bows and arrows, nor of many years after; neither durst they scarce handle a gun, so much were they afraid of them. And the very sight of one (though out of kilter) was a terror unto them. But those Indians to the east parts, which had commerce with the French, got pieces of them, and they in the end made a common trade of it. And in time our English fishermen, led with the like covetousness, followed their example for their own gain.
> (p. 204)

It is these reflections that introduce the most famous rogue in the history, Thomas Morton of Merrymount, whom Bradford excoriates for selling arms to the Indians.

Prosperity, moreover, has a major role in causing conflict among the Pilgrims themselves. Although Bradford is naturally troubled by the events, he seems to have a clear understanding of their causes, economic and social, and he presents them unmistakably as natural consequences of human actions in a world that is just as complex for Pilgrims as for others:

> Also the people of the Plantation began to grow in their outward estates, by reason of the flowing of many people into the country, especially into the Bay of the Massachusetts. By which means corn and cattle rose to a great price, by which many were much enriched and commodities grew plentiful. And yet in other regards this benefit turned to their hurt, and this accession of strength to their weakness. For now as their stocks increased and the increase vendible, there was no longer any holding them together, but now they must of necessity go to their great lots. They could not otherwise keep their cattle, and having oxen grown they

must have land for plowing and tillage. And no man now thought
he could live except he had cattle and a great deal of ground to
keep them, all striving to increase their stocks. By which means
they were scattered all over the Bay quickly and the town in
which they lived compactly till now was left very thin and in a
short time almost desolate.

And if this had been all, it had been less, though too much; but
the church must also be divided, and those that had lived so long
together in Christian and comfortable fellowship must now part
and suffer many divisions. First, those that lived on their lots on
the other side of the Bay, called Duxbury, they could not long
bring their wives and children to the public worship and church
meetings here, but with such burthen as, growing to some compe-
tent number, they sued to be dismissed and become a body of
themselves. And so they were dismissed about this time, though
very unwillingly. But to touch this sad matter, and handle things
together that fell out afterward; to prevent any further scattering
from this place and weakening of the same, it was thought best
to give out some good farms to special persons that would promise
to live at Plymouth, and likely to be helpful to the church or
commonwealth, and so tie the lands to Plymouth as farms for the
same; and there they might keep their cattle and tillage by some
servants and retain their dwellings here. And so some special
lands were granted at a place general called Green's Harbor, where
no allotments had been in the former division, a place very well
meadowed and fit to keep and rear cattle good store. But alas, this
remedy proved worse than the disease; for within a few years those
that had thus got footing there rent themselves away, partly by
force and partly wearing the rest with importunity and pleas of
necessity, so as they must either suffer them to go or live in
continual opposition and contention. And other still, as they conceived themselves straitened or to want accommodation, broke
away under one pretence or other, thinking their own conceived
necessity and the example of others a warrant sufficient for them.
And this I fear will be the ruin of New England, at least of the
churches of God there, and will provoke the Lord's displeasure
against them. (pp. 252–54)

Clearly, then, the Puritan historian was able to recognize a pattern
that has become common in our secular history. Mobility and prosperity harm the community. New remedies bring on new diseases.
Throughout the history, Bradford also records a dialectic in which
the chosen people (acting out Christian typology) struggle to find
God's will as they move between the perils of disease and remedy,

prosperity and adversity, friend and enemy. In the long passages I have cited here the people are often trapped in a logical predicament that finds superb expression in the coordinate antitheses of Bradford's rhythmic syntax. That admirably flexible instrument is capable of showing us the Puritan's ideal community, the covenanted church "knit together as a body," the pilgrims whose "dearest country" was in heaven, and the pious but inevitably troubled reality in the actual country of the New World, where complex historical forces transform church and commonwealth.

Bradford's style also serves him admirably in many pages of circumstantial description. Though often abstract, and though occasionally confused by ambiguous pronoun references, his prose has a tough particularity that regularly grounds his typology in explicit Biblical references and specific facts of New England life. His typological reading of the smallpox epidemics that devastate Indian nations but pass over the English would be much more vulnerable to criticism if he had not balanced it with a sympathetically detailed picture of the suffering Indians, and with some effort to explain the terrible consequences:

> . . . they fear [smallpox] more than the plague. For usually they that have this disease have them in abundance, and for want of bedding and linen and other helps they fall into a lamentable condition as they lie on their hard mats, the pox breaking and mattering and running one into another, their skin cleaving by reason thereof to the mats they lie on. When they turn them, a whole side will flay off at once as it were, and they will be all of a gore blood, most fearful to behold. And then being very sore, what with cold and other distempers, they die like rotten sheep. The condition of this people [in Windsor, Connecticut] was so lamentable and they fell down so generally of this disease as they were in the end not able to help one another, no not to make a fire nor to fetch a little water to drink, nor any to bury the dead. But would strive as long as they could, and when they could procure no other means to make fire, they would burn the wooden trays and dishes they ate their meat in, and their very bows and arrows. And some would crawl out on all fours to get a little water, and sometimes die by the way and not be able to get in again. (pp. 270–71)

An amazing hurricane; a dying sailor cursed by his own shipmate for expiring too slowly; a fatal shoot-out over fur-trading rights in the Penobscot River; a rogue whom the Indians (with Bradford's consent) capture when he loses control of his canoe as he tries to shoot at them—these and other phenomena come through to the modern reader with equal vigor and detail.

It would be foolish to claim that Bradford's history is faultless. The book is marred at times by an appalling indifference to the Indians and by the kind of narrow perspective and partisanship that one might expect of the "puritanical." But it is an admirably faithful work as well as an eloquently "mythical" statement about plain pilgrims on a journey through the world, and its continuing value depends as much on Bradford's historical intelligence and skill as on his celebrated modesty and style. It gives the best picture that I know of Puritan piety in action in the New World, and it owes much of its success to the obligations imposed on every believer by that piety: to search faithfully for an understanding of God's revealed will in the ambiguous evidence of the historical world.

BIBLIOGRAPHY

Editions

History of Plymouth Plantation. Edited by Samuel Eliot Morison. New York: Knopf, 1952. Reprinted, New York: Modern Library, 1967.
History of Plymouth Plantation, 1620–1647. Edited by Worthington C. Ford. 2 vols. Boston: Houghton Mifflin, 1912.

Scholarship and Criticism

Bradford, E. F. "Conscious Art in Bradford's *History of Plymouth Plantation.*" *New England Quarterly* 1 (1928): 133–57.
Gay, Peter. *A Loss of Mastery: Puritan Historians in Colonial America.* Berkeley and Los Angeles: University of California Press, 1966.
Grabo, Norman S. "William Bradford: *Of Plymouth Plantation.*" In *Landmarks of American Writing,* edited by Hennig Cohen, pp. 3–19. New York: Basic Books, 1969.
Howard, Alan B. "Art and History in Bradford's *Of Plymouth Plantation.*" *William and Mary Quarterly,* 3d ser., 28 (1971): 237–66.
A Journal of the Pilgrims at Plymouth: Mourt's Relation. Edited by Dwight B. Heath. New York: Corinth, 1963. Another edition: Edited by Henry Martyn Dexter. New York: Garrett Press, 1969.
Kraus, Michael. *The Writing of American History.* Norman, Okla.: University of Oklahoma Press, 1953.

Langdon, George D., Jr. *Pilgrim Colony: A History of New Plymouth, 1620–1691.* New Haven, Conn.: Yale University Press, 1966.

Murdock, Kenneth B. *Literature & Theology in Colonial New England.* Cambridge: Harvard University Press, 1949. Reprinted, New York: Harper, 1963.

Rosenmeier, Jesper. "'With My Owne Eyes': William Bradford's *Of Plymouth Plantation.*" In *Typology and Early American Literature,* edited by Sacvan Bercovitch. Amherst, Mass.: University of Massachusetts Press, 1972.

Smith, Bradford E. *Bradford of Plymouth.* Philadelphia: Lippincott, 1951.

2

Anne Bradstreet

ANN STANFORD

Anne Bradstreet stands on the threshold of American letters as the first colonial to write out of the conscious desire to be a poet. Though she lived at the far edge of European culture, her poems cover a broad range of religious, social, political, intellectual, and domestic subjects. They show an active concern with the world of affairs and also with the inner life. They reflect wide reading and put to use her knowledge of most of the literary forms of her era. Through its use of the tradition, her work forms a link with English and Continental literature. But she adapts the tradition to the circumstances of life in the new world. She stands at the very beginning of that divergence of American from British literature which was to grow ever wider as Americans identified their unique concerns and represented them in their own forms. It is significant that Anne Bradstreet's book of poems was published first in London in 1650, then in seventeenth-century Boston, and again shortly before the Revolution.

Though isolated in space, she was never isolated in time. Her writing contains the tensions, sometimes in still shadowy form, that remained long in American life and literature. She is the civilized European facing the wilderness; she is the colonial gradually gaining roots in the new land and finally sloughing off the old world. She sides with democracy against the establishment, Parliament versus king, yet without giving up her belief that the upper, educated class should rule over those in the steps below. She represents the right,

Ann Stanford, professor of English at California State University, Northridge, is a poet, scholar, translator, and critic. Her five volumes of poetry include *The Descent* (1970). She is translator of the *Bhagavad Gita* and co-editor of the CSUN Renaissance Editions.

still sought, for woman to shape her potential beyond the narrow confines of an ordained role. She represents the Protestant against the Catholic, and in her own faith, the spirit over dogma. In her handling of all these, she is a vigorously American poet.

Anne Bradstreet's intention to be a poet is avowed in several poems. In her elegy "In honour of Du Bartas," the French Calvinist poet whom she greatly admired, dated 1641, she said:

> But barren I my Dasey here do bring,
> A homely flour in this my latter Spring,
> If Summer, or my Autumn age do yield,
> Flours, fruits, in Garden, Orchard, or in Field,
> They shall be consecrated in my Verse,
> And prostrate offered at great *Bartas* Herse.*

And the next year she presented to her father her witty defense of the woman poet in "The Prologue" to the "Four Elements" and "Four Humours." Apparently her neighbors had found fault with her for daring to write, and the criticism hurt enough to prompt her to reply:

> I am obnoxious to each carping tongue
> Who says my hand a needle better fits,
> A Poets pen all scorn I should thus wrong,
> For such despite they cast on Female wits.

She seeks elsewhere a judgment less stern:

> And oh ye high flown quills that soar the Skies,
> And ever with your prey still catch your praise,
> If e're you daigne these lowly lines your eyes
> Give Thyme or Parsley wreath, I ask no bayes.

And in 1658 she wrote: "Mean while my dayes in tunes Ile spend, / Till my weak layes with me shall end."

The determination to be a writer, along with certain other aspects of Anne Bradstreet's work, can only be accounted for by the particular circumstances and ideas that shaped her life. Like many another early settler, she was not trained for the role of pioneer. She grew up in the household of the Earl of Lincoln, where her father, Thomas Dudley, held the important post of steward and manager of the estates. The earl was one of the Puritan nobles, and

---

* Except where otherwise noted, all quotations from Anne Bradstreet are from the John Harvard Ellis edition of *The Works of Anne Bradstreet in Prose and Verse.*

his household at Sempringham was in close touch with others of the Puritan nobility, such as Lord Saye and Seale and the Earl of Warwick. John Winthrop and Roger Williams came there during the organization of the migration to the Bay Colony, and John Cotton was the preacher in Boston nearby. The Dudleys were themselves distantly related to the family of Sir Philip Sidney, or at least claimed to be. The household must have been an enlightened and exciting place, in which the reading of books vied with the stir of important events. In 1628 Anne Dudley married a protegé of her father's, Simon Bradstreet, and the young couple entered the household of the Countess of Warwick, where Bradstreet served as steward. This aged and pious lady was the widow of Lord Rich, whose first wife had been none other than Stella, the lady of Sidney's sonnets.

But the young couple were not to remain for long in the role of English country gentry. On April 8, 1630, Anne Bradstreet had her last glimpse of England, when the Bradstreets and the Dudleys sailed as part of the first large migration to the Massachusetts Bay Colony. They arrived in June, at the beginning of summer, but even so, Anne Bradstreet's impression of the New World was unfavorable. She later recorded her apprehension in a letter "To My Dear Children": "I found a new world and new manners, at which my heart rose." The context indicates that her heart rose against what she found.

The Bradstreets spent the first winter in Charlestown (Boston) and the next spring moved to Newetowne (Cambridge). Within the next few years, they moved to the new frontier town of Ipswich, and, between 1640 and 1644, on to the inland plantation of Andover (now North Andover), where Anne Bradstreet spent the rest of her life. Thus, though she belonged to a family of some wealth and standing, Anne Bradstreet, no less than later pioneers, lived constantly at the thin edge of European civilization. It has been said that Anne Bradstreet's perseverance in writing was an attempt to hang on to that civilization. But Anne Bradstreet was a realist, who was quick to take stock of where she was and what she might do there. After admitting that her "heart rose," she added, "but after I was convinced it was the way of God, I submitted to it and joined the church at Boston."

The first winter was a hard one, and many colonists grew ill and died. Anne Bradstreet survived, though her first extant poem was written after a "Fit of Sickness" in 1632. The poem is not very original, but it shows that she already had achieved considerable skill in handling rhyme and meter.

Her next dated poems are the three elegies written in 1638, 1641, and 1643 and dedicated to Sir Philip Sidney, Du Bartas, and Queen Elizabeth, all of whom she greatly admired. There is one very odd thing about these poems: Anne Bradstreet chose for them a form of elegy plus epitaph generally used for persons recently dead, whereas these three had died more than forty years before. The reason for her choice lies in a book of the poems and translations of Joshua Sylvester, titled *Du Bartas His Divine Weekes and Workes, with a Compleat Collection of all the other most delight-full Works Translated and written by the Famous Philomusus Joshua Sylvester Gent*. Anne Bradstreet doubtless had the 1631 edition of this book with her in New England. Here in Sylvester's elegies on Prince Henry and William Sidney she found the models for her own poems of praise. She follows Sylvester not only in his form, but also in his puns and wordplay. These are found more often in the elegy on Elizabeth than anywhere else in her work. The wordplay includes such lines as: "She's Argument enough to make you mute"; "Since time was time, and man unmanly man"; "She wrackt, she sackt, she sunk his Armado"; "She frankly helpt, *Franks* brave distressed King"; and ". . . proud *Cleopatra*, whose wrong name, / Instead of glory, prov'd her Countryes shame."

None of these elegies represents her best work, but the poem on Queen Elizabeth has some flashes of the sharp wit with which she defended her sex. After comparing Elizabeth to the great queens of history, she asks:

> Now say, have women worth? or have they none?
> Or had they some, but with our Queen is't gone?
> Nay Masculines, you have thus taxt us long,
> But she, though dead, will vindicate our wrong.
> Let such as say our Sex is void of Reason,
> Know tis a Slander now, but once was Treason.
>
> (ll. 95–100)

In these early elegies there is a remarkable lack of emphasis on any Christian dogma. The characters and references found in them come from Greek mythology or from history, not from the Bible. The epitaphs promise to Sidney, Du Bartas, and Elizabeth not a Christian resurrection, as Sylvester posits for his subjects, but renown and lasting fame. They reflect the Cavalier mode in elegies, not the Puritan. They are more pagan than Christian.

About the time she was writing the elegy on Du Bartas or shortly afterwards, she embarked upon an ambitious project—a long poem describing the four elements and the four humours. Didactic poems encompassing large bodies of information were popular in the period. Anne Bradstreet's father had written such a poem, too. It has been lost, but according to his daughter, it presented four sisters representing the four parts of the world. These four contested over their wealth, their arts, their age. Anne also chose to write her poem as a debate in which each character boasts of her nature and virtues. Her choice was fortunate, for the dramatic form adds much to the readability of the poem. The opening lines of "The Four Elements" are lively, and as each element rejects the claims of the others and advances her own, the result is a poem of some vigor. The material for the second of the quaternions, "The Four Humours," is drawn from a book on anatomy, the *Microcosmographia* of Dr. Helkiah Crooke (1615). The poet mentions the "curious, learned *Crooke*" in her poem and some passages are versifications of portions of that work. Dr. Crooke subscribed to the Hippocratic but still current theory of the four humours, each of which governs specific portions of the body. Every man is composed of elements and their corresponding humours in different proportions, and the characters of the choleric, sanguine, melancholic, and phlegmatic man are common in seventeenth-century literature.

Later, in a poem praising Anne Bradstreet's book, Nathaniel Ward was to call her "a right *Du Bartas* Girle." Though condescending in so referring to the matron of thirty-eight, he did make the point that Anne Bradstreet was the equal of Du Bartas. This was high praise, for most literate Englishmen of the time held the French poet in great esteem. But the phrase, together with Anne Bradstreet's own references to Du Bartas, has given undue weight to but one of the many writers whose work Anne Bradstreet read and assimilated. The strongest impact of Du Bartas on Anne Bradstreet occurred around 1642 when she was writing "The Four Elements" and "The Four Humours." There are some images drawn from Du Bartas, notably the joining of hands by the Humours near the end of their colloquy to form "A golden Ring, the Posey, Unity" and the description of the mullet in "As loving Hind." But there are many differences in style. Anne Bradstreet is much more direct; she does not use the many figures of speech, compound epithets, puns, or classical characters to be found in Du Bartas, nor does she follow him in making moral comments.

Anne Bradstreet herself consciously avoided too close a parallel with Du Bartas. In March 1642 she sent the two quaternions to her father, accompanied by a letter in rhyme; she had intended to write more, she said, on "how divers natures, make one unity," but "fear'd you'ld judge, one *Bartas* was my friend." Apparently Thomas Dudley received her poems with appreciation, for she added two more quaternions—"The Four Ages of Man" and "The Four Seasons." In these, her style, when it is not plain and direct, is closer to Spenser than to Du Bartas. The Ages and Seasons are related to the Elements and Humours: Childhood goes with Winter and is "son unto flegm, Grand-child to water"; Youth, related to Spring, "claims his pedegree from blood and air"; Middle Age, like Summer, "of fire and Choler is compos'd"; and Old Age, resembling Autumn, is made of "earth, and heavy melancholy."

In "The Four Elements" the poet had stated her version of the ancient idea of the composition of the universe. In "The Four Humours," she expounded the old theory of the composition and physiology of man as a little world. In "The Four Ages" she gives the Puritan idea of the moral nature of man in relation to sin and death. And in "The Four Seasons" she describes the New England landscape. The last of the quaternions are far better than the first pair for they are closer to Anne Bradstreet's own experience.

The theme of "The Four Ages" is the vanity of man, his accomplishments and desires, as found in every time of life. The poet begins with a conventional emblematic description of the first speaker:

> Childhood was cloth'd in white & green to show
> His spring was intermixed with some snow:
> Upon his head nature a Garland set
> Of Primrose, Daizy & the Violet.
> Such cold mean flowrs the spring puts forth betime
> Before the sun hath throughly heat the clime.
> His Hobby striding did not ride but run,
> And in his hand an hour-glass new begun.
>
> (ll. 11–18)

Childhood's monologue mingles Puritan dogma regarding the innate depravity of man, who is "stained from birth with *Adams* sinfull fact," with Anne Bradstreet's own observations on child-rearing. Of his mother, Childhood says:

> With wayward cryes I did disturb her rest,
> Who sought still to appease me with the breast:
> With weary arms she danc'd and *By By* sung,
> When wretched I ingrate had done the wrong.
>
> (ll. 73–76)

And of the ills of childhood (and we remember how many children then died in infancy):

> What gripes of wind mine infancy did pain,
> What tortures I in breeding teeth sustain?
> What crudityes my stomack cold hath bred,
> Whence vomits, flux and worms have issued?
> What breaches, knocks and falls I daily have,
> And some perhaps I carry to my grave,
> Sometimes in fire, sometimes in water fall,
> Strangly presev'd, yet mind it not at all:
> At home, abroad my dangers manifold,
> That wonder tis, my glass till now doth hold.
>
> (ll. 131–40)

"The Four Ages" and "The Four Seasons" contain many examples of such moving from symbolic or emblematic figures to more realistic scenes or portraits. The latter are kin to the prose characters of Bishop Hall, Sir Thomas Overbury, and John Earle. The characters of these and other writers as they developed in the seventeenth century portrayed stereotypes or parodies of men of varying dispositions or humours, or people of different occupations or beliefs, as "The Malcontent," "The Milkmaid," "The Puritan." But later they moved toward portrayals of real people. Anne Bradstreet's poem includes both stereotypes and portraits that suggest she used real people as models, however sketchily she drew them. The most interesting are those in "Youth," where Anne Bradstreet describes the follies of youth, a catalog which ends:

> If any time from company I spare,
> 'Tis spent in curling, frisling up my hair . . .
> Cards, Dice, and Oaths, concomitant, I love;
> To Masques, to Playes, to Taverns stil I move;
> And in a word, if what I am you'd heare,
> Seek out a Brittish, bruitish Cavaleer.
>
> (ll. 199–200, 203–6*)

In the second edition (1678) the "Cavaleer," in tune with the new fashion, wears a wig, and the second line quoted reads: " 'Tis spent to curle, and pounce my new-bought hair."

The harsh portrait of the Cavalier is in contrast to that of the ideal youth, undoubtedly a portrait of Sir Philip Sidney, for in addition to claiming other Sidneyan virtues, Youth says:

---

* This quotation is taken from the Josephine K. Piercy edition of *The Tenth Muse;* hereafter cited as Piercy.

> I cannot lye intrench'd before a town,
> Nor wait till good success our hopes doth crown:
> I scorn the heavy Corslet, musket-proof;
> I fly to catch the bullet thats aloof.
>
> (ll. 159–62)

So Sidney, casting off part of his armor, was caught by a bullet during the seige of Zutphen.

Though the Cavalier is here shown as morally, socially, and religiously opposed to virtue, he was also at this time a political opponent of the Puritans, and her description is at least partially politically motivated. Satirical portraits of political groups had been included in the collections of characters since Elizabethan times, and the number of these increased around 1642. In her portrayal of the Cavalier, Anne Bradstreet was undoubtedly aware of current political writing.

In "Middle Age" she pictures the middle-class family man and his many responsibilities with great sympathy:

> Yet all my powers for self ends are not spent,
> For hundreds bless me for my bounty lent.
> Whose backs I've cloth'd, and bellyes I have fed
> With mine own fleece, & with my houshold bread.
>
> (ll. 253–56)

She speaks in particular of the good done by the just magistrate, the good pastor, the skillful captain, the soldier, and the cheerful laborer, types often used by the writers of characters. Here we have a list of the characters of a small town such as Ipswich, where her husband was a magistrate and her brother-in-law a captain. At his worst, the middle-aged man was subject to the usual vanities. He is represented by a farmer with his "dunghil thoughts," and her realistic description of the farmer's life contrasts with the more idealistic portrayal given in "Spring."

Old Age recounts the conflicts between Protestant and Catholic on the Continent and in England as he recalls his life. Perhaps he represents Anne Bradstreet's father, who, like his father before him, had fought in France on behalf of the French Protestants. Perhaps he speaks for the poet, too, when he states that knowing much is the pleasantest life of all. His speech rounds out the theme of vanity that has unified this quaternion by a paraphrase of Ecclesiastes 12 : 1–8 on the vanities of life. This is the first long incursion of a Biblical element into Anne Bradstreet's work, an element that was to become increasingly strong.

"The Four Seasons," especially "Spring" and "Summer," are in large part an appreciation of the life and activities of a New England household and farm. Though the travel literature which drew many settlers to the New World was rich in praises of plenty, Anne Bradstreet's appreciation is perhaps the first of that line of literary productions which celebrated America as a homeland. Half a century before Samuel Sewall composed his famous passage on Plum Island, Anne Bradstreet describes the land and her new home with affection. She no longer seems conscious of the mysterious wilderness and the loss of her native country; her description makes the New World seem a satisfactory home. And England, after more than a dozen years in the New World, must have seemed far away. "Spring" is probably the best of these early public poems. In "Autumn" she moves once again toward an imagined landscape, for she includes oranges and lemons among the fruits of autumn. Here she is using the landscape as emblem and is describing autumn as the month in which Adam was created in the garden of Eden. She includes in her poem a defense of wine:

> The vintage now is ripe, the grapes are prest,
> Whose lively liquor oft is curs'd and blest:
> For nought so good, but it may be abused,
> But its a precious juice when well its used.
> (ll. 171–74)

The quaternions of the elements, humours, ages, and seasons are followed by another poem of fours. Despite its title, "The Four Monarchies" is not a continuation of the preceding group. This longest and dullest of her poems is an abridgment of Raleigh's *History of the World*, taking the Assyrian, Persian, and Grecian empires from the reign of Nimrod to the death of Cleopatra. The fourth monarchy, the Roman, is incomplete. Whole passages are versifications of Raleigh, though she did consult other historians. The poem answered in her time the then commendable purpose of teaching through the "delight" of rhyme, and the lessons of history were, of course, especially important to the Puritans and to the sixteenth and seventeenth centuries generally. As in the preceding quaternions, however, Anne Bradstreet usually presents her material without the moralizing found in her source.

More interesting to us is the history that she repeats in "A Dialogue between Old *England* and New; concerning their present Troubles, *Anno*, 1642." The troubles referred to were of course the opening battles of the English Civil War. In the dialogue between Old Eng-

land and her daughter New England the reader is given a quick
sketch of the history of England's wars under various conquerors and
kings from the Saxons on, and he is brought up to date on the latest
news from England, including the beheading of the Earl of Strafford
and the retirement of Charles I to York. There is no question that
Anne Bradstreet is on the side of Parliament in the dispute. But in the
character of New England she is forced to defend the Puritans who
had crossed to America in the migrations of the 1630s; by this time
some English Puritans had accused their colonial brethren of de-
serting their fellows rather than staying to purify the church at home.
Thomas Shepard was to answer such accusations in 1648 with his
pamphlet, *A Defence of the Answer*, and Anne Bradstreet's earlier
poem contains similar arguments. She describes the injuries to the
saints in those days, and ponders the doom that hung over England
for its irreligious ways:

> The Sermons yet upon record doe stand,
> That cry'd, destruction to my wicked Land:
> These Prophets mouthes (alls the while) was stopt,
> Unworthily, some backs whipt, and eares cropt;
> Their reverent cheeks, did beare the glorious markes
> Of stinking, stigmatizing, Romish Clerkes.
>
> (Piercy, ll. 125–30)

The Puritans of Massachusetts Bay had hoped, among other goals,
to be a model of the Congregational system for the English churches
when the time came for their release from Romish prelates. Some
had conceived of themselves as going to the new world to prepare
an army to fight in the battles which would liberate the church, as
Edward Johnson dramatically described in *The Wonder-Working
Providence of Sion's Savior in New England* (1654). Neither of these
hopes were realized. New England can offer Old England only prayers
and sympathy, for the sudden ceasing of immigration into the colonies
at the beginning of the forties caused a serious depression. Anne
Bradstreet takes note of this:

> Your humble Child intreats you, shew your grief,
> Though Arms, nor Purse she hath for your relief,
> Such is her poverty.
>
> (ll. 53–55)

This poem and the historical portion of "Old Age" indicate how
interested the colonists were in the events going on in England. Anne
Bradstreet put into these poems references to events very current;

she had apparently read pamphlets and sermons dealing with the crisis. A mention of Mero's curse in her poem is a reference to a sermon on that theme preached in Westminster by Stephen Marshall in February 1642 and reprinted several times during the Civil War. She also in this poem shows a vengefulness not present in other portions of her work (except in her comments on reports of atrocities in Ireland):

> But those that hurt his people and his Crown,
> By force expell, destroy, and tread them down:
> Let Gaoles be fill'd with th'remnant of that pack,
> And sturdy *Tyburn* loaded till it crack.
>
> (Piercy, ll. 240–43)

She ends the poem with a bit of millenarianism. Once peace in England is won and Charles has submitted to Parliament, she calls for a holy war against the church of Rome and against the Turks, and for the conversion of the Jews. Then in this millennium the whole Western world as she knows it will be at peace, united in the worship of God in the Puritan way.

It was during the following year (1643) that she wrote the elegy on Queen Elizabeth. Doubtless one reason for her writing in praise of the great queen at that time was to contrast her reign with that of the Stuarts. Sylvester, in dedicating his book to James I, had called Elizabeth a Phoenix from whose ashes "a new true Phoenix" arose in the form of James. Anne Bradstreet denies this, saying: "She was a Phoenix Queen, so shall she be, / Her ashes not reviv'd, more Phoenix she." And she goes on to say: "But happy *England* which had such a Queen: / Yea happy, happy, had those dayes still been."

The millenarianism of "Old *England* and New" is reflected in the elegy when she says of the queen:

> No more shall rise or set so glorious sun
> Untill the heavens great revolution,
> If then new things their old forms shall retain,
> *Eliza* shall rule *Albion* once again.
>
> (ll. 107–10)

The concern with Biblical subjects developed here in the millennial passages and in the vanity theme of "The Four Ages" is continued in her next two poems. Neither of these reveal much of the author. "*Davids* Lamentation for *Saul* and *Jonathan*" is a paraphrase of the passage of 2 Samuel. "Of the vanity of all worldly creatures" is a gracefully written assertion of the theme that there is a greater good than that which the senses reveal—a theme to be pursued later in "The Flesh and the Spirit," "Contemplations," and "As weary pilgrim."

The quaternions, with their introduction and prologue, "The Four Monarchies," "A Dialogue between Old *England* and New," the elegies on Sidney, Du Bartas, and Elizabeth, "*Davids* Lamentation," and "Of the vanity of all worldly creatures" comprise all of Anne Bradstreet's long, predominantly didactic poems. With the exception of "The Prologue," and an apology at the end of the quaternions, they are all in heroic couplets. With the possible exception of part of "The Four Monarchies," they were probably all written during the Bradstreets' residence in Ipswich. All of them represent an active concern with the events of the world and with books.

Though at its founding Ipswich was "thirty miles by Indian trail from Boston," it quickly became a center for some of the most educated and liberal people of the colony. Nathaniel Ward, who had a wide acquaintance on the continent of Europe and who later returned to England and preached before Parliament, wrote *The Simple Cobler of Aggawam* there. John Winthrop, Jr., lived there for a time, bringing with him his library of over a thousand books. Richard Saltonstall, Jr., the son of Sir Richard Saltonstall, lived there too, as did some members of the Dudley family. Another resident was Richard Bellingham, who is perhaps most famous for his appearance as the governor in *The Scarlet Letter*. Simon Bradstreet himself was a magistrate, required to go to meetings of the Great and General Court at Boston. The leaders of Ipswich were educated and well informed on what was going on in the homeland and on the continent. The public poems of Anne Bradstreet reflect this alertness and concern with worldly things.

After Parliament seized power in the Civil War, New England ministers were much sought after by congregations in England, and many of them returned there. Among these were Nathaniel Ward and Anne Bradstreet's brother-in-law, John Woodbridge. In 1647 Ward's *Simple Cobler* was published in London by Stephen Bowtell at the sign of the Bible in Popes Head Alley. Three years later, in 1650, Stephen Bowtell published *The Tenth Muse Lately sprung up in America . . . By a Gentlewoman in those parts.* The manuscript was delivered to the printer by John Woodbridge, and it contains the encomium by Nathaniel Ward, among others.

Anne Bradstreet reacted to the publication of *The Tenth Muse* with a poem which combines the expression of her dismay at being published—and with so many errors—and the acknowledgment of

pride in her work. In his introductory poem John Woodbridge had
likened her book to a child, saying:

> If't be a fault, 'tis mine, 'tis shame that might
> Deny so fair an Infant of its right,
> To look abroad; I know your modest mind,
> How you will blush, complain, 'tis too unkind:
> To force a womans birth, provoke her pain,
> Expose her labours to the Worlds disdain.

Catching up the image of the child, Anne Bradstreet sent a good-
natured reply in the often reprinted poem which begins:

> Thou ill-form'd offspring of my feeble brain,
> Who after birth did'st by my side remain,
> Till snatcht from thence by friends, less wise then true
> Who thee abroad, expos'd to publick view.

The poem ends on a note reminiscent of Spenser's "Goe little booke"
at the beginning of *The Shepheardes Calender:*

> If for thy Father askt, say, thou hadst none:
> And for thy Mother, she alas is poor,
> Which caus'd her thus to send thee out of door.

Anne Bradstreet was probably acquainted with that work of Spenser,
for she mentions him elsewhere in her poetry and without doubt
knew his other little volume *Astrophel.*

Despite her claims of embarrassment over the publication of her
poems, Anne Bradstreet immediately set to work making corrections.
She says:

> Yet being mine own, at length affection would
> Thy blemishes amend, if so I could:
> I wash'd thy face, but more defects I saw,
> And rubbing off a spot, still made a flaw.
> I stretcht thy joynts to make thee even feet,
> Yet still thou run'st more hobling then is meet;
> In better dress to trim thee was my mind,
> But nought save home-spun Cloth, i'th'house I find.

She must have hoped for another chance to present her poems in
"better dress." Perhaps she already had in mind such a book as "The
second Edition, Corrected by the Author," which was eventually to
appear in 1678, some six years after her death.

Sometime between the completion of the poems in *The Tenth Muse*
and its publication in 1650, the Bradstreets moved to the new inland

plantation of Andover. This was not so cosmopolitan a town as
Ipswich. It contained several families related to the Dudleys, but
the houses were more scattered. It was in the comparative isolation
of Andover that Anne Bradstreet wrote most of her private poetry,
the poetry which reflected her own inner feelings and her relationship
to her family. There are five earlier poems written at Ipswich, however, which were not published in *The Tenth Muse* and which form
a part of this domestic poetry. These are the poems written to her
husband. Sincere, yet cast in the most complicated of her metaphors,
they are among the best of her work. They express an ardent love for
her husband, whose love she prizes "more then whole Mines of gold."

The group includes three poems written as letters to her husband
"absent upon Publick employment." He had probably gone to Boston,
for she uses in one of them the metaphor of his having gone south-
ward while she remains in the north, her only solace being to look
upon her children, "those fruits which through thy heat I bore."
These poems are metaphysical arguments. They are not based so
much on fact as in the argumentative bouncing of the image conceived by the poet. In the first she represents herself as the earth,
her husband as the sun. In the second she begs Phoebus to carry
a message to her husband of her sorrows at his absence. Using the
elaborate tear imagery often found in the period, she says: "Tell him
here's worse then a confused matter, / His little world's a fathom
under water." The last and best of the three begins with a play on
words: "As loving Hind that (Hartless) wants her Deer," and depicts
the poet successively as a hind, a dove, and a mullet. The mullet,
according to legend, when her mate is lost, cast herself on the shore.
The poem concludes with the witty and delightful request:

> Return my Dear, my joy, my only Love,
> Unto thy Hinde, thy Mullet and thy Dove,
> Who neither joyes in pasture, house nor streams,
> The substance gone, O me, these are but dreams.
> Together at one Tree, oh let us brouze,
> And like two Turtles roost within one house,
> And like the Mullets in one River glide,
> Let's still remain but one, till death divide.

The poem is admirably constructed. Eight lines are devoted to
each of the three controlling images—the first four describe the deer,
dove, or mullet looking for its mate; the second four draw the
parallel to the poet. The last eight lines collect the three images

into two arguments. Though the rhyme is that of couplets, the syntax
gives the effect of quatrains. The image-and-argument structure is
similar to that she was later to use so effectively in "Contemplations."
The poem is far from being as homespun as it pretends. It is a
skillful metaphysical love poem.

The remaining poem to her husband is more serious. Mindful of
the many deaths of women in childbirth, Anne Bradstreet composed
the poem "Before the Birth of one of her Children," in which she
begged her husband to remember her and to protect her babes
"from step Dames injury." This poem appears to have been written
before 1647. "In reference to her Children," written in June 1658,
contains imagery similar to that of the love poems though it again
is much more serious. In it, the poet writes in the character of the
mother bird "I had eight birds hatcht in one nest." The metaphor is
not as complicated as that in the earlier love poems, for it simply
transfers the human situation of family to bird situations ("house"
becomes "nest," etc.). It ends on a note of love and continuing concern for her children.

> When each of you shall in your nest
> Among your young ones take your rest,
> In chirping language, oft them tell,
> You had a Dam that lov'd you well,
> That did what could be done for young,
> And nurst you up till you were strong,
> And 'fore she once would let you fly,
> She shew'd you joy and misery;
> Taught what was good, and what was ill,
> What would save life, and what would kill?
> Thus gone, amongst you I may live,
> And dead, yet speak, and counsel give:
> Farewel my birds, farewel adieu,
> I happy am, if well with you.

As did so many other Puritans, Anne Bradstreet at times kept a
journal, and there still exists a notebook containing entries for the
years 1656–57 and 1661–62. The entries were made for the spiritual
benefit of her children, and the opening letter contains words reminiscent of lines from the poem "I had eight birds," which was
written at about the same time. To her children she says that she
wishes to "bequeath to you, that when I am no more with you, yet
I may bee dayly in your remembrance, (Although that is the least

in my aim in what I now doe) but that you may gain some spiritual Advantage by my experience. I have not studied in this you read to show my skill, but to declare the Truth—not to sett forth myself, but the Glory of God. . . . The method I will observe shall bee this—I will begin with God's dealing with me from my childhood to this Day."

There follows a short biography and some prose meditations, together with poems of prayer and thanksgiving for God's various mercies, mostly the granting of recoveries from illness. The prose passages reveal her struggles with the acceptance of Christian dogma: "I have often been perplexed that I have not found that constant Joy in my Pilgrimage and refreshing which I supposed most of the servants of God have; although he hath not left me altogether without the wittnes of his holy spirit, who hath oft given mee his word and sett to his Seal that it shall bee well with me." She confesses that many times she has been troubled by the question of whether there is a god, but "That there is a God my Reason would soon tell me by the wondrous workes that I see, the vast frame of the Heaven and the Earth, the order of all things, night and day, Summer and Winter, Spring and Autumne, the dayly providing for this great houshold upon the Earth . . . ." Yet, knowing there is a god, how does she know that she worships the true god? "May not the Popish Religion bee the right?" Rejecting this thought, she returns to "this Rock Christ Jesus . . . and if I perish, I perish."

The telling of her spiritual experience and her doubts is the kind of recital required for admission into a congregation; other Puritans both in England and America, including Thomas Shepard and John Bunyan, tell of similar religious doubts. However common the subject, Anne Bradstreet's letter is convincing and remains one of the finest pieces of colonial prose.

The poems of praise and thanksgiving found in the notebooks are in the iambic tetrameter or alternate tetrameter and trimeter of the *Bay Psalm Book* and the Sternhold *Psalms,* rhyming *abab* or *abcb,* a form seldom seen in Anne Bradstreet's work until this time. Though they seem written more for piety than for art, they bear a clear music. In this they may be contrasted with their model, for the versification of the *Bay Psalm Book* is noted for its awkward inversions of syntax. Anne Bradstreet's poems of praise, on the other hand, are direct. In their simplicity of diction they foreshadow that later New Englander, who also wrote in the meters of the hymns, Emily Dickinson.

Two of Anne Bradstreet's poems of prayer stand out as especially fine. One is that of May 13, 1657, which begins:

> As spring the winter doth succeed,
> And leaves the naked Trees doe dresse,
> The earth all black is cloth'd in green;
> At sun-shine each their joy expresse.

The other is "Upon my dear and loving husband his goeing into England, Jan. 16, 1661" (N.S. 1662). This is a fervent prayer for the protection of her husband. It contains the last of the poet's political allusions, for her husband's mission was to gain the acceptance by the newly restored monarchy of the colony's patent and former privileges. Anne Bradstreet is aware of the mission:

> Unto thy work he hath in hand,
> Lord, graunt Thou good Successe
> And favour in their eyes, to whom
> He shall make his Addresse.

And then come the moving lines by the gentlewoman looking out at the bleak wintry woods:

> Remember, Lord, thy folk whom thou
> To wildernesse hast brought;
> Let not thine own Inheritance
> Bee sold away for Nought.

During her husband's absence Anne Bradstreet found consolation in a spiritual aid available to Christians of all faiths, the practice of meditation. In the seventeenth century this practice had become widespread. The New England minister Thomas Shepard recounts in his *Autobiography* his going out to the fields to meditate: "I took out a little book I have every day into the feelds & writ down whut god taught me least I should forget them." In the poem "In my Solitary houres in my dear husband his Absence" Anne Bradstreet writes of finding consolation in a colloquy with God:

> And thy Abode tho'st made with me;
> With Thee my Soul can talk
> In secrett places, Thee I find,
> Where I doe kneel or walk.

She mentions the practice also in her more formal dialogue "The Flesh and the Spirit":

> In secret place where once I stood
> Close by the Banks of *Lacrim* flood

> I heard two sisters reason on
> Things that are past, and things to come;
> . . . .
> Sister, quoth Flesh, what liv'st thou on
> Nothing but Meditation?
> Doth Contemplation feed thee so
> Regardlessly to let earth goe?
> Can Speculation satisfy
> Notion without Reality?
>
> (ll. 1–4, 9–14)

The formal practice of meditation had been described by a long series of Catholic and Anglican writers, beginning with Ignatius Loyola. These Catholic and Anglican methods were transcribed to forms suitable for Puritans by Richard Baxter in *The Saints Everlasting Rest* (1650). There is no reason to believe that Anne Bradstreet had read Baxter, but she was undoubtedly acquainted with the practice itself and with some of the poetry which grew out of it. In its briefest form, meditation involves the vivid picturing in the imagination of a scene called the "composition of place." The scene may be drawn from the Old or New Testaments, the details of the life of Christ, the terrors of hell, or a more present situation. Baxter explained the value of meditating on the creatures as well as on the Scriptures: "There is yet another way by which we may make our senses serviceable to us, and that is, by comparing the objects of sense with the objects of faith; and so forcing sense to afford us that medium, from whence we may conclude the transcendent worth of glory, by arguing from sensitive delights as from the less to the greater." The thought that the creation is visible proof of the existence of God also appeared repeatedly in New England sermons and was accepted, as we have seen in the passage previously quoted from the notebook, by Anne Bradstreet. It was therefore natural that she would turn to the creatures for her meditation. For her, as for others, the creatures not only proved the existence of God but were symbolic of his eternal truths.

After imagining a scene, or seeing the subject of meditation before one in the fields, the meditator draws arguments from it regarding eternal truths or his own relation to God. The last step is a colloquy with God or with the creature, theoretically involving the will, in which the meditator determines to have more faith, to cease from sin, to abide by God's laws, or comes to some moral discernment.

Related to the production of poetry in the form prescribed for meditation was another kind of poetry popular in the seventeenth century. This was the poetry found in the emblem books, such as those of Quarles and Wither. These consisted of pictures accompanied by a text, usually in verse. The text explained the symbols or characters involved in the picture and drew a moral from them.

In her major poem "Contemplations," Anne Bradstreet reflects her knowledge of both meditative and emblematic poetry. Beginning with a description of place, the poem moves through a series of commentaries on the objects seen, and concludes with an exclamation involving Time. Within this broad structure is a whole series of smaller meditative or emblematic poems which move naturally from one to another. Taken together, they express the double theme that the creatures of earth tell of the glory of God and are in many ways stronger and more lasting than man, whose life is short and full of care. Yet man alone of all the creatures may achieve immortal life.

The composition of place is established in the first two stanzas which describe the glory of autumn and assert: "If so much excellence abide below; / How excellent is he that dwells on high?" Then the poem shifts to a more detailed look at the scene, first at an oak, then at the sun. From each of these, the truths which they symbolize are drawn. The poet then shifts to a completely imaginary scene to depict various stories and characters from the Old Testament: the fall of Adam and Eve, Eve holding the infant Cain, the murder of Abel. The conclusion of this section compares the shortness of life of modern man to that of his ancestors, the idea that man had decayed since the fall being still a vital one. The shortness of man's life continues as a theme through the next group of stanzas (18–20), where the poet returns once more to the scene before her, and, using the emblems of heavens, trees, and earth, comments on the mortality of the creatures. Stanzas 29–32 describe the woes of mankind. The last stanza, which holds the position of the colloquy in the meditative poem, begins with an exclamation "O Time the fatal wrack of mortal things," which is close to an apostrophe and which sums up the moral of the whole series of meditations.

In the whole of the poem or series of poems, Anne Bradstreet is following a sequence which she has adapted from the writers of meditative and emblematic poetry. The whole series may be read as a poem in meditative form, for it moves from a description of a real or imagined scene, through a drawing of analogies to moral truths, to a final summing up of the moral in the exclamation addressed to Time. Within the long meditation are shorter meditations on the trees, fishes, birds, and insects, with their moral or spiritual implications and colloquies, as well as partial meditations in which the pictorial is stressed, as in the descriptions of Old Testament characters. Anne Bradstreet has in her usual eclectic way used existing genres of poetry for her purposes.

In doing so she has made excellent use of her seven-line stanza form. The lines are in iambic pentameter, rhyming *abab ccc*. This rhyme scheme lends itself to a division in the stanza between the quatrain and the triplet. The poet observes the division by a break in syntax and in context. The quatrain generally paints the picture, describes the scene, or asks a question. The triplet interprets the picture or draws the moral lesson or the truths to be known from the creatures depicted. Thus the individual stanza does in small space what the groups of stanzas do and what the poem does as a whole.

An extra foot in the last line of each triplet makes for an easy flow into the next stanza. The same stanza form with its long last line was used by Phineas Fletcher for his *Purple Island* (1631), a long poem in which the human body is described in geographical and political terms. However, the *Purple Island* stanza has runovers of syntax and context into the triplet, which Anne Bradstreet usually avoids. Her stanza form is ideally adapted to the contemplative poem.

Anne Bradstreet was aware that she was writing an emblematic or meditative poem. In stanza 23 she mentions the emblem during an apostrophe addressed to the stream ("O happy Flood"):

> Thou Emblem true, of what I count the best,
> O could I lead my Rivolets to rest,
> So may we press to that vast mansion, ever blest.
>
> (ll. 159–61)

She uses the term "emblem" again in one of her prose "Meditations" (no. 40): "The spring is a lively emblem of the resurrection, after a long winter we se the leavlesse trees and dry stocks (at the approach of the sun) to resume their former vigor and beauty in a more ample manner then what they lost in the Autumn."

It has sometimes been said that Anne Bradstreet was an early forerunner of the Romantics in her descriptions of nature found in "Contemplations." Her appreciation of nature, however, is always subordinated to the purpose of the poem. In "Contemplations" it is bound to the structure of the emblem. She appreciates nature because it is the visible sign of the invisible Power behind it. There is not the panoramic sweep that is often found in Wordsworth's or Bryant's scenic pieces. Her step-by-step use of emblems is closer to Bryant's "Waterfowl," a type of poem which derives from such a late meditative writer as Vaughan, through Wordsworth, to the Romantic moral poem.

In "Contemplations" Anne Bradstreet achieves a balance between the tensions that appear in some of her other poems and in her prose. There is an appreciation of the natural scene, what had once been to her wilderness. There is an acceptance of the importance of the eternal and invisible life, of which the visible scene is a temporal representation. Here are no critical neighbors or political disturbances. This is Anne Bradstreet's most serene poem.

An even greater acceptance of religious teaching is to be found in her series of prose "Meditations Divine and morall" begun in March 1664. These are aphoristic paragraphs, many of them in the form of analogies or metaphors. The late nineteenth century regarded these as the best of Anne Bradstreet's work, but there is little in them beyond proper moralizing. Few show much of the poet; most repeat without question the dogma of her time. A few, containing remarks on rearing children, show a pleasing awareness of human differences. One (72) is rather poignant. It suggests that Anne Bradstreet may have been looking back over the long journey from her first home with an acceptance of reality: "As the brands of a fire, if once severed, will of themselves goe out, altho you use no other meanes to extinguish them, so distance of place, together with length of time (if there be no intercourse) will coole the affectiones of intimate friends, though there should be no displeasence betweene them."

More interesting than "Meditations" is "The Flesh and the Spirit," which follows "Contemplations" in the second edition of her poems. It reflects once more the struggle between the visible and the belief in the invisible which animates the prose of the notebooks. The Flesh, having criticized the Spirit's interest in contemplation, meditation, and speculation continues her scornful diatribe:

> Dost dream of things beyond the Moon
> And dost thou hope to dwell there soon?
> Hast treasures there laid up in store
> That all in th' world thou count'st but poor?
> Art fancy sick, or turn'd a Sot
> To catch at shadowes which are not?
>
> (ll. 15–20)

Flesh then describes the pleasures of the world, the "true substance." The treasures are fame, riches, and pleasure. They may be attained, says Flesh, by "industry," that basic Puritan virtue, and there is no indication in the poem that the fame, riches, and pleasures she speaks of are of a dishonorable nature, though Spirit calls the pleasures "sinful." The Bradstreets were well off and they took part in such modest pleasures as the colony afforded. Fame must have been the greatest temptation, however, to Anne Bradstreet. We remember the conclusions of the early elegies, which promised, not eternal life, but fame. We remember her request for a modest parsley wreath, and her claim, in the first edition, to be kin to Sir Philip Sidney. These sisters arguing, are the two parts of Anne Bradstreet herself, and the struggle runs through all her poems from 1665 to her last dated poem in 1669. These are among her best and most often reprinted poems.

The tension is illustrated in her poem "Upon the Burning of Our House." In 1666 the Bradstreet house at Andover burned down and along with it the Bradstreet's library of over 800 books and Mrs. Bradstreet's papers, among them part of her long poem on the Roman monarchy. The poem Anne Bradstreet wrote after the disaster is not a dialogue, though the movement is similar to that in "The Flesh and the Spirit." The first two stanzas describe the noise and shouts of "fire" and her coming out to watch her house burn down. She continues with the proper religious statement:

> And, when I could no longer look,
> I blest his Name that gave and took,
> That layd my goods now in the dust:
> Yea so it was, and so 'twas just.
> It was his own: it was not mine;
> Far be it that I should repine.

The Spirit here seems to have a hard time convincing the Flesh of the justice of her loss. The poem continues: "He might of All justly bereft, / But yet sufficient for us left." The Flesh recounts her losses:

> When by the Ruines oft I past,
> My sorrowing eyes aside did cast,
> And here and there the places spye
> Where oft I sate, and long did lye.

> Here stood that Trunk, and there that chest;
> There lay that store I counted best:
> My pleasant things in ashes lye,
> And them behold no more shall I.
> Under thy roof no guest shall sitt,
> Nor at thy Table eat a bitt.

> No pleasant tale shall 'ere be told,
> Nor things recounted done of old.
> No Candle 'ere shall shine in Thee,

> Nor bridegroom's voice ere heard shall bee.
> In silence ever shalt thou lye . . . .

But the Spirit gains the upper hand for the rest of the poem: "Then streight I gin my heart to chide, / And did thy wealth on earth abide?" and goes on to praise her permanent house "on high erect, / Fram'd by that mighty Architect."

The response of the Flesh to the promises of the Spirit came with even more difficulty in the case of the loss of her beloved grandchildren. Between the years 1665 and 1669 Anne Bradstreet wrote three elegies on such losses. These are far different from her early elegies already discussed. They are, too, far different from and vastly superior to other elegies written by her New England contemporaries. The funeral elegy, which was pinned to the hearse of the dead or passed around among the mourners, was a popular form of poetry among the New England Puritans. But the funeral elegy most often written was full of puns on the decedent's name and other kinds of word play together with apologies for the writer's lack of skill. We need only recall as examples that by E. B. on Samuel Stone, in which the departed is called a whetstone, a loadstone, a ponderous stone, etc., and the elaborate tribute to Anne Bradstreet herself in which John Norton says:

> Her breast was a brave Pallace, a *Broad-street*,
> Where all heroick ample thoughts did meet,
> Where nature such a Tenement had tane,
> That other souls, to hers, dwelt in a lane.

In contrast, Anne Bradstreet's elegies are sincere outpourings of grief, checked and held in balance by her asserted belief in the everlasting.

The procedure followed in the poem "In memory of my dear grandchild Elizabeth Bradstreet, who deceased August, 1665. being a year and half old" is similar to that in the poem on the burning of her house. It is a movement between grief and the proper attitude toward death. It is written in the "Contemplations" stanza, which lends itself remarkably well to the tensions of the elegy. The first four lines express farewell and sorrow, the triplet replies:

> Blest babe why should I once bewail thy fate,
> Or sigh the dayes so soon were terminate;
> Sith thou art setled in an Everlasting state.

The second quatrain describes how it is natural for mature things to die, and the triplet responds with what comes close to criticism of the Almighty:

> But plants new set to be eradicate,
> And buds new blown, to have so short a date,
> Is by his hand alone that guides nature and fate.

The feeling of the strength of grief in this poem, conveyed by so appropriate a form, makes this one of the finest elegies in American literature.

In 1669 and 1670 the family of Anne Bradstreet's son Samuel suffered a succession of tragedies. Moreover, the poet herself seems to have fallen into either an illness or a despair with this earthly life much different from her usual strong response. Samuel's daughter Anne died in June 1669 at a little more than three years of age, and the poet's elegy on that occasion remarks resignedly: "Farewel dear child, thou ne'er shall come to me, / But yet a while, and I shall go to thee." However, when the third of Samuel's children died in November of the same year, Anne Bradstreet came as close as she ever had to criticism of the Lord. She elaborates the motif she had used for the ending of the elegy on Elizabeth: "Three flours, two scarcely blown, the last i'th'bud, / Cropt by th'Almighties hand . . . ." The statement of fact is almost an accusation, especially when it is followed by the almost ironic "yet is he good," and by her characteristic but stubborn acceptance:

> With dreadful awe before him let's be mute,
> Such was his will, but why, let's not dispute,
> With humble hearts and mouths put in the dust,
> Let's say he's merciful as well as just.

If the word "say" is emphasized, this is indeed close to blasphemy. Anne Bradstreet closed the elegy with four conventional lines, a settling back into dogma after her outburst of feeling.

Anne Bradstreet's last important poem other than the elegies, "As weary pilgrim," was written in that discouraging summer of 1669. In it she finally accepts, even embraces, the everlasting state she had never seemed quite sure of. She begins with the metaphor of the pilgrim which gives its title to the poem—the pilgrim who traverses a wilderness of briars, thorns, hungry wolves, erring paths, rugged stones, stumps, and rocks, and who eats wild fruits instead of bread. But the metaphor is not entirely imaginary, for Anne Bradstreet herself has experienced the actual wilderness. She too is a weary pilgrim, her "Clay house mouldring away." She brings to the poem some of the realistic detail characteristic of her work:

> This body shall in silence sleep
> mine eyes no more shall ever weep

> No fainting fits shall me assaile
>   nor grinding paines my body fraile
> With cares and fears ne'r cumbred be
>   Nor losses know, nor sorrowes see.

She continues with the image of Christ as a welcome bridegroom:

> What tho my flesh shall there consume
>   it is the bed Christ did perfume
> And when a few yeares shall be gone
>   this mortall shall be cloth'd upon
> A Corrupt Carcasse downe it lyes
>   a glorious body it shall rise

and concludes: "Lord make me ready for that day / then Come deare bridgrome Come away." Once more, the same heart that "rose" when she came into the new world accommodated itself to the inevitable after long struggle. The tension that so often appears in her private poems between what she saw and what she believed, between the visible and the invisible, is one of the lasting strengths of Anne Bradstreet's work.

Anne Bradstreet was an eclectic writer; she drew upon a wide variety of reading for use in her own work. But she always adapted what she read to her own purposes. Thus, in her three early elegies, she shifted the formal memorial purpose of Sylvester's elegies to poems of praise, and even, in the case of that on Queen Elizabeth, to a partly political poem. She transformed the encyclopaedic and didactic material of Du Bartas to semidramatic form as a response to a poem by Thomas Dudley. She used the witty argument of the metaphysical love poem, but imbued her metaphoric arguments with a lasting genuineness of emotion. She combined what she learned from meditative and emblematic poetry in the poem "Contemplations." Her poems of prayer surpassed their models in *The Bay Psalm Book*. And she made of the Puritan elegy, often a formal exercise in verbal ingenuity, a lasting statement of human grief.

In the early poems—those up to the early 1640s—Anne Bradstreet used wit as a method. Just as the Elements and Humours used wit in the repartee one against another, so Anne Bradstreet used it in "The Prologue" to defend herself against those who thought her "hand a needle better fits." She used it in her apology for her book and in the love poems written from Ipswich to her husband. As time went on her poetry became more direct and realistic.

In the observer of the "clocking hen" of "Spring," the fussy babies of "Childhood," and the sufferer of "fainting fits" in "As weary pilgrim," we have glimpses of a real personality establishing itself in a real landscape. The literary responses of the earlier poems gave way to an almost shocking outspokenness in her dealings with God in her later work. In the musical lines of her best poems and in her observations of nature, she catches overtones of the Elizabethan age behind her and the Romantic age that was to come. Anne Bradstreet deplored the harsh new world into which she had come. But submitting herself to it, she came to celebrate her life there in poetry and prose that is worthy to stand at the beginning of our literature.

BIBLIOGRAPHY

Editions

Poems of Anne Bradstreet. Edited by Robert Hutchinson. New York: Dover, 1969.
The Tenth Muse. Edited by Josephine K. Piercy. Facsimile reproductions. Gainesville, Fla.: Scholars' Facsimile & Reprints, 1965.
The Works of Anne Bradstreet. Edited by Jeannine Hensley. Cambridge: Harvard University Press, 1967.
The Works of Anne Bradstreet in Prose and Verse. Edited by John Harvard Ellis. Charlestown, Mass.: Abram E. Cutter, 1867. Reprinted, New York: Peter Smith, 1932; Gloucester, Mass.: Peter Smith, 1962.

Scholarship and Criticism

McMahon, Helen. "Anne Bradstreet, Jean Bertault, and Dr. Crooke." *Early American Literature* 3 (Fall, 1968): 118–23.
Morison, Samuel Eliot. "Mistress Anne Bradstreet." In *Builders of the Bay Colony.* Boston: Houghton Mifflin, 1930, 2d ed., rev. and enl., 1964.
Piercy, Josephine K. *Anne Bradstreet.* New York: Twayne, 1965. Reprinted, New Haven, Conn.: College and University Press, 1965.
Richardson, Robert D., Jr. "The Puritan Poetry of Anne Bradstreet." *Texas Studies in Literature and Language* 9 (1967): 317–31.
Rosenfeld, Alvin H. "Anne Bradstreet's 'Contemplations': Patterns of Form and Meaning." *New England Quarterly* 43 (1970): 79–96.
Stanford, Ann. "Anne Bradstreet: An Annotated Checklist." *Early American Literature* 3 (Winter, 1968–69): 217–28.
——. "Anne Bradstreet: Dogmatist and Rebel." *New England Quarterly* 39 (1966): 373–89.
White, Elizabeth Wade. *Anne Bradstreet "The Tenth Muse."* New York: Oxford University Press, 1971.

3

Edward Taylor

DONALD E. STANFORD

Edward Taylor composed his poems in the late seventeenth and early eighteenth centuries. They were not made available to the reading public until over two hundred years later. This is the only case in American literature where the twentieth-century reader is confronted by an important body of poetry written so many years ago for which he does not have the aid of intervening centuries of scholarship and critical judgment to help in understanding and appreciating it. At least two adjustments have to be made before we can appreciate Taylor's poetic accomplishment. We must be willing to place ourselves imaginatively in the world of seventeenth-century Puritan Calvinism, where the devil is taken seriously and literally and a few saints are battling a great many sinners, and we must be willing to accept the artificial rhetorical style of the seventeenth-century metaphysical poets, which often seems confused and awkward to us today, particularly if we have recently been reading the more harmonious verses of the popular Romantic and Victorian writers.

Furthermore, as we read Edward Taylor we should keep in mind the fact that poetry was not Taylor's primary preoccupation. He was, for over fifty years, from 1671 until his retirement in 1725, a Puritan parson in the small frontier town of Westfield, Massachusetts. In church polity he was a Congregationalist. In religious doctrine he was a Calvinist—that is, his fundamental religious ideas were identical

Donald E. Stanford is professor of English at Louisiana State University and editor of *The Southern Review.* He is the author of two volumes of poetry and the editor of the comprehensive edition of the poems of Edward Taylor. He has held a Guggenheim fellowship (1959–60) and was a visiting professor at Duke University (1961–62).

with those set forth in the *Institutes* (1536) of John Calvin and rephrased in the Westminster Confession of 1645–47. In both polity and doctrine he was in accord with the leading Massachusetts ministers of his day—such as the famous Increase and Cotton Mather. He fought against all deviations from his own conservative orthodox views, particularly against the practice of Solomon Stoddard of Northampton in admitting the unregenerate to the sacrament of the Lord's Supper. In his poems and sermons he attacked various "schisms" and churches not his own, especially the Anglican and Roman Catholic.

It has sometimes been said that a Puritan of narrow dogmatic views (such as Taylor) cannot compose important poetry, and that a man whose primary attention is devoted to the salvation of his own soul and the souls of his parishioners and whose life is circumscribed by the strict moral code enjoined by his faith does not have the range of human experience to create a literature of permanent and wide appeal. In a way, Taylor is a test case. Can a Calvinistic Puritan write successful poetry? Taylor wrote entirely on religious subjects. His education included the study of Hebrew, Greek, and Latin poetry, but one gets the impression that it was mainly a textbook knowledge and not the wide-ranging humanism of a scholar and poet like Milton. We know from poems copied out in his notebooks and from internal evidence in his own verse that he had read a few English poems, but, in all probability, only a few. His library contained only one book of poems in English (by Anne Bradstreet) and most of the books he owned or copied were sermons or were on religious subjects. Yet it will be the argument of this chapter that in spite of the limitations of his time, place, and education he succeeded in composing a remarkable body of poetry and is quite properly considered America's first important poet.

He was born of yeoman parents (who were in all probability nonconformist) in Sketchley, England, about 1642. Sketchley, a small hamlet a few miles from Coventry, was a farming community. (It has disappeared, but the name is still prominent in advertisements for the Sketchley dye works.) Taylor was brought up in a thatched cottage and undoubtedly learned the rudiments of farming at an early age. There is a possibility that he learned the newly developed weaver's trade in nearby Hinckley. His poems make frequent use of the technical terms of farming and weaving. He went to a nonconformist school, but there is no real evidence that he attended a university in England. He taught school for a short time in his native country, but the Act of Uniformity of 1662 by which King Charles II required all school teachers and ministers to acknowledge their faith

in the Anglican mode of worship deprived Taylor of a chance to earn
his living by either teaching or preaching. Consequently, in 1668, at
the age of twenty-six, he embarked for the New World, and from that
time on his story belongs to American history. He entered Harvard
College, taking the usual courses which were considered good training
for the ministry, and upon his graduation in 1671 he accepted the call
to Westfield. He preached his weekly sermons to a farmer congregation
from 1671 until his retirement in 1725. He died in 1729 and was buried
at Westfield. He was married twice—to Elizabeth Fitch of Norwich,
Connecticut, and, after her death, to Ruth Willys of Hartford. He
had fourteen children—eight by his first wife, six by his second. Five
of his children by Elizabeth Fitch died when they were babies. One
of his most moving poems, "Upon Wedlock, and Death of Children,"
records his grief.

Taylor's place in the literary history of America will be determined
by two groups of poems: the *Preparatory Meditations* and *Gods
Determinations*. Both groups (in very different ways) promulgate
Taylor's Puritan Calvinism. The basic doctrine of Calvinism may be
summarized as follows: Before the foundations of the world were
laid God had foreordained that a few men, the elect, would be saved
through the intercession of his son, Jesus Christ. The rest of mankind
would justly suffer in hell as a result of the pre-ordained Fall in the
Garden of Eden. Those pre-ordained to be saved were in a covenant
relation with God, the Covenant of Grace, so called because salvation
was granted by God's Grace alone and was not merited by any
works man might do. The emphasis among all Calvinists, including
Taylor, was on the overwhelming majesty and power of God as contrasted with the insignificance and weakness of natural man. Those
who were of the elect could discern the working of saving Grace in
their hearts and be assured of salvation. (The certainty of assurance
was a matter of debate among the Puritans. Taylor himself sometimes
expressed fear that he might be unregenerate.) Those assured of
salvation or at least of the probability of salvation were allowed to
partake of the Lord's Supper, which was considered a seal of the
covenant of Grace.

THE *PREPARATORY MEDITATIONS*

In 1682 Taylor wrote the first poem of a group which he described
on his title page as *Preparatory Meditations before my Approach to*

*the Lords Supper. Chiefly upon the Doctrin preached upon the Day
of administration.* He continued composing at intermittent intervals
until 1725. By this time he had completed over two hundred
meditations.

The Lord's Supper for which these poems were spiritual preparation
was one of two sacraments which the Congregational Church inherited from Anglican and Roman Catholic worship. It was admin-
istered to his congregation by the pastor—at irregular intervals in the
case of the Westfield church, although the evidence available at
present seems to indicate that Taylor would have liked to administer
the sacrament at least once every two months. Illness may have
prevented maintaining the original schedule. Also, it appears that on
more than one occasion Taylor withheld the sacrament from his congregation for disciplinary reasons.

Taylor considered the Lord's Supper to be a most important part
of Congregational worship. Although the Puritans did not believe in
transubstantiation (the changing of the whole substance of the bread
and wine into the body and blood of Christ), they did believe in the
real spiritual presence of the Lord at the sacrament—and in a sense—
the real physical presence also. The sacrament was for the regenerate
only (in Taylor's opinion)—that is, it was reserved for those alone
who were assured that they had received and experienced saving
grace. At the time of the partaking of the Lord's Supper the devout
Puritan experienced a real spiritual union with Christ. The most frequently expressed emotions in these meditations are *wonder* and *joy:*
wonder that God would suffer himself to be united to worthless
humanity corrupted by original sin, and joy that the union has been
achieved and that the believer is purified and saved.

The Style of the Meditations

To express these feelings of wonder and joy, Taylor employed a
poetic style that was derived chiefly from two sources: the Bible (particularly the Song of Solomon and the Book of Revelation) and the
poetry that Taylor read as a schoolboy and later during his early years
in England. His use of colloquial diction and rhythms, his juxtaposition of the learned words of the scholar with the technical terms of
weaving and with the common diction of the farmer and the rural
cottage remind us of the metaphysical style of John Donne and his
"school." Probably the greatest single poetic influence on Taylor was

a volume of poems, *The Temple* (1633), by the metaphysical poet George Herbert, although he is never mentioned by name in any of the Taylor manuscripts. John Cleveland, one of the last of the metaphysical poets and famous in his day for his extravagant wit, is mentioned once in a poem by Taylor. Cleveland, educated in Hinckley, not far from Taylor's native hamlet of Sketchley, was esteemed during the seventeenth century more than Milton. It is almost certain that Taylor read him, and he may have been a minor influence on Taylor, who was the last of the important English and American poets to write in the metaphysical style.

The influence of the Bible is pervasive—each meditation is based on a text from the Bible or on doctrine derived from the text. One of Taylor's favorite books must have been the Song of Solomon or Canticles (as he called it). A long series of poems (Meditations 115–53 of the second series) composed toward the end of Taylor's life is derived exclusively from the texts of Canticles, and there are a number of other meditations also derived from this book of the Bible. Taylor, like other Puritans, interpreted the Song of Solomon allegorically, and what was, in the original Hebrew, erotic love poetry becomes a celebration of the "marriage" or "wedden" as Taylor called it between Christ (the bridegroom) and his church (the bride). Thus the Lord's Supper is frequently described as a "wedden feast" and the spiritual preparation for the feast is referred to as the putting on of the "wedden garment," the bridal clothes being thought of as signs of sainthood:

> Seing, Dear Lord, its thus, thy Spirit take
>   And send thy Spokes man, to my Soul, I pray.
> Thy Saving Grace my Wedden Garment make:
>   Thy Spouses Frame into my Soul Convay.
> I then shall be thy Bride Espousd by thee
> And thou my Bridesgroom Deare Espousde shalt bee.*
>
> (1 : 23)

Commentators have noted the sensuous language used in describing the mystical union between the poet and Christ. The sensuousness comes chiefly from the Bible and not (as far as we can judge) from personal sexual experience or from secular books. These lines from Meditation 2 : 149:

---

* Unless otherwise indicated, all quotations from Taylor are taken from my edition of *The Poems of Edward Taylor.*

> Thy Spirituall Navill like the Altars Bowle
> Filld full of Spirituall Liquor to refresh
> The Spirits babes conceived in thy Soule

and

> Her Belly where her Spirituall Offspring's bred
> Is like an heap of Wheate most Choice and fine
> With fragrant Lillies richly selvidged
> Making the whole most beautifully shine

appear strange coming from a Puritan parson until we remember that Canticles 7 : 2 in the King James version reads, "Thy navel is like a round goblet, which wanteth not liquor: thy belly is like an heap of wheat set about with lilies." But the figure "to refresh / The Spirits babes conceived in thy Soule" is not in Canticles. It is obviously a conceit derived from reading the more extravagant metaphysical poets, perhaps Crashaw or Cleveland. Similarly in Meditation 1 : 4 Taylor, taking the words "I am the Rose of Sharon" from Canticles, indulges in various sensuous appeals. To the sense of smell:

> Lord lead me into this sweet Rosy Bower:
> Oh! Lodge my Soul in this Sweet Rosy bed:
> Array my Soul with this sweet Sharon flower:
> Perfume me with the Odours it doth shed.

To touch: "Lord, with thy Oyle of Roses Supple mee." To taste: "Lord let my Dwindling Soul be dayly fed / With Sugar of Sharons Rose, its dayly Bread." To taste and touch:

> God Chymist is, doth Sharons Rose distill.
> Oh! Choice Rose Water! Swim my Soul herein.
> Let Conscience bibble in it with her Bill.
> Its Cordiall, ease doth Heart burns Causd by Sin.

God is a chemist (that is, in modern-day terms, a druggist), and conscience is a duck. The juxtaposition of the apothecary's shop, the farmyard, and the rose of Sharon from the Bible is typical of metaphysical poetry and of much of Taylor's verse. Also typical of the metaphysical style is the amount of work the rose is made to do in this poem. It furnishes a bower for lovers, a bath for the soul, and a medicine (cordial) to cure the heart of sin. (Roses were in fact made into purges in the seventeenth century.) The rose in Christian typology was Christ, Christ's blood, and Christ's grace. And so, fastening words to things in the style advocated by Ramistic handbooks of rhetoric, Taylor wrote the following stanza in this same poem:

But, oh! alas! that such should be my need
   That this Brave Flower must Pluckt, stampt, squeezed bee,
And boyld up in its Blood, its Spirits sheed,
   To make a Physick sweet, sure, safe for mee.
   But yet this mangled Rose rose up again
   And in its pristine glory, doth remain.

But yet this mangled Rose rose up again! The Christian typology, the pious pun so frequent in the seventeenth century, the schoolboy reading of George Herbert, the firsthand experience with medicine (Taylor was the town's physician), the constant meditation on the Song of Solomon (Taylor must have known it by heart) produced a line, and indeed an entire poem, which is quite unique in American literature, unique, that is, except for other poems by Taylor himself. After Taylor's death, this style was not seen again in America or England.

When Taylor was educated in England and at Harvard, he was required to study the standard rhetorical handbooks of his time. There he found examples of such figures or tropes as synechdoche, metonymy, meiosis, amplification, ploce, polyptoton, etc., all designed to enhance the style of the would-be poet and preacher. Some of these figures (and others) are referred to by name in his "Declamation" read at his graduation exercises in 1671; a poem which praised the English language as superior to Latin, Greek, and Hebrew:

   Our Web thus wrought, rich Rhetorick steps in
   As golden Lace a Silver Web to trim.
   There's scarce a single thrid but doth entwine
   A Trope or Figure in't to make it fine.
   Here lies a Metonymy; there doth sculke
   An Irony; here underneath this bulke
   A Metaphor; Synecdoche doth reare
   And open publickly Shopwindows here.*

And so on. Before the poem is finished he has listed a dozen figures of speech. It is fair to say that the influence of these "rhetorical style sheets" was as pervasive as that of the Bible or as that of any other single source. A few examples will have to suffice. Amplification, the device of reinforcing a proposition by the piling up of specific repetitious detail, is frequently used by Taylor, too frequently for modern taste. The most usual employment of this figure occurs when the poet is depicting the glory of God or Christ. Thus in Meditation 1 : 17 the

---

* Thomas H. Johnson, "The Topical Verses of Edward Taylor," *Publications of the Colonial Society of Massachusetts* 34 (1943): 524.

glory of God is stated to be superior to that of any earthly king—but this simple idea is extended by amplification through seven stanzas, that is, through the entire poem. The first two stanzas read:

> A King, a King, a King indeed, a King
>   Writh up in Glory! Glorie's glorious Throne
> Is glorifide by him, presented him.
>   And all the Crowns of Glory are his own.
>   A King, Wise, Just Gracious, Magnificent.
>   Kings unto him are Whiffles, Indigent.
>
> What is his Throne all Glory? Crown all Gay?
>   Crown all of Brightest Shine of Glory's Wealth?
> This is a Lisp of Non-sense. I should say,
>   He is the Throne, and Crown of Glory 'tselfe.
>   Should Sun beams come to gilde his glory they
>   Would be as 'twere to gild the Sun with Clay.

For the modern reader this is rhetoric run wild. It would probably have been more acceptable to the average seventeenth-century reader.

The contrast of amplification, diminishing (meiosis or "abasing a matter")—the repetitious use of pejorative terms—is employed again and again to portray the sinful nature of fallen man. Thus Meditation 2 : 18 begins:

> A Bran, a Chaff, a very Barly yawn,
>   An Husk, a Shell, a Nothing, nay yet Worse,
> A Thistle, Bryer prickle, pricking Thorn
>   A Lump of Lewdeness, Pouch of Sin, a purse
>   Of Naughtiness, I am, yea what not Lord?
>   And wilt thou be mine Altar? and my bord?
>
> Mine Heart's a Park or Chase of sins: Mine Head
>   'S a Bowling Alley. Sins play Ninehole here.
> Phansy's a Green: sin Barly breaks in't led.
>   Judgment's a pingle. Blindeman's Buff's plaid there.
>   Sin playes at Coursey Parke within my Minde.
>   My Wills a Walke in which it aires what's blinde.

Augmenting and diminishing were, in fact, considered a single device (amplification) when used in juxtaposition, and this figure came naturally to the Calvinist poet when he was promulgating his favorite topic—the glory of God contrasted to the sinfulness of natural man, and concomitantly, the vileness of fallen nature contrasted to the beauty of regenerate man. Meditation 2 : 75 is one of a group of meditations which contrasts the state of fallen man with that of the saint. The entire poem is simply one long amplification. Natural man is a "varnisht pot of putrid excrements," a "Mudwall tent," a house tainted with leprosy. Regenerate man is a cabinet of sparkling gems, a house made with walls of precious stones overlaid with gold leaf, and so on. Often amplification employs a series of similes and metaphors which appear to be hopelessly mixed, as in "The Return," where Christ in one stanza is a spout, a stepping stone, and a ladder:

> Heavens Golden Spout thou art where Grace most Choice
> Comes Spouting down from God to man of Clay.
> A Golden Stepping Stone to Paradise
> A Golden Ladder into Heaven!

Central to Taylor's Christian doctrine is the paradox of the incarnation—the belief that Taylor refers to as "blessed Theanthropie," the union of an omniscient God, who is everything, with powerless human nature, which is nothing. As Taylor expresses it "Thou Full, and Empty art: Nothing, yet ALL" (Meditation 1 : 2). Hence paradox becomes an important element of his poetry, a stylistic device he shares with the metaphysical poets but which, regardless of the influence of metaphysical poetry, he probably would have employed anyway. Paradox is frequently expressed by puns, and it should be noted that the pun in Taylor's poetry is usually pious and not mere word play, as in Shakespeare's famous line "When first your eye I eyed." The most obvious and extravagant example of the pious paradoxical pun is Meditation 2 : 48, where "might" expresses the power of God and "mite" expresses the weakness of man:

> My Mite (if I such Solicisms might
> But use) would spend its mitie Strength for thee
> Of Mightless might, of feeble stronge delight.

Some form of the word *might* (or *mite*) is used forty times in this poem of seven stanzas.

Such a repetition of words (named ploce by the rhetoricians) and a repetition of a single word root in different inflectional forms (polyptoton) also occur frequently to reinforce figures other than paradox. Meditation 1 : 7 presents the conceit of Christ as a distillery. His body is the "Golden Still," his "Holy Love" is the heat whereby the "Spirit of Grace" is distilled, and the soul of the poet is the "Violl" which he hopes will be filled with the distilled spirit. All this is in the first stanza. The second stanza continues:

> Thy Speech the Liquor in thy Vessell stands,
> Well ting'd with Grace a blessed Tincture, Loe,

Thy Words distilld, Grace in thy Lips pourd, and,
Give Graces Tinctur in them where they go.
Thy words in graces tincture stilld, Lord, may
The Tincture of thy Grace in me Convay.

The repetition of "Grace" is an example of ploce; "ting'd," "Tincture" and "distilled," "stilld" are examples of polyptoton. It will be observed that the metaphor has changed somewhat. In the first stanza Grace is the distilled spirit. In the stanza quoted, Grace has become a tincture, a medicinable substance dissolved in the alcohol of Christ's words. The third stanza begins: "That Golden Mint of Words, thy Mouth Divine." Christ's mouth has now become a mint coining gold, whereas in the first stanza it was: "Thy Mouth the Neck through which these spirits still." Taylor attempts to bring the two metaphors together in the final lines of the poem: "Grace in thy Lips pourd out's as Liquid Gold. / Thy Bottle make my Soule, Lord, it to hold." Grace is thus both gold and a spirituous liquid.

Nevertheless by modern standards the figures in this and in most of Taylor's poems are badly mixed. It is a fact of life one has to live with in order to appreciate Taylor and much other poetry of the seventeenth century, and by an act of the historical imagination we have to remind ourselves that sensibilities change through the centuries, that the seventeenth-century sensibility perceived similarities in the midst of differences and seems not to have been perturbed by the presence of the differences, that is, the mixed figures of speech. Evidently Taylor, in using symbolic language, did not visualize his images in quite the same way we do, because if he did he would have easily perceived the ludicrousness of some of his figures: a surrealistic rose, for example, equipped with knife and fork, carving up a roast of beef: "Dost thou sit Rose at Table head, where I / Do sit, and Carv'st no morsell sweet for mee?" These lines are from the famous "The Reflexion" and if we can read them with little or no visualization as Taylor intended, the poem can become a moving performance. There is considerable complexity in this passage and indeed in the entire poem (confusion of the sexes, for example). According to the usual allegorical interpretation, the Song of Solomon celebrates the marriage between the bridegroom (Christ) and the bride (the church). Sometimes, as in 2 : 1 of the Song, the woman speaks, "I am the rose of Sharon." Sometimes, as in 7 : 1, the man appears to be speaking, "How beautiful are thy feet with shoes, O prince's daughter!" Taylor appears to be reversing the usual interpretation and identifies Christ with the woman, the rose of Sharon, yet the confusion is easily overlooked because it seems natural for the male poet to be writing love poetry to a woman rather than to a man. It has been pointed out by at least one critic that there also may be sexual overtones in the figure of the "conduit" in a preceding stanza. How aware Taylor was of the possible sexual implications of this love song to Christ is a matter of conjecture.

Taylor's Mysticism

"The Reflexion" seems to record an intense personal experience amounting perhaps to a hallucination or a vision:

Once at thy Feast, I saw thee Pearle-like stand
'Tween Heaven, and Earth where Heavens Bright glory all
In streams fell on thee, as a floodgate and,
Like Sun Beams through thee on the World to Fall.

The poem stands near the beginning of the *Preparatory Meditations,* is not entitled "Meditation," is undated, and has no Biblical text as the meditations have. It is preceded by two companion poems which perhaps record the same mystical experience. "The Experience" describes a moment of union with Christ which occurred during prayer over the Lord's Supper:

Oh! that I always breath'd in such an aire,
As I suckt in, feeding on sweet Content!
Disht up unto my Soul ev'n in that pray're
Pour de out to God over last Sacrament.
What Beam of Light wrapt up my sight to finde
Me neerer God than ere Came in my minde?

Because he is actually united to God he is superior to the angels:

I'le Claim my Right: Give place, ye Angells Bright.
Ye further from the Godhead stande than I.
My Nature is your Lord; and doth Unite
Better than Yours unto the Deity.
Gods Throne is first and mine is next: to you
Onely the place of Waiting-men is due.

In the next poem, "The Return," he appears to be writing of the same experience and wishing for its return. Most of the stanzas have the refrain: "Oh! that thou Wast on Earth below with mee / Or that I was in Heaven above with thee," and the penultimate stanza states definitely

I do say
That thou hast been on Earth below with mee,
And I shall be in Heaven above with thee.

It may not be too fanciful to suggest that the desire to accomplish "The Return" to that one overpowering mystical moment that occurred during prayer at the Lord's Supper was the prime motivation for the entire sequence of *Preparatory Meditations* written over a period of forty-three years. Although the three poems in question are undated, their position in the manuscript indicates that "The Experience" occurred in 1682, the year in which Taylor started writing his *Preparatory Meditations*.

The Structure of the Meditations

These meditations are what their title suggests—an act of contemplation expressing profound and pious emotions, certainly, but by no means exhibiting that "spontaneous overflow of powerful feelings" in the romantic sense. As we have seen, they are written in a fairly complex and formal style with the frequent and conscious (sometimes self-conscious) use of conventional rhetorical devices. Most of them are structured according to certain demonstrable patterns. For instance, the very act of meditation had its rules in both Catholic and Protestant practice, and when these rules were followed the result was a poem with a clearly definable organization. Richard Baxter in his *Saints Everlasting Rest* (1650) formulated the conventional method which involved the three faculties of the soul—memory, understanding, and will. The subject matter of the meditation (or the poem) is heavenly doctrine supplied by the memory. This doctrine is analyzed and comprehended by the understanding or reason. Once understood the affections of the will (the emotions) are aroused in this order: love, desire, hope, courage, and joy. Louis Martz has demonstrated that Taylor's Meditation 1 : 29 follows this pattern. The first two stanzas present the "heavenly doctrine"—that Christ is the Tree of Life and natural man is a "Withred Twig," destined for destruction unless he is grafted onto the Tree of Life. The next three stanzas analyze and amplify the doctrine and the central image. The final two stanzas express the emotions aroused by an understanding of the doctrine. Besides a logical development, the poem has a basic unity achieved by the employment of the Tree of Life image, which is consistently maintained through every stanza. This threefold development combined with a fundamental image is employed in a number of meditations.

We do not have to go to Baxter, however, to describe the structure of many of these meditations. Taylor's method is frequently this: He begins with a depiction of man's fallen estate, of original sin, and of his own personal sins. The concomitant emotion is despair. Next, he depicts Christ and his redemptive power, frequently with a vision of the elect in heaven. The concomitant emotion is joy. He concludes with a plea to Christ that he be numbered among the elect. The concomitant emotion is hope. Frequently, the final lines state that if he is saved he will sing the praise of Christ, that is, compose verses in his honor. He usually employs terms of abasement in referring to his own verses ("my rough feet," "my ragged rhymes"), together with the notion that he needs Christ's aid to improve them.

The emotional progression is from despair (that man has fallen) to joy (that some are saved) to hope (that the poet will be saved). The pattern may be schematized:

Subject	Emotion
1. Original sin	Despair
2. Christ's saving grace	Joy
3. Possibility of personal salvation	Hope

The vision of the elect which motivates the feeling of joy is dramatically juxtaposed to the depiction of original sin with its expression of despair; hence, the climactic moment of the poem comes in part 2 instead of part 3.

Three meditations, among many, may be analyzed to demonstrate this procedure. Meditation 1 : 39 has as its Biblical text "If any man sin, we have an Advocate." The first two stanzas depict the poet's sins: "My Sin! my Sin, My God, these cursed Dregs, / Green, Yellow, Blew streakt Poyson hellish, ranck," and Taylor's inability to cope with them:

> I cannot kill nor Coop them up: my Curb
> 'S less than a Snaffle in their mouth: my Rains
> They as a twine thrid, snap: by hell they're spurd.

The next four stanzas set forth the doctrine of Christ the Redeemer, who has purchased salvation for some men through his death on the

Cross. In contemplating this doctrine the poet expresses *joy:* "Joy, joy, Gods Son's the Sinners Advocate / Doth plead the Sinner guiltless, and a Saint." The two last stanzas are a plea to Christ to number the poet among the saved, and if Christ does so, the poet will be enabled to sing his praises:

> My Sins make thine, thy Pleas make mine hereby.
> Thou wilt mee save, I will thee Celebrate.
> Thou'lt kill my Sins that cut my heart within:
> And my rough Feet shall thy smooth praises sing.

The poem has logical development, emotional progression, and is given an overall unity by the fundamental metaphor of Christ as attorney, who is pleading the sinner's case before the bar of divine justice, a metaphor which is introduced in the third stanza and maintained throughout the remainder of the poem.

Meditation 1 : 33 has a similar pattern. It is dated July 7, 1689, the day on which Elizabeth Taylor, the poet's first wife, died, and it has, for that reason, been sometimes misinterpreted as an elegy on his wife's death written in honor of her memory. However, we know from the elegy he wrote later that Mrs. Taylor died in the evening of July 7 about "two hours after sunset." July 7 was a Sunday. Taylor, according to the title page of his meditations, composed these poems in preparation for his administration of the Lord's Supper. Hence he must have finished Meditation 1 : 33 Sunday morning *at the latest,* before his wife died, and therefore the poem cannot be about her death. Furthermore, a careful reading shows that this poem is a conventional meditation on salvation through Christ. It makes no mention of his wife. The Biblical text is "Life is youres." The first four stanzas are a meditation on sin. The first three stanzas depict the poet's own sins—he has set his heart on worldly things instead of divine. He addresses Christ:

> Oh! what strange Charm encrampt my Heart with spite
>   Making my Love gleame out upon a Toy?
> Lay out Cart-Loads of Love upon a mite?
>   Scarce lay a mite of Love on thee, my Joy?

The fourth stanza makes a statement about original sin and the devil—the cause of all sin and of death: "Hells Inkfac'de Elfe black Venom spat upon / The same, and kill'd it. So that Life is gone." The second part of the poem consists of only one stanza, the fifth, which defines Christ's redemptive power with the figure of the golden Ark: "Life thus abusde fled to the golden Arke, / Lay lockt up there in Mercie's seate inclosde." The third division of the poem (the last two stanzas) is a conventional plea to Christ that the poet be saved— that is, included in the golden Ark: "Lord arke my Soule safe in thyselfe, whereby / I and my Life again may joyned bee."

The threefold patterns described above, deriving from the faculties of memory, understanding, and will of the Catholic and Protestant meditative tradition or from the contemplation of sin, of Christ's redemptive power, and of the possibilities of personal salvation, patterns which are sometimes unified by a single concept or metaphor (Christ as attorney, for example) account for the structure of most of the meditations.

Typology as a Unifying Device

Within the structures described above there may occur an extremely loose and "wild" associational progression from image to image which reminds us of the most extravagant "baroque" techniques of Crashaw and Cleveland. Meditation 2 : 78 is an example of this kind of associational development unified by typology. Like many poets of the seventeenth century, Taylor was thoroughly versed in typology—the finding of events, persons, or things (the types) in the Old Testament which foreshadowed events, persons, or things in the New Testament (the antitypes). For example, the ram which was provided by God to be sacrificed in place of Isaac was considered the type of Christ. The Jewish Passover is the type of the Lord's Supper. John Bunyan in his "Light for Them That Sit in Darkness" (1675) divides the types of Christ into three groups: men, beasts, and insensible creatures. Men who are types of Christ are: Adam, Moses, Aaron, Melchisedic, Samson, Joshua, David, and Solomon. The beasts considered types of Christ are the Paschal Lamb and the red cow of Numbers 19 : 2 because, says Bunyan, it was without blemish and was sacrificed. Objects in the Old Testament that are types of Christ are the manna in the wilderness, the rock that gave out water, and Mount Moriah.

Taylor makes use of these types and of metaphors derived from typology. Christ is the antitype of the rose of Sharon; hence Christ is frequently referred to as a rose or as a medicine (cordial) derived from roses. The bunch of grapes found by the scouts in Canaan was considered a type of Christ. Therefore, Christ is not only grapes, but wine pressed from the grapes. The notion that the virgin Mary was a cabinet enclosing a jewel was common in Christian typology and accounts for the many enclosing images in Taylor's poetry.

Keeping these matters in mind, it is now possible for the twentieth-century reader to consider Meditation 2 : 78 from Taylor's own point of view:

> 78. Meditation. Zech. 9.11. By the Blood
> of thy Covenant I have sent forth
> thy Prisoners out of the Pit wherein
> is no water.

Mine Eyes, that at the Beautious Sight of Fruite
  On th'Tree of, Knowledge, drew black venom in
That did bemegerim my brains at root
    That they turnd round, and tippled me int' Sin.
    I thus then in t'Barath'rick pit down fell.
    Thats Waterless and next doore is to Hell:

No water's here: It is a Springless Well.
  Like Josephs Pit, all dry of Comforts Spring.
Oh! Hopeless, Helpless Case: In such I fell.
    The Creatures buckets dry, no help can bring:
    Oh, here's a Spring: Indeed its Lethe Lake
    Of Aqua-Infernales: don't mistake.

This Pit indeed's Sins Filthy Dungeon State,
  No water's in't, but filth, and mire, Sins juyce.
Wherein I sinke ore Head, and Eares: sad fate,
    And ever shall, if Grace hath here no Sluce.
    Its Well Coards whip Coards are: not Coards to draw
    (Like Pully Coards) out of this Dungeons maw.

Yet in the upper room of Paradise
  An Artist anvill'd out Reliefe sure, Good,
A Golden Coarde, and bucket of Grace Choice
    Let down top full of Covenantall blood.
    Which when it touches, oh! the happy Cry!
    The doores fly ope. Now's jayle's Deliverie.

This is a Spring of Liquor, heavenly, Cleare.
  Its Streams oreflow these banks. Its boundless Grace
Whose Spring head's Godhead, and its Channells where
    It runs, is Manhood veans that Christ keeps Chase
    For it, and when it makes a Springtide Flood
    This Pit is drown'd with Covenantall blood.

And now the Prisoners sent out, do come
  Padling in their Canooes apace with joyes

Along this blood red Sea, Where joyes do throng,
    And sayling in the Arke of Grace that flies
    Drove sweetly by Gailes of the Holy Ghost
    Who sweetly briezes all along this Coast.

Here's Covenant blood, indeed: and't down the banks
    Of this dry Pit breakes: Also 'tis a key
T'unlock the Shackles Sin hung on their Shanks
    And wash the durt off: send them cleane away.
    The Pris'ners freed, do on this Red Sea swim
    In Zions Barke: and in their Cabbins sing.

Lord let this Covenantall blood send mee
    Poore Prisner, out of Sins dry Dungeon pound.
And on this Red Sea saile mee safe to thee
    In which none Israelite was ever drown'd.
    My Sayles shall tune thee praise along this coast
    If waft with Gailes breath'd by the Holy Ghost.

The poem has the usual three-fold structure: The first three stanzas are a meditation on original sin and particularly on the poet's own sinful nature, which arouses a feeling of despair. The next four stanzas make statements about Christ's redemptive power and present a picture of the salvation of the elect. The emotional climax of the poem occurs in stanza six and expresses (as we would expect) the feeling of joy:

    And now the Prisoners sent out, do come
        Padling in their Canooes apace with joyes
    Along this blood red Sea . . . .

The final stanza is a plea to Christ to save the poet and enable him to sing praises in his honor.

The basic unifying figure is that of the pit, cited in the Biblical text and referred to in every stanza. The imagery, inextricably involved with typology, which at first glance appears hopelessly confused, probably would seem less so to the seventeenth- or early eighteenth-century reader. It may be analyzed as follows:

Stanza one: The poet (man) has eaten the forbidden fruit. The fruit has envenomed him with sin until his brains are thoroughly tippled. In this state he falls into the pit of Barathrum (a pit near Athens where condemned criminals were thrown). The pit is waterless.

Comment: The forbidden fruit and the venom are, of course, standard figures of sin. The pit, any pit, may represent hell.

Stanza two: The pit of Barathrum is identified with Joseph's pit. It is dry; God's grace is not to be found in it. The poet's bucket is dry. The pit, however, is not dry. It is full of the mire of Lethe Lake, of Aqua-Infernales.

Comment: The dry bucket refers to man's inability to save himself without grace from above. The Aqua-Infernales calls to mind, by contrast, the aqua vitae which is a common figure for God's grace. The seventeenth-century typological mind found no difficulty in a pit which was "dry" (devoid of God's grace) and at the same time full of Aqua-Infernales.

Stanza three: The pit is full of sin's juice; the poet is drowning in it and will drown unless Grace opens the sluice and drains off the filth. The well cords which descend into the pit are of no help. They are, rather, like whip cords.

Stanza four: In paradise an Artist (God) has fashioned a golden bucket full of blood. The bucket of blood, when let down into the pit, frees the prisoner.

Comment: Taylor, as he is frequently in the habit of doing, abruptly changes his metaphor. In the preceding stanza the poet is drowning and Grace to save him must open a sluice and draw off "sin's juice." In this stanza Grace becomes a bucket of blood which if added to sin's juice would of course simply increase the poet's predicament. The typological mind, however, moved with ease from one figure to the next, the appropriateness of the figure being determined by traditional usage (typological or otherwise) and not by whether or not it logically coalesced with the preceding figure.

Stanza five: The bucket of "Covenantall" blood is a clear spring of liquor (aqua vitae) whose source is the Godhead and whose channels are Christ's and man's veins. In the springtime this spring makes a flood and drowns the pit.

Comment: The notion that blood is a "clear spring" offered no difficulty to one who believed that blood and water poured from Christ's side. The "Springtide Flood" refers to seasonal floods and to the season of Christ's Passion and Resurrection. The abrupt transition from the figure of the bucket to the figure of the channels as carriers of God's grace is typical of Taylor's method.

Stanza six: The prisoners (they are now plural) escaping from the pit paddle joyfully in their canoes along the blood red sea; they enter the ark which is driven along by gales of the Holy Ghost.

Comment: The blood red sea calls to mind the Red Sea, traversed by the escaping Israelites. In typology, the Red Sea was a standard type of Christ's blood, which drowns sins as the Red Sea drowned the Egyptians. Noah's ark and the ark of the covenant were often identified, and Noah was considered a type of Christ. The Indian canoes are a New England innovation. The notion of the Holy Ghost as a breath or a breeze is commonplace.

Stanza seven: The Covenant blood washes sins off; it is also a key to unlock the shackles of sin. The freed prisoners swim in "Zions Barke" and sing in the cabins.

Comment: The allegorical mind can consider blood as both a liquid and a key, and sin as both dirt and shackles, without being disturbed by the obvious incongruity.

Stanza eight: The poet prays to the Lord to free him from the dungeon of sin and sail him in the ark along the Red Sea to paradise. If the Lord does this, the poet will tune his sails to praise God. The poet identifies himself with the Israelites who escaped from Egypt.

Comment: The mind that can call the Red Sea a key is not perturbed by the notion of tuning sails as if they were a harp. Taylor's intention is not to shock the reader by violent juxtaposition of imagery. Nor does he expect the images to coalesce. Nor are the images supposed to suggest connotations and meanings beyond the strictly limited and conventional typology from which they are drawn. Taylor's procedure is this: to illustrate and define his ideas by means of symbols drawn from typology, or by means of images drawn from almost anywhere, with attention only to the concrete particulars of the image relevant to the idea he is illustrating, and without any attention to the irrelevant or "suggestive" particulars of the image, and without any consideration as to whether the concrete particulars of one image are congruent with the concrete particulars of preceding and following images.

We have been attempting to consider Meditation 2 : 78 from the point of view of a contemporary reader of Taylor's poetry. The fact remains, however, that for most of us the style of this poem will seem bizarre and extravagant. It is probable that Taylor's reputation will rest on meditations which are closer to the restrained style of Herbert or to the plain style of Ralegh and Ben Jonson. Meditation 1 : 6 makes use of several rather complicated conceits but without the incongruous mixture of figures that we find in Meditation 2 : 78. The tone is that of a quiet, subdued, yet moving prayer.

Another Meditation at the same time.

Am I thy Gold? Or Purse, Lord, for thy Wealth;
Whether in mine, or mint refinde for thee?

Ime counted so, but count me o're thyselfe,
  Lest gold washt face, and brass in Heart I bee.
I Feare my Touchstone touches when I try
  Mee, and my Counted Gold too overly.

Am I new minted by thy Stamp indeed?
  Mine Eyes are dim; I cannot clearly see.
Be thou my Spectacles that I may read
  Thine Image, and Inscription stampt on mee.
If thy bright Image do upon me stand
I am a Golden Angell in thy hand.

Lord, make my Soule thy Plate: thine Image bright
  Within the Circle of the same enfoile.
And on its brims in golden Letters write
  Thy Superscription in an Holy style.
Then I shall be thy Money, thou my Hord:
Let me thy Angell bee, bee thou my Lord.

We do not have here the threefold division of the typical meditation. Rather, the poem is a prayer to Christ to make the poet one of
the elect. It may have been intended as the final three stanzas of a
longer and more conventional meditation which was not successfully
completed. At any rate, Taylor liked these three stanzas well enough
to preserve them as an independent poem. The title "Another Meditation at the Same Time" indicates that Taylor was writing at least
two poems simultaneously.

The poem is unified by the fundamental image and pious pun of
the angel—a golden coin which became obsolete about fifty years
before these verses were written. The touchstone of the first stanza
is a black stone formerly used to indicate the genuineness of a gold
coin by the kind of mark it made on the metal. The entire prayer is
completely consistent with Calvinist Puritan doctrine. In stanza one
the poet says, I am counted true gold; that is, as a minister of a
Congregational Church I am considered by the world to be one of the
elect. But I am not truly so unless you, Lord, find me so. When I
test myself, I fear that my touchstone touches too overly, that is, it
makes the kind of mark that indicates my gold is counterfeit.

The second stanza raises the same question: Am I true coin or
counterfeit? At the same time it stresses the Calvinist doctrine of the
complete inability of natural man. The poet does not have clear
enough eyesight to read the stamp of the coin (himself) to determine
its true value: "Mine Eyes are dim; I cannot clearly see. / Be thou
my Spectacles . . . ." The last stanza is a plea that God make him

a genuine coin, one of the elect, so that he will indeed become God's angel. It should be noted again that the poet is expressing his own complete inability; not only does his election depend entirely upon God, but he does not even have the ability to know if he is one of the elect unless God gives him that ability. In its consistency of imagery and tone, in its quiet Herbertian piety, the poem seems to me to be completely successful.

In the more than two hundred meditations written over a period of almost half a century it is difficult to discover an overall plan or pattern, although the fact that Taylor began renumbering them after the first ten years would indicate that he may have had a plan in mind for each of the two "series." Taylor himself did not use the titles "First Series" and "Second Series." These were supplied by modern editors. When Taylor came to the end of Meditation 49 he simply numbered the next Meditation 1 without explanation. There are certain poems which appear to fall into groups—the first thirty or so poems of the second series, for example, are concerned with typology. Also in the second series is a group of poems written on sequential texts from Canticles. Nevertheless, neither the first series as a whole nor the second series as a whole seems to have a unified plan. However, it is evident from the foregoing discussion that there is a recurrent theme, explicit or implicit, running through both series of meditations from beginning to end—the pitiful condition of man as a result of the Fall, the wonderful power of God's Saving Grace, the hope that the poet will be a recipient of this Saving Grace: "Oh! Grace, Grace, Grace! this Wealthy Grace doth lay / Her Golden Channells from thy Fathers throne" (Med. 1 : 32).

The *Preparatory Meditations* are a poetic record of Taylor's prayers to Christ, a kind of spiritual diary. They are essentially private poetry— perhaps the finest body of private poetry in American literature.

GODS DETERMINATIONS

We now turn to a remarkable poem (or group of poems) which, at the time of composition, may have been intended for publication as a kind of handbook or guide to those members of his own congregation or of other congregations who were having difficulties in assuring themselves of the experience of saving grace and who therefore were reluctant to accept full covenant relationship with any church. The poem has as its title page: *Gods Determinations touch-*

ing his Elect: and The Elects Combat in their Conversion, and Coming up to God in Christ together with the Comfortable Effects thereof. It is didactic in intention and tone. It justifies God's ways to fallen sinners. It is designed to comfort those of God's people who have doubts of their election and to show them the way to Christ. The doctrine which is explicated throughout the poem is, of course, the same as that of the *Preparatory Meditations,* but here the doctrine is made more explicit and the style and quality of the verse are often quite different from that of the meditations. *Gods Determinations* is public rather than private poetry.

Because the doctrine and the action of the poem which exemplifies the doctrine have sometimes been misinterpreted, it is necessary to summarize the action before considering style and technique.

The Content and Structure of Gods Determinations

The argument of the poem is based upon the following division of mankind:

A. The damned
B. The elect—those who ride to glory in God's coach. The elect are divided as follows:
   1. The saints—those who have sinned little. They receive grace quickly and easily.
   2. The converts—those who come to Christ through varying degrees of difficulty. They eventually become saints. The converts are subdivided into:
      a. The first rank—those who are captured by God's mercy.
      b. The second rank—those who are captured by God's justice.
      c. The third rank—those who are captured after considerable difficulty by God's justice.

As we shall see, Taylor gets rid of the damned early in the poem and then concentrates on his real subject, the various ways in which God brings his predestined elect to salvation.

The "Preface" describes the Creation in orthodox terms. The physical universe was built by God out of nothing and is maintained by his sustaining presence. God also created "nothing Man" so that "nothing Man" might glorify Him. From the very beginning of the poem the omnipotent power of God and the complete inability of man are emphasized:

> Oh! what a might is this Whose single frown
> Doth shake the world as it would shake it down?
> Which All from Nothing fet, from Nothing, All:
> Hath All on Nothing set, lets Nothing fall.
> Gave All to nothing Man indeed, whereby
> Through nothing man all might him Glorify.

In "The Effects of Mans Apostacy," man, as a result of the Fall, finds God his enemy. He flies from God in fear, and Justice and Mercy, the two cardinal attributes of God personified, fall into debate about what to do with sinful man.

In "A Dialogue between Justice and Mercy," Justice at first seems determined to condemn man to eternal punishment but he is partially dissuaded from his vengeance by Mercy who, to pay man's debt, promises to become incarnate (in the person of Christ) and suffer death, to fill man with inherent grace, righteousness, and faith. Justice pronounces himself satisfied. Both Justice and Mercy foresee excessive humility in some men and excessive pride in others. Justice will frighten and humble the proud by reminding them that only saints are saved—all others must burn in hell. Mercy will encourage and comfort the humble and weak by convincing them that all are saved who have true faith. All men are now called to account for their sins in "Man's Perplexity when calld to an account." In "Gods Selecting Love in the Decree," God, after offering a general call to all men to attend his "sumptuous feast," in "Special Grace" sends his royal coach to carry only his elect to the banquet. Those who "slite the Call" stay behind and go to hell. Thus "all mankind splits in a Dichotomy," into the elect and the damned. The damned are now forgotten and the rest of the poem is concerned with the various ways in which God brings his elect to salvation. The point must be stressed that we are now concerned with the elect only and not with all mankind. Some readers have wrongly interpreted *Gods Determinations* as being universalist in its implications, thinking that Taylor was demonstrating that all men were saved. Taylor of course always believed that only a few among many men would reach heaven.

In "The Frowardness of the Elect in the Work of Conversion" the elect are divided into four groups. The "saints" go to Christ easily and quickly. The second group (called the first rank) are captured by Mercy. The other groups (called the second and third ranks) are captured by Justice. These three captive ranks are now attacked and tempted by the devil in "Satans Rage at them in their Conversion." This attack and the intervention of Christ occupy the next three sections of the poem. Failing in his attacks on all three ranks, Satan now turns his attention to the first rank and in "First Satans Assault against those that first Came up to Mercys terms" he engages in one of his most subtle temptations, that those of the first rank have not truly experienced saving grace because they were converted *too easily*, a line of attack which is maintained through "The Accusation of the Inward Man," "The Outward Man accused," and "The Soul accused in its Serving God," where Satan almost convinces the soul of the enormity of its sin and the impossibility that God would ever pardon it. In "The Souls Groan to Christ for Succour" the soul asks the Lord to break the teeth of the cur, Satan, and in "Christs Reply" the soul is assured that Satan acts like a sheep dog by God's permission to drive the repentant soul to Christ. The soul expresses "An Extasy of Joy let in by this Reply in Admiration," and Satan, failing with the first rank, now turns his attention to the rest of the captured sinners. In "The Second Ranke Accused," Satan reverses his method of temptation. Instead of accusing the sinners of coming to Christ too easily, he argues that because they held out against Mercy's terms, they had demonstrated to God that they were hardened sinners deserving eternal punishment. In "The Third Ranke Accused" he employs one of the subtlest temptations of all, and one that caused considerable difficulty to the Puritan ministers—that these hardened sinners would be *guilty of the sin of presumption* if they dared to consider themselves saved, and such presumption was sin enough to send them to hell. Other arguments are also introduced, including the probablity that Hell, God, and the existence of the soul itself were all delusions.

After "A Threnodiall Dialogue between The Second and Third Ranks" the sinners in despair enter "Their Call in this Sad State for Mercy" and seek advice of God's people, the saints. In the following six sections all of Satan's temptations are analyzed and refuted by the saints or by their spokesman. The final seven poems, beginning with "The Effect of this Discourse upon the second, and third Rancks," depict the final defeat of Satan and the triumph and eternal joys of the elect.

It can now be seen that *Gods Determinations* is in three parts: (1) an account of man's fall and of God's selecting love whereby the elect are saved; (2) an account of Satan's various temptations by means of which he intends to destroy the elect; and (3) an account of the failure of Satan and the salvation and joy of the elect. In part 2, the major section of the poem, Taylor is undoubtedly making use of the spiritual difficulties which he had found among members of his own church and is attempting to reassure them that they have not fallen from Grace, that they should retain full communion in the church, and if they had not yet come into full communion they should do so.

Gods Determinations *and Stoddardeanism*

As we have seen, this poem is very different in intention and execution from the *Preparatory Meditations*. The meditations are primarily acts of spiritual introspection in which the poet prays to Christ to enable him to discern in himself the Lord's body and thus make him worthy of administering the sacrament to his congregation. *Gods Determinations* is hortatory; it is designed to console and reassure believing Christians that it is possible to find in themselves the signs of saving grace and so, rejecting the temptations of Satan, partake of the Lord's Supper—that "sumptuous feast" mentioned early in the poem, a feast restricted, according to Taylor, to the elect only. To put it simply, the *Preparatory Meditations* prepared the author for administering the sacrament. *Gods Determinations* may have been written to prepare the congregation for the sacrament but then, for reasons unknown, Taylor failed to publish it, although he may have read some or all of it to his congregation. Taylor's chief opponent, Solomon Stoddard of Northampton, argued in a long controversy that: (1) it was impossible to be absolutely assured of salvation, and therefore (2) the Lord's Supper could not be restricted to those who considered themselves regenerate. It should be, rather, a converting ordinance available to all believing Christians. *Gods Determinations*, which was probably written during the height of the controversy, may well have been intended as a poetic refutation of Stoddard as well as a guide to those Christians who were experiencing doubts of their salvation. Taylor also preached a series of eight sermons against Stoddardeanism. They are discussed below.

The Style of Gods Determinations

Because this is a didactic poem written with a definite kind of reader in mind, the style is somewhat different from that of the *Pre-*

paratory Meditations. Gods Determinations is meant to persuade the Christian reader of God's mercy and justice. The dialogues between Satan and the elect probably owe something to the virulent and polemical religious pamphlets of the seventeenth century written to defend or attack nonconformity, Catholicism, or Anglicanism. We know that Taylor was interested in this pamphlet warfare for he copied into his Diary Book a poem entitled "An Answer to a Popish Pamphlet" as well as a polemical "play" (more a debate in verse than a play) by Robert Wild entitled "The Recantation of a Penitent Proteus." Wild was also engaged in pamphleteering, and his "A Friendly Debate between a Conformist and a Non-Conformist" (1672) is written in a style similar to that of the debates in *Gods Determinations.* The following lines from this poem concerning the future of Roman Catholicism in England after the declaration of liberty of conscience by Charles II are typical of the style and tone of seventeenth-century religious controversy:

Conformist

We fear, the *Papists* will grow proud and swell;
Give them an *Inch,* and they will take an *Ell.*
The *Popes Supremacy* will soon be Trump,
'Tis he must be the *Head,* and CHARLES the *Rump.*

Non-Conformist

The *Papists* swelling is the way to burst,
Let them have *Rope* enough, and do their worst.
And for the *Popes* Supremacy, Alack!
'Tis but the *Bunch* upon the *Camels* back.

Because of the central conflict in Taylor's poem between Satan on the one hand and Christ and the elect on the other, it has been suggested that Taylor attempted to dramatize his material under the influence of medieval morality plays and perhaps of Elizabethan and Jacobean drama. There is no evidence, however, that he had read any of these plays. Certainly, as a Puritan, the secular drama would have been anathema to him. It is more probable that he found suggestions for his portrayal of Satan and for his personified abstractions in homiletic and devotional literature, where in such books as Downame's *Christian Warfare* and John Bunyan's *The Holy War* allegorical devices and battle terminology were used to depict the struggle and salvation of the soul. It should also be remembered that battle imagery came naturally to Taylor. He was born amid the turmoil of the English Civil War. During his early ministry at Westfield he was close to King Philip's War. And as a Puritan believing in the church militant he read such works as Edward Johnson's *Wonder-Working Providence* (1654), which advised Christians to prepare for the battle of the Lord, to "store yourselves with all sorts of weapons for war, furbish up your Swords, Rapiers, and all other piercing weapons." The "dramatic" characteristics of *Gods Determinations,* therefore, were probably not derived from Taylor's reading or from observing medieval or later plays.

There is considerable variety in the style of the individual poems, ranging from the sonorous rhetoric of the preface, with echoes of Joshua Sylvester's translation of Du Bartas's *Divine Weekes,* to the extremely colloquial diction of the polemical and virulent speeches by Satan. Because *Gods Determinations* seems to have been intended as public and didactic poetry, the plain style of direct statement is frequently used and the more complex and baroque conceits of the *Preparatory Meditations* are less in evidence. One of the finest poems, "Christs Reply" is written in this plain style:

Christs Reply.

I am a Captain to your Will.
You found me Gracious, so shall still,
Whilst that my Will is your Design.
If that you stick unto my Cause
Opposing whom oppose my Laws
I am your own, and you are mine.

The weary Soule I will refresh
And Ease him of his heaviness.
Who'le slay a Friend? And save a Foe?
Who in my War do take delight,
Fight not for prey, but Pray, and Fight
Although they slip, I'le mercy show.

Then Credit not your Enemy
Whose Chiefest daintie is a lie.
I will you comfort sweet extend.
Behold I am a sun and shield
And a sharp sword to win the field.
I'l surely Crown you in the End.

His murdering Canons which do roare
And Engins though as many more
Shoot onely aire: no Bullets fly.
Unless you dare him with your Crest,

> And ope to him the naked breast,
> Small Execution's done thereby.

> To him that smiteth hip, and thigh,
> My foes as his: Walks warily,
> I'le give him Grace: he'st give me praise.
> Let him whose foot doth hit a Stone
> Through weakness, not rebellion
> Not faint, but think on former dayes.

The line "Fight not for prey, but Pray, and Fight" with its pious pun neatly sums up the Calvinist doctrine of the necessity of struggling for one's own salvation, not for one's own advantage but for the glory of God, together with the paradoxical notion of the inability of man to fight without God's aid. God saves the elect so that the elect may glorify him: "I'le give him Grace; he'st give me praise." In this predetermined and predestined battle for salvation, God assures the sinner that he will be merciful so long as the sin is not rebellion against God:

> Let him whose foot doth hit a Stone
> Through weakness, not rebellion
> Not faint, but think on former dayes.

The final line is designed to encourage those members of Taylor's church who, once certain of election, are now experiencing doubts.

Considered as a whole, *Gods Determinations* is uneven in tone and texture. It has a unifying theme—the salvation of the elect—but the reader has the final impression of an anthology of poems all written on the same subject but in different styles at different times rather than of a coherent composition. Nevertheless there are individual poems and passages of great merit.

THE MISCELLANEOUS POEMS
AND PROSE WORKS

The Occasional Poems

Taylor's chief contribution to American literature has now been discussed, but some reference should be made to the other poems and to the sermons, although detailed comment will not be attempted here. Taylor wrote a series of eight occasional poems prompted by events ranging in importance from the trivial (a wasp chilled with

cold) to the tragic (the deaths of two of his children). "Upon Wedlock, and Death of Children" is the most memorable of these verses
on "occurrants" as Taylor called them. As the town physician, Taylor
felt doubly responsible for the health of his own infants. Of Abigail,
who died at the age of one year, he wrote: "But oh! the tortures,
Vomit, screechings, groans, / And six weeks Fever would pierce hearts
like stones." The poet's grief is assuaged by his firm belief that his
dead children have gone to heaven. Referring to his daughter Elizabeth, who also died at the age of one year, he remembers both
the glory and the grief:

> But oh! a glorious hand from glory came
>   Guarded with Angells, soon did Crop this flowre
> Which almost tore the root up of the same
>   At that unlookt for, Dolesome, darksome houre.

His children are in paradise. The poem ends with the poet seeing
himself as sharing in their eternal joy: "I piecemeale pass to glory
bright in them."

For the Puritan, the power of God is manifest everywhere. The
minister-poet, constantly preoccupied with his place in the divine
scheme of things, may seize on almost any subject or event for
spiritual meditation and improvement. Thus the sight of his wife
spinning was the probable "occurrant" for his famous poem "Hus-
wifery," in which he prays that God will make him His spinning
wheel and His loom so that the divine cloth will become the poet's
"Holy robes for glory." The sight of a half frozen wasp warmed back
to life by the sun prompts him to write a charming versified prayer
comparing the wasp who

>   . . . hoises sails
>   And hu'ming flies in thankfull gails
>   Unto her dun Curld palace Hall
>   Her warm thanks offering for all

to his own soul which, experiencing the sun of saving grace, will
". . . upraise/An Heavenly musick furrd with praise."

The Metrical History of Christianity

Toward the end of his poetic career Taylor set about composing a
long poem of over twenty thousand lines which he bound in a
manuscript without his name and without a title. The poem is at-

tributed to Taylor on internal evidence and on the evidence of the handwriting. The title was supplied by the present writer. Using as his primary source the *Magdeburg Centuries,* a sixteenth-century history of the church in Latin written from the Protestant point of view, Taylor versified the history of the Christian church from the beginnings until the twelfth century and then composed a short final section describing the martyrdoms in the reign of Queen Mary of England. *The Metrical History* is a dogged, determined perform-ance composed in a style which is frequently crude and dull and which sometimes descends into extremely coarse and abusive lan-guage in the description of those popes whom Taylor especially dis-liked. There are a few flashes of genuine poetry here and there, particularly in intervening sections dealing with God's justice and mercy.

The Sermons

There are twenty-five sermons by Taylor extant which, with three exceptions, have been collected and edited by Norman Grabo in *Edward Taylor's Treatise Concerning the Lord's Supper* and in *Christographia.* The *Treatise* (the title has been supplied by the editor; it is not in Taylor's manuscript) consists of a series of eight ser-mons preached at Westfield in 1693 and 1694 on what Taylor con-sidered to be the proper Christian attitude toward the Lord's Supper, his chief points being that the Sacrament is central to Christian worship, celebrating not only the Last Supper but the "wedden," as Taylor calls it, between the church and Christ and the spiritual union between the individual saint and Christ. It is not a converting ordinance but a seal of the Covenant of Grace for the regenerate elect only. Here he parts company, as we have seen, with Solomon Stoddard, particularly in the final four sermons where he attempts to give a point-by-point refutation of Stoddardeanism. In so doing, however, he is careful to prove to his listeners that with the proper preparation they will find in themselves the signs of saving grace, which (like the later Jonathan Edwards) he enumerates in detail. Once assured that he is regenerate, Taylor argues, it is the duty of the church member to approach the Lord's table. The sermons form an important chapter in the history of the Stoddard controversy and are also of importance in the light they shed on the doctrinal back-ground of *Gods Determinations* and the *Preparatory Meditations.* A series of meditations (2 : 102–2 : 111), written in 1710 and 1711, are devoted to explicating Taylor's position on the Lord's Supper and to refuting Stoddardeanism and the Roman Catholic and Lutheran concepts of the Eucharist.

One of Taylor's doctrinal preoccupations was Christological—the belief in the perfect union of the divine and human natures in the single person of Christ. Taylor, as we have seen, referred to this union as "blessed Theanthropie," the state of being God-Man. The-anthropie is the subject of a number of meditations, and it is the theme of fourteen sermons entitled *Christographia*, which he preached at Westfield in the years 1701–3. Taylor was primarily concerned with demonstrating the *excellency* of Christ's person, which resulted from this perfect union of the human and the divine. He makes two major points: (1) Christ as God-Man is the necessary and completely efficacious redeemer of the elect; and (2) Christ as God-Man is the perfect ideal on which every individual saint should attempt to model his earthly life.

These *Christographia* sermons are learned, allusive, and abstruse. They must have been frequently above the heads of his farmer congregation. There are a few eloquent passages which may move the twentieth-century reader, but their chief value is to reinforce our appreciation of the principal motivation of the *Preparatory Meditations*—Taylor's love of the *person* of Christ and the conviction that at the time of partaking of the Lord's Supper he was uniting himself to Christ's person.

Viewed as a whole, Taylor's published sermons may be considered the equal of those by Cotton and Increase Mather. They are probably inferior to those of the earlier John Cotton and Thomas Shepard, and they are far inferior in style to the sermons of the later Jonathan Edwards. Their importance is historical rather than literary.

CONCLUSION

It was pointed out at the beginning of this chapter that to understand and appreciate Taylor requires an act of the historical imagination. Such an act is, of course, necessary in the reading of all poets who wrote several centuries ago, but a greater effort is required in reading Taylor than in reading a number of British poets of the same period

or earlier, such as Pope, Dryden, Milton, Donne, and Fulke Greville
Consider the following lines:

> Downe in the depth of mine iniquity,
> That ugly center of infernall spirits;
> Where each sinne feeles her owne deformity,
> In these peculiar torments she inherits,
> > Depriv'd of humane graces, and divine,
> > Even there appeares this *saving God* of mine.

This is the opening stanza of a poem by Fulke Greville (Sonnet 99), who was, like Taylor, a Calvinist in doctrine although he stayed within the Anglican church. He antedated Taylor by about one hundred years, yet he seems to speak across the centuries directly to our own time, while Taylor only rarely escapes being "dated." *Gods Determinations*, with its outworn machinery—its roaring devil, personified Mercy and Justice, and God's coach—its self-conscious use of rhetorical devices, and its obsolete and esoteric words is, after all, a rather archaic poem with occasional passages of great beauty and power. The *Preparatory Meditations* suffer less from the limitations of time and place. They are a valuable poetic record of the experience of saving grace.

Although there is an impressive body of religious poetry from sixteenth- and seventeenth-century England, there is practically none from colonial America except for Taylor's. It is evident from journals, diaries, sermons, and letters that there were a number of American Puritans leading lives of intense and honest piety. Edward Taylor is the only one of these American Puritans who expressed his spiritual experience in verse of a quality that can stand comparison with major poets like Donne, Herbert, and Crashaw. This is the measure of his unique achievement.

BIBLIOGRAPHY

Editions

Christographia. Edited by Norman S. Grabo. New Haven, Conn.: Yale University Press, 1962.
Edward Taylor's Treatise Concerning the Lord's Supper. Edited by Norman S. Grabo. East Lansing, Mich.: Michigan State University Press, 1966.
Metrical History of Christianity. Edited by Donald E. Stanford. Wooster, Ohio: Micro Photo, 1962.

The Poems of Edward Taylor. Edited by Donald E. Stanford. Foreword by
Louis L. Martz. New Haven, Conn.: Yale University Press, 1960; [some-
what abridged, with new introduction by Stanford] 1963.
The Poetical Works of Edward Taylor. Edited by Thomas H. Johnson.
Princeton, N.J.: Princeton University Press, 1943.

Scholarship and Criticism

Ball, Kenneth R. "Rhetoric in Edward Taylor's *Preparatory Meditations.*"
Early American Literature 4 (Winter, 1970): 79–88.
Bercovitch, Sacvan, ed. *Typology and Early American Literature.* Amherst,
Mass.: University of Massachusetts Press, 1972. [Includes three essays
on Taylor's typology.]
Colacurcio, Michael J. "*Gods Determinations* Touching Half-Way Member-
ship: Occasion and Audience in Edward Taylor." *American Literature* 39
(1967): 298–314.
Grabo, Norman S. *Edward Taylor.* New York: Twayne, 1961.
Keller, Karl. "The Example of Edward Taylor." *Early American Literature*
4 (Winter, 1970): 5–26.
Manierre, William R. "Verbal Patterns in the Poetry of Edward Taylor."
College English 23 (1962): 296–99.
Stanford, Donald E. *Edward Taylor.* Minneapolis, Minn.: University of
Minnesota Press, 1965.
Thorpe, Peter. "Edward Taylor as Poet." *New England Quarterly* 39
(1966): 356–72.
Warren, Austin. "Edward Taylor." In *Major Writers of America,* edited by
Perry Miller, 1: 51–62. New York: Harcourt, Brace, and World, 1962.

4

Cotton Mather

SACVAN BERCOVITCH

Lead me, my Lord upon mount Lebanon,
    And shew me there an Aspect bright of thee.
Open the Valving Doors, where there upon
    I mean the Casements of thy Faith in mee.
. . . .
Then I shall see these precious square wrought Stones
    Are to thy Zion brought, foundations laid,
And all these Cedars Choice, of Lebanon
    Are built thereon and Spirituall Temples made.
. . . .
Lord let me stand founded on thee by grace
    And grow a Cedar tall and Upright here.
And sweeten me with this sweet aire apace
    Make me a grape of Leb'nons Vine up peare.
    Let me then see Thy glory Lebanon
    And yield the Smell of those sweet vines thereon.
. . . .
Lord, make thine Aspect then as Lebanon.
    Allow me such brave Sights and Sents so sweet
Oh! Ravishing Sweet pour'd out my Soule upon.
    Fill all its empty Corners and there keep
    That so my breath may sing thy praise divine
    All smelling of thy Lebanons rich wine.
          Edward Taylor, "His Countenance is like Lebanon.
          Excellent as the Cedars," Med. 2 : 125

Sacvan Bercovitch, professor of English at Columbia University, formerly taught at the University of California, San Diego, and at Brandeis. He is the author of a monograph entitled "Horologicals to Chronometricals: The Rhetoric of the Jeremiad," published in *Literary Monographs*, vol. 3, by the University of Wisconsin Press (1970), and numerous studies in European and American literature, most

IMAGES FOR MYSELF: COTTON MATHER
IN HIS DIARIES (1724)

*Once History inhabits a crazy house, egotism may be the last tool
left to History.*

                              Mailer, *The Armies of the Night*

Increase Mather died in August 1723, rich in years and honors, widely mourned as the foremost American Puritan of the age. Several months later his eldest, best-known, and most devoted son, now *de facto* heir to the theocratic dynasty, took stock of his own life and works. He had early and eagerly accepted the greatness to which he had been born, had assiduously prepared himself for the high destiny which his very name blazoned forth, proclaiming as it did his pre-eminence among the remnant that God had sifted two generations before and directed under the aegis of his grandfathers, Richard Mather and John Cotton, to establish a specimen of New Jerusalem in the Western wilderness. At the age of twenty-two—five years after his victorious debut in the family pulpit, and already acknowledged "an Excellent Preacher, a great Writer, next in Fame" to Increase alone—he had secured divine assurance of his calling. From the Throne of Christ, his face shining like the noonday sun over Damascus, an angel had brought him special prophecies of the *magnalia* which he, Cotton Mather, should do not only in America but the world over to usher in the millennium. It was reserved for him, he learned, as he humbled himself in the dust of his study floor, to fulfill the messianic vision of Ezekiel 31: *"Behold hee was a Cedar in Lebanon, exalted above all the Trees of the Field, because of the Multitude of Waters when hee shott forth. Thus was hee fair in his Greatness in the Length of his Branches for his Root was by*

---

recently on the Puritan imagination and concepts of history. His latest work, a collection of essays on typology which he edited and to which he contributed an extensive bibliography, was published in 1972.

The author would like to thank Kenneth Silverman for a careful and sympathetic reading of this essay, and The Johns Hopkins Press for permission to use (in substantially revised and condensed form) parts of his "New England Epic: Cotton Mather's *Magnalia Christi Americana,*" *English Literary History* 33 (1966): 337–50.

This essay is dedicated to Quentin Anderson.

*the great Waters. Nor was any Tree in the Garden of God like unto him in his Beauty."**

Cotton Mather had subsequently received many visits and messages from his "particular angel." And he had often reminded himself of that "strange and memorable" prophecy. He had invoked it two years later when the citizens of Boston selected him their spokesman against the royalist-Anglican Governor Andros. Soon after he had cited the text to preface the book with which he hoped to rescue Massachusetts from its witchcraft enchantments. He had called it to mind in 1689, when, considering the hermeneutic through which he was preparing to expound New England's errand, he found "the Types, like the Waters in Ezekiel's *Vision, Growing and Rising still.*" He had developed the image into a central theme of his paean to Harvard College (the introduction to book IV of the *Magnalia*), where he was then serving as its youngest overseer and where at fifteen, as its youngest graduate, he had heard President Chauncey declaim his peerless ancestry and prospects. He had returned to it throughout the first quarter of the eighteenth century, in his efforts to sustain the Good Old Way at home and to further the Reformation abroad: in his defense of the Half-Way Covenant (*A Tree Planted by the Rivers of Water*), his missionary ventures in providing *Another Tongue* for the heathen Indians or a *Temple Opening* for frontier settlements, his political *Observanda* and *Icono-clastes* against Catholicism, his descriptions of *Baptismal Piety*, the proper *Resort of Piety*, and the country's *Shaking Dispensations*. The "Emblem of the *Goodly Cedar*" had become a standard for his daily self-appraisals, whether at prayer ("*Lord*, Let me be Fruitful"), or in moments of despondency ("My Barrenness! My Barrenness!," how long "has this unprofitable tree been Standing in the Field of the Lord!"), or in token of public recognition, as when he commemorated his honorary D.D. with a signet ring bearing a tree and the legend *Glascua Rigavit*, "the University of Glascow has watered

---

* Here and throughout this essay, I have decided not to use ellipses to indicate omissions made in passages quoted from Mather's writings. Mather's habitual elaborations, citations in the "learned tongues," and baroque redundancies of expression would have made full quotation (in most cases) unduly extensive—indeed, positively cumbersome—for the purpose of a critical essay. It would have been equally distracting, I believe, to record the numerous omissions by the use of ellipses. Of course, I have tried at all times to be faithful to Mather's precise meaning and, wherever possible, to suggest the ornate quality of his style.

Unless otherwise indicated, quotations from Mather's writings have been taken from the first edition of each work, or, if the work has not been published, from the manuscript.

it." His son Samuel tells us that "The Cast of his Eye upon this, constantly provoked him to pray, O GOD, *make me a very fruitful tree.*" He was summarily to urge Samuel from his deathbed on February 13, 1728, to "Remember only that one word *Fructuosus.*"

Now on the ides of March 1724, at the age of sixty-one, in the fortieth year of his pastorate at Boston's North Church (whose direction he was assuming at last), Cotton Mather confided to his diaries the fruits of his long labors. It is surely one of the grimmest accounts of lost expectations in American letters. What had he not done to promote God's Kingdom, both in the Old World and the New! Setting aside the more than four hundred books he had published while shepherding the colony's largest congregation, his good deeds spread across every sphere of society, like branches of a towering cedar over all the garden within its reach. He had devised projects to aid sailors and "the poor *Negro's*," had worked tirelessly for Harvard's improvement, had distributed alms to the needy (above one-seventh of his income), had established societies to advance piety and strengthen civic authority, had given generously of his time to the distressed and the errant, had written treatises "for the Profit and Honor of the *female Sex*," dispensed tracts, hundreds of them, to his neighbors and acquaintances, tendered support of all kinds to his parents and children and destitute relatives. "AND YETT"—at each point, with a relentless self-lacerating tough-mindedness that rivals Henry Adams's *Education*—Mather recorded the disastrous reversals:

> AND YETT, there is not a Man so cursed, among the *Sailors.* . . .
> AND YETT, some, on purpose to affront me, call their *Negro's,* by the Name of *Cotton Mather.* . . .
> AND YETT, where is the Man, whom the *female Sex* have spitt more of their Venom at? . . .
> AND YETT, where is the Man, who has been tormented with such monstrous *Relatives?* . . .
> AND YETT, How little *Comfort* have I seen in my *Children?* . . .
> AND YETT, the Discountenance I have almost perpetually received from the *Government!* . . .
> AND YETT, the *Colledge* forever putts all possible Marks of Disesteem upon me. . . .
> AND YETT, my *Company* is little sought for. . . .
> AND YETT, I see no man for whom all are so lothe to do good *Offices.* . . .
> AND YETT, I have had *Books* written against me. . . .
> AND YETT, I am a very *poor Man.* . . .
> AND YETT, Every Body points at me, as by far the most afflicted

Minister in all *New England*. And many look on me as the *greatest Sinner* because the *greatest Sufferer*.*

Undoubtedly, Mather's complaint tends toward melodrama. Set as it is alongside his chronicle of accomplishments, it conveys an unsavory egotism, a mixture of self-pity and self-congratulation which has repelled most readers of his diaries. These character traits, in fact, or their equivalents—spiritual rigidity, narrow and reactionary dogmatism, a lust for affliction wedded to a petty and pompous complacency—form the core of the stereotype through which he has come to represent Puritanism in the popular mind: a stereotype promulgated by his contemporary enemies, embellished by nineteenth-century historians, and reaffirmed in our time by influential scholars and critics. Like most stereotypes, this one expresses a measure of truth; like all stereotypes it is essentially misleading.

In the first place, it obscures the fact that Mather's charges are accurate in substance. If he sometimes exaggerates he also understates. Regarding his achievements, he omits mention, *inter alia,* of his crucial part in the founding of Yale, his mastery of the Iroquois language (in addition to the six others he already knew) so as to help integrate the Bay Indians, his scientific investigations which earned him membership in Britain's famed Royal Society and acclaim in our time as the first significant figure in American medicine, his considerable contribution to the persecuted Huguenots and to German Pietist charities. More striking yet is his restraint in enumerating his most painful setbacks. We know from other sources that during 1724 he not only abandoned hope of the Harvard presidency—which the College Corporation then offered to three obviously less qualified candidates—but resigned himself to leaving his "Biblia Americana" unpublished, the massive twenty-year compendium of scripture commentary which he treasured as his *magnum opus* and for which he had solicited subscribers with increasing desperation for some three decades. We know, further, that in the same year he found himself threatened with imprisonment for debts incurred by his wife's former husband, and that Lydia Lee Mather herself was, if not insane, decidedly psychopathic. He had been happily married twice before; all evidence indicates that he was a devoted father and husband, "agreably temper'd with a various mixture of Wit and Chearfulness," in an age of paternal severity disposed toward persuasion or compromise, careful to instruct his daughters as well as his sons, deeply affected by the succession of illnesses that by 1724 had proved fatal to twelve of his

* *Diary,* ed. Ford (1957), 2: 706–8.

fifteen children. His silence about Lydia on this occasion reveals something of his forbearance toward her in the face of public shame and private distress. Similarly, the absence of explicit grievances against his son Increase may be taken as testimony (elsewhere made abundantly clear) of his patience and readiness to forgive, his abiding faith in the young man despite the anxieties he caused him. We can hardly blame what resentment we do feel in the muted contrast between his own lifelong sacrifices for his father—whom he had honored always and thrice eulogized in biography—and the intractable prodigality of his favorite child. Later that year he learned that "Cressy" too was dead, drowned in a storm at sea.

The genuine pathos that informs Mather's statement suggests another, more serious limitation in the stereotype. When we juxtapose his disappointments with his unremitting sense of mission, the recurrent "AND YETT" takes on a distinctive purity and force. It comes to signify—beyond its cry of private indignation—a representative gesture of defiance, the righteous anger of a Jeremiah against the betrayal of the promise he somehow still embodies. Of course, Cotton Mather was not a sackcloth prophet in the wilderness. His biographers have justly portrayed him as a contradictory figure, at once a "primitive Puritan in a Boston that was becoming Yankee" and the most cosmopolitan of Yankees, champion of the New Science, fashionable in dress and decorum, stylistically (at times) a model of Augustan refinement. Like Henry Adams, that primitive Yankee in a Boston hurling into the twentieth century, he functioned as a sort of customs-house through which the latest European notions entered the country, from plant hybridization and Newtonian optics to Milton's theory of unrhymed verse. But like Adams he was a casualty of change. Intellectually, that is, he was not so much transitional as schizophrenic, a dispossessed leader caught between two eras, one dead, the other beyond his moral and emotional comprehension. For in his basic convictions Mather belonged in toto to the former era. His very sophistication seems from this perspective to have hardened his allegiance; in effect, it sharpened the shocks of reality that impelled him inward, toward the shelter of the imagination. The more he discovered how thoroughly his education had failed him—the further he drifted into the supersensual chaos of the Age of Reason— the closer his identification grew with the vanished theocracy which for him enshrined the true meaning of the country. It is this commitment, this visionary's No-in-thunder to the way of the world, which adds, I think, a redeeming suprapersonal dimension to Mather's outrage. More largely, it is this self-concept which welds the fragmentary entries in his "Testimony"—along with his constant revision of them and later insertions—into a spiritual autobiography of remarkable coherence and extraordinary cultural import.

Mather's stubbornly archaic moral idealism pervades every aspect of his self-portrait. It accounts for his astounding naiveté, his inability not only to cope with but to grasp the meaning of new social-ideological trends: the reasons, for example, for the clergy's loss of political influence after the Andros revolt, or (in theological matters) for the rise of Stoddardism, or again, on a more intimate level, for the depletion of his flock and his ostracism from the councils of government. It underlies his courage in defense of certain old friends (like the discredited Sir William Phips) and under public attack, as when he pioneered the use of inoculation despite violent general resistance, issuing in at least one attempt on his life. Indeed, it helps explain why he should have been so much a prey for attack: why he should have stood as scapegoat for the witchcraft debâcle when his conduct then was at worst representative and in sum notably moderate; why he should have become an exemplum of bigotry although, at "the Hazard of much Reproch," he repeatedly condemned persecution for civil or religious dissent. Finally, his emotional commitment explains the curiously static character of his thought. The diaries exasperate even the sympathetic reader by their unflagging intellectual monotony. Notwithstanding Mather's international correspondence, varied concerns, and prolific reading, notwithstanding also the series of crises (diplomatic, theological, scientific) that marks his career, his outlook remains virtually unaltered. Nor does this impression misrepresent his attainments. His sermon of 1724 that set out his plan for benevolent societies he had delivered verbatim at the age of sixteen. The same didactic and hermeneutic strains run throughout the corpus of his work. His interest in medicine, which resulted in the widest-ranging colonial inquiry into the subject, derives from his earliest adolescence. The obsessions of his last years—with the spectre of death, with his professed slothfulness and much-lamented "ambitious Affectation of Praeheminencies" —abound in his first manuscripts. The persecution itself which he detailed at sixty-one he decries so often previously that it seems part of a deliberate course of martyrdom.

His development lies in the realm of the imagination. It consists simply, astonishingly, in his capacity to transform public defeat into private triumph by recourse to metaphor and myth. If, as we are told, we can glean so little from the diaries of concrete historic value, that in a sense is precisely their intent. They trace the growth of a prophet's mind in opposition to, not within, a recalcitrant world. The mystical rapture with which they open returns time and again ("glorious," "incredible," "triumphant, weeping," ultimately "inexpressible") to raise the author with a "Supernatural and Immediate *Efficacy*" into "an high, a sweet, an heavenly" plane of "*Joy unspeakable and full of Glory*," returns after every adversity carrying "wondrous Assurances" of "a rich Compensation for all the Sorrows, which are appointed for me." In this dialectic, Ezekiel's vision flows into a whole configuration of epiphanies through which Mather gradually discerns, or unveils, the nature of his calling. He offers, in short, not a self-examination but a cosmic self-affirmation, in the Calvinist meaning of the word a "justification" of his life. His reflections on periods of public distress picture him an epic hero in "a dismal Emblem of Hell." "This Assault of the *evil Angels* upon the Country," he concludes at one point, "was intended as a particular Defiance, unto *my* poor Endeavors"; a subsequent analysis demonstrates that "Extraordinary Things were done for me, that cannot be related. I will only say, the Angels of Heaven are at work for me." Within this mythopoetic framework, the diaries present with gathering confidence a procession of *figurae* which all but submerge the actual man within the metaphorical—specifically, within the dual image of John the Baptist and Christ, alternately (and in the end, simultaneously) messenger of the New Day and Man of Sorrows, the greatest of sufferers misjudged as the greatest of sinners.

Through the image of John, Mather sought to recover the social role that history denied him. As he conceived of the parallel its prophetic meaning, its *sensus plenior,* absorbed the literal meaning, bespeaking a procession of seers from Daniel, the Baptist, and the writer of Revelation to Cotton Mather, climactically, as witness for the chiliad at hand. The basis for his conception lay at the roots of New World Puritanism. Millennial anticipations had played a central part in the Massachusetts Bay Colony venture. As motive, as teleology, and as psychological support they formed a key source of the vitality which wrought the New Canaan out of the howling American desert. In his famous definition of *New-England's Errand into the Wilderness,* John Danforth described the Baptist as a forerunner not only of the Incarnation but of the Second Coming and compared his wilderness mission in the latter regard with that of the theocracy. Other ministers before and after Danforth announced the good news with the same visionary enthusiasm. When "John the Baptist arose like a bright and shining light," Jesus appeared to him "at the end

49774

of the Jewish world *in the end of the world* [i.e., the wilderness]" as
a partial fulfillment of the last and great day; accordingly, another
light shone forth more clearly to reveal Christ when the Reformation
dawned after the long night of the Roman Antichrist; to bring that
light to its full brilliancy was "the end of our coming hither" across
the Atlantic—and now, considering our accomplishments, "you may
conclude that the Sun will quickly arise upon the world" and New
Jerusalem come down from heaven to the American strand.

By the time Cotton Mather had grown to manhood that vitality
had largely dissipated, or at any rate radically changed. No one
knew that better than he; but he could retain the source itself—
"the Cause of God and his People in *New England according to its
divine Originall and Native beautie*"—in rich compensation for the
authority that by heavenly as well as human right he ought to have
inherited. Had not God called him "as a John, to bee an Herald of
the Lord's Kingdome now approaching"? Did he not "feel the Lord
Jesus Christ most sensibly carrying on, the Interests of His Kingdom,
in my Soul, continually," and so directing him, "as poor and as vile"
as he was, to "become a *Remembrancer* unto the Lord, for no less
than whole *Peoples*, Nations and Kingdomes"? He especially liked to
contemplate the prospect on the Sabbath. Since the Lord's Day was
"a Peculiar Type of the Blessed *Millennium*," it invited his researches
into the prophecies concerning the Great Sabbatism, his prayers for
their swift fulfillment, and his preparations for "being eminently
serviceable in the *mighty Changes*." Together, these activities inspired him to assume an oracular political clairvoyance, to declare
himself at once interpreter, personification, guide, and forecaster of
the corporate future. In the death of England's King Charles II he
read the beginning of the Resurrection of the Witnesses; religious
turmoil in Europe meant variously "a wondrous *Revolution*" in Scotland and Ireland, an end-time convulsion in France, and a "notable
Reformation" in the Spanish Indies; the civic instability of late seventeenth-century Massachusetts pointed to the collapse of the Ottoman
Empire and the imminent conversion of the Jews.

Such prognostication was by no means unusual. Indeed, it had
become something of a Reformation pastime ever since Luther had
announced the *clavis Apocalyptica* in the equation of Roman Catholicism and the whore of Babylon. What distinguishes Mather from
other chiliasts is the intense responsibility he takes for the shape of
things to come. To judge by the diaries, it is *his* tears that will
liberate France, *his* "Prayers and Pains" that will shortly enlighten the

Jewish nation, *his* "Goods Devised" that will ready the colony for the Second Coming. It is, comprehensively, in *him* that we are to locate the burgeoning *"Manifestations* of what the Lord is *going to do in the Earth."* European Puritans studied the prophecies for either personal or political reasons, either as an independent scholarly undertaking or (like the founders of the city on a hill) as part of their adherence to a collective enterprise. In Cotton Mather, particularly after 1690, both motives are joined and transmuted. The "great Revolutions expected in the Dayes approaching" become for him a substitute for a manageable political context; the "Consuming of the Ten Kingdomes"—and all the other doomsday cataclysms that he predicted in 1724 would "suddenly come upon us"—constitutes an ambiguous retribution-reward meted out to the backsliding New Israelites from whom he willfully divorced himself *and* whom he was directing into the Theopolis Americana. I have "made Sacrifices of all, even my dearest Enjoyments," he wrote at several different moments during that bleak time, and so "I went to the Lord; and cried unto Him that the Ministry of His holy ANGELS might be allowed unto me, that the holy ANGELS may make their Descent, and the Kingdome of the Heavens come on." Refusing to resign himself merely to a proud isolation, glorying in the "sacrificing Stroke" that bespoke his solitary midnight watch, Mather established within the apocalyptic imagination per se his mastery over the forces of history, the unique insight and supernatural efficacy that revealed him the unacknowledged legislator of the New World.

In his private afflictions Mather cast himself in the image of a suffering Savior. No image is more familiar to Christian tradition; the diaries stand out among Puritan journals, however, for their insistence on the *imitatio Christi* and in personal literature generally for their conscious, diversified, and transparently compensatory application of the concept. If we can trust Mather's "Paterna"—his manuscript autobiography, composed mainly of diary extracts chosen to edify his sons (first Cressy and then Samuel)—the application dates from his childhood. "When I was about seven or eight years old," he writes, "I rebuked my play mates for their wicked *words* and *ways;* and sometimes I suffered from them, the persecution of not only *Scoffs* but *Blows* also for my Rebukes, which when somebody told your Grandfather, I remember he seemed very *glad,* yea, almost proud of my Affronts."

The anecdote has provoked a number of caricature-renderings of the preacher as a young prig; it remains valuable nonetheless as the first recorded instance in a dominant pattern of Mather's thought. No doubt he did not mean to associate his father with God, as the logic of his rhetoric here suggests.* But the explicit fusion of himself and Jesus recurs with growing frequency and amplitude: in Jesus's persecution and temptations, in His ministry, habits of prayer, and behavior toward kinsmen, even in His relations with His consort, the church, and above all in His resignation to the scoffs and blows of the wicked. When Mather's congregation dwindles (like "the Withdrawal of the Disciples"), when during the inoculation crisis Mather sees, with Christ, only malice for his efforts to heal the diseased, when in 1724 he finds himself (like "the Sheep before the Shearers" and "the Stone, which the Builders have refused") deserted by his consort and rejected by Harvard, he wears the affronts with jubilant thanksgiving: "A comformity to Him in Sufferings, Injuries, Reproaches from a malignant world, causes me, even to rejoice in those Humiliations"; by leading "mee to entirely submit unto the Will of GOD," it makes all but inevitable "those Things, wherein Satan will be marvellously bruised under my Feet." If it also made martyrdom inevitable, as he felt throughout the last decade of his life, he could only rejoice the more. "I beheld myself nailed unto a Cross. My spirit is reconciled unto this condition: 'tis welcome to

---

* Certainly such conjecture should not be pressed too far; but the implicit association is pervasive enough to warrant comment. It may be fairly discerned in his eulogies to the abused but forgiving saint (*"These are my Brethren, they and I have the same Father"*), in the recurrent tree-imagery of his trinitarian discourses ("God the *Father* as the Sacred *Root,* Christ, as a *Trunk* issuing from it, [and] the Holy *Spirit* as a *Sap* running thro' it"), and even perhaps (considering the biographical parallels) in his references to *"the Glorious Pattern of the Blessed Jesus, Readily and Cheerfully Submitting to take the Cup, which His Father had given Him."* "It is impossible," he wrote, "that the SON should be without the FATHER, or the FATHER without the SON, or both without the HOLY SPIRIT." We ought to recall in this connection his numerous private expressions on the subject —his reiterated urgency to embrace "the Spirit of Adoption in the *Abba, Father*" and to penetrate "the Sweet Mystery of Going to God as my Father, and crying *Abba, Father*"—as well as his excessive zeal against Arianism, and his strange attraction to it in moments of despair. When he was a young man he recorded a "little Accident" that he believed emblemized his "own Transactions with Heaven": his son displeased Increase one day, and Cotton Mather, as father-become-son, pleaded "as an Advocate for the Child [become mankind] in his Infirmity. So the Child was presently received into Favour with my Father; my Father look'd on him with a pleased Aspect, and bestow'd aggreable Illuminations upon him." In his old age he customarily referred to Increase as "Adoni Avi," "my Lord, my father."

me, in regard of the glorious Designs which my SAVIOUR has, in ordering such a Conformity unto Himself." Thus in 1717; seven years later
he was still luxuriating in that "incomparable Satisfaction. And I am
willing," he added, drawing perhaps upon his boyhood memory for
the crowning analogy, "that my Crucifixion should go on, [so] that
I should be made a Spectacle which the glorious GOD will with
delight look down upon."

Mather supplemented this beatific conformity with an assortment
of scriptural precedents (Jeremiah and Isaiah in the Old Testament,
Paul and Stephen in the New); he augmented it through a variety of
typological guises. In different scenes during his *agon*, his combat
with the Devil, he appears an obedient Adam or a defiant Elijah, a
persevering or an assertive Job, another Samson combating the con-
spiring Philistines abroad, or, ill in bed, a shorn Samson awaiting a
renewal of strength to vex the Dragon. This therapeutic-exegetical
technique forms a structural principle of the diaries. His early identification with Moses enabled him to overcome the most severe trauma
of his youth, the stammer which almost foreclosed his clerical vocation.
The Hebrew, he noted in his initial entry (March 12, 1681, one month
after his eighteenth birthday), had not heeded God's promise that
He would *"bee with his Mouth*. And now, because I would not so sin,
therefore I trust in thee! Thou dost send mee forth, as thou didst
Moses, and thou wilt bee with my Mouth." When the stammer persisted
he took courage by recalling how "Moses complained that the Infirmitie
of his *Utterance* continued, after his Entrance upon his Ministry"; he
sought sustenance from the parallel over and again, until, confident
at last in God's promise to *him,* feeling that he would henceforth
"speak with Fruitfulness," he could hymn his vow "to make my *Tongue
/ A Tree of Life."* At sixty-one he was relying on the same approach
to gird himself against adversity. Faced with the possibility of arrest,
he remembered that *"Joseph* was a Type of our admirable JESUS, in
this among other things, that the very Methods which their Enemies
took to defeat the Purposes of Heaven concerning them, did but
help to fulfill those very Purposes." And in the autumn of that year,
his elaborate, moving threnody over his "poor beloved Absalom"—
"Ah! My son *Increase!* My Son! My Son! My Head is Waters, and
my Eyes are a Fountain of Tears! I am overwhelmed!"—came not as
a spontaneous outburst of grief but as the *finale* of a figural drama
he had long engaged in, mentally, as director and main actor, in an
effort to bring under control the most traumatic personal frustration
of his old age.

From Moses to David the diversity of types highlights the Christ-image which unifies Mather's presentation of his private life. To some extent this image conflicts with that of millennial herald. One is essentially self-contained, the other sweeps the protagonist into the dynamic, ineluctable, all-encompassing movement of history. What links the two is their common basis in the outlook that prompted the Great Migration, the joint personal-social eschatology that flourished (for a generation or two) as the New England Way. It may be valid, therefore, to speak of Cotton Mather as representing *in extremis* the thrust and tensions of American Puritanism—if we recognize that his representative attributes are nourished as wish-fulfillment. They blend and reinforce one another not, as his grandfathers had planned, in a community of saints on a historic errand, a church-state where the stages of inner preparation reflect the settlement's temporal progress, but in a process of self-definition designed to create a well-nigh archetypal figure, the embodiment of things past and to come, para-doxically insulated from the present and symbolic of his culture. Broadly considered, the figure evokes a number of earlier heroic models, such as the postexilic Hebrew seer. Most directly and pointedly, its counterpart appears in the isolatoes who through the nineteenth century shaped the nation's literary tradition: the "keepers of the dream," who, unlike their European counterparts—whether Puritan (like Milton) or Romantic (like Blake and Wordsworth, Hölderlin and Schelling)—*refused* to substitute an apocalypse of the mind for a disappointed historic expectation, and whose epic-autobiographies, accordingly, transform personal failure into social ideal.

This is not the place to speculate on the cultural continuities that underlie such continuities in imaginative strategy. It must suffice to recall our recurrent crises of national identity, and the recurrent emergence of Jeremiahs seeking to set the crazy house of history in order by invoking the idea of America and finding instead "rich compensation" for an untoward political reality in the self-contained, all-encompassing, exemplary American self. In this tradition Mather has an honorific place both as a colonial Puritan and as a man of letters. "The Cross is a dry sort of wood," he once remarked in recording a Lord's-Day epiphany; "but yett it proves a *fruitful Tree*." However deceived he was in his mystical assurances, whatever our *ad hominem* judgment of his "Martyrdom," his diaries—and his major published writings, each of them in some form an extension of the diaries—vindicate his trust in the image-making imagination.

IMAGES OF MYSELF: COTTON MATHER
IN HIS WRITINGS (1683-1700)

*History is never, in any rich sense, the immediate crudity of what
"happens," but the much finer complexity of what we read into it.*
Henry James, *The American Scene*

Few Puritans more loudly decried the bosom serpent of egotism than
did Cotton Mather; none more clearly exemplified it. Explicitly or
implicitly, he projects himself everywhere in his writings. In the most
direct compensatory sense, he does so by using literature as a means
of personal redress. He tells us that he composed his discussions of the
family to bless his own, his essays on the riches of Christ to repay his
benefactors, his tracts on morality to convert his enemies, his funeral
discourses to console himself for the loss of child, wife, or friend. More
often, his self-projection serves to magnify some intimate problem
into a tenet of the system he is defending. His first sermons expound
texts on "the noble faculty of speech" from Psalms and the life of
Moses; subsequent sermons establish a continuing parallel between
personal concern and public exhortation. At the appropriate point in
the chronology of his affairs, Mather speculates about the nature of
angels, the holiness of the children of saints and their filial responsibilities,* how properly to "take arms against adversity" or, in other

---

* At times, these sermons betray a deep ambivalence. It lies beyond the scope
of this essay to trace Mather's complex, shifting attitude toward his father, but
the reader should be aware of the personal implications in his obsessive use of
the filial bond for subject and simile. On the one hand, we can doubt neither his
abiding respect and affection (which he summarized in his funeral eulogy and
embodied in his lengthy and very readable *Parentator* [1724]) nor his marked tem-
peramental affinities to Increase (their diaries resemble one another in their mil-
lennialism, their mystical assurances, their laments over spiritual barrenness, and
their hypersensitivity to persecution). On the other hand, we know that the relationship must have entailed severe emotional strains, not least of which lay in its
incalculable cost to Mather's political ambitions. The strains appear even in the
polemics which espouse his parent's quarrels, such as *Political Fables* (1692),
where he plays Orpheus to his father's Mercury, the "divine harpist" obliged to
protect the "not much concerned" celestial messenger. Most vividly, they are
manifest in his contradictory thematic or metaphorical applications. Although, for
example, he often invokes his parentage to justify himself, he constantly asserts
the superiority, in elect families, of son to father: "*Young* People are more fit
than *Old*"; they radiate a "Double Glory" and the Lord "will do more for them
than ever He did for their elders," since "the *Covenant-Mercy* of God, oftentimes

cases, to resign oneself to it (in accordance with *The Religion of the Cross*), the advantages of a successful marriage or the temptations of bachelorhood and widowhood, the dangers of vanity, the mutability of earthly goods—envisaged in revealing particulars of fire, illness, debt, or the loss of a son at sea—and, finally, the solacements of *A Good Old Age* and *Death Approaching*, including prospects of heavenly discourse with the heroes of the Bible.

It would be easy from this vantage point, and not entirely inaccurate, to see in Mather's enormous literary productivity a compulsive and omnivorous self-involvement. But here as in the diaries the clue to his creative energy (as distinct from whatever psychoses we think we discern) lies in his persistent stress upon the images through which he forged his identification with Puritan New England. Thematically considered, conformity to Christ and the hastening apocalypse delineate his main areas of concern. The *imitatio Dei* forms the basis of his practical theology. His millennial politics, he tells us, follow from "the signalizing Advantage the *John Baptist* had, in an Opportunitie, to tell [his countrymen], *what they are to do.*" He took the opportunity at every public ceremony—before the artillery company, at times of thanksgiving and humiliation, from the election-day desk—speaking through the phrases of Ezekiel, drawing upon Isaiah to justify his chiliastic "medlings," turning to a variety of predecessors (Moses, Jeremiah, Daniel, John the Divine, the angels at the Incarnation) to prove that the "long line of *Inter-Sabbatical Time*" is coming to a close. "Le Coeur du Sage," he wrote at the head of his prophetic summons to France, "connoist le temps."

In his most ambitious works he invokes both these images of himself and builds his argument upon the tension or harmony generated by their dual perspective. One such example is *The Wonders of the Invisible World* (1693), his once-notorious assessment of the Massachusetts witch-scare, recently defended as a cautionary, level-headed effort at reconciliation. The defense unquestionably improves upon the former view: like his father, Cotton Mather tried to curb the use

---

the *further* it Rolls, the *bigger* it grows." Or again, he seems too much to protest his concern with his "dying parent," not only because of his insistence on the image, but, more strikingly, because of his many allusions to *Vatersmord*. "*You are Murderers of your Fathers!*", he cries time after time to the unconverted; "*You murder your Fathers!*"; and on several occasions he refers to the story of Croesus' "Dumb Son, who tho' he never spoke before; yet seeing a man go to kill his Father, his Agonies made him shriek, *O don't kill my Father!*" The relationship was of course further complicated by Mather's intense feelings for his own first and favorite son, whom he named Increase, after his father.

of "spectral evidence," which lay at the heart of the crisis. But the
book itself is as far from sweet reasonableness as it is from self-
serving hysteria. Its purpose rests in its impassioned affirmation of the
colonial cause. As it portrays the descent of Satan and his legions,
all details of court procedure are subsumed in what becomes, like
Milton's *Paradise Regained*, a "brief epic" of eschatological tribulation.
The preface presents the author as an amalgam of suffering servant
and seer, a saint subjected to "buffetings from Evil Spirits" and a
prophet whose fortitude and foresight "countermine the whole PLOT of
the Devil." The narrative transfers these terms to the settlement at
large. "The Errand of our Fathers into these Ends of the Earth,"
Mather explains, fulfilled "the Promise of old made unto our Blessed
Jesus, *That he should have the Utmost parts of the Earth for his
Possession*." What wonder, then, "that never were more *Satanical
Devices* used for the Unsetling of any People under the Sun"? Those
devices, from the outbreak of heresy in the 1630s to King Philip's
War in 1675, had hitherto collapsed, and the inevitable finale was
hastening: "Wherefore the Devil is now making one Attempt more
upon us," "a thing, prodigious, beyond the Wonders of former Ages,"
a war "so *Critical*, that if we get well through, we shall soon Enjoy
Halcyon Days with all the *Vultures* of Hell *Trodden under our Feet*."

In accordance with this prospect, Mather turns for his text on
witchcraft not to the Hebrew law (as in Exod. 22:18) but to the Book
of Revelation: "*the Devil is come down unto you, having great Wrath;
because he knoweth, that he hath but a short time*." His application
pictures the settlers as another David, afflicted from his youth, and
as a second Job, his dwelling "Hurricano'd" and his wife inciting him
to curse God, pleading with his friends for compassion: "*Have pity
upon me, for the Wrath of the Devil has been turned upon me*."
Here, however, the wrath has a much farther-reaching significance,
"such an one as is indeed Unparallelable." Recalling the Baptist's
times, Mather notes "That just before our Lords *First Coming*, there
were most observable Outrages committed by the Devil upon the
Children of Men." Surely, therefore, the present "unusual Range of
the Devil among us, a little before the *Second Coming*" means that
we shall deliver "the last stroke." Did not Israel go "further in the
two last years of their Journey *Canaan-ward*, than they did in 38
years before"? Drawing together the Apocalyptic time schedule,
the progress of the Reformation, God's miraculous protection of His
American vineyard, the political and natural occurrences abroad—in
short, the totality of human history—Mather proclaims

Good News for the *Israel* of God, and particularly for His *New-English Israel*. The Devil was never more let *Loose* than in our Days; and it proves the *Thousand Years* is not very *Far Off*. SHORTLY didst thou say, Dearest Lord! O Gladsome word! I may Sigh over *this* Wilderness, as *Moses* did over *his*, We are consumed *by thine Anger*, [yet] if God have a Purpose to make here a Seat for any of *Those Glorious Things, which are spoken of Thee, O Thou City of God;* then even thou, *O New-England,* art within a very little while of Better Dayes than ever yet have Dawn'd upon thee. Our *Lord Jesus Christ shall have the uttermost parts of the Earth for his Possession,* the *last* [shall] be the *first,* and the *Sun of Righteousness* come to shine *Brightest,* in Climates which it rose *Latest* upon!*

Thus, as Jonathan Edwards was to render Northampton, Salem village becomes the setting for the climactic drama in the story of redemption. *"The Walls of the whole World are broken down!,"* Mather exults; "the very *Devils* are broke in upon us, to seduce the *Souls,* torment the *Bodies,* sully the *Credits,* and consume the *Estates* of our Neighbours, as if the *Invisible* World were becoming *Incarnate.*" When he considers the specifics of the situation he urges restraint. Many of the accused, he fears, are innocent. As in "a *Blind Mans Buffet,*" encircled by "the *Ty-dogs* of the Pit," terrified by *"the Fires that are upon us,"* we are "hotly, and madly, mauling one another In the dark." But in the main it is the invasion from the Pit that seizes his imagination. In the fires of diabolism, consuming alike the virtuous and the possessed, he sees the conflagration from which, phoenix-like, will arise a new heaven and a new earth. And he highlights the dialectic by blending the American wilderness and the wilderness of Christ's agon. This conjunction (intimated by the figural trials of Moses, David, and Job) links all aspects of his sermon-treatise-narrative, makes Salem a paradigm of New England, each of the bewitched a representative of the suffering community, every untoward act symbolic of the entire snare, and New England itself, summarily, an emblem of the invisible universal church. Mather's introductory discourse on the "Enchantments Encountered" ends with a prayer to the Savior in His anguish; the last section ("The Devil Discovered") concludes with a lengthy comparison of each of the three temptations with the Devil's present wiles. What more need be said of the tidings which all this "Hints unto us"? At the dawn

---

* *Wonders of the Invisible World* (Boston and London, 1693), pp. 36–37, 43–45.

of the Christian era the Tempter was repulsed and the Eden of the redeemed soul raised in the wilderness; some seventeen hundred years later the full ramification of that defeat is to be made manifest, in the antitypical Eden, New Jerusalem, shining like the meridian sun over a renovated creation from the uttermost ends of the earth.

The harmony that Mather asserts here between his public and his private worlds is in some measure deceptive. Reaction against the trials had already set in (as he tacitly concedes at several points in the book) and was beginning to erode not only his family's dynastic claims but the theocracy's very foundations. By 1700 the counteroffensive came to focus upon him in particular. Why he should have thus been made *bête noire* of the entire episode remains a matter of conjecture. Even after we acknowledge his excessive zeal, even as we comprehend the enormity of his naiveté, it seems undeniable that most of the accusations were extrinsic, or tangential, to his stand on the trials per se. His critics assailed him because he upheld the authority of the court (while dissenting from its more reprehensible tactics and decisions); because *Wonders* paraded an approving preface by Lieutenant Governor William Stoughton, with Hathorne the sternest of the "hanging judges"; because Mather had too confidently trumpeted his cure, four years earlier, of a "possessed" Boston girl, and then, by methods some considered suspect, tried to repeat his success at Salem (though it is worth noting that the cure itself anticipated the psychosomatic treatment of hysteria); because he authored the official, collectively formulated clerical position on the proceedings; because he was later reluctant to recant, and, when he did, persisted nonetheless in his apocalyptic interpretation; and fundamentally perhaps because he was the youngest, least experienced, and hence most vulnerable of the old-guard spokesmen involved in what came to be considered the triple misfortune of the 1690s: the Salem trials, the new colonial charter, and the appointment of Sir William Phips as governor.

Whatever importance we assign these factors individually, in general Mather had good reason, I think, to complain of persecution. In any event, as the reaction turned more and more into a vendetta against him, his writings increasingly strike up an antiphonal movement, reminiscent of the diaries, between prophet and people. We can follow its rising counterpoint through his various treatments of witchcraft, from *Memorable Providences* (1689), his sanguine, straightforward tale of the Goodwin children of Boston, to *Triumphs over Troubles* (1701), his reply to Robert Calef's slanderous satire-denunciation of 1700, *More Wonders of the Invisible World.* For instance, in *Wonders* Mather likens the colony to Joseph importuned by Potiphar's wife, Satan's instrument, and to a martyr at the stake who had the Book of Revelation thrown at him "by his Bloody Persecutors"; in *Triumphs* he transfers the figures from history to biography. Taking his text from Joseph's response to his adversaries ("*ye thought evil against me;* But God meant it unto Good"), he compares the Mathers to the martyr Constantine cast into a dungcart. By a "*Strange and Fierce Assault,* All the Rage of Satan against the Holy Churches of the Lord falls on us," he exclaims—meaning now his father and himself in *opposition* to the colony—and yet we will prove instead to "be a precious Odor to God."

This is by no means to say that the Salem experience reversed Mather's convictions. Insofar as he deals only with the witches—outside the circle of private recriminations, so to speak—his outlook retains its former unity. What he learned in essence solidified the role for which, I have suggested, he had been preparing from childhood. He entered into the witchcraft debate in 1688 in his mid-twenties, with public honors thick upon him. He emerged from it, less than a decade later, something of a political exile (in his own eyes the victim of "*Contempt,* & Cruel Mockings"), but determined to uphold in his writings the "Utopia that was NEW-ENGLAND" despite (or beyond) history, to *use* his isolation as a means of revealing himself foremost among "those Watchmen that God hath sett upon ye Walls of Jerusalem, which never hold their peace, & give Him no rest, until He make Jerusalem a praise in the earth." The basis of this development lies in the aesthetic formula through which, in the diaries, he resolved his identity crisis: the interchangeability, and mutually sustaining import, of the images of Christ and the Baptist. The passion which his new-found assurance elicited suggests itself in sheer quantity of publication: seventy-nine titles between 1692 and 1700. At best, it is embodied in the most forceful political sermons of the age, worthy precursors of a national genre that culminates in Whitman's *Democratic Vistas* (1871).

Some of these sermons devolve upon witchcraft; others deal with parallel disturbances: Indian battles, natural disasters, threats of invasion. In each case the strategy builds upon the same model. All the temptations or injuries recapitulate those of Christ (Satan "would *run* us over the most amazing Precipice in the World"); every encounter assumes epic proportions ("Our *Air* has an *Army* of Devils in it," with "marvellous *Energy*" to "*Crack* and *Craze* the Soul"); in every circumstance the lesson for the individual as for the community is that God's American remnant must "travel through the valley of Baca, that is of weeping, unto their everlasting happiness." Together, these elements constitute a view of history which absorbs even the traditional doom-clauses of the federal covenant within a profoundly optimistic framework, an absolute against which this world's temporal evils cannot prevail.

The framework had been established long before. It was intrinsic to the rhetoric of John Cotton and Richard Mather, with its interlinking of the providential and the predetermined; it was embellished and elaborated by their colleagues and successors. What their grandson more than any other colonial Puritan contributed was an emphasis upon the mythical. Scholars have traced the evolution of seventeenth-century New England thought as a process of compromise and distintegration, step by stubborn step, under the exigencies of actuality. Only in the realm of the imagination could the idea remain intact. Mather's practical misfortune became his most formidable literary asset. It not only stimulated but, in self-protection, compelled him to draw *ad extremis* upon the metaphorical. Of course he was also temperamentally suited for the task. His first published sermon, *The Call of the Gospel* (1686), is rich in figural expression and fired with the significance of "this Wilderness, that like *Gideon's* fleece, enjoyes the Dewes of Heaven when the rest of the world is dry"; his first political *Declaration* (1689), expands the issues at hand—the abuses of authority during the Andros regime—to incorporate the "horrid *Popish Plot*" against Protestantism, and sees in matters like taxation without representation (as certain Americans were to do a century later) a conspiracy instigated "by the great *Scarlet Whore*"; he could not repress this sense of drama even in the little almanac he issued in 1683 (*"for the year of the Worlds Creation 5632"*) and supplemented with a disquisition on time and eternity.

The authorial stance he created for himself in the next decade brought these tendencies to full flower. "If *this* world will deny me," repaying love with asperity, he wrote, he could "appeal to the *other*," as a prophet-leader bearing the cross of New England's sacred Old Principles. It was, in effect, an appeal to the legendary past and future, a method (rather like Whitman's) of establishing his connection with the present by dissolving and then reconstituting it in accordance with his self-concept. That the new generation was sinful he could not but admit; God's "Ax is laid unto the Roots of the Trees," His "*Knife* ha's been cutting and Pruning of us," "*Every thing looks*

Black." But it was a narrow literalist view that despaired at such setbacks. *Sub specie imaginationis,* as Mather understood them, they opened out into a magnificent overarching plan, one that pronounced the colonists the long-typed-out Israel *redivivus.* His public addresses transform the "vicious Body of mockers" he rails against in his letters and diaries into a beleaguered but "Precious *People* of God," a "people which may say before the Lord, as they in Isa. 63:19. Lord *We are thine,*" the blessed remnant of which "it was said Rev. 18:20. *Rejoice over her, thou Heaven.*" A veritable "cloud of witnesses," he claims, attests to his position, including the fact of the colony's supernatural growth into a second Paradise. How, then, can any thoughtful New Englander submit to pessimism? How can he not "*Venture his all, for this Afflicted people of God,*" how fail to "say as the Martyr once, *Alas That I have but one Life to loose! 'Tis Immanuels Land* that we Venture for."

Politically considered, Mather's grandiloquence seems naively hyperbolical; considered as literature, it serves an important double function. First, it superimposes upon the facts of declension a corporate essence which effectually eradicates the threat of reality; and secondly, it conjures up an ideal auditory through which he can seize the present, after all, for his historiography. For though the younger generation in many ways stands inferior to the moral giants who "laid the Foundation of our *Heaven* and our *Earth,*" nonetheless, as they appear on Mather's pages, they have shown themselves deserving of their inheritance. The founders' goal depended on continuity from father to son, like the Hebrew exodus, and, on a mystic plane, like the scheme of redemption. In celebrating past and future, therefore, Mather is obliged to come to terms with his own times; he does so by transferring his emotional energy to the rhetoric that affirms his vision. We are now, he argues, in these closing years of the seventeenth century, like our ancestors "a *People* which has proportionately more of God among them than any part of mankind beside." In particular, "the youth in this country are very sharp and early ripe in their capacities, above most in the world," so that it seems likely "our little New England may soon produce them that shall be commanders of the greatest glories." In general,

> *He that looks upon these Colonies, will see them filled with precious and Holy* Churches. *He will see a great Instance of the* Protestant Religion, *in its purest, and fullest* Reformation, *maintained, by the Children which are the product and Off-spring of that* Choice Grain, *which God sifted [from] Three Nations, to*

bring into this Wilderness; *and he must have his* Eyes not open
if he do not make that Exclamation, How Goodly are thy Tents,
O New-England, and thy Tabernacles, *O thou American* Israel!*

  In this context, Mather finds solace in God's very displeasure. We
are not the first to suffer thus, he points out. "Endless" punishments
were meted out to our forebears, "Awakening and Horrible Calam-
ities" which anywhere else would have brought a speedy ruin to
the enterprise. Our punishment is so harsh, then and now, because
the Lord, Who loves us above the rest of mankind, will *not* let us fail.
He has pledged as much in chastising His elect; and for us, as for
them, reversals are an inspiriting sign, a token of divine affection. In
short, the substance of federal condemnation—the lament itself over
promises forsaken—becomes for Mather a vehicle of affirmation. God's
"corrective" rod demonstrates the unbroken, unbreakable, tie between generations. And hence it presages a far greater fulfillment.
Had not Daniel, for one, foretold that *"There shall be a Time of
Trouble, and at that Time thy People shall be delivered"?* Granting
then that the colony had regressed from its original luster, supposing
even that the evil had spread like a cancer beyond human control—
what of it? God has also revealed to us that His end-time mercy would
gratuitously redeem his chosen. "Hee'l then give Peace to His un-
sanctified [but justified] people, and make this Peace to be the means
of Sanctifying them. *Not for your sakes,"* as He had declared in
Isaiah and Revelation, *"but for my Holy Names sake!"* The "contrary
and Terrible Appearance of Things" was no more than that—appearance; reality lay in Scripture and in things to come. "So, then, the
Blacker you see the *Troubles* of the Age to grow, the sooner and the
surer may be the *Peace* which we are hoping for." What seems "a dismal *Tragedy"* is really a prothalamium, Christ's preparation for the
marriage of heaven and earth. All humanity ought to be concerned in
the event, but we especially: " 'Tis the prerogative of New-England
above all the countries of the world."

  On the strength of that prerogative, Mather salutes the Sun of
Righteousness glowing from behind the clouds of wrath, the American City of God emerging through the mists of history, and (in
what surely required the most audacious leap of the imagination)
Christ's New England host standing, as it were beyond the pews of
hostile faces, *"terrible as an Army with Banners"* at the very threshold

---

* *A Companion for Communicants; Discourses upon the Nature, the Design,
and the Subject of the Lords Supper* (Boston, 1690), dedication, sigs. A²verso–
A³recto.

of the millennium. *"O what has God wrought?,"* he exclaimed in 1690 and again in the year following. "My brethren, we shall very quickly see those *glorious things which are spoken of the City of God"; "*I now speak to some Hundreds, who are like to live unto the Day, when mankind shall no more be Inebriated with the *Cup of Abominations* in the Hand of the old Romish *Whore"; "*I am verily perswaded, A great part of this Assembly may live to see those Blowes given to the *man of Sin."* In 1696, in his sermon *Things for a Distressed People to Think upon,* his fervor rose to a higher pitch still:

> *The number of years,* for the Church to ly under its Desolations, is very near to its Accomplishment, and the bigger part of this Assembly, may in the course of Nature, Live to see it: There stand those within these Walls this Day, That shall see, *Glorious Things done for* the City of God! An Age of Miracles is now *Dawning* upon us. My Fathers, and Brethren of this *New-English Israel,* you are concerned [in this] more than any men living.*

Here again Mather's confidence reflects the outlook of early New England, and again with the same crucial difference. In the first decades, the mingling of providential and redemptive history flowed logically from a profoundly social ideology, one which embraced church and state, individual purity as well as temporal mission; which yoked together (under the uneasy label of "nonseparating congregationalism") the glory of Separatism and the grandeur of national election. Accordingly, what gives dramatic force to the literature of the emigrants is the tension it expresses. We sense that their relentless quest for coherence entails a deep insecurity, not of purpose but of adjusting means to ends within a recalcitrant day-by-day reality. What gives dramatic force to Cotton Mather's work is, on the contrary, the resolution or relaxation of tension. This absence of conflict, I believe, accounts for his much-noted indifference to theory, his focus on synthesis and interpretation as opposed to theology proper. In any event, it explains the facility with which he shifts from one level to another, from prophecy to history, from texts on the saint's wayfaring and warfaring to admonitions about details of behavior. "We have seen a *great* REVOLUTION," he writes in *Eleutheria,* "and we are e're long to see a *greater";* and then, almost without transition, he connects the latter with theocratic principles of conduct. He begins *The Duty of Children* by proclaiming that the final triumph of the church is at hand; he continues with a parallel (reserved by European Puritans for solely temporal purposes) between Israel and New England, but

* (Boston, 1696), pp. 32, 34, 38.

magnifies it into "a Figure and Shadow" of the imminent fall of Antichrist; and only when this framework has been established does he address himself to his main theme, the necessity of conversion, linking it firmly, however, to his prefatory remarks.

The finest sermon-length illustration of these shifts of perspective, which blend (rhetorically) the functions of savior and seer, is *A Midnight Cry* (1692). The subtitle speaks of the *"peculiar things* [occurring] *in THIS TIME for our AWAKENING,"* the dedication then defines the preacher's office as "that of a WATCHMAN," the text (from Rom. 13:11) announces: "now is our *SALVATION* nearer." Each capitalized word deliberately carries the many-layered implications noted above (temporal and atemporal, personal and communal), as does the title itself, which exhorts both reformation and regeneration through the doomsday parable of the ten virgins (Matt. 25). The sermon brings these disparate areas together by the sheer breadth of its controlling metaphors. It opens by linking justification and sanctification implicitly through the negative metaphor of sleep: the moral sleep of the quiescent reason, the spiritual sleep of the soul (when it lies unresponsive to its principle of grace) and the *"Corporal Sleeping"* which delays good works. On all levels, the sinners are avoiding the same ultimate question. Or more accurately, they have committed themselves, on every level, to the same dread choice. To sleep is finally to die, not to be; and their not-being at *this time* foreshadows a terrifying consummation, reveals them to be hanging "by a Rotten Thread over the Mouth of that heated *Furnace* from whence the smoke of Torment ascends for ever." Mather invokes this Calvinist sight of sin, however, as a watchman's ruse, the more dramatically to prelude the "Ravishments" of *waking*. As he proceeds, his picture of declension fades into an altogether different prospect for the New World. The colonists appear, as of old, in the aura of the humbled servant: Samson amidst the Philistines, Daniel in the lion's den, Joseph in prison, Jacob wrestling the angel. Their wakening terrors, Mather assures them, herald their *salvation*. And he invites them in *this time* to rouse their sluggard intellect from the long sleep of linear time.

The vista of glory he opens thus transfigures his metaphors, and by extension history itself, to accord with his midnight watch. It enables him to cope with time's complexities and contrarieties by relegating them to the realm of not-being. Having "measured the *Last Hours,"* he sounds the great final alarum in the world's "heavy Ears, *Behold, the Bridegroom comes! THE TIME OF THE END,* seems just going to lay its Arrest upon us. May we now *Awake* unto it, KNOWING

THE TIME!" To the hypocrite, the unconverted, and the transgressor alike, he reiterates the same eschatological challenge: "In what condition would we desire to be found, if we were sure that within a very little while our Lord should come to take his *Kingdome?*" Well, precisely that condition is "to be *Now* Endeavored; and I say *NOW*, with an emphasis." The cosmic revolution we are engaged in (for already "we are got into the *Dawn* of the Day") suggests the stakes we face, and, specifically, teaches us in *this time* how "to walk in its *Light.*" To enforce the instruction, Mather proposes in conclusion that the congregation join in a renewal of convenant, a "voted" declaration by those under the convenant of grace, that they bind themselves to the laws of the community. This proto-revivalist procedure first appears (in colonial literature) in Winthrop's *Arbella* sermon; it became something of an institution after the Indian massacres of 1675, when the clergy began calling on their flocks to rededicate themselves to the Good Old Way. But in *A Midnight Cry* it serves not (as before) to admonish, but to celebrate; joyfully to reassert the relation between the bonds of works and of grace and to advance the marriage of heaven and earth as a paradigmatic course of action for the settlers.

The once thorny question, "What is to be done?," raises no real problem here. "*Labour to be found in such* Wayes," Mather invariably counsels, "*as the State of PEACE now advancing upon the world, would oblige us unto. Awake, out of this unbecoming Sleep*" so that "the *Father of Lights* may give you some *Light* of those *Prophecies*" together with "*a large measure of Grace in your Souls.*" Thereafter the road ahead is irresistibly clear. As Christ will then, so we may now drive the Devil from our land. Like the saints then, so now we can "assay to do every Thing in the whole of both our Callings": each man by his continual inward query, "Am I in a *Fit STATE* to appear *BEFORE THE JUDGMENT SEAT,*" and the whole of New England by a unanimously positive response to its watchman's demand: "Suppose that before to morrow Morning, the Lord Jesus Christ were to become visible, and make the Sky to rattle, the Mountains to tremble, the Hills and Rocks to melt; could we *Rejoyce?*" In sum, *waking* for the settlers means, individually, living in the present as though they were already in the future, and collectively, restructuring experience in light of the terrestrial-otherworldly church-state-to-be, prefigured by the golden sheen of the Great Migration.

Thus if Mather could not reconcile history with myth, he could sunder them as Christ had sundered the dead world from the life of faith. And if the apodictic turned out to be nothing more than imaginative assertion, that served his purpose well enough. It enabled him to recreate a dormant New England in his own likeness—through the dual image of righteous affliction and messianic mission—so as to preserve it against not only the crudity but the complexity of history. It allowed him, furthermore, to bind his social role inextricably with his literary calling. Most broadly, it led him to develop a rhetorical form which continued to inspire the watchmen of God's Country long after Puritanism gave way to new and alien modes of thought. It may be found in Thoreau, for example, who substituted for the "list of failures" he recorded in a draft of *Walden* his famous proposal "to wake my neighbors up," or in Walt Whitman, who, sensing that "the Almighty had spread before this nation charts of imperial destinies, dazzling as the sun, culminating time," sensing too "the people's crudeness, vice, caprices," offered his "prophetic vision" (in which speaker and subject merge) as guarantee of the rising glory of America.

Whitman's vision leads back through Barlow's *Columbiad* (1807) to Edwards's *Thoughts on the Revival* (1742). It is explicit in the self-justifying dialectic of Mather's *Midnight Cry*, as the sermon graduates from the opening jeremiad toward the peroration: toward Mather's summons to a national greatness which (in Melville's phrase) "was predestinated at creation," and, simultaneously, to a revival of the soul whereby "the suddenly awakened sleeper" (in the words of Emerson and Margaret Fuller) "is instantly apprised not what part of dead time, but what state of life and growth is now arrived and arriving." "I affirm," Mather concludes, "that all the *Peace* of *New* England," and of each one of her inhabitants, "lies in her *going forth* to meet this *Blessed Reformation. Awake, Awake, put on thy Strength, O* New-English *Zion, and put on thy Beautiful Garments, O* American *Jerusalem.*"

THE ESCHATOLOGY OF SERVICE: COTTON MATHER'S ESSAYS TO DO GOOD (1700–28)

Throw a stone into the stream, and the circles that propagate themselves are the beautiful type of all influence.

Emerson, *Nature*

To interpret Mather's shifts of perspective as a slackening of Puritan principles overlooks his meaning; much less should we read them as a covert capitulation to Arminianism or as a conscious transition from piety to moralism. Undoubtedly, they were so adapted later in the eighteenth century, but we ought not to burden the author with the sins of his readers. He held adamantly to Orthodox Calvinism, the system erected by the master's Swiss, Dutch, and English disciples, which, despite basic modifications, built upon the notions of man's depravity and impotency. A year before his death, Mather denounced the Arminians as vigorously as had his grandfathers. Deism he regarded as a front organization for the atheist conspiracy. He respected the intellect, like the earlier Puritans, as a dignified but decisively limited faculty. With his father, he supported the Half-Way Covenant because he believed it carried forward the theocracy's original design. When he directed the saints' unconverted heirs to will themselves to heaven, he was articulating what he considered, with good reason, to be a theory indigenous to the New England Way. Virtually every major first-generation theoretician (as Increase argued impressively in 1675) had assumed that church-membership tests reliably segregated the sheep from the goats, and that, for the most part, the line of election ran "through the loins of godly parents." Virtually all of them believed that the spiritual seed passed genetically from father to son. By this logic (a consequence or extension of the doctrines of preparation, visible sainthood, and providential-teleological historiography), the unconverted-but-baptised children were saved in all ways but one, their unthawed wills, just as their once-repentant-but-backsliding parents were already redeemed, though in need of corrective affliction, and just as the colonial errand, which by God's time was long since accomplished, demanded their present services.

To that unique community, and not to the world at large, Mather thundered the duty actively to seek after salvation. For them alone he stressed social responsibilities in sermons on *Free-Grace Maintained* (1706) and *The Salvation of the Soul* (1720), only before an American Puritan congregation did he claim that baptism indicates that God "has *Prae-ingaged* those Children for Himself." What elsewhere would be flat self-contradiction, what had in fact been denounced abroad as well-nigh heretical presumption, became a paradox of faith in the pulpit of Boston's North Church: "it is *Grace*, pure *Grace* that helps us; *God is with you, while you are with Him*"; or again: "there is a COVENANT OF GRACE; And by our *Consent* unto this most gracious *Covenant*, we are to *make choice* of the Great GOD for *Our God*, and [thereby] *make sure* of His being so"; or once again, at the close of a covenant-renewal ceremony: "Let us Request for, and Rely on, the Aids of Grace for a Self-Reformation" *and* for "ALL the [outward] Designs of *Reformation; the Land mourns and fades because we have broken the everlasting Covenant.* Wherefor if we would be recovered," one and all, now and *ad aeternum*, "tis the *Covenant* that must Recover us, the *Covenant of Grace*, which is Brought unto us all as have been Admitted unto any [!] *Ecclesiastical Priviledges among us.*"

Mather's approach varies not so much in thought as in expression from that of his forebears: in the confident, easy sweep of his language. Yet here too the variance betokens a qualitative distinction. Transferred to the domain of letters, the struggle for a Holy Commonwealth issues in the foregone triumph of the absolute over the temporal. By means wholly of rhetoric Mather subdued reality in his political sermons and accredited himself as prophet-watchman; by those means elsewhere, especially after 1700, he integrated that role with his functions as pastor. Forced back from the political arena, he absorbed himself in the possibilities for public awakening provided in his vocation, turned increasingly to the "watchfulness in particulars" which led Samuel to say that "the Ambition and Character of my Father's life was Serviceableness," and Ben Franklin to acknowledge Mather as an inspiration for his own way to wealth, benevolence, and moral self-improvement. This tendency also underlies the familiar charge that Mather launched the national success ethos, with its unsavory alliance of grace and cash, and the popular definition of the Puritan as an inveterate meddler, driven by the fear, as Mencken put it, that someone, somewhere, might be enjoying himself.

Whatever justification these charges may have in Mencken's America, they belie the character of Mather's writings. In the first place, insofar as doing good expresses an immemorial Christian attitude (reinforced anew by the Reformation), Mather's preoccupation reveals him as a conservative rather than an innovator. He modeled his views, as he takes pains to point out, upon scores of earlier authorities, and in this sense his sermons on serviceableness stand with his political sermons as an effort to recover the theocratic ideal. "We live in faith in our vocations," said John Cotton, "in that faith in serving God serves men, and in serving men, serves God." Secondly, judged from a practical standpoint, Mather's well-doing is genuinely well-meant. When we read of him as "a Man of *Whim* and *Credulity*," dangerously eager "to make Experiments on his Neighbours," we should remember that those phrases originated during the smallpox epidemic with the opponents of immunization. His own words suggest at least a different motivation: "They have lived longest in the world, who have done the most good in the world; whatever contributes unto the welfare of mankind, and a relief of their miseries, is to glorify God." His pastoral advice follows his precept. In sermon and treatise he urges the practice (not merely the profession) of charity, denounces the slave trade, extols the benefits of ecumenism. He instructs parents to look to their own ways before mending those of their children, and to discipline, when necessary, by example rather than brute authority. So, too, he would have teachers attend to "not only the *brains*, but also the *souls*" of their pupils, supplementing instruction with tutorials designed to bolster the student with "*expectations and encouragements.*" He applies similar strictures to the relations between master and servant, ruler and subject, minister and layman, lawyer and client, physician and patient.

Bonifacius (1710) is Mather's classic formulation of the nature and meaning of these "essays to do good." At some level, predictably, he intended the book as an advertisement for himself. His exhortations about rising to an "*afflatus* that will conquer *temptations*," about being such "a son that the best surname for the glad father would be, *the father of such an one*," about responding with Christ's meekness to "vile INGRATITUDE from Communities as well as *individuals*"—these and many other imperatives (buttressed by quotations from his previous writings) unmistakably mirror his most private aspirations. Most telling of all in this respect is the tree image which grows into the controlling metaphor of the work. According to its preface, "to *plant trees of righteousness* is the hope of the book now before us"; its first section argues that "we begin to bring forth *good fruit* by lamenting our own *unfruitfulness*"; the next section explains how "to live fruitfully" for others; subsequent sections make the obligations specific: ministers must seek "pardon for *unfruitfulness*," the prosperous must remember that "gathering the fruit relieves the tree," the educated must share their learning like "a *tree that brings forth fruit.*" In every instance, the delegated function becomes the means of replanting oneself, in unity with all men, within the garden of God, like the Second Adam "abounding in the fruits of *well-doing.*"

The harvest, Mather promises, will yield blessings both in this world and the next. In light of current criticism, it needs to be re-emphasized that the promise does not mark a departure from orthodoxy. It was standard fare in the early colonial churches, intrinsic to the rationale for corporate calling and for preparation for salvation. Like his forebears, Mather circumscribed the discussion by positing first that sanctification is not a means to redemption ("*Woe unto us if it were!*"), and then by limiting it effectually to the visible saints. "Though we are *justified*, yet good works are demanded of us to *justify* our *faith*," he puns; the agency of free grace compels us (in time) and, simultaneously, disposes us (from eternity) to the outward forms of Chris-

tianity. To be sure, the staggering difference between the principle
and its local application—and the problematic distinction in the latter
context between the virtues and vices of wealth—required delicate
exposition to the world at large; his predecessors had tread warily in
the realm of theory. Like them, he sought to hedge his position with
traditional denunciations: "Riches are a Fine, Gay, speckled Bird; but
it is a Bird in the *Bush*"; he who "*has nothing but Gold & Silver in his
mouth*" is a fish swimming into "*the Nets of Perdition.*" But because
he knew that prosperity might follow the labor of the convenanted
(in the New Israel above all other lands), he set his sights upon its
positive ramifications; and because he could not resolve the tension
between dogma and practice, between a flourishing New England as it
should be and as it was, he turned as usual to rhetoric in order to
dissolve it. With an effortless fluency which has shocked later theologians, he elaborated on the metaphor that the righteous are the
trustees of God's world, on the parable of the bread thrown upon the
waters, and on the prophecies concerning the blessed remnant. In these
terms he measured the distance between the saintly rich and those
who rise by fraud, and, affirming the correspondence between God's
providential and absolute aid, he urged parents never to "*Concern
themselves more to get the World than Grace for their Children,*" since
"if God giveth them Grace, Earthly blessings shall never fail."

In *Bonifacius* he incorporates these various explanations into an
imaginatively more heightened and more comprehensive approach,
one which absorbs the transitory, at all levels, into the eschatological.
As he develops his argument, every good work becomes magnified into
a momentaneous demonstration of the judgment to come. When he
states that "the more good any man does, the more he really *lives*," he
means "life" as an emblem of eternity, wherein "the only wisdom of
man" lies in his union with God. When he terms "GOOD DEVICES the
most *reasonable religions,*" he does so to persuade the reader to embrace them "with *rapture,* as enabling him directly to answer the
great END of his being." On these foundations he proposes beneficence
as a bridge between the visible and the invisible. "To do *good,* is a
thing that brings its own *recompense,*" he writes; it stands of itself
as "your powerful, and perpetual vindication." It must begin, like conversion, in the soul-struggle to be perfected in the image of God.
Subsequently, of its own accord it leads outward to others; but its
essential motive, "the *greatest* and *highest* of its glories," remains
first and last atemporal. Thus morality seeks no worldly remuneration
(in fact, "your conformity unto Him, yet *lacks one thing*" if you are
not "*despised and rejected of men*"); thus also it may be said to win

heaven ("the more you consider the *command* in what you do, the more assurance you have" of redemption); and thus, finally, the elect may find material recompense. As the saint in solitude prepares himself for life by meditating upon death, so conversely the well-doer, by eschewing the *gloria mundi*, shows himself worthy of the earthly blessings vouchsafed to certain servants of the Lord.

Even on a practical level Mather's notions merit our respect. They signify a wholesome if chimerical reaction against the *"Private Spirit"* he had long lamented, an effort to impose some spiritual cohesion upon a community that was disintegrating under the "liberating" ruthlessness of enlightened self-interest. Appropriately, one of the key terms in *Bonifacius* is *relatedness*. The section on "Home and Neighbourhood," for example, reminds us that not only family members but *"Neighbours* stand *related* unto one another," and that in both spheres the relationship entails duties: "relieving the afflicted with all agreeable kindnesses," assisting the destitute with gifts or loans (the latter to be repaid not on a certain day but when the borrower should find himself able to repay it, without inconvenience). Emanating from the center of one's concern for his soul, such circles of relatedness, as Mather conceived them, would widen progressively to envelop the whole body social. His most ambitious conception devolved upon "reforming societies." None of his projects has come under sharper attack, and none more unjustly. His intent was neither repression nor prurience but the desire to curb expediency by attaching the mean to an ideal—without, however, discarding the notion of the mean: he asked for temperance, not prohibition, and taught his "sodalities" (the prototypical graduate seminars he inaugurated) "rather *Socratically than Dogmatically*," aware that "what is now most in vogue may anon be refuted like its Predecessors." If he required zeal of his "Societies of Young Men Associated," he sought to temper excess through compassion and discretion. What he envisioned at most was a "blessed concord" of visible saints, "bound up in one *bundle of love*," "charitably watchful over one another" and rejoicing in *"opportunities to do good."*

His scheme had immediate precedents in Augustan England; more important for him, certainly, was the parallel it offered with the bonds of church-covenant which knit together, "as one man with one soul," the citizens on a hill. To the degree that we grant him the validity of the parallel, *Bonifacius* stands, Janus-faced, as a crucial document in the continuity of the culture. Hopelessly nostalgic from one perspective, it looks forward from another not only to Franklin's "Clubs for Mutual Improvement" but to Edwards's "Blessed Unions."

Its connection with the Great Awakening, indeed, appears to be the more basic of the two. I refer to *Bonifacius*'s consuming eschatological thrust, personal and social, its emphasis alike upon conversion and upon groups animated by "the wondrous force of *united prayers*," with "the *savor* on them of the saints" of old, seeking to revivify a dead land by doing that only, in Edwards's words, which added to "the glory of God or the good of men." Above all, I refer to the book's pervasive millennial expectations. That Mather never abandoned those expectations is evident everywhere in his published and unpublished works; and if after 1700 he had little or no following at home he found support abroad. Through his enormous European correspondence, to which he increasingly gave his energies, he aligned himself with the millenarians in Scotland. In 1709 he came into contact with August Hermann Francke and German Pietism, whose influence was extending through many regions of Europe, including England and Scotland, and whose missions had reached across the Atlantic to the East Indian Islands.

The full impact of Franckean Pietism upon colonial thought remains to be explored. It may be gleaned in different ways from Samuel Mather's *Vita Franckii* (1733) and from Edwards's tribute in his *History of the Work of Redemption* to Francke's leading role in the events which led to the Revival. Cotton Mather was especially affected by Francke as a kindred spirit whose efforts (unlike his own) met with "amazing" success. To further their "Marvellous Effects" he contributed to Pietist enterprises at Halle and advocated their emulation in America. He had himself urged similar enterprises often before. Now, however, he felt emboldened by the support of a gathering international movement, one that based its social beneficence on the same chiliastic Reformed historiography as that which informed the Great Migration (though transferred to a *spiritual* migration from local corruption). Like Edwards, he carefully insisted on the priority in all this of the New World theocracy; the American church, he pointed out, was "*pulcherrima inter mulieres*," the most beautiful of Christ's brides, and so had "the Honour of making the *First*, Right, Fair and Genuine *Beginning*."* But he was eager to express his

* The point was crucial to Mather because it allowed him at once to embrace German Pietism and to fit it into the framework of New England historiography. Thus he feels obliged even in his flowery epistles to Francke and Boehme to affirm that "There is not a place in which true Christianity is more cultivated than here in New England," and to note that "*American Puritanism* is so much of a Peece with the *Frederician Pietism*" that his *Magnalia* would prove "serviceable to [your] glorious intentions." Indeed, he introduced Francke to the "true

gratitude and solidarity. He did so most notably by assimilating the Pietists' techniques and terminology: their integration of homilectic "uniting maxims," for instance, with the neo-Joachite "Everlasting Gospel," their emphasis on the "prophecy of Joel" in conjunction with the emergent "Age of the Holy Spirit," and, in general, their shifting sense of the apocalypse, from the premillenarianism of the New England planters toward something approaching the postmillenarianism that characterizes American thought from the Great Awakening onwards—toward a view, that is, which sees the chiliad *within* history rather than as the result of a cataclysmic, supernatural break with history.

The shift was not a radical one. With the other Franckean concepts he espoused, it was consonant with the emigrants' gradualistic-typological soteriology, in which the church-state served both as antitype of the Old Testament Jerusalem and as *figura* of the Jerusalem-to-be. What German Pietism offered Mather was in essence what Coleridge and Carlyle offered Emerson: the potential for a renewed activism within an established national mythos, as well as a means of reaffirming the mythos within a contemporaneous intellectual-spiritual *Zeitgeist*. It was too late in life, too far into the Yankee apostasy, for Mather to recall his political ambitions. (Though he continued to interfere in public affairs, he recognized that he would never command the authority he once dreamed of, and exercised momentarily two decades before, in his father's absence). But he could transfer the momentum of Pietism's burgeoning success into literary summons and "Goods Devised." "I am dismissed from any expectation of much encouragement," he confessed in 1717 to an English correspondent. "And the truth is, I have dismissed and even divorced myself in a great measure from every party, but one which is now going to be formed." Yet that party of the future, *already* combining as it did

---

American Pietism" in 1710 as a system which embodied the "Principles and Practices of the Immanuelan People" (adding privately that, "admirable" as they are, the German "Professors are not without their Errours"); and in reprinting Francke's resumé of the Pietist missionary triumphs, he points out that those undertakings followed the lead of the emigrants: of John Eliot in particular ("no One is wronged if it be confessed, that our ELIOT shone as the *Moon among the Lesser Stars*"), and in general of the theocracy's "Pure MAXIMS of the *Everlasting Gospel*," harbinger of the *"Mighty Showers* to be expected in the *Latter Days."* The relations between German Pietism and American thought merit close study, not only in their direct manifestations (e.g., Mather and Edwards) but in their later indirect influences—through the writings of Schiller (for example)—in the nineteenth century.

the best of the past and the present (the New England Way and the
Franckean revival) provided encouragement enough.

Its impact upon his schemes for doing good appears in his revived
enthusiasm for local reform, particularly in the ministry and in education.* It is evident, too, in his reanimated call for missionary endeavors, to awaken not only the Indians but the Jews. Through the 1690s
he had made several gestures, as another "Evangelical Elias," toward
bringing about the restitution of Israel. A ten-year silence on the issue
followed. When he then returned to it, his new-found fervor, he explained, stemmed from the "Tokens for Good" at Halle, and the
"miraculous" conversion of several Jewish children in Berlin. He set
forth his convictions in 1718 in *Faith Encouraged*, an expanded version
of the Berlin miracle, and, most dramatically, in *Psalterium Americanum*, whose preface and commentary magnify the enterprise of translation into a concerted missionary service, preparatory to the Marriage
of the Lamb with His first-and still-beloved spouse at the altar of the
apocalypse.

Of course, Mather stresses that the Psalms also pertain to every
spiritual Israelite. Insofar as they continuously invoke Christ, they
may ensure the Christian reader "here the Character of those who are
to be admitted into the *Messiah's* glorious Kingdom." And insofar as
they contain the "*Key of David*" to "the *Mysteries* of the *Great Salvation*," they illuminate the contours of Christian history, from the
church's persecution under Antichrist to its victory on the fields of Gog
and Magog. But beyond such private aids, they may also provoke the
reader to a sublime serviceableness, one that concerns the mightiest
of the end-time events. Nowhere, cries Mather, is the progress of the
Jews more vividly depicted and (metaphorically) enacted than in
the Psalter. Indeed, "the Design of the PROPHETIC SPIRIT in the PSALMS

---

* *Manuductio ad Ministerium* (1724), his chief contribution in this area, owes
much of its pungent forcefulness to that enthusiasm. Fundamentally, like all his
books, it is a personal testament, at once the product of his pastoral experience,
an *apologia* for his style, a paean to the persecuted Christ-like servant, and compensation for his failure to attain the Harvard presidency. But the sublimating
process is undergirded by the appeal to an immediate historic thrust: specifically
to the curriculum in use at Halle; generally, to the "new type of ministerial leadership," admittedly modeled upon Francke's *Manuductio*, which would control "the
lives of the people through pietism." The appeal begins with the familiar do-good
eschatology (subordinating all studies, actions, and intentions "to an union with
God"); it proceeds through the maxims of pietism—seconded by a "dear brother
of mine, a professor in the Frederician University"—which raises the well-doing
minister into the "state of Paradise"; its crown and essence is proclaimed in the
book's running title: *The Angels Preparing to Sound the Trumpets.*

all along has been to describe the Sufferings" and "predict the Recovery of the *Jewish Nation*." What nobler service, therefore, could
a second Baptist aspire to, what surer means for making way for
the City of God, than to render their meaning intelligible? What
time could be more suitable than the present, when "the condition of
the *Jewish Nation* is like to be"—by that very nation—"more considered
than in the former Ages"? What place, finally, could be more advan-
tageous for the task than the New World, since the Psalms specifically
hold out "Hopes for *Americans*," predicting (Ps. 18:43) that after
"Our Saviour had seen and known *Asians, Africans, Europeans*," He
would turn, at the close of history, to the unknown continent at the
world's fabled fourth corner? Taking all this into account, "the Psalms
put into the hands of the *Jews* with so Entertaining a *Commentary*
thereupon, may be a powerful and perswasive Engine" for guiding
them into "the Grand Revolution which concludes our Bible."

To that end Mather gears the whole machinery of translation and
commentary, recasting the Psalter into a divine comedy of the wandering House of Israel. Substantiating his figural and Christological
readings by way of rabbinical opinions (his most frequently used
source), he expands the poetry into a prophetic saga of decline and
recovery: the destruction of Jerusalem and Babylonian captivity; the
Hebrews' stiff-necked disobedience, culminating in their rejection of
Christ; their subsequent pitiful persecution, wonderful preservation,
and happy restoration. Threading the narrative is the theme of National
Conversion; over one-third of the Psalms (by Mather's account) center
on this concept. The focus alternates, that is, between linear advance
and vertical revelation, in what becomes a dialectic of human action
and divine will, promise and fulfillment. The process itself takes several forms. Sometimes it shapes the meaning of an individual set of
verses, as in Psalm 69, which is said to relate the *agones* of Christ and
the Jews. More often it evolves by juxtaposition, so that the Jews' songs
of praise upon their rejuvenation (Psalms 96 and 97) seem to flow
logically into the cosmic jubilee at the Second Coming (Psalm 98).

Characteristically, the process unfolds in separable series or blocks
of poems, all built around the same theme, though following one another with rising intensity. Thus Psalms 125 through 136 describe successively the grounds of Israel's perseverance, its retrospective lament
for sins past, and its thankful devotions to the Lord of its salvation;
the next series (137–50) opens by recapitulating the sorrows of the
dispersed Jews, then recounts their prayers for help, announces their
redemption, and ends in an extended encomium to the New Jerusalem.
In every case the movement proceeds from the urgency for conver-

sion; and through the book as a whole the reiterated "Miracles to be wrought when *Israel* shall be returned from Exile" increasingly broaden to encompass the well-doer, beneficent societies, and, in the "transcendent efficacy" of the end-time wedding-ritual, "the supreme and final true PIETY" whose signs have already appeared:

> DOUBTLESS, *the Day approaches* wherein the *Kingdom of* GOD will appear in brighter displays than the World has ever yet been Enlightened withal. There are certain MAXIMS of PIETY wherein all Good *Men* are *United.* GOD will bring *His People to receive one another* upon these generous MAXIMS. An admirable *Peace* and *Joy* will arise from the operations of the *Holy Spirit;* and *Joels* Prophecy will be accomplished. ANGELS shall *Fly thro' Heaven,* having the *Everlasting Gospel.* That cry *Babylon is fallen* will ensue upon it; and wondrous Changes upon the World [reflecting in grander form the accomplishments of New England] will turn an horrid and howling *Wilderness* into a *Paradise.**

The strains of *Psalterium Americanum* thus lead back *to Bonifacius,* as do most other aspects of Mather's pietism. Written in the first flush of his contact with Halle, *Bonifacius* unites his earlier concepts of doing good with the possibilities newly opened by the Franckean revival. His proposals here for missionary undertakings extol those of the Pietists—they should "animate us, to imitate them"—and affirm New England's superiority in this respect by a detailed summary of the work *"formerly done* for the Christianizing of our *Indians."* Now, he promises, our missions will extend much further. The Holy Spirit will clear our path, as it did in the infancy of Christendom, with irresistible influences which will "cause whole *nations* to be *born at once"* and "render this world like a *watered garden."* A century before, the Bay emigrants had carried those influences to a new continent; the children of that exodus are to amplify the joyful sound to all peoples. As for the Hebrews, Mather would seem here to summon them primarily by the example of the reborn New World garden (as Increase did in 1669, in *The Mystery of Israel's Salvation,* and Edward Johnson in 1654, in *Wonder-Working Providence*). In general, he refers over and again to rabbinical dicta: partly to prod the colonists to "outdo *Judaism,"* as a rule to remind all his readers of the way of living which the rabbis foretell for "the *generation wherein the Messiah comes,"* the perfect serviceableness which will characterize

---

* *Psalterium Americanum* (Boston, 1718), introduction, pp. xxxii–xxxiv.

that *"illustrious state of the Church of God, which is to be expected, in the conversion of the Jews."*

This millennial way of living most fully embodies Mather's essays to do good. It also serves most lucidly to explain his position as precursor of Franklin and Edwards. The rags-to-riches stories he recounts (in a number of biographies as well as in *Bonifacius*) become "charming examples" of godliness chiefly in terms of his pietistic eschatology. It is a distinction which separates him from the conventional Protestant apologists for laissez-faire; and it is a distinction which applies, in different ways, to the spirit of the Great Awakening, and, later, to the concept of national mission. For Mather's vision of well-doing, beyond the material benefits it brought, beyond its excellence per se, beyond even its value as a private passport to heaven, carried forward the standard of the Everlasting Gospel. The chosen heirs of the uttermost parts of the earth could hardly consider their redemption merely as single, separate persons; assuredly, too, their "relatedness," under the ascending sun of the Holy Spirit, would never stop short at secular goals. "In engaging as many others as we can, to join with us," *Bonifacius* insists, we are "promoting His Kingdom among the children of men." The *"springs of usefulness"* we dig open by each act, "having once begun to run, will spread into *streams*, which no *human foresight* can comprehend"; each proposal realized, "like a *stone* falling into a *pool*," will cause "one *circle* (and *service*) to produce another, until they extend" ad infinitum. So our magistrates will enact solely those laws by which the reign of holiness may be advanced; so our universities, charged with *"collegia pietatis*, like those of our excellent *Franckius*," will accomplish *"wonders* in the world"; so our societies, "Propagating the *Maxims* wherein His *Will* shall *be done on Earth as it is in Heaven*," will by that "blessed symptom be together associated in the *Heavenly City"*; and so, comprehensively, we will reconstitute ourselves, what once we were, what God wishes us to be again, a serviceable light to the world, a knot of saints associated whose *"works of the day* fall in with the designs of *Divine Providence."*

In this perspective, as in subsequent American millenarianism, secular employment contrasts as unequivocally with the "work of the day" as does the house built upon sands with the stone cast upon the waters of eternity. The one stands self-contained, trapped in the limits of space and time; the other swells *sui generis* into an image of the entire human-divine order, dilating concentrically, ineluctably, from the personal sphere to the "federal" and the universal, imaging simultaneously the Neo-Platonic circle of salvation and the spiralling movement of Christian teleology.* By the same dynamic the work of the day comes also to image the order of nature. "Serious and shining *Piety,*" Mather writes in *Bonifacius,* "will glorify the *God of Nature.* Nothing so *unnatural* as to be *irreligious.*" He notes that the concept derives from Thomas Browne's *Religio Medici* (1643); its larger context is the "natural theology" which developed in the seventeenth century, the belief that creation, as the New Science revealed it in all its majestic, intricate symmetry, embodied God's goodness and wisdom. Mather was the first American actively to espouse the belief, in league with European religious scientists and scientifically minded clerics: William Derham, for example, author of *Physico-Theology* (1713), and Halle's Philip Spener, and, of course, Sir Isaac Newton, physicist and chiliast (as he was popularized in Richard Bentley's *Confutation of Atheism* [1693]). In *Bonifacius* Mather projects as part of this tradition his own *Angel of Bethesda,* designed to "instruct people how to improve in agreeable points of piety; and at the same time, inform them of the most experimental, natural, specific *remedies* for diseases." He might already have included his *Wonderful Works of God* (1690), his eloquent *Winter-Meditations* (1693), and perhaps the "Declamations on Natural Philosophy" he delivered as a student at Harvard. His most important undertaking of this kind, begun within a few months of *Bonifacius,* was published a decade later as *The Christian Philosopher: A Collection of the Best Discoveries in Nature, With Religious Improvements.*

In his scientific pursuits, Cotton Mather (again like Edwards and Franklin) was an avid dilettante, with an encyclopaedic range of interests and a predisposition toward the experimental and the pragmatic. His manuscript "Curiosa Americana," together with his communications to the Royal Society, reveal an amusing credulity. As historians of the subject have recognized, they also display a "striking ability to select, from the maze of 'natural philosophy,' those discoveries and problems which were eventually to prove of major

---

* The concept of the circle in these terms needs fuller treatment than the present essay can allow. Briefly: the metaphor of the circle of redemption stems from the philosophy of Plotinus as this was absorbed into Christian thought from the Church Fathers through the Renaissance; the circle-as-spiral comes to symbolize the repetitive yet forward-moving history of redemption, especially as this was expounded by progressivist-typologists from Eusebius and Orosius to the Bay emigrants. Mather's conflation of the two images may be seen in his dual self-concept in the diaries, in the rhetoric of his political sermons (such as *A Midnight Cry*), and above all in the notion of "representative men" he set forth in his biographies (discussed below).

importance." *The Christian Philosopher* unites this ability with his still more striking ingenuity in extracting "religious improvements" from the selections, drawing upon the discoveries and problems to erect a monument to the God of his fathers. The discoveries celebrate the reaches of man's mind; the problems teach him not to exceed his grasp: demonstrate that his "*Reason* is too feeble, too narrow a thing to comprehend the *infinite*," leave him "so transcended" that he will not "cavil, but adore" the "*Mysteries* altogether beyond [his] *Penetration.*" The interaction between the two strains, resembling the theocracy's blend of mysticism and rationalism, conveys Mather's purpose. As in *Bonifacius,* he was not so much adapting Puritanism to the Enlightenment as trying to dam up the excesses of the latter by recourse to orthodoxy: in effect, updating the Ptolemaic providential-natural theology that ran from (say) Augustine's *Confessions* to John Cotton's *Briefe Exposition upon Ecclesiastes.* And as in *Bonifacius,* his contributions to the humanitarian-scientific outlook of Franklin and Jefferson forms the lesser aspect of his legacy. In its quality of imagination at least, *The Christian Philosopher* belongs to a different national tradition—meta-scientific and at some level counter-rationalistic —which includes Edwards's *Images or Shadows of Divine Things* and Emerson's *Nature.*

This is not to deny *The Christian Philosopher* its transitional importance in the transformation of the earlier cosmology. Unquestionably, it is a crucial expression (in the New World) of the configuration of Puritanism, Pietism, and science which has been identified as a mainstream of American thought. Unquestionably, too, Edwards's epistemology, insofar as it derived from either Berkeley or Locke, is as difficult to reconcile with Mather's spiritualizations as it is with Emerson's transcendentalism. The similarity between the three preachers hinges on the fact that their subordination of science proper to divinity resulted in comparable symbolic modes. In part, this manifests itself in terms of natural theology: in certain common sources, for example, such as Thomas Browne; or in the effort to restrain the tide of materialism stirred up by the New Science; or in the "feeling akin to the poet's" which their passages evoke (for one critic, Mather's "artistic effects" recall the method of many of Walt Whitman's poems); or in the anachronistic inconsistencies which insinuate themselves into their technical expositions (Edwards's strangely medieval notes, Mather's obstinate belief in discrete providences). But such parallels may be found in scores of European works. What distinguishes *The Christian Philosopher,* and what seems specifically to relate it to later American works, is the theocratic confluence of personal and social eschatology, transferred now to the mind of the awakened observer of Nature. "The whole *World*," writes Mather, "is a *Temple* of GOD," where "Every thing about me Preaches unto me" concerning "the grand End of man's Being," the "*Evangelical* Spirit of *Charity*," and "the Blessedness of the *future State*." This threefold pattern, integrating salvation, serviceableness, and history, informs Edwards's response to the Newtonian universe; it appears, in one secular guise or another, in Emerson's (as well as Whitman's and Thoreau's) internalization of the meaning of America; to a large extent it defines the method of *The Christian Philosopher*.

Mather's fundamental assumption is the correspondence between the Book of Nature and the Book of God. "We will now for a while read in the *Former* of these *Books*," he explains, "'twill help us in reading the *Latter*." But of course he means equally that (in Edwards's words) "the Book of Scripture is the interpreter of the Book of Nature," and he organizes his material in accordance with Genesis 1, proceeding from light to the celestial bodies to the elements to the forms of life on earth, and concluding, in the longest section, with man. Hermeneutically and rhetorically, the creation story conveys his meaning on all of its three levels. Its literal-naturalistic aptness allows him to set the progress of science within the biblical framework. On a figural plane, the first seven days shadow forth the seven ages of man, so that the natural wonders he records bespeak the impending Judgment Day and the Sabbatism to follow, when "our Saviour may *feast* His *Chosen People* with Exhibitions of all these Creatures, in their various *Natures*." Anagogically, the mystery of creation, like the mystery of the Scriptures, stands revealed in the Incarnation; all things refer ultimately to Christ, from the magnet to the laws of gravity a "shadow" of His parturient love. Man's cognitive process follows this paradigm in that it recreates the individual in harmony with the cosmos. The principles of plant growth or of light are bare statistics "unto him that has no Faculty to discern *spiritually*." Granted that agency of inner renewal, he finds the light to be correlative to his own reason, his capacity (in Christ) to overcome the powers of darkness, and his claims to the inheritance of the saints in light; he discerns in the plants' physical structure "the Analogy between their States and ours" and, spiritually, in their revival in the Spring an emblem of the resurrection and "of the *Recovery* which the Church will one day see from a *Winter of Adversity*."

Right perception, then, reconciles man simultaneously with Creation, with history, and with his Redeemer. And in so doing it unites him with himself as paragon both of Nature and of the Bible: as "a *Machine* of a most astonishing Workmanship," which is also "the most exquisite Figure for an *holy Temple*"; as "the highest link in the *golden chain*, whereby *Heaven* is joined to *Earth*," who is at the same time "the *Microcosm*" of all being. "*Opera Creationis externae habent in se Imaginem Creationis internae*," Mather declares, anticipating Emerson's "every appearance in nature corresponds to some state of mind." Our inner and outer worlds are synonymous: "he that speaks to MAN, speaks to *every Creature*"; the Me and the Not-Me reflect one another through their common generative divinity. But beyond both, for Mather, circumscribing and delimiting their linked analogies, stand the Scriptures and ecclesiastical authority. As though he divined the anarchic subjectivism, the "imperial selfhood," potential in his outlook, he requires the observer to uncover meaning rather than invent it, to guage his spiritualizing faculty by an objective hierarchy of values which lies beyond his understanding and yet communicates itself to him through concrete, restrictive obligations: the maxims of piety that "the whole creation of GOD would mind us of," the good works that result from his homage to the sun as "*An Image of the Divine Goodness*," the services he will render when he can feel toward his neighbor the "*Law of Attraction*, whereby all the Parts of *Matter* embrace one another."

The Christian Philosopher fails in this attempt to bridge science and pietism. Its inadequacies have been discussed from a scientific or a theological standpoint. They seem to me most glaring in the haphazard proliferation of literary modes. Allegory and analogy, sacred and secular similitude, *figura* and trope follow indiscriminately from one another, often within the same context. Some such confusion appears in every Bible culture; but here it tends conspicuously toward chaos, palpably betokens a dissolution of external controls (in contrast to medieval Catholicism with its boggling excess of imposed categories). It issues in a kind of democratic blur of traditionally distinct forms: a universal levelling (not unlike a Whitmanesque catalogue) which (unintentionally) discards the differences between wit, metaphor, and hermeneutic, and invokes moral authority equally through the notion that faith is a telescope to the heavenly world, that ornithology affords a norm of filial devotion, and that typology highlights the botanical *curiosa* of a well-tended garden. It is this collapse of rhetorical distinctions, I believe, that most clearly marks the cultural significance of the book. For one thing, it offers an interesting perspective on the failure of natural theology and, more broadly still, on the aesthetic revolution implicit in Reformed thought, which cleaved literal from spiritual, set man vis-à-vis God without an officially sanctioned intermediary network of human-divine meaning, and so opened the road to modern symbolism. In particular, it serves—precisely in its levelling of symbolic dimensions as reality is ingested and "improved" in the microcosmic imagination—to highlight the beginnings of a movement which continues through Edward's "subjective idealism" to mid-nineteenth-century "American romanticism." The continuity here should not obscure the many differences between Mather and later writers. But neither should the differences discourage us from tracing the lines of development, especially, perhaps, through the affinity Mather draws, in the metaphor of creation, between Nature, the symbolic observer, and the exemplary American, the book's autobiographical-suprapersonal protagonist who explores himself in exploring the world, and for whom, as for Emerson's Poet, the world-self "is a temple whose walls are covered with [hermeneutic] emblems, [aesthetic] pictures and [moral] commandments of the Deity."

It is true that *The Christian Philosopher* does not have a pronounced American setting. It does not, like (say) Thoreau's "Walking," apply the individual's spiritual rebirth in Nature to the "true tendencies" of the renovated, or renovating, wilderness. Its historiographic implications emerge in context of related undertakings, as those in Emerson's *Nature* may be discerned in "The American Scholar," and as those in Edwards's *Images or Shadows* reveal themselves by way of *Thoughts on the Revival* and *The History of the Work of Redemption*. Probably the relevant texts in this particular connection are the passages (in *Bonifacius* and elsewhere) dealing with American Pietism, and the manuscript "Biblia Americana," which Mather advertised in a concluding appendix to *Bonifacius*, and within which he intended to incorporate *The Christian Philosopher*. As the advertisement describes the organization of "Biblia Americana," the sixth and central section deals with "*Natural Philosophy, called in to serve Scriptural Religion*," where "*the best thoughts of our times*" on science combine with those concerning the three "*grand revolutions, the making*, and the *drowning*, and the *burning* of the world." Surrounding this section are a history of Jerusalem (until its "present and wretched condition, in which it waits *the set time to come on*"), the saga of Israel, concluding with its imminent recovery, a discussion of types and prophecies—all of which (except those pertaining to the chiliad) "have had their most punctual *accomplishment*"—and an exhortation on the advantages of "*experimental piety*." The entire configuration explains Mather's emphasis on "Americana"; his last proud words apply with equal force to *Bonifacius* and *The Christian Phi-losopher:* "All done By the blessing of CHRIST on the Labors of an American."

THE VISION OF HISTORY: COTTON MATHER'S *MAGNALIA CHRISTI AMERICANA*

As he made no compromise with Time, Time kept out of his way.
Thoreau, *Walden*

From an American perspective *The Christian Philosopher* is a germinal symbolic work; to what degree Mather may be called a literary artist, in this or any of his major writings, is a matter of emphasis and definition. Certainly, he would consider himself an artist (if at all) only in the strictest didactic terms. Yet his lifelong concern with *belles-lettres* betrays a commitment to the aesthetic that exceeds the usual Puritan clerical confines. His chapter on poetics in *Manuductio,* the first large-scale New World critique of the subject, demonstrates not only a wide knowledge of literature but a salient liberality of taste. Notwithstanding his warnings against the "pagans," he recommends Horace's *Ars Poetica* enthusiastically and quotes everywhere from "the beauties" of Greek and Latin poetry, as well as from contemporaries like Herbert and, the first American to do so, the poet Milton. His own verse rarely rises above the mediocre, but he wrote a great deal of it, from his initial publication (1683) to the hymns he composed to cheer his last days. Indeed, his service to the New England psalmody was a considerable one. In addition to his lost *Songs of the Redeemed,* he adapted hymns from Isaac Watts, wrote a treatise on melodics, commented astutely on the formal defects of the Bay Psalm Book, and, in the preface to his own *Psalterium,* offered a careful exploration of the possibilities of language that pioneered prosodic theory in the colonies.

If these interests do not themselves prove artistic intent, they point to a more persuasive fact: Mather's sophisticated sense of style. His sensitivity to form is manifest in his diverse, adroit use of rhetorical effects in his sermons; critics have only begun to speak appreciatively of his astonishing range of technique, his ear for good phrasing, his conspicuous flare for the dramatic, and his sure sense of rhythm. Most significant in this respect is his choice of the baroque as a vehicle for content and self-expression. While he pays due homage to the plain style, he also praises the "piercing eloquence" of embellished prose: the oratory that captivates with "a *silken line* and a *golden hook*," the writing that dazzles by its "easie fluency bespangled with glittering figures." "Every man will have his own *Style*," he notes, "which will distinguish him as much as his *Gate*," and at its most ambitious, when he wished to reach the widest audience, his prose is distinctively, almost belligerently ornate—the "massy way" which he compares to a marble monument, a "great musical harmony," or a Byzantine "Cloth of Gold" adorned with jewels and "*choice flowers.*"

He did not mean these analogies to suggest a standard for his own work. Overburdened with duties and overzealous to communicate his every thought, he could hardly permit himself to strive for anything like formal perfection. (He regularly apologizes for the haste with which he wrote.) Unduly anxious, furthermore, as an American, to prove himself before his European peers, his allusions, citations, and verbal "ingenuities" sometimes wax rather grossly ostentatious. And self-consciously alienated from his American contemporaries, he tends characteristically toward hyperbole. Yet insofar as his analogies to art bespeak a concern with the interaction of manner and substance, they imply an important aesthetic rationale for his "massy" style. His grandfathers had advocated simplicity of language to combat the "florid and carnal" Anglicans. But their outlook itself was far from simple, and the discrepancy was made painfully evident after the Restoration, when the plain style came under attack from the proponents of a still starker purity: the Moderns who denigrated book-learning, the Hobbesians who scorned elocution, the coffee-house blades who cultivated an urbane, conversational wit, the enthusiasts who spoke directly from the heart, the Deists who demanded a sparse scientific exactness. The Puritan *Weltanschauung* stood antithetically opposed to each of these tendencies of the new era. Eschewing uninformed "prophecying," it placed a virtually scholastic primacy upon erudition. In acknowledgment of human imperfection it encouraged eloquence as a wholesome psychological aid to the reason ("fit bait to catch the will and affections"). Its view of providence invested each human and natural phenomenon with symbolic import. Its system of logic required arguments adduced from every branch of intellectual endeavor. Its mode of scriptural interpretations was founded upon the premise of interlinking congruities in sacred, fabulous, and secular history.

When, therefore, Mather took upon himself the mantle of his forebears he chose in the same instant his style, his subject, and his intellectual gait. His display of learning, culled from his prodigious "Quotidiana" (the notebooks in which he recorded *memorabilia* from his reading), his fondness for puns and anagrams, for esoteric authorities and digressive anecdotes—all his "multiplied references to other and former concerns" are bent toward one end, the affirmation of a world view rooted in the concept of the unity of knowledge. They constitute, that is, variations upon a central *rhetorical*—not pedantic, nor even pedagogic—strategy. As logical argument they are arbitrary (even superfluous), as moral instruction excessive, as history unreliable, or hazy, or blatantly biased. Their value lies in their cumulative imaginative impact. They are meant to convince by indirection and participation: by bringing the reader face to face with the vast tradition that culminated in the New England theocracy, and, through that encounter, by engaging him, symbiotically, in a fluid but coherent universal design. It was a design that incorporated nature, as in *The Christian Philosopher*, and moral eschatology, as in *Bonifacius*. It is most amply embodied in Mather's largest and greatest book, which he labored over from 1693 to 1697 (the pivotal period in his literary development) and published in 1702 under the title of *Magnalia Christi Americana*—"the mighty acts of Christ in America"—*or, The Ecclesiastical History of New England.**

Mather intended the *Magnalia*'s very "massiness" to repudiate the outlook of the age. He expected contempt and he received it. From the start "a supercilious generation" ridiculed the immense work—packed with narratives, sermons, church decrees, and biographies—as "a mighty chaos," flung together huge and undigested and groaning with ostentatious erudition and verbal bombast. For Mather it amounted to nothing less than a confirmation of his role. He anticipated the hostility by introducing himself over and again as the isolated artist. At one point he adopts the *persona* of Orpheus, "whose song might [Christ-like] draw his disciples from perdition"; but mainly he emphasizes the bleakness of his position. Scoffers, he cries, dismay him no more than they did Virgil when he "read his *Bucolicks* reproached and his *Aeneids* travestied." Like the poet Antomachus he continues his declamation though "the assembled auditory all left in the midst of his reading," like the sculptor Policletus he will persevere in the face of calumny: "let the impotent cavils nibble at the *statues* which we have erected; the statues will out-live [them] all."

* Quotations made from this work have been taken from the edition of Thomas Robbins (Hartford, 1853–55), 2 vols.

His "recompense, which will abundantly swallow up all discourage-
ments," lies in the work itself, simultaneously in its manner and
substance, as it did for David, who "built a House of God in his
psalms."

He underscores these comparisons by likening the composition of
the book to the process of artistic creation, in music and portraiture,
sculpture and theater. Especially, he parallels his task with that of
the epic poets: Du Bartas, Tasso, Blackmore, Homer, and, most
extensively, Virgil and Milton. From *Paradise Lost,* where he found
his supreme example of the Puritan literary imagination, Mather
quotes at length, "taking the colours of Milton to describe our story";
and he alludes throughout to *The Aeneid,* in which he saw the pagan
counterpart to his own undertaking. For though he never says so
explicitly, and though of course he was also writing in the tradition of
ecclesiastical history (as well as that of the jeremiad), the *Magnalia*
itself bears out what these numerous references suggest, that its
author *intended* to celebrate a great legend in epic form. Conflating
theology, fact, and metaphor, he draws the lives of Adam and
Aeneas into the "typical pattern" of the American church-state, lifting
his story into a heroic world in which, as Hawthorne pointed out,
"true events and real personages move before the reader with the
dreamy aspect which they wore in Cotton Mather's singular mind."

The epic form was eminently appropriate to his designs. Its vision
grew naturally from the theopathic euphoria of his political sermons
(several of which he incorporates into the work). The *Magnalia,*
says Mather, describing as it does the colonial venture from its pristine
origins to the last conflict with Antichrist, is "an history to anticipate
the state of the New Jerusalem." As such it integrates the rhetoric
of the New England jeremiad with the apocalyptic thrust of Protestant
ecclesiastical history, and so attempts—what *The Aeneid* did for
Rome—to establish an inviolable corporate identity for America. In
more personal terms, the epic form provided Mather with the widest
scope for his role as solitary watchman and as the afflicted well-
doer. He suspected by 1693, and knew by 1697, that the colony had
strayed beyond recall, that "hardly any but my Father, and myself,"
as he complains in his diaries, "appear in Defence of our invaded
Churches." He had also learned from his Salem experience to accept
the burden of the legacy. When, sporadically, he turns in the
Magnalia to the world about him, it is to reject it for the world of
his creation. With the "stones they throw at this book," he declares
with a bitter pride, "I will build my self a monument. Whether New-

England may *live* [in fact] any where else or no, it must *live* [as epic] in our History!"

Accordingly, he starts with an elevated invocation of his muse and theme, emphasizing his chosen literary convention by pointed allusions to *The Aeneid.* Assisted by Christ, not Clio, he sings in "all conscience of Truth" rather than in a *furor poesis,* and glorifies not a fabled hero but a convenanted community directed by Divine Providence to the ends of the earth. His church history, that is, parallels but surpasses Virgil's poem—as the founding of New England antitypes the founding of Rome, as the Puritan emigrants resemble but excel the Trojan exiles (not only as pious men but as sea-farers and conquerors of hostile heathen tribes), and as the millennium toward which the Reformation is moving will immeasurably outshine the Augustan *Pax Romana.* Within this framework, the opening lines combine every aspect of colonial historiography as it had evolved from John Cotton through Increase Mather: the renunciation of Europe, the brilliant achievements that irradiated the heathen darkness, and the wonders yet in store for the American strand. But where his forebears had at least confronted the dichotomy between anticipation and actuality, he transforms both into myth. America, he explains, remained so long under Satan's exclusive dominion so that the Lord might more awesomely reveal His power when, "in the fulness of time," He undertook the renovation of the church. Thus the two most luminous contributions of modern civilization, the printing-press and the Reformation, "dawned upon the miserable world, one just *before,* the other just *after,* the famed navigation hither," a navigation inspired by heaven to herald the transcendent moment, some hundred and thirty years later, in which Christ carried a chosen number of His "faithful servants unto an American desart, on purpose that He might there, *to* them *first,* and *by* them, give a *specimen*" of the thousand-year reign of the saints.

Thus, too, His servants had proceeded to usher in another "*golden Age.*" "There are golden Candlesticks (more than twice times seven!) in the midst of this 'outer darkness,'" Mather exults; "unto the upright children of Abraham [i.e., the elect], here hath arisen *light in darkness.*" The image, which looks back to Eden and forward to the millennium, stands as a comprehensive symbol of his enterprise. He refers to the *aetas aurea* throughout the narrative, from the theocracy's "small beginnings," when "there were [but] *seven* Churches, all of them golden candlesticks," to its most recent triumphs, which announce "a time of wondrous *light.*" The candlestick as *figura* envelops the church-state in a configuration relating the Hebrews, the primitive church, the city on a hill, and the Old-New Jerusalem of the redeemed remnant. And its seven branches, emblem of the *Magnalia's* seven-fold division, outline the seven stages of mankind's development from creation to the Sabbatism ("within the last few sevens of years nearer to accomplishment"), sound the seven trumpet blasts that bring down the walls of Jericho, stronghold of Satan, and foreshadow the seven end-time trumpets that are to ring in the consummation of the New World mission, thus fusing the colony's past and future into an ahistoric aesthetic whole.

Mather's style provides a fitting Cloth of Gold for his epic theme. His pedantry and rhetorical devices (pun and paradox, repetition of key words, the metaphorizing of proper names) function here not only to convey the Puritan outlook, but to adjust the very concept of time to his vision. The plethora of learned citations, for example, in Hebrew, Greek, and Latin, present themselves as choice moments of truth, fragmentary revelations of God's will, reordered in accordance with the nature of the Holy Commonwealth. As they are infused into a given action, they tend to draw it out of its immediate context into a realm of universal relevance which (for the author) mingles the best insight and experience of all peoples. Cumulatively, they provide a kind of Matherian anthology of epiphanies, whose purpose is to erode historic lines while establishing a past for the country, rendering New England at once a timeless ideal and the heir of the ages.

The *Magnalia's* New England, then, transcends all material boundaries, its past shaped by the imagination and its future antedated in prophecy. And more intensely than in most of Mather's works, its presence is charged with apocalyptic energy. If *Wonders of the Invisible World* is Mather's brief epic, the *Magnalia's* action (which subsumes the witchcraft episode within other, larger events) stands equal but opposite to the action of *Paradise Lost;* it precisely inverts Satan's anti-heroic errand. Mather begins the narrative in the old world inferno, seen under the aspect of the Exodus motif. As he describes Europe in the first three books, it is an extension of Egypt, Babylon, and pagan Rome; flying its deprivations, the emigrants, like the Hebrews or early Christians escaping their persecutors, shut behind them the gates of a lost world. The terrors of the Atlantic (another River of Lethe or Old Chaos) reveal their unprecedented courage and faith, while their "divine deliverances" surpass the miracles that carried the Israelites through the Red Sea or Aeneas through the supernatural Mediterranean. And their progress in the New World, finally, as it reverses Satan's conquest of earth (rendering the continent in this sense an ensign for the entire planet), is portrayed through the overriding metaphor of the Garden of God.

Though Mather devotes some space to the Puritans' early hardships, primarily he stresses how quickly they converted the barren strand into a greater Canaan. The triumph of Milton's Satan all at once lays waste the world; the New Englanders complete the first stage of their calling when the wilderness, as in dream or legend, springs suddenly into full bloom. Mather presents the metamorphosis through variations on the image of the plantation as the Tree of God; he amplifies the rich Edenic echoes of the image in his "History of Harvard College" (book IV). Established by the emigrants and continued by their sons, the college becomes a "fit emblem" of both fructification and fruition. The *Magnalia* personifies the harmony between generations through the lives of ten Harvard graduates (the number of perfection), all "cedars" of filiopietism, who "had their whole growth in the soyle of New England." So "the *root* gives verdure to the *branches* and the flourishing *branches* again commend the root," in an organic process which proves that the theocracy supersedes the holy communities of the past. "Where God had before planted his church," the harvest had withered and lay desolate upon the hard ground, "overgrown with thorns and nettles." But in New England "the proverb 'that vinegar is the son of wine' and 'that the son of heroes are trespassers' has been contradicted"; here only has the paternal "vine that took deep root and filled the land" borne abounding filial "clusters of *rich grapes*." Having set before us the founding of the colony (book I), the magistrates' achievements (book II), and the superior attainments of the divines (book III), Mather now displays the lines of continuity in the theocracy—the perpetuation of the New England paradise—in assurance of the paradise to come.

He affirms this development most graphically by his biographical method. Its abundance of biographies places the *Magnalia* in the mainstream of Protestant ecclesiastical history through Foxe's *Book of Martyrs;* it diverges in its conscious, aesthetic interweaving of hagiography and historiography. Obviously drawing upon the parallel between these genres and the two facets of his self-concept in the diaries, Mather discovered in metaphor a cogent and inclusive method of integration. To some degree the exodus and garden motifs (from the Church Fathers onward intrinsic to the vocabulary of spiritual pilgrimage) entered inevitably into his saints' lives. Mather's impressive contribution was to make the pilgrimage a persistent reflection of

New England at large, and vice versa: to gather both into the same literary ambiance, so that one supported, and was realized through the other, the epic of the soul lending credence to the social epic and the latter substantiating the works of the day by which justification was made manifest.

This union of the personal and the communal expresses various tenets, already discussed, of American Puritan thought, and, for quite different reasons, of Mather's in particular. The *Magnalia* builds upon both of these elements. On the strength of colonial eschatology, it fuses the morphology of conversion (in the biographies) and the flourishing of the theocracy (in the narrative) into alternate perspectives on the work of redemption. Because of its author's predisposition toward the imaginative, it seizes on the unique implications of that approach. For European writers from Augustine to Bunyan, *exodus* and *garden* signified states of mind. In the *civitas terrena,* that is, sacred history became meaningful by becoming biography: the pilgrim's progress in time was allegorical and universal, his historical encounters *visibilia* denoting hope, conflict, and salvation. For the American Puritans the highpoints of the pilgrimage—flight from corruption, sea-crossing, "wilderness-condition," conquest of Canaan— were all too real. And yet, *for them* if not for others it reverberated at all times with mystical import. Their corporate growth, in short, was symbolic. The more closely they examined the actual, the more clearly they perceived the Grand Design, which, they kept telling a deaf or incredulous world, rendered New England's progress the historical analogue to the private, interior movement of grace.

To be sure, they tried hard to equalize the value of allegory and symbol. They sought support in this from the inherently ambiguous vocabulary of grace, whereby Christ antitypes the elect individually and collectively, and from their dual allegiance to congregationalism and to the concept of national election. Were they not, they argued, as visible saints one man in the body of Christ? And did not sacred history (in conjunction with Revelation and the prophecies) adumbrate the whole story of mankind, thus applying as surely to their terrestrial calling as it did to the *itinerarum mentis?* Nonetheless, so long as they wrestled with the untoward facts of backsliding, hypocrisy, and schism, they could never quite discard the possibility of error. Beneath the aggressive optimism of their rhetoric, the emigrant ministers convey an unmistakable disquietude. As in the course of the century dream and reality veered farther apart, the orthodoxy came more and more to rely on rhetoric; but even the second generation acknowledged (however obliquely) that the affinity between the allegory of saint's life and the story of the New Canaan, as this manifested itself in their common reference to the biblical Israel, might be provisional, perhaps misleading: that, after all, one mode represented an objective, absolute truth while the other depended on will and interpretation. For Cotton Mather, the correspondence in imagery was sufficient unto itself. In the epic world where his New England "lived" he was free to collapse allegory and symbol, tradition and invention, dream and reality into metaphors that with equal authority defined saint and society.

He had laid the foundations for this strategy not only in the diaries but in such sermons as *A Midnight Cry*, with its shifting personal/ social perspectives. He was to magnify it, interestingly but unsuccessfully, in *The Christian Philosopher*. In its limited application in the *Magnalia* it gave him an important means of control over his material. Perhaps the most striking of its effects appears in his reversals of context. Not infrequently, the biographies stress public issues, whereas the narrative builds on images of the journey of the soul. For example, Mather minimizes the conversion experience (traditionally a central focus of hagiography) and places the emphasis instead on the saint's conversion to Puritanism, his subsequent persecution, and his decision to migrate; predictably enough, the corporate emphasis becomes still more pronounced in the saint's American career. Conversely, but with similar intent, Mather often represents the theocracy as the archetypal Christian. Thus he permeates his descriptions of the Atlantic crossing with allusions to baptism which lend an allegorical dimension to the contrast between the New World and the Old. So, too, his narrative of the settlers' privations, probations, and perseverance render them as a pilgrim entering upon the *vita nuova*, venturing "into the wilderness to a sacrifice unto the Lord," finding life "well stocked everywhere with the thorns of vexations," and radiating in all his/their trials the image of Christ.

Mather uses this technique effectively elsewhere; it is especially appropriate, I think, to the *Magnalia*. The Christ-figure in *Wonders* transparently reveals the author's attempt to impose himself upon the events (or rather, to absorb and remold them within his psyche). He makes the same attempt here, of course, and on a far more comprehensive scale. But he also objectifies his self-projection by portraits of "exemplary actors," all attesting to the author's dynastic rights (either indirectly, as loyal theocrats, or directly, as his regal Cotton and Mather forebears), most of them in varying degrees reflections of John the Baptist and the suffering servant, and each of them compared, further, to hosts of modern, classical, and scriptural

figures. These "biographical parallels," set at the start and end of the
Life—generally an emphatically "American" Life—invest the subject
with a magnitude and diversity which, as in the diaries, seem to spring
from the subject himself, and by implication from his "American-
ness." In sum, they reveal him a representative man: representative of
the pagan virtues (though superior to them), representative of the
godliness of the Old Testament Israelites (but building upon their
precedent), representative, above all, of a culture that rises above
temporal limitations as the crown and essence of human history. On
all these levels, he comes to embody, and hence to justify, New England's "special appointment." John Mitchel, writes Mather, "was a
circle, whereof the circumference took in all New-England"; and
again; "I shall now invite my readers to behold *the wonders of New
England,* in one *Thomas Hooker*"; and once more: "the New-English
principles and practices are found in the character of our celebrated
Eliot." This approach to biography, which extols the individual not as
an exceptional being, not even as an individual, but *as the community,*
as a circle encompassing the country's wonders, principles, and practices, would seem to preview Emerson's notion of representative men
and Whitman's personalism. In any case, it allows Mather to redeploy
hagiography, martyrology, and ecclesiastical history for his own epic
purposes.

In narrower structural terms, it allows him to establish the proper
tone of jubilation for the fifth book, "The Acts and Monuments" of
New England, in which he virtually abrogates the course of history.
To that end, he organizes the documents thematically rather than
chronologically. He opens in 1680 with the "Confession of Faith," the
orthodoxy's lament for a wayward people, which he interprets as a
general thanksgiving for half a century of *"rest* and *growth."* He then
turns to the Cambridge Platform (1648), the defunct *magna charta*
of the theocracy, explaining that "the churches have cheerfully embraced it, practised it, and been prospered in it, unto this very day";
and upon the basis of this "vigorous unanimity" he proceeds to the
church decrees of the second generation. The Half-Way Covenant
(1660), which scholars have designated as the *locus classicus* of
colonial decline, bears out for him the "expectations of our *seers,"*
consecrating the divine bond between father and son. There then
follows a festive parade of synods that with undeviating faithful-
ness to first principles guides the plantation to "an exactest unity" in
which all controversy is resolved "unto the general joy." The New
World garden, displayed hitherto in its physical lushness and godly
inhabitants, appears now in its brightest spiritual splendor—the whole

of time encompassed within its mythical-green glow—against the background of an ecclesiastical harmony that Mather likens to the music of the spheres.

Though the theocracy thus flowers physically and spiritually, it never quite becomes (what Mather sometimes calls it) a sanctuary. To the end the natural perils of the new world mar its prosperity, and neither its guard of angels nor its wall of fire can keep it safe from heretics, Indians, and witches. Milton's epic concludes with paradise lost; Christ's mighty acts in America form the road to the New Jerusalem. The theocracy, like the saint, advances by overcoming a series of obstacles that grow progressively more formidable, more cataclysmic. Our topmost glory, Mather reiterates over and again, lies in our direst test, one in which the legions of hell will gather from every corner of the universe for "a furious but a fruitless attempt" upon the children of light. He orders the *Magnalia's* last actions accordingly. It begins (book VI) with minor skirmishes— vignettes of suffering and regeneration at sea, on the settlements, in the relations between father and son—so structured as to recapitulate the colony's progress. How far the latter had gone toward ending the Devil's long reign Mather dramatizes in thirteen scenes of witchcraft, unified implicitly by analogy to Christ's exorcizing of the demons (apocalyptically interpreted) and explicitly by typological association with Christ's wilderness temptation. He expands upon this "most particular prefiguration for us" in the *"Ecclesiarum Praelia"* against the heretics, proceeding with a swelling note of victory from Roger Williams through the more dangerous Antinomians to the Quakers, who constitute all "the *vomit* cast out in the by-past ages" now "lick'd up again for a *new digestion.*" Their banishment, therefore, together with the expulsion of the witches, shows the "heirs of salvation" literally "treading Satan underfoot." Moreover, it exhibits the unabated doctrinal solidarity, civil power, and clerical wisdom which girds the theocracy for its most arduous and most splendid trial, the Indian wars.

For several reasons, these battles provide the right conclusion to Mather's epic. First, they serve to round out his parallel with *The Aeneid* (as he emphasizes by entitling the section "ARMA VIROSQUE CANO"). Secondly, they had not yet reached a decisive end, as had the heresies and witchcraft, and so imply the settlers' continuing ascendancy over the forces of evil. Thirdly, because the Indians, again unlike the heretics and witches, were indigenous to America, their destruction could better symbolize the near completion of the Puritan mission. Most important, the Indian conflicts afforded a fitting finale to the *Magnalia's* dominant exodus-garden motif. As "Wars of the Lord" against primitive tribes, they enforce the resemblance between Christ's American army and the wandering Hebrews. And as prelude to total victory, they reveal the crucial distance between New England's destination and the Good Land won by the "erratick church of Israel." Elsewhere Mather had urged, and had himself participated in, the "civilizing and Christianizing of the savages." Here, following the logic of his vision, he identifies them with the Canaanite peoples conquered by Joshua (not only as parallel but as genealogical fact). And he goes further than this: Joshua, he explains, is Jesus; the Indian king is the Old Serpent; and the theocracy is Christ's *true* Church. In short, the struggle to dispossess America's native inhabitants is the struggle not simply for territory (as in *The Aeneid* or the Pentateuch) but for a renovated earth. Having secured its temporal Canaan, the New Israel, as Mather unveils its full meaning in this seventh book of the *Magnalia,* stands at the van of mankind, engaged in a fatal enterprise against all the devils and the damned.

In terms of metaphor, the enterprise allows Mather to fuse the temporally distinct (because sequential) concepts of exodus and garden into an aesthetic absolute which in his epic *is* New England. In terms of Puritan historiography the enterprise terminates the *magnalia* God had worked in America even before the *Arbella* arrived, when He decimated the Indians by pestilence to prepare the land for His particular people. In the view of redemptive history, as Mather intimates by citing *Paradise Lost,* it brings to the verge of completion the cosmic combat initiated by the war in Heaven. As it was to be seen in a later, secular American perspective, the enterprise prepared for the westward movement, which (said Representative Robert Winthrop of Massachusetts in 1846) made manifest the destiny of "the universal Yankee nation." Mather sketches the outcome for us in phrases that apply no less to Robert Winthrop's outlook than they do to John Winthrop's. He had begun his general introduction with the Ark of God en route to the New World, changing geography into *"Christiano-graphy";* throughout the narrative he had hinted at the proximity of the millennium. Now, as his epic draws to a close, he sets the church-state directly within the halo of "THINGS TO COME." Quoting from his own and others' sermons, he announces "a REVOLUTION AND A REFORMATION at the very door, which will be more wonderful than any yet seen from the beginning of the world"—and, he adds, my *"fancies* and *juggles* have their foundations laid in *realities."* He means, of course, to refer us to the verities of scripture and history: the juggles of Revelation, the prophetic fancies still to materialize, the types which saw a partial realization in the Great Migration and its consequences. What his achievement reveals is the self-contained coherence of his vision. Built as a monument *against* realities, founded upon myth and fortified by hermeneutics-become-symbolism, the *Magnalia* survives as a testament to its author's ability to incorporate New England, the world, and time itself within the image-making imagination.

As such it remains, for all its many flaws, an essential part of American letters. As epic, it differs from *The Aeneid* and *Paradise Lost* in a way which may be said to begin a distinctive national mode, through *Leaves of Grass* into our own time. Latium and Eden come to us from an irrevocable past; Mather's New England, like Whitman's "fervid and tremendous IDEA" of the United States, is a golden age which remains perpetually "near, even at the door," requiring one last great act in order to realize itself. It is (to quote Whitman again) "a passageway to something, rather than a thing concluded," its hodge-podge of allusions trying to establish an American past commensurate with America's "infinite" (and indefinite) future, its disparate metaphors of Garden and Exodus dialectically entwined in the country's perennial quest for fulfillment, and its apparent structural chaos controlled by a dream which looks always beyond the present. As historiography, the *Magnalia*'s definition of the dream (capping a half-century of similar formulations) may be traced in all its basic elements, such as the contrast between old Babylon and New Israel, or the divine rationale for the continent's "discovery," in the exuberant national eschatology that runs from the Revolution through the Civil War. Finally, Mather's rhetorical strategies, bespeaking as they do a fundamental cultural polarity between prophet and people, presage those of a long line of American Jeremiahs; while in their aesthetic implications, as a symbolic method which fuses objective and subjective, plural and singular, internalizing history as a defense against time, they may be seen to have found their highest creative expression in the American Renaissance.

This is not to say that Cotton Mather's significance consists in his adumbration of later writers. It consists in his resolution of a profoundly cultural dilemma in a way that was dictated by his cultural allegiances and by the dilemma itself. As it turned out, this was also the way Puritanism came most fully to be absorbed in the national consciousness: as image and metaphor, as mythico-historiography, and, paradigmatically, as the dream of an ideal personal-corporate identity which perpetuates itself—in different forms corresponding to the vocabularies of different cultural moments—as an apocalyptic wakefulness destined to overcome the sleep of time, a temporal exodus designed to obliterate temporally rooted anxieties in the end-time Garden of God as this was embodied simultaneously in the ever-new nation and its representative men. In this ironic-prophetic sense, Mather's resolution stands in all its symbolic richness and historical vacuity as the literary *summa* of the New England Way. When, shortly after his death, his son Samuel (following family tradition) wrote his father's biography, he recalled that "while Cotton was yet young, he bid fair to *be great*, for he *believed* he should be so; he *expected* it; and therefore he *bore and did many things*." In this conviction at least Mather was not altogether deceived. Out of his failure and his faith he wrought a number of works which have prospered, in the realm of the American imagination, better than he expected or believed.

BIBLIOGRAPHY

Some Modern Editions

Bonifacius: An Essay upon the Good. Edited by David Levin. Cambridge, Mass.: Harvard University Press, 1966. [Important introductory essay by the editor.]

The Diary of Cotton Mather. Edited by Worthington C. Ford. Massachusetts Historical Society *Collections*, 7th series, vols. 7–8. Boston, 1911–12. Reprinted, New York: Frederick Ungar, 1957.

The Diary of Cotton Mather, D.D., F.R.S., for the Year 1712. Edited by William R. Manierre II. Charlottesville, Va.: University Press of Virginia, 1964.

Selected Letters of Cotton Mather. Edited by Kenneth Silverman. Baton Rouge, La.: Louisiana State University Press, 1971. [Includes a valuable commentary by the editor.]

Selections from Cotton Mather. Edited by Kenneth B. Murdock. New York: Harcourt, 1926. 3d ed., New York: Hafner, 1965. [The editor's introduction provides a wide-ranging biographical and literary evaluation.]

Scholarship and Criticism

Beall, Otho T., Jr., and Richard H. Shyrock. *Cotton Mather: First Significant Figure in American Medicine*. Baltimore: Johns Hopkins Press, 1954.

Benz, Ernst. "Ecumenical Relations Between Boston Puritanism and German Pietism: Cotton Mather and August Hermann Francke." *Harvard Theological Review* 54 (1961): 159–93.

Brumm, Ursula. *American Thought and Religious Typology.* Translated by John Hoaglund. New Brunswick, N.J.: Rutgers University Press, 1970.

Hansen, Chadwick. *Witchcraft at Salem.* New York: Braziller, 1969.

Holmes, Thomas James. *Cotton Mather: A Bibliography of His Works.* 3 vols. Cambridge, Mass.: Harvard University Press, 1940. [Includes brief essays by several prominent scholars, among them Theodore Hornberger on *The Christian Philosopher,* Perry Miller on the *Manuductio,* and Kenneth B. Murdock on the *Magnalia.*]

Levin, David. "The Hazing of Cotton Mather: The Creation of a Biographical Personality." *New England Quarterly* 34 (1963): 147–71.

Lowance, Mason I., Jr. "Typology and the New England Way: Cotton Mather's Exegesis." *Early American Literature* 4, no. 1 (1969): 15–37.

Manierre, William R., II. "Cotton Mather and the Biographical Parallel." *American Quarterly* 13 (1961): 153–60.

Middlekauf, Robert. *The Mathers: Three Generations of Puritan Intellectuals, 1596–1728.* New York: Oxford University Press, 1971.

Warren, Austin. "Grandfather Mather and His Wonder Book." *Sewanee Review* 72 (1964): 96–116. Reprinted in considerably revised form, as "Dr. Cotton Mather's *Magnalia,*" in Warren, *Connections,* Ann Arbor, Mich.: University of Michigan Press, 1970.

Wendell, Barrett. *Cotton Mather: The Puritan Priest.* New York: Dodd, Mead, 1891. Reprinted, New York: Harcourt, 1963, with an introduction by Alan Heimert.

Woody, Kennerly M. "Cotton Mather's *Manuductio ad Theologiam:* The 'More Quiet and Hopeful Way.'" *Early American Literature* 4, no. 2 (1969): 3–48. Supplemented by a separate issue (also published by *Early American Literature*) of very extensive "Bibliographical Notes to Cotton Mather's *Manuductio ad Ministerium*" 6, no. 1 (1971): 1–98.

5

William Byrd
Taste and Tolerance

RICHARD BEALE DAVIS

The best known of southern colonial writers, William Byrd II (1674–
1744), stands at the beginning of an intellectual as well as social
golden age in the Chesapeake Bay country. Too often considered
atypical of both society and literature in his time and region, he is
more nearly archetypal. His earliest writing is close to the fashionable effusions of the English Restoration era in which he was born
and educated, and his last bears clear resemblance in form and
style to the literary composition popular in the reigns of Queen
Anne and the first Georges. Yet his recorded interest in poor white
and slave and red Indian, in colonial society and government, in
New World fauna and flora, in the economics of the agrarian way
of life (including tobacco and investment in frontier lands), and
in his country's future mark him as genuinely American. Indeed, his
interests and his approach to them are perhaps closer in character to
those of the majority of writers in the new United States at the end
of the eighteenth century than are those of any other colonial writer
save Benjamin Franklin.

Though a native Virginian, Byrd received all his education between
the ages of seven and twenty-one in Europe, most of it in England.
Sent by his father, the public official and Indian trader William Byrd

Richard Beale Davis is Alumni Distinguished Service Professor of American
Literature at the University of Tennessee. The author of *George Sandys, Poet-
Adventurer* (1955), *Intellectual Life in Jefferson's Virginia* (1964), and editor or
author of sixteen other books, he has held Huntington Library, Folger Library,
Fulbright, and two Guggenheim fellowships. In 1955 Randolph-Macon College
awarded him the degree of Litt. D. He reviews regularly for the Phi Beta Kappa
Key Reporter and is undertaking an intellectual history of the colonial South.

I, to live with or near relatives in rural England, William II attended an excellent classical private school and then studied business for a time in the Netherlands with some of his father's associates and in the counting house of the great London firm of Perry and Lane. In the 1690s he came under the protection of the statesman and scientist Sir Robert Southwell. In 1692 he entered the Middle Temple and three years later was formally admitted to the bar. In the Temple he formed lifelong friendships with noblemen, playwrights, and a future chief justice of Massachusetts, among others. In 1696, probably through retiring president Sir Robert Southwell's nomination, he was elected to membership in The Royal Society and within a year had a short essay, "An Account of a Negro-Boy that is dappel'd in several Places of his Body with White Spots," published in its *Philosophical Transactions.* Also in 1696 he was called home to Virginia for a short period, notable only for the fact that he served a term in the House of Burgesses. In 1697 he was back in London on business both public and private. Among his political duties was service as attorney for Governor Andros in a hearing before the Archbishop of Canterbury and the Bishop of London to answer Virginia Commissary James Blair's complaints that Andros was blocking the clergyman's ecclesiastical and educational program. Byrd remained in London until 1705, when he was called home at his father's death. In 1706 he married Lucy Parke, the handsome daughter of the profligate and dashing Colonel Daniel Parke.

Byrd settled for a time into the life of a Tidewater planter, improving his house and garden at Westover on the James, corresponding with friends in England, and, as a member of the Governor's Council (in addition to lesser offices), playing a part in colonial government he was not to relinquish until his death. His earliest extant diary gives the details of family, business, and official life. He was already gathering and arranging the library which was to be, with Cotton Mather's and James Logan's, the greatest in the colonies in quality and quantity. In 1714 or 1715 he returned to England for the second of his three missions as agent for the colony. His wife died there of smallpox, but his two elder daughters acquired a taste for fashionable entertainment they carried back with them to the colony.

Much of Byrd's time was for several years spent in a search for a suitable second wife, preferably an heiress. Many gallant—and despairing—letters and a second portion of the diary reveal much of these years. They record his daily life in the city of Addison and Steele and Congreve, including his amours with women of high and low degree. In 1718 he had an audience with George I, representing the Virginia Council in a feud with Governor Spotswood regarding provincial courts. Frequently he was writing, probably on the history of Virginia (of which he left copies with two noble friends) and the verses published under the pseudonym "Mr. Burrard." By February 13, 1720, he was back in Virginia.

In 1721 he undertook his third mission as Virginia agent in England and married Maria Taylor, who brought him only the rather weak prospect of a fortune he never obtained. In 1726 he was back in America for good. He always planned to revisit the mother country; but financial concerns, a growing family, and finally age prevented him. From a literary point of view the last eighteen years of his life were the most interesting and the most fruitful. In 1728 he was the senior Virginia commissioner appointed to settle the dividing line between Virginia and North Carolina. From the notes and official reports of the sea-to-mountains expedition he was in later years to shape his finest prose. In 1732 he visited various mines and in 1733 surveyed, figuratively and literally, his recently acquired acres in Governor Eden's North Carolina. Again from notes and reports he was to write two travel-observation accounts of significance. In 1735–36 Byrd once more acted as king's commissioner, this time to determine the true bounds of the Northern Neck, Lord Fairfax's proprietary. His records of this expedition, except for a letter or two, have disappeared.

Obtaining settlers for his vast frontier lands was the great business problem of the last fifteen years of his life. The story of his attempts lies principally in letters and in a promotional tract, a polyglot assemblage of data from many sources, published in German and signed Wilhelm Vogel. With his old friend, the surveyor William Mayo, he laid out on his own land the future Richmond and Petersburg, building in typical American fashion cities, instead of castles, in the air. About a year before his death he succeeded his venerable friend and former enemy Commissary Blair as president of the Council, the most eminent political office a native Virginian was to achieve in that province during the colonial period.

Such in barest outline (some of it will be filled out as his writings are discussed) was the social, political, and intellectual career of a southern colonial most literary historians have insisted was a biological "sport," a freak, the great exception among his contemporaries in the Chesapeake Bay region in the eighteenth century. This he distinctly was not. There were dozens of Virginians and Marylanders who had received their education in Great Britain or on the Continent. In his own time his brothers-in-law John Custis and Robert Beverley II were, with several members of the Maryland Carroll and Dulany families, among them. One and two generations later William Stith, Robert Munford, Robert Bolling, Jr., the Lee brothers, a number of Wormeleys, Carters, and Ogles, with many others, attended English classical schools, Oxford or Cambridge, Edinburgh, and the London Inns of Court. Some, like Sir John Randolph and his sons Peyton and John, visited England in public and private capacities more than once.

The Wormeleys, several Carters, the Dulanys, the Randolphs, the Blands, and a dozen others had impressive libraries, several of them apparently rivalling Byrd's, and in two more generations there were greater libraries than his. Virginians Richard Bland, Landon Carter, and John Mercer are among those who seem to have written all their lives. In Maryland Dr. Alexander Hamilton, printer Jonas Green, and other rural and urban members of the Annapolis Tuesday Club apparently drove the quill steadily throughout their allotted years. Except for the clergy among them, most published even less than Byrd. Fortunately some of their manuscripts survive. When they are published they will show not only these authors, but Byrd, in new perspective. Some parallel him in style, some in satiric intent, several in catholicity of interests, several in their representations of the needs and rights of the colonies before kings, bishops, or committees on trade and the plantations. The same men could be as gallant in their prose or metrical addresses to ladies as could the master of Westover. In other words, William Byrd II as writer is but the tallest tree in a forest of considerable size and modest variety.

MISCELLANEOUS MINOR WRITINGS

As writer and man William Byrd has been labelled belated Restoration cavalier and satirist, Queen Anne wit, pamphleteer, promoter, American Pepys, virtuoso, travel writer, and historian. He is most of these things in some degree, and more. His varied interests, occupations, and recreations are represented in brief pieces he probably considered trifles or professional exercises of no literary significance.

But even without his letters, diaries, and the well-known histories, his surviving compositions would entitle him to at least a minor place as a man of letters.*

Too often Byrd's legal training and the literary uses he made of it are overlooked. During his three tours of duty in London as agent for Virginia he prepared arguments, petitions, and addresses which show him to have been an unusually able legal writer. In defending Governor Andros before the mature ecclesiastics at Lambeth in 1697 the twenty-three-year-old barrister acquitted himself well. His extempore remarks are preserved with the rest of the hearing in nineteenth-century print. But the formal defense of Andros he had written out and never had an opportunity to deliver is excellent legal prose in both style and reasoning. The next year, as agent for Virginia, Byrd submitted to the lords of trade and plantations "Proposals . . . for sending the French Protestants to Virginia," a kind of petition in legal form on a subject which was to interest him all his life, the settlement of Continental Europeans in the great open spaces of his own colony. A year later he made a "Representation concerning Proprietary Governments," arguing the abuses of fair trade and settlement under the proprietary colonial governments, including the harboring of pirates, and urging that the control of these governments be vested in the king as quickly as possible. Perhaps his most eloquent and effectively argued as well as politically significant legal piece is the brief address he delivered before the lords of trade in 1718 on the subject of oyer and terminer courts.

There are other politico-legal papers mentioned in the diaries which do not appear to have survived. And he certainly had a hand in several official addresses to and arguments before the governor and council during his long tenure in public office. Closely related are the quasilegal arguments in certain letters to Governor Gooch, and in the official reports of the 1728 and 1735–36 boundary commissioners, documents which demonstrate the author's legal background and experience in public service.

Intensely conscious of his Virginia origin, especially when he was in London, William Byrd tried his hand several times at writing a history of his native province. Some time before 1708, perhaps several

---

* Much of what I have quoted from Byrd's works is still in manuscript form or is taken from excerpted passages in various journals. See the bibliography for a listing of the more important printed sources used in the preparation of this essay. A fuller bibliography may be found in my *American Literature Through Bryant, 1585–1830* (New York: Appleton-Century-Crofts, 1969), pp. 24–25.

years before, Byrd had written a sketch of Virginia which was used by John Oldmixon in the 1708 and 1741 editions of *The British Empire in America*. In the second edition Oldmixon acknowledged that he was indebted to Byrd for much of his material in the Virginia chapter. One should recall that Robert Beverley's excuse for writing his own *History and Present State of Virginia*, first published in 1705, was that he had seen Oldmixon's manuscript and was so indignant at the errors regarding Virginia contained therein that he felt compelled to set matters straight. Since there was a considerable interval between Beverley's sight of the manuscript and its first publication, it may be that Oldmixon, having seen Beverley's book, asked the latter's brother-in-law for assistance in improving his work. Or it may be, though unlikely on several counts, that Beverley believed Byrd to be the promulgator and perpetuator of error.

That Byrd was still working on, or had completed some sort of draft of a history of the Old Dominion, is borne out by his diary entry of November 20, 1719, when he mentions that he left copies of his "description of Virginia" for Lord Islay and his brother the Duke of Argyle. Then there is the delightfully sardonic outline of Virginia history that forms the introduction to "The History of the Dividing Line" and does not appear in "The Secret History." As Louis B. Wright has pointed out in his introduction to *The Prose Works*, the promotion-tract published in 1737 as *Neu-gefundenes Eden*, the compilation already noted as signed Wilhelm Vogel, may have been much the same as Oldmixon's source or the Islay-Argyle "description," though it seems unlikely. What evidence there is seems to point to the probability that from the beginning of the century to 1740, about the date of completion of "The History of the Dividing Line," Byrd worked at least intermittently on a fairly ambitious history of Virginia. It would be interesting to compare what he did compose with Beverley's *History and Present State of Virginia*.

As Royal Society virtuoso or eighteenth-century son of the Enlightenment, Byrd had to be interested in science. His observations botanical, zoological, ethnological, geological, meteorological, pharmaceutical, and otherwise are scattered through dozens of letters, the two Dividing Line histories, the *Neu-gefundenes Eden* (though most of these are second-hand), and the diaries. But there were at least two scientific pieces published in his lifetime. One is the Royal Society published essay (in 1696) noted above. *A Discourse Concerning the Plague, with some Preservatives Against it, By a Lover of Mankind* (1721), recently identified through the diary and internal evidence as Byrd's, is more significant. This is ostensibly a learned treatise, loaded with allusions to ancient and modern medical practices, and proposing that the government take specific precautions to prevent the spread of the plague. The principal antidote proposed is tobacco. Since it has already been chewed, smoked, or snuffed in every rank of society since 1665, the author writes, England is free of the plague. To insure further this immunity, tobacco should be worn on the person, hung in coaches and apartments, burned in dining rooms, and chewed daily. Though the *Discourse* has been taken seriously as a medicinal-cum-tobacco-promotion tract, the mock-serious, sly, deadpan, satiric irony of Swift's *A Modest Proposal* or some of Franklin's essays seems also to be here. It is difficult to believe that Byrd's contemporary reader could take the author seriously, but then Swift and Franklin were so taken by many.

The recently discovered commonplace book now in the Virginia Historical Society, clearly one of a number he kept alongside the diaries, covers some of the years between 1722 and 1733. It contains a little of anything that interested its compiler, from love letters to "Charmante" to a random assortment of ribald anecdotes, epigrams, verse, and puns. There are even "Some Rules for preserving health" faintly suggestive of Franklin's rules in his *Autobiography*.

A Description of the Dismal Swamp and a Proposal to Drain the Swamp (printed in 1841 and 1922), both a promotion piece and an engineering proposal, was probably drawn from the same notes as the descriptions in the Dividing Line histories and resembled them in style. Outlined is a joint stock company and the necessary steps to be taken in setting up the procedures for the draining operation.

Capable of reading more than a half-dozen languages ancient and modern, Byrd wrote at least one letter in Greek and used Hebrew and Latin phrases whenever he felt them appropriate. His daily reading in foreign languages resulted in a number of translations, several mentioned in his diaries and a few actually preserved among his manuscripts. His version of "The Ephesian Matron" of Petronius is among his best.

Perhaps as early as his days at the Inns of Court, Byrd drew character sketches of his friends, his enemies, and himself. He was following a seventeenth-century tradition as well as a form popular among the Queen Anne essayists. Many of the earlier English caricaturists were represented in his library, and, perhaps as significantly, Theophrastus, La Bruyère, and his own contemporaries Addison and Steele. The latter two's Sempronia, Clorinda, Amaryllis, Sabina, Cleora, and Monimia are also among the tag names Byrd assigned the ladies in his sketches or to whom he addressed certain letters. There is good evidence that the tags used by Byrd were in every case mere appropriate disguises for the names of real people.

His "characters" are panegyrics or sharp caricatures, though sometimes, as in "Dr. Glysterio" (Dr. Samuel Garth, poet-physician), he strikes a balance. "Cavaliero Sapiente" is an affectionate but accurate portrait of the amiable and able Sir Robert Southwell, but "Duke Dulchetti," his friend the Duke of Argyle, is probably overly favorable. The majority of his analyses are, however, satirical, a quality natural to both the man and his time. Byrd does not indulge in cruel invective. Normally he employs irony with an edge, expressed in those beautifully balanced antitheses he was to employ even more effectively in his later writings.

By far the most interesting to the modern reader is his relatively long self-analysis "Inamorato L'Oiseaux," the essential truthfulness of which is attested in diaries and letters. He begins by lamenting his lifelong amorousness, or sexuality, which has been an embarrassment and—cryptically—the hindrance to his achievement of "Eminence in the World." His surface look of pride he recognizes and passes off with the comment "Hardly any body liked him that did not know him, and nobody hated him that did." He parades his good qualities, such as sincerity, frugality, abstinence in food and drink, his perfectionism, his love of retirement, and his conviction that a taste for the company of the ladies is necessary to prevent a scholar being a mere pedant or a philosopher a cynic. He notes his sympathy for "all brute creatures" who are without protection in a hostile universe. He sums up thus:

> His memory is in nothing so punctual as in performing of Promises.
> He thinks himself as firmly bound by his Word as by his hand &
> seal . . . . He knows the World perfectly well, and thinks himself
> a citizen of it without the [. . .] distinctions of kindred sect or
> Country. He has learning without Ostentation. By Reading he's
> acquainted with ages past, and with the present by voyaging and
> conversation . . . .*

Though these words taken out of context may seem to make Byrd pompous, in context they point up the whimsical irony of his attitude. All together he shows a sophisticated introspection as indicative of his meditative cerebration as any of the self-probings of the theologically centered saints of New England. Nowhere else in his writing does this

---

* *Another Secret Diary,* ed. Woodfin and Tinling, p. 280.

gentleman planter come nearer to lowering his guard, though in many places one learns more of his external self.

Most of these "characters" seem to be more British than American in subject and certainly in form, though in one of them Byrd refers to his "Indian" way of expressing himself. But they were useful preliminary exercises for the remarkably perceptive, ironic, mildly satiric portraits he was to draw in the prose of his great period, the American.

His sincere religious belief, neither Presbyterian-Puritan nor deistic, is spelled out in the "creed" written on the first leaf of the 1709–12 diary. His was the moderate or middle way of his time, a fairly normal Anglican Trinitarianism with a rational tinge. The patriotism suggested in his legal pieces and "The History" is nowhere more evident than in the epitaph he was asked to compose for the tombstone of the popular governor Nott, Spotswood's predecessor, who died after only a few months in office. The final lines, unrecorded on the stone which bears the rest, probably because of their reflection on Spotswood, are at once eloquent and patriotic: "Whoever thou art that readest the sad tydings of his death, if a Stranger, pity the Country: if a Virginian, thy self."

In none other of his minor writings is Byrd more in the spirit of Queen Anne's London than in the few and scattered verses we can assign to his pen. One should recall that his diaries assure us he wrote more, such as lampoons upon the House of Burgesses or Williamsburg gentlemen, or amusing pieces he read to a circle of ladies not too delicate to enjoy the sexual innuendos. Over a span of twenty years, from 1700 to 1719, he composed light vers de societé on the ladies who thronged to such watering places as Bath and Tunbridge Wells. The surviving lines are gallant or mocking and quite conventional.

Of better quality is the elegiac poem on the deceased "Malantha," or the elegiac acrostic (probably his) on his daughter Evelyn printed in the *Virginia Gazette*. The five- and eight-line pieces imbedded in letters to "Facetia" are worth studying to determine their intention. But there can be no doubt about the bawdy intent of "Upon a Fart," a burlesque of Anne, Countess of Winchelsea's, "Upon a Sigh," both included in Byrd's letter to "Bellamira."

Perhaps in imagery and meter the best of Byrd's known verse is his short eleven-line epigram upon his old enemy, former Governor Spotswood, later his friend, which is included in "The History of the Dividing Line" and is a compliment to Spotswood's efforts to chris-

tianize and educate the Indian youths of the colony. The balanced
antithesis of his best prose is combined with apt historical and
classical figures in a nicely disciplined, graceful little poem.

DIARIES AND LETTERS

It was not known that Byrd was a diarist at all until 1939, when the
discovery of one portion of his shorthand journal was announced,
and it was not until two years later that the decoded work appeared
in print. Two other sections promptly turned up and were printed in
1942 and 1958, respectively. The three cover the years 1709–12, 1717–
21, and 1739–42. Other portions may yet be discovered. As it is, the
three printed segments are historically and literarily significant in
themselves, though they hardly raise Byrd to the rank of an American
Pepys. In some ways they are most interesting as glosses or commentaries on his major work, the histories. And they combine with
his letters to fill out the story of the life and times of one of the most
eminent of colonial Americans.

The young Byrd studying in England must have been quite aware
that many men kept daily journals, though he may not have known
of those kept by his fellows of the Royal Society, Samuel Pepys and
John Evelyn, that of the former in shorthand. He is much more likely
to have seen the log-like records of men who had been at sea,
records which in form remind us of Byrd's own. In America New
Englander Samuel Sewall kept a diary, as did Byrd's Virginia son-in-
law, Landon Carter, though both the Puritan and the Cavalier
were much more introspective, and usually much more detailed,
than was the master of Westover. And several other Virginia, as
well as many more New England, diurnal jottings survive from the
eighteenth century.

As literary pieces per se Byrd's diaries have little merit. They are
merely thin segments of life, not the rounded and relatively complete
story represented by an autobiography or long and continuous
diary. The schedule of the day's activities, from early rising to exercise
and to reading in any of his acquired languages, through the name of
each kind of food he ate, to the concluding nightly prayers—or the
forgetting of them—becomes so monotonous that one edition of the
earliest diary has appeared which omits the methodical repetitions.
The daily business life of the plantation is more varied, for it concerns
agriculture, health of slaves, shipping, mining, or land purchases.

Occasionally he noted what he had been reading. Social life at Westover or in Williamsburg or London follows fairly regular patterns, though the persons with whom Byrd converses or indulges in recreations innocent or illicit are fascinatingly varied and impressively prominent in the literary, political, military, or fashionable circles of colony or kingdom. Sabbath observance is meticulously recorded, whether of reading Tillotson on a dreary day at home, hearing a visiting parson at Westover or Commissary Blair in Williamsburg, or listening to a famous preacher in London. His conjugal and extra-marital sexual relations are noted with the matter-of-factness of one who never expected his diaries to be read by any other than himself.

Of the roughly nine years covered in the extant diaries more than seven were spent in Virginia. Almost all of plantation and village-capital life is at least outlined here. Political and personal contention with Governor Spotswood or Commissary Blair in the early years and warm friendship with both when he was sixty-five is noted without comment. Arranging books and laying out gardens, planning the new brick house, playing games with the ladies, and plying family and friends or servants with purgatives or quinine tell us a good deal about this plantation life on the James. As a record of life during the "publick times" in the capital at Williamsburg it is just as informative. Meetings of council and General Court and the Board of Governors of William and Mary, face-to-face encounters pleasant and unpleasant with Governor Spotswood (in the earlier two segments), dinners and balls are briefly observed, but often with a personal anecdote revelatory of observed and observer. They are rich in historical value, indicating, when taken chronologically, the development of the colony from frontier fears to sophisticated political arguments in an established society, a nation in embryo.

Byrd's sense of humor never deserts him, though in the diaries it is rarely as close to the surface as in most of his other writings. Cheating his first wife at cards and quarreling with her concerning her eyebrow-plucking are inherently comic situations, but Byrd's commentary is dead pan, as "got the better of her, and maintained my authority." His curious dreams, faithfully recorded along with speculation as to their portent, were apparently taken seriously. But if one keeps in mind the age and Byrd's other writings he can never be sure that the diarist is not smiling as he describes the figments of his subconscious.

The life of the London man-about-town (all in the second diary in the interval between his two marriages) is as significant for the

English social historian as for the American. It is even more interesting as an indication of how easily a Virginia colonial might slip into English high society, and it explains some of the habits, attitudes, and amusements of Byrd in America. He has been called a social climber, but there is no indication that the Virginian was ever to feel that he was not to the manner born, as that other diarist Pepys may have felt. Byrd's schooling, his intimacy with a score of noble and eminent men, and his entree to all the best houses and to the royal court seem to have been taken as a matter of course, though he took pride as well as pleasure in the friendship of Sir Robert Southwell and Sir Hans Sloane, and in being a member of the Royal Society.

Byrd's diary was not kept out of mere narcissism or out of the desire to create a public image. He enjoyed all of life, and in keeping a record of its fleeting days he could, as he grew older and reread his jottings, place its events in proper perspective. That he did reread he attests in his last diary and in his commonplace book. But probably his strongest motivation was the feeling that some day when he had leisure and lacked hedonistic and business distraction, he would transform most of it into more enduring prose. That he did turn his notes and journals of most of 1728 and portions of 1732 and 1733 into such prose is the great fact of his life. Perhaps he planned to utilize other portions of his diaries, by telling the story of his English tour with Sir John Perceval, or of his own literary and social activity amidst the circle of London gallants who were also poets, scholars, and playwrights. But seventy years was hardly enough time for a writer such as Byrd, a reviser and perfectionist, to transmute the dross of diurnal jottings into the polished silver of prose in the age of Anne.

Byrd's letters scarcely compare in literary quality with those of his greatest British contemporaries, but among colonial American epistolarians he must be given high rank. The letters are a necessary complement to and gloss upon his other writings, especially the diaries. They fill gaps in his colonial and London life that the extant diaries do not cover, they shed light on persons mentioned in the diaries, they are documentary evidence of his remarkably diverse interests, they indicate that he was a master of several epistolary forms, and they afford our best evidence of their author's concomitant love of England and patriotism for Virginia. They contain passages equal in style and feeling to the best of the histories, and they include a number of ordinary business and polite social notes.

Many of Byrd's epistles, most of them undated, follow the literary conventions of the late seventeenth and early eighteenth centuries. They are most often to ladies, sometimes mere frames for character sketches, sometimes playfully flirtatious, sometimes piteously plead-ing for the lady's hand or for her favor. "Preciosa," "Vaporina," "Zeno-bia," "Lucretia," "Fidelia," and the rest (as we have noted, actual ladies) were addressed in tones sharply satirical, mocking, semiseri-ous, or serious, though even in the last with sardonic overtones. The epistolary courtship of "Facetia" by "Veramour" (Byrd in his youth) is a series of pleadings interspersed with the malicious or droll gossip of the town. In middle age he addresses "Minionet" and the cruel "Charmante" in much the same fashion. In the same period his epistolary wooing of "Sabina" reveals a serio-comic situation worthy of being turned into a sentimental comedy by one of his numerous playwright friends—if Byrd himself lacked sufficient detachment to undertake it. As Byrd observed in "Inamorato L'Oiseaux," he was usually at his worst—his most ridiculous—when he was in love.

But to others, as "Fidelia" (Lucy Parke), the lady he won, or to his kinswoman-by-law, "Cousin Taylor," he is courtly, gallant, amusing, sure of himself, though, especially in his letters to the latter, gently satiric, not of the lady but of the rest of human kind on whom he touches, and simply witty. The balanced clauses, paradoxical images, alliterative phrases, the frequent reliance on assonance so charac-teristic of his fully developed style in the histories is also here, from the letters of 1700 to the last forty-one years later.

Byrd was already an effective and witty letter-writer by 1701, when he and the recuperating Sir John Perceval (later Earl of Egmont) began a tour of eastern and northern England and part of Scotland. Apparently Byrd's Scottish letters have not survived, but those giving his impressions of provincial England, scholars and antiquarians, university life, and the appear-ance of cathedral towns are almost as entertaining as his later travel accounts of the expedition from Currituck Inlet to the Blue Mountains. Conversing frequently in French and sometimes relieving the tedium of horseback travel with Sir John's songs, Byrd men-tions table-talk with such still-remembered scholars as Drs. Humphrey Prideaux of Norwich and John Colebatch of Cambridge. In the latter university city they were much entertained: "We din'd yesterday at Mr Vice-Chancellor's, where Philosophy flew about the table faster than the wine." Interesting is the contrast with the picture of Oxford Byrd drew two years later in a letter to "Facetia." He had stayed in this university town when the troupe of players led by Mrs.

Bracegirdle and Mrs. Prince were entertaining the undergraduates, while the advanced theology students contended for their doctorates. Though Byrd loved the theater, he found student rowdiness too much, and concluded, "I was perfectly sick of the confusion & impertinence of Oxford, & thought every day a month til I could return hither [to London]."

As an observant lover of nature and a member of the Royal Society, Byrd continued to show in his letters as late as 1741 his enormously varied interest in the physical world about him in Virginia. He corresponded with Sir Hans Sloane for at least thirty-five years (1706–41), sending to the great scientist boxes of seeds, plants, skins, and live birds and animals. To Sloane he expatiates on various medicinal plants, including ginseng and snakeroot. He frequently alludes to the Royal Society and sends other members as well as personal friends, among them Lord Pembroke, boxes of plants they may try in their gardens. In exchange he asks for English flowering shrubs and trees for his own use. The great naturalist Mark Catesby frequently visited him at Westover and gave advice on laying out what the Quaker naturalist Peter Collinson called the finest garden in Virginia. Byrd corresponded with Catesby when the latter was back in England and with Collinson, as well as with the latter's friend John Bartram, who also visited him at Westover.

For thirty-five years Byrd begged Sloane to persuade some young naturalist, preferably a physician, to come over and do several years of field work in searching for medicinal plants. Both John Lawson of North Carolina and Mark Catesby did some of this kind of work, as did the two John Claytons and other "curious" gentlemen. But they had not gone far enough inland, Byrd felt, to have discovered significant new species. In his letters Byrd also shows his interest in minerals, meteorology, astronomy, and other phases of science, and comments upon them, much as he does in the histories.

Among Byrd's best letters, literarily and historically, are those addressed to his close friends and relatives. Among his London friends, in addition to the scientists and Sir Robert Southwell mentioned above, were Edward Southwell, secretary of state for Ireland; Sir Charles Wager, First Lord of the Admiralty; Charles and John Boyle, successively Earl of Orrery; John Campbell, Duke of Argyle, and his brother Lord Islay; the Earl of Egmont; Lord Carteret; and Colonel Martin Bladen. It should be noted that all these were in some way men of letters, at least three of them having dashed off plays—all professionally produced—in their spare moments. Among his Virginia correspondents were his brothers-in-law the horticulturist-planter John Custis and the historian-planter Robert Beverley II, Virginia governors Nicholson, Spotswood, and Gooch, North Carolina governors Burrington and Johnston, and his neighbors Benjamin Harrison and Sir John Randolph. English relatives, usually through his second marriage, were Colonel and Mrs. Francis Otway, Lady Sherrard, and Mrs. ("Cousin") Taylor. With them all he shares the interests he displays elsewhere: with his British friends his anxiety at the state of the empire, news and gossip about mutual acquaintances, and details of his own activities in a far-away corner of the world; with Custis family affairs and plants; with Sir John Randolph local politics and amateur theatricals at Williamsburg. Mrs. Taylor, Mrs. Otway, and Lady Sherrard are addressed with playful gallantry. To Mrs. Taylor, who appears to have enjoyed a spicy story, Byrd relates the ribald tale of a Williamsburg actress who artificially enhanced her feminine charms and came to public grief thereby.

In letters to people in England he frequently jeers at the saints of New England, who carry on smuggling in the Chesapeake Bay region, sell Kill-Devil rum, and are the principal movers in the fiendish slave trade. To Byrd, as to James Fenimore Cooper a century later, the Puritans were canting hypocrites. Even to his old friend and fellow Middle Templar Benjamin Lynde, Chief Justice of Massachusetts, he makes the charge directly, though in jesting tones. This anti-New Englandism is the same quality as that he shows frequently in the Dividing Line histories. His abhorrence of the slave trade is most trenchantly expressed to Lord Egmont (July 12, 1736), when he begins his discussion with "this unchristian Traffick, of making Merchandise of our Fellow Creatures . . . ."

To these close friends and to others, from Sir Robert Walpole to his librarian at Westover or a penniless fellow Virginian in London, Byrd writes in graceful phrase and witty anecdote. So frequently does he write tongue-in-cheek that the unwary must read carefully. One letter contains a tale/sketch of a lady and a parson in a mail-coach that might well match a Hogarthian print. The devastating irony of his letter to John Fox upon receipt of a volume of trifling verse Fox had without permission dedicated to him is worthy of comparison with Dr. Johnson's classic reply to Chesterfield. The playful irony of his "Most hypochondriack Sir" reply to librarian Proctor's complaint about firewood and candles is as unanswerable as his letter to Fox.

Emotionally and perhaps intellectually the most appealing of the themes developed in Byrd's letters is his record of conflict within himself as to whether he was Englishman or American, gay Londoner or busy and patriotic Virginian. He is one or the other in different moods. The scale is definitely unbalanced, for most of his extant letters were written from Virginia to London friends, and he consciously and unconsciously rationalizes his rural existence as a sojourn in Eden.

But he wants his first wife on a visit to England "to see the town [London] in all its glory," and in his later years he confided to the Earl of Orrery that he longed to return once more "to that Enchanted Island," even with its smoke and fog. And he mentions earlier that his older daughters find the colony lifeless after the balls and masquerades of London. Begging for letters from "home," he tells Mrs. Otway that "Our lives are uniform, . . . till the Season brings in the Ships. Then we tear open the Letters they bring us from Our Friends, as eagerly as a greedy Heir tears open his Rich Fathers will."

Nevertheless the other side of the coin is usually uppermost. To Custis, from London, he declared that he longed to be in America, for "my heart is in Virginia," and a little later from the colony he describes the second Mrs. Byrd's first impression of the country in spring. Again and again he refers to "our sun-shiny country," where "the Heavens put on a Cheerful Countenance." A dozen times he portrays himself in the role of pater familias in a natural paradise. This passage, from a 1726 letter, is fairly typical, including its biblical imagery:

> I have a large Family of my own, and my Doors are open to Every Body, yet I have no Bills to pay, and half-a-Crown will rest undisturbed in my Pocket for many Moons together. Like one of the Patriarchs, I have my Flocks and my Herds, my Bond-men and Bond-women, and every Soart of Trade amongst my own Servants, so that I live in a kind of Independence on every one but Providence. . . .
>
> Thus my Lord we are very happy in our Canaans if we could but forget the Onions and Fleshpots of Egypt.*

In a more pagan idyllic mood he notes that "We [who] are banished from those Polite Pleasures are forct to take up rural entertainments. A Library, a Garden, a Grove, and a purling Stream are the Innocent Scenes that divert our Leizure."

Byrd's familiar letters then, like other epistles of the English Augustan age, offer instruction, advice, love, gallantry, ribald entertainment, and scientific information, among other things. His mood is sometimes playful, sometimes happily serene, but most often satiric.

---

* *Virginia Magazine of History and Biography* 32 (1924): 27.

He liked to exercise the repartee of his time even in his letters: "I love to have the Ball tost directly to me & catch it before it reaches the ground." The turn of phrase is always graceful. He looked at himself and his fellow men with a certain equanimity, sometimes tinged with the cynical or the serene: "We play the Fool . . . 50 or 60 Years, what Prodigys then should we grow up to in double that time? And why should the figure of our constitutions be lengthened out when the odds are great, we should make a bad use of them." This was in 1739. Twenty years earlier he had been in a less disillusioned mood when he wrote:

> God almighty is ever contriving our happiness, and does many things for good which appear to our short sight to be terrible misfortunes. But by the time the last act of the play comes on, we grow convinced of our mistake, and look back with pleasure on those scenes which first appeared unfortunate.*

THE PUBLIC PROSE

William Byrd's four best-known writings, "The Secret History of the Dividing Line," "The History of the Dividing Line," "A Progress to the Mines," and "A Journey to the Land of Eden," appeared together for the first time as recently as 1966. This edition, based on the original "Westover Manuscripts," the one manuscript of "The Secret History" in the American Philosophical Society, and a few odd pages to fill lacunae, is the first textually satisfactory publication of these prose travel accounts. Taken together, or as a unit, this is the first classic work by a native southern American. Some of the manuscripts were well known in 1803 and 1817, portions were published in 1822, 1841, 1866, and 1900. A parallel-text edition of the two histories first appeared in 1929, though a few pages of text since filled were lacking. A new printing of this edition, with the missing pages supplied, appeared in 1967. A modern authenticated text based upon a complete study of the variants among the manuscripts in the Virginia Historical Society, the American Philosophical Society, Colonial Williamsburg, Inc., and the Henry E. Huntington Library, and the printed 1822 fragments of a different manuscript version of "The History" now apparently lost or disintegrated is still needed.

---

* To "Irene," c. 1716, in *Recollections and Private Memoirs of Washington,* ed. B. J. Lossing (New York: Derby & Jackson, 1860), p. 29.

The reworked fragments of drafts in Byrd's own handwriting, especially when compared with the almost complete fair copy of "The Secret History" in the American Philosophical Society and the fair copy of the other three travel accounts in the Virginia Historical Society, graphically illustrate Byrd's habit of revising and filling out.

The Westover (Virginia Historical Society) version of "The History," a fair copy not in Byrd's hand but with emendations in his hand, was apparently about ready for the printer at the time of Byrd's death. Quite evidently, as already noted, Byrd kept the same sort of diary we have for other years, during the two parts of the Dividing Line expedition, the visit to the Germanna mines, and the excursion to North Carolina, and almost surely additional notebooks loaded with statistics and descriptions of fauna, flora, and topography. Two documents, "A Journal of the Dividing Line Drawn between the Colonies of Virginia & North Carolina begun March 5: 1728 . . . [by] Col. Byrd & Others" and "A Journal of the proceedings of the Commissioners," in the British Museum and Public Record Office respectively, rough-note reports submitted by Byrd in 1728 and 1729 as leader of the Virginia group of the expedition, were clearly among the sources for his expanded accounts of his travels. There is no real evidence as to the date of composition of the shorter "A Progress to the Mines" or "A Journey to the Land of Eden," but they too were drawn from diaries and rough notes kept during the excursions.

That Byrd waited several years before he began at least one of the two histories is probable. With some pride, as early as 1728–29, he gives Lord Orrery and others a capsule account of the expedition in his letters. Not until July 1736 (in a mutilated letter probably to Lord Egmont) does Byrd mention that he is shaping his rough notes into something more, for he protests that his activity in founding the cities of Richmond and Petersburg and promoting Switzer colonization along the Roanoke has prevented his finishing the work identified in a manuscript note as "The History" (version unknown) and "A Journey." In the same month, in a letter to Peter Collinson, he apparently declines to send a copy of a version of which Collinson has heard: "I own it goes against me to deny you such a trifle, but I have one infirmity, never to venture anything unfinished out of my hands." Byrd does offer to send the rough journal, possibly "The Secret History," for it "is only the skeleton & Ground Work of what I intend, which may some time or other come to be filled out with vessels, & flesh, & have a decent skin drawn over all to keep things tight in their places and prevent their looking frightful. I

have the materials ready, & want only leisure to put them together."
A year later he informs Collinson that he still intends to "cover this
dry skeleton" and that, since he will occasionally mention plants
and animals, he would like for Mark Catesby to do the "figures," or
illustrations, of them.

Internal evidence also aids in the conjectural dating of "The
History." Byrd mentions in it a natural catastrophe occurring in
1736, but no one appears to have noted his comparison of throngs
at an outdoor religious service to the multitudes who gathered in the
open fields to hear George Whitefield preach. The great evangelist's
first visit to America was in February-August 1738, though his preaching to great crowds had begun in England the year before. These two
references may have been interpolations in a completed manuscript,
but they do not so read, and neither appears in "The Secret History."
"The History" was most probably begun about 1732 and finished
some time between 1738 and 1740.

Almost surely "The Secret History" is the earlier version. It is one-
half as long as "The History," omits the prefatory history of Virginia,
uses tag names for the principal participants, and is much more
sharply satirical, even sarcastic, than "The History." It includes a
number of speeches by Byrd to the whole group of surveyors and
assistants, and a number of letters and other documents passed
between the Virginia and North Carolina commissioners, none of
these appearing in "The History." It could have been the skeleton he
intended to flesh out, though the travel account he sent Collinson
may have been closer in content and tone to the longer "History."

What the two histories have in common is that they are both
travel accounts of the same expedition and that both possess a
mock-heroic quality, though in the case of "The History" mock-epic
unobtrusively merges into genuine epic. Both may be promotion
pamphlets, though the propaganda quality is much stronger in
"The History" than in "The Secret History." The latter apparently was
written for the reading and delectation of a private circle of
friends, and American friends at that, as attested by the casual
comparison of Moseley to "the Commissary" (James Blair), an
allusion which might have been lost upon an English reader or
listener. The basis for most of the humor in both versions is sex, as
in much Restoration and eighteenth-century English literature and in
the work of neighboring Marylanders George Alsop and Ebenezer
Cook. But the sex is much more abundant and much coarser in
"The Secret History." It is not difficult to visualize Byrd, with his kin

and neighbors, the Harrisons, Banisters, Beverleys, Stiths, and Bollings, sitting before a winter fire in a plantation house along the James reading and laughing at "The Secret History."

Stylistic qualities in general are held in common. Antithesis; analogy; witty disparagement; puns; short, balanced, paradoxical, and epigrammatic statements the two histories share with the familiar letters and the character sketches. "The History" is in general the more urbane, sophisticated, and polished and thus has less of an air of spontaneity. In both, the saints of New England receive a number of glancing blows—at their sanctimonious hypocrisies in trading, and, in the instance of "Puzzlecause" (North Carolina Commissioner Little), their debased and hypocritical lechery, with perhaps more anti-Puritanism in "The History." Disparaging allusions to North Carolina appear in plenty in "The Secret History," chiefly in the form of caricatures of that colony's commissioners and anecdotes about its people, but they are much more frequent in "The History." And more sweeping and generalized condemnations of Carolinians and other more northern colonists are employed in "The History" to accentuate Virginia as earth's only paradise—for prospective settlers.

As clearly as "The Secret History" was intended as witty social satire, "The History" was at least in part a redirecting of the same materials for propaganda purposes. The learned descriptions of unusual American plants and animals, from ginseng to buffalo and beaver, the detailed descriptions of beautiful rivers, flowery meadows, and odoriferous woods, the disquisitions on Indian life, customs, and costumes often appear in germinal form in "The Secret History," but the extrapolations of all these in "The History" are evidently aimed at the European reader, most probably the potential emigrant. Yet "The History" remains essentially a work of art, the projection of a not too unusual colonial official enterprise into a travel-adventure symbolic of the frontier experience. Byrd adorned and furnished it from his wide reading in many languages and with even more of his personal experience in other contexts than he had employed in "The Secret History."

The basic material for the two histories sprang, of course, from the two-stage Dividing Line expedition authorized by the king and implemented by the governors of Virginia and North Carolina in 1728 to determine the exact location of the boundary between the two colonies. It was an old problem, at least once before having been undertaken with unsatisfactory results, and involving such important matters as titles to land and squatters who evaded taxes from either colonial government. Byrd and two fellow commissioners from

Virginia met their North Carolina counterparts at Currituck Inlet on the Atlantic Ocean. With them were surveyors, pioneers (engineer-chainbearers), and woodsmen-hunters. They began work in late February and stopped on April 9, as the snakes began to appear. They resumed their labors in September, and the Virginia party continued on until late November and reached the foothills of the mountains, though they had long since been deserted by their Carolina colleagues. They had crossed sandspits and what is still the jungle quagmire of the Great Dismal Swamp, forded flooding spring rivers, endured torrents of rain and scarcity of food, visited Indian villages, narrowly escaped some potentially fatal accidents, and made observations of topography, red men, and fauna and flora. Byrd as senior member of the Virginia party had to prevent open conflict between members of his own group, endure some treachery, and occasionally mete out justice. According to his own modest statements and those of the two colonial governors, he showed his probity by awarding North Carolina more territory than it had ever expected and his leadership by returning all his men in comparatively good health, with his instructions fulfilled. That he should profit personally by purchasing many thousands of acres in the territories he had first "discovered" was in no way incompatible with the spirit or letter of his mission.

As already noted, Byrd's friends who heard or read "The Secret History" must have found this account of the journey as entertaining as a Restoration or sentimental comedy. Byrd himself was "Steddy," his Virginia compatriots Dandridge and Fitz-William appeared as "Meanwell" and "Firebrand," their surveyors as "Orion" and "Astrolabe," and the North Carolinians Moseley as "Plausible," Lovick as "Shoebrush," and Little as "Puzzlecause." The vignettes are apt and cutting: "Puzzlecause [Harvard-educated] had degenerated from a New-England preacher, for which his Godly Parents design'd him, to a very wicked, but awkward rake." The vignette becomes a full portrait as the journey continues and "Puzzlecause" shows his rabid and indiscriminate sexuality. "Shoebrush" was a merry, good-humored man who had acquired his good manners while he was employed as valet de chambre to North Carolina governor Hyde. "Plausible," a learned and forceful character, Byrd treats with more respect but toward the end professes himself disillusioned by this commissioner's "treachery." If the Carolinians' portraits are unflattering, so are those of "Firebrand" and "Orion," the one lascivious, vicious, and conniving, the other ineffective, untrained, sycophantic, and cowardly. "Meanwell," the author's good friend and principal aide, is

portrayed sympathetically. But if there are any heroes other than
the narrator in either history, they are the rank and file, the men
who cheerfully and uncomplainingly carried the chains through
quicksand and jungle, slept in soaked clothing, and in general carried on. They were the frontiersmen who were making America,
but they were also Virginia yeoman farmers who as hunters or
craftsmen put their past experience to significant use. In "The
Secret History" the villainy or knavery of "Firebrand" and "Shoebrush" are often in the foreground, but frequently in the same
scenes were the first described American poor whites, the inhabitants
of Lubberland, where the men were indolent and boorish, the women
careworn and slovenly. In both histories Byrd usually calls these
latter folk North Carolinians, perhaps because they do appear for the
most part to have come first to the easternmost section of that
colony, even though they actually lived on both sides of the old and
new boundary lines. Naturally it suited his propaganda purposes in
"The History" to label them as non-Virginians. But another point he
makes implicitly and occasionally explicitly is that some of these
people occupy good lands which, under the management of such
thrifty immigrants as Swiss or German or French, might be
turned into prosperous and perhaps eventually opulent farms. He
makes the same point more explicitly in his letters promoting colonization.

Included in "The Secret History," as noted above, were "Steddy's"
letters to various officials and his speeches to encourage his men.
Both kinds of documents were certainly taken from notebooks or
journals, the original rhetoric perhaps a little embellished in the
retelling. The speeches especially suggest epic intent in that they
roughly parallel the patriotic or council-of-war speeches Byrd knew
from classical or Renaissance work in his library. All this documenta-
tion, the tag names, and the individual sexual adventures of certain
of the party are omitted from "The History." Yet the latter is twice
as long.

To flesh out "The History" Byrd used several devices. He added
the rather long prefatory resumé of Virginia history, emphasizing
the colony's steady shrinkage in size, as broken promises carved
from it new provinces. Thus he gave potential European readers a
sense of situation as his story opened. He took what is in "The
Secret History" a brief entry about the Saponi Indians and expanded it into a detailed account of numbers, dress, hunting habits,
and manners, some of it drawn from sources such as John Lawson's
A New Voyage to Carolina (1709) and his own experience. The

well-known account of "Bearskin's" (the Indian hunter's) religion occurs in both versions, but it is expanded in "The History" and completely rewritten, with more picturesque adjectives and nouns throughout the discourse, and is concluded with an observation not even suggested in "The Secret History":

> This was the Substances of Bearskin's Religion, and was as much to the purpose as cou'd be expected from a meer State of Nature, without one Glimpse of Revelation or Philosophy.
>
> It contain'd, however, the three Great Articles of Natural Religion: the Belief of a God; the Moral Distinction between Good and Evil; and the Expectation of Rewards and Punishments in Another World.
>
> Indeed, the Indian Notion of a Future Happiness is a little Gross and Sensual, like Mahomet's Paradise. But how can it be otherwise, in a People that are contented with Nature as they find Her, and have no other Lights but what they receive from purblind Tradition?*

So with the accounts of plants and animals, which Byrd amplified in "The History" from the scientific books in his library and his earlier observations in other parts of Virginia. His natural description is not always objectively scientific, for like certain of his contemporaries Byrd intensifies or heightens the colors with a tall story, usually tongue-in-cheek or deadpan, but at times taken half-seriously even by this sophisticated teller. Literary allusion to drama, verse, curious and learned tomes, and especially the classics is frequent. Religion is taken seriously at least by Byrd and "Dr. Humdrum" (Parson Fontaine), and its absence among frontier whites evokes serious concern and disdainful satire. Graphic figures emerge from his own experience, as "We then kindled a rousing fire in the center of it, and lay round it, like so many Knights Templars," a vivid juxtaposition of frontier reality and the evoked memory of the round Temple church in London. Other emotions are rekindled in tranquillity. "The Secret History's" already poetic commentary "I hardly knew how to behave myself in a Bed, after having lain a week in the Open Field, & seeing the Stars twinkle over my head," becomes in "The History," "A clear Sky, spangled with Stars, was our Canopy, which being the last thing we saw before we fell asleep gave us Magnificent Dreams."

The prose of "The Secret History" may be poignant, as the early "I often cast a longing Eye towards England, & sigh'd"; or piquant,

---

* *William Byrd's Histories of the Dividing Line*, ed. Boyd and Adams, p. 202.

as the "Commissioners of Carolina . . . [were] much better provided for the Belly than the Business." Perhaps "The History" suffers
in liveliness as the author sacrifices this terseness for more explicit
explanations of Carolinian uncouthness or ineptitude. But the pervasive ironic tone of "The History," which displaces the shorter work's
forthright satire, makes for an equality, or balance, between the two
accounts. As more than one critic has observed, the two histories
complement each other. Most readers will find the parallel-text edition, despite the slight distractions of glancing from one page to that
opposite, better reading than taking the two one after the other.

Similar in tone to "The History" are the two shorter pieces from
the Westover manuscripts, "A Journey to the Land of Eden in the
Year 1733" and "A Progress to the Mines in the Year 1732." The
former is really an appendix or afterword to "The History," for in it
Byrd relates his experiences in surveying with his friend Major
Mayo the lands acquired in the boundary region. The tone retains
a slight tinge of irony, but the characterizations of individuals are
less lively than those of "The History." "A Progress" to see and be instructed in the working of the mines of former governor Spotswood is livelier, with portraits of such people as Miss Theky, the old
maid, entertaining anecdotes such as the story of the tame deer
plunging into a full-length mirror, and interesting information on
mining and smelting. Both add to our knowledge of the author and
his world. But they are, after all, merely travel accounts.

"The Secret History" and "The History" are more conscious works
of art. In the end, "The Secret History" remains a remarkably lively
comic satire, extremely personal, half London wit and half New
World situation. "The History" is something more, a superior work
of both intention and accomplishment. Here is the southern planter of
the golden age seeing his native Virginia world through the eyes of
European experience and education. He ornaments his picture with
his learning and his knowledge of the world of men. Above all, he
sees it as he should, as an actual journey which was also the
symbolic progress of the American experience. As in Leatherstock-
ing's gradual trek westward or Huck Finn's voyage down the Mis-
sissippi, the epic significance of the journey is largely implicit. But
the epic quality, however shadowy, is definitely in the consciousness
of the man who describes playfully (in both histories) the founding
of the noble order of Ma-ooty, with wild turkey beards as cockades,
a spread-winged turkey in gold suspended from a ribbon-collar about
the neck, and a Latin motto signifying that through this bird these
chosen ones were supported in the wilderness. And who, more seri-

ously, records in his last diurnal entry in "The History" his sense of the heroic quality of American destiny in the simile: "Thus ended our second expedition, in which we extended the line within the shadow of the Cherakee mountains, when we were obliged to set up our pillars, like Hercules, and return home."

CONCLUSION

Byrd wrote for a variety of reasons in a variety of forms. His entirely serious writings, including his legal briefs and petitions, his proposal to drain the Dismal Swamp, his business letters, and his scientific epistles afford evidence of his depth of learning, his eager curiosity, his practical sagacity, and his Christian rationalism. But he lived in an age when the comic spirit reigned, and the diaries, "characters," many of his letters, and travel accounts, however factual, are marked by "an indulgent irony" which on rare occasions sharpens into somewhat disdainful but never cruel satire.

Byrd, like other great planters of his own and the succeeding age, lived by the golden mean, which meant that he wished to see his world in balance. Others employed the yardstick of the middle way without humor, men like William Fitzhugh or Landon Carter or even Thomas Jefferson. But for the master of Westover deviations from the middle way, whether of pompous Carolina commissioners, lawless denizens of the boundary line, or the saints of New England, were droll. For a talent nurtured in Queen Anne's London, incongruities must be shaped into congruity, or order, by the mightiest of weapons, wit. His observant eye caught everything in Williamsburg or Westover or the wilderness, and he usually found it out of proportion. He was quite aware that he was laughing at himself as he laughed at things around him in Virginia. His mood and his intention thus sprang from his rationalism.

He united wit with utility, or usefulness. His wit might win a lady's favor, destroy a rival, or persuade Europeans that they should migrate to his Eden. He exercised the combination most effectively, as we have noted, in his most ambitious work designed to attract settlers. But the conscious artist in him would not allow him to limit "The History" to the function of promotion pamphlet. It was also planned to satisfy the natural curiosity of the European concerning the strange New World and to supply scientists with interesting data on every conceivable object of his regard. Above all, it provokes volleys of silvery laughter.

Byrd was modest and, despite his satire or perhaps through it, tolerant. For he could and did ridicule and accept in the same passage. One could wish him less modest, both in the histories and the diaries, by telling us more about what he was writing, of his table talk with the coffee house immortals of his years in the London of Addison and Pope and Swift, of his founding of cities, or of his opinions of the books he was reading. Nowhere does he pass critical judgment on a book he has read, on the abilities of a playwright or an actress he knew intimately, and very rarely on those blurred or dim figures of the American past, such as commissary Blair, governors Spotswood and Gooch, or the distinguished Sir John Randolph. His diaries remain, at least when compared with Pepys's or Evelyn's or Landon Carter's, curiously superficial. Byrd was not given to introspection even in the privacy of shorthand, perhaps because restraint went hand in hand with tolerance. Though he may have been as imaginative as his son-in-law Landon Carter, he did not possess the latter's sensitivity or sensibility.

Byrd, at least as a writer, was a perfectionist, as his quoted letters and rough drafts and versions of his histories demonstrate. The unfinished would never, if he could help it, go from his hands to the printer's. He wrote with grace, symmetry, in rhythms at once his own and his era's.

The aristocrat William Byrd, like that later Virginia aristocrat Jefferson, looked with sympathy at all kinds of his fellow Americans and with perceptive curiosity at the uncouth and marvelous land in which they lived. More than did the Massachusetts theologians, he projected the future United States, not as a city set upon a hill, but as a happy valley of plenty and a beehive of fruitful industry—despite the natural and acquired indolence of some of its inhabitants. And it is through William Byrd that the sprightly charm of eighteenth-century English literature entered colonial American writing.

BIBLIOGRAPHY

Editions

Another Secret Diary of William Byrd of Westover, 1739–1741. Edited by Maude H. Woodfin and Marion Tinling. Richmond, Va.: Dietz, 1942. [Also includes essays and poems.]

The London Diary (1717–1721) and Other Writings. Edited by Louis B. Wright and Marion Tinling. New York: Oxford University Press, 1958.

The Prose Works of William Byrd of Westover. Edited by Louis B. Wright. Cambridge, Mass.: Harvard University Press, 1966. [Best text of four major works.]

The Secret Diary of William Byrd of Westover, 1709–1712. Edited by Louis B. Wright and Marion Tinling. Richmond, Va.: Dietz, 1941.

William Byrd's Histories of the Dividing Line between Virginia and North Carolina. Edited by William K. Boyd. New introduction and textual additions by Percy G. Adams. New York: Dover, 1967. [Parallel-text edition.]

Scholarship and Criticism

Beatty, Richmond C. *William Byrd of Westover.* Boston: Houghton Mifflin, 1932.

Dolmetsch, Carl. *William Byrd.* New York: Twayne, in press.

Marambaud, Pierre. *William Byrd of Westover (1674–1744).* Charlottesville, Va.: University Press of Virginia, 1971.

Masterson, James R. "William Byrd in Lubberland." *American Literature* 9 (1937): 153–70.

Weathers, Willie T. "William Byrd: Satirist." *William and Mary Quarterly,* 3d ser., 4 (1947): 27–41.

Wright, Louis B. "William Byrd's Defense of Sir Edmund Andros." *William and Mary Quarterly,* 3d ser., 2 (1945): 47–52.

———. "William Byrd's Opposition to Governor Francis Nicholson." *Journal of Southern History* 11 (1945): 68–79.

6

Jonathan Edwards
Historian of Consciousness

DANIEL B. SHEA, JR.

Intellectual responses to the work of Jonathan Edwards divide between two possibilities. It is not only Calvinists who have derived pleasure from the harmony of his mind, a mind which, in its first flourishing, appeared to contain the seeds of all its later development. Such admiration may also extend to the gathered assertions of the mature mind, an accomplishment of scrupulous consistency in which doctrine comes to the support of doctrine, networks of cause and effect are stitched together, science and metaphysics blend smoothly and are assimilated to the higher purposes of divinity.

A detailed examination of Edwards's thinking, however, dissipates this impression of consistency. As a student of others' thought, Edwards paid homage to his most important secular teachers, Newton and Locke, by sampling judiciously from among their major ideas. His earliest philosophical speculations achieved a largely intuitive reconciliation between an atomistic materialism and an idealistic immaterialism. And whether students of Edwards now read theology or behavioral psychology, they must be aware how brief and precarious was the harmony Edwards created in treating the problem of evil or in defining an element of freedom in man's bondage to his own nature.

Daniel B. Shea, Jr., is associate professor of English at Washington University, St. Louis. He is the author of *Spiritual Autobiography in Early America* (1968). He was a Woodrow Wilson fellow at Stanford and has taught at the Universities of Caen and Nice and the Claremont Graduate School. Most recently he has studied continuities between Puritanism and American literature with the aid of a National Endowment for the Humanities fellowship.

An impulse either to praise the meshing of Edwards's intellectual systems or to carp at weaknesses in his argument must be checked against Edwards's comments on harmony of mind. There is, first of all, the autobiographical testimony that he felt his own mental life to be discontinuous, at least in the sense that his earliest notions of divine things seemed like a blind man's conception of color in comparison with views he later enjoyed. Considered alone, harmony had limited attractions. Edwards could muster no praise for a merely self-sufficient consistency. A world "nicely contrived that the parts might nicely hang together," whose only end is that "it might be a nicely contrived world . . . is good for nothing at all," he observed in his *Miscellanies.* "Who can't see this?"*

Eclectic, pragmatic, oriented toward experience rather than theory, the American mind has been able to see Edwards's point very well, perhaps even better than Edwards. American contempt for a foolish consistency among abstractions was most pungently expressed by Emerson, whose ideas and career so often parallel Edwards's. William James, whose *Varieties of Religious Experience* suggested the keenness of his interest in Edwards, found particularly abhorrent any attempt to translate religious experience into "spread-out conceptual terms." Josiah Royce, linking together Edwards, Emerson, and James as our only contributors to philosophy, preferred to speak of Edwards's "synoptic vision" rather than his intellectual synthesis.

As Royce's term suggests, it is appropriate to consider Edwards's thought, not as system, but as the expression of a profound experience of the interrelatedness of things or as the intellectual symbol of his pious passion for unity, especially since, for Edwards, to study history was to study the religious consciousness, among masses of men and in individuals. From the same inner perspective, Edwards's ideas may be found less intriguing than the rigid totalism of personality which holds them all together and for which his definition of the atom—that which resists division infinitely—is an appropriate image. From any view it is evident that while Edwards took care to articulate consistent arguments, he devoted himself utterly to maintaining their consistency with the sovereign demands of his deity, an allegiance won from him just as his intellectual

---

* In quoting from Edward's writings, I have drawn most heavily on the Williams and Parsons edition of *The Works of President Edwards* (1968). The reader should also consult the other works listed in the bibliography for this essay, especially vol. 1 of the Dwight edition for Edwards's early writings, and the authoritative volumes of the Yale edition now in progress.

development crested. If equating Edwards's ideas with his personality makes too simple a formula, his ideas are nevertheless inseparable from his piety, as Edwards asserted they should be, and his piety arose from the crystallization of personality which took place in him before he ever preached a sermon.

I

More than biographical interest attaches to the writings of Jonathan Edwards as child prodigy. The mind itself fascinates, disguising its youth and inexperience in an essay on "The Soul" through its amused contempt for the "notion that the Soul is matereal," adumbrating a mature controversial manner in its relentless pursuit of an opponent's absurdities. The most remarkable of Edwards's writings before he entered college in the fall of 1716 purpose discovery rather than refutation. A brief essay, "Of the Rainbow," confirms Newton's experiments with the refraction of light. Once in possession of the principle—Newton's *Opticks* had its first edition in 1704—one possessed all the analogies stemming from it. Taking a mouthful of water, "spirting of it into the Air," anyone could give back to nature as "Plain a Rainbow with all the Colours as ever was seen in the heavens." But the principle became evident only through an "Ocular Demonstration." The operations of nature, while minute and of a marvellously refined complexity, exist to the eye, and must finally beseech a consciousness in order to be realized.

Edwards's best known observations of natural phenomena occur in his essay, written at age twelve, on the movements of the flying spider. Here, especially, his essential habits of mind reveal themselves. No one who has read "Sinners in the Hands of an Angry God," with its spider-sinner dangling over a fiery pit, can suppress a sense of the premonitory in Edwards's disposition of these "most despicable" creatures, who are "Swept and Wafted into the sea and buried in the Ocean," a sense further troubled by knowledge that in this detail, though not elsewhere, the young observer presumed beyond his evidence.

As yet, Edwards's language is thoroughly ductile and stretches easily from a cautious empiricism to expressions of wonder and delight, balancing objective and subjective realities. Indeed, it is the spider's very "way of working" which evokes such outbursts as "wonderful," "still more wonderful," and "very Pretty and Pleasing." Delight has an objective reason for being, and the mind can find it out. The truth that proves to be is more marvellous than anything that might have been imagined beforehand. And yet the phenomenon of the spider's flight, previously unexplained by anyone, did not exist until brought near an observer's eye: "but then I Plainly Percieved another such a string to Proceed Out of his tail I now Concieved I had found out the Whole mystery."

Already, Edwards had benefited greatly from his study of Newton, whom he mentions in three of his four earliest writings; and from his continued emphasis on such Newtonian subjects as gravity, light, and atoms, it seems likely that Edwards reviewed Newton throughout his time at Yale. Given Edwards's virtually congenital assumption of spirit's priority to matter, as suggested in "The Soul," one might have expected him to recoil from Newton's description of physical cause and effect in a material universe. But as historians of science point out, Newton often begins with gravity and concludes with God, and the second edition (1713) of the *Principia* had been recommended by Roger Cotes, Trinity's professor of astronomy and experimental philosophy, as "the safest protection against the attacks of atheists."

In the *Principia*'s third rule for reasoning in natural philosophy, Newton granted that the mind can think matter into successive halves ad infinitum, as Edwards demonstrates in an exercise aimed at exposing "The Prejudices of the Imagination." But, Newton continued, we cannot so easily determine whether the particles constituting matter, "may, by the powers of Nature, be actually divided . . . ." By the time he was speculating again on the nature of atoms, in query no. 31 of the second edition (1717) of the *Opticks*, Newton had drawn back from any suggestion that these "solid, massy, hard, impenetrable, moveable particles" might be divided to infinity—"no ordinary power being able to divide what God himself made one in the first creation." Edwards may already have been aware that Henry More, Newton's acquaintance at Cambridge, found such a description of atoms compatible with Neo-Platonism. In any case, he now moved boldly to construct a philosophical basis for his immaterialism, associating the idea of divine power operating on matter with the idea that atoms endure by an infinite force. Elaborating on hints from Newton, he argues that an absolute plenum, occupying all the space within its limits, can no more be divided in one place than another; or let one imagine its being broken in any part, it must be broken in all parts simultaneously, that is, suffer annihilation. Atoms endure, then, by a force no less than infinite, and the power to dissipate this force would be the power to annihilate God himself.

What men usually understand by solidity is not, after all, so solid: "for aught we know, the most dense bodies we are acquainted with, do not take up about the 10,000,000,000th part of the space they are in." And those particles called atoms, which do occupy all the space they are in and which compose at last the apparently solid furniture of our existence, must be understood as the locus of an infinite force rather than as a quantity, as resistance rather than mass. In his "Notes on Natural Science," Edwards gives this force a proximate name—"Solidity is gravity; so that, in some sense, the Essence of bodies is Gravity."

Newton himself had avoided making this identification, but here as elsewhere Edwards unhesitatingly transformed a mechanical principle into a spiritual one. From his earliest reading in Newton, he had accepted the notion that colors do not exist in things themselves but in the mind. Was solidity alone exempt from this principle, as the undifferentiated substance which supported all perceived qualities? If color *happens* to a perceiver, and cannot happen to him in the dark, why may not the same be said of solidity, which happens to us as resistance, and would not if there were no motion? Through a series of corollaries to this proposition, the essay titled "Of Atoms and of Perfectly Solid Bodies" becomes a demonstration that "there is no proper substance but God himself," communicating resistance throughout the "corporeal universe" in a manner which we codify as the laws of nature.

By the time he entered on these speculations, of course, Edwards had probably also absorbed Locke's distinction between primary and secondary qualities. But he read Newton first, and his reluctance to accept Locke's identification of primary qualities—solidity, motion, figure, number, extension—with the substance of material objects, appears to have been strengthened by his prior exposure to Newton and by the conception of substance as force.

Edwards thus assimilates Newton and Locke according to his own nature. From Newton's physics, he derives a basis for immaterialism; from Locke's psychology of sensation, he fashions his idealism and a way of describing the relation between divine and created mind. After his study of Locke, the ways of knowing and the experience of consciousness become of paramount importance to Edwards, especially in the notion that sense experience is the source of all our ideas, either directly or as the basis for the mind's reflection upon its own operations. Sense ideas may be simple or compounded, and the manner of their association sometimes hidden, but for Edwards they share a common obedience to the laws governing atoms, and man's consciousness of them is his surest guarantee of his own and God's existence.

Let the process of perception run backwards, Edwards suggests in his essay "Of Being," until the mind is totally emptied of its ideas. An idea of space, the closest Edwards comes to granting an innate idea, must nevertheless remain. (The mind is, thus, fortunately prevented from undoing itself by thinking of "the same that the Sleeping Rocks Dream of.") What is necessary is necessarily infinite, and to speak plain, Edwards admits, "I have already said as much as that Space is God." By which he meant, of course, not simply the space within the universe but the space into which the universe is expanding.

The trial may also be reversed. Suppose an entire roomful of ideas, set apart from any perceiving mind. How can these ideas be said to exist? In no way, states Edwards, unless God be thinking them. And therefore, he concludes, "those beings which have knowledge and Consciousness are the Only Proper and Real and substantial beings . . . spirits Only Are Properly Substance." Those who attribute substance to matter are guilty of a "Gross mistake," he adds, in an anticipation of Thoreau's metaphysical punning. Or in Ishmael's hopeful phrase, "Methinks that what they call my shadow here on earth is my true substance."

Without agreeing perfectly, then, Edwards's two ways of doing philosophical homage to divine primacy exhibit a pleasing convergence. God is both a force and a mind; his thinking the universe is its resistance against annihilation. Although the world exists only to our minds, as we exist only to God's, ideas are communicated to us in such an orderly way that it makes no practical difference if we continue to describe it in the old language of materialism. Edwards's use of the term "space" seems a verbal testimony to the irreducibility of the concept of God, rather than a symptom of pantheistic tendencies. As Douglas Elwood suggested in *The Philosophical Theology of Jonathan Edwards*, Edwards is better described as a panentheist, one who sees the material universe as within God and manifesting God, but who does not identify God with his creation.

By the time he received his A.B. from Yale in 1720, Edwards had developed a set of premises, in his notes on "The Mind," which would last him a lifetime, and which dealt to his own satisfaction with the implications of Newton's science and Locke's psychology for his Calvinist Christianity. At about the same time, he was cherishing an enormous intellectual ambition. His dual interest in psychology and natural philosophy led him to project an exhaustive study of both the human mind and the natural world. Under the heading, "The Natural History of the Mental World," he would consider all those topics which a reading of Locke had created for him: sensation, the emotions, the effects on judgment of prejudice and vogue. And in the more modestly titled "Things to be Considered, or Written Fully About," often referred to as his "Notes on Natural Science," Edwards was following the example of Newton, whose "Queries," appended to the *Opticks,* were both a stimulus and a challenge to him. In addition to questions that remained from childhood—why lightning is crooked and the ocean salty, what lies under the earth, and how clouds cohere—there were optical phenomena not yet described; "and if we can discover them, it is probable we may be let into a New World of Philosophy." Edwards has often been dismissed as a serious thinker for choosing to frighten children and defend predestination rather than explore that New World, but he had seen something else in the project which caused it to remain only a project: "the greatness, distance, and motion, etc. of this great universe has almost an omnipotent power upon the imagination; by it will man be chilled with the vast idea."

The cognitive range of any created consciousness is limited, and the terror which accompanies this discovery of limitation startles the mind into considering, alternatively, the emotional relation between perceiver and perceived. Consciousness without feeling is unimaginable to Edwards. Consciousness "is a sort of feeling within itself. The mind feels when it thinks; so it feels when it discerns, feels when it loves and feels when it hates." The essay on the flying spiders compels attention less for its discovery of fact than through its sustained delight that facts should be harmonious with one another: "why there's a web for him to go over upon." In comprehending the "sweet harmony" of the world, the naturalist may be "filled with such astonishment that the soul is ready to break." Yet he derives his pleasure from a mere shadow of reality, inferior in all its extent to any of "the many millions of little worlds," the saints, in whom dwells grace as the very principle of beauteous and holy harmony. Edwards's leave-taking from "the glories of astronomy and natural philosophy" in Miscellany 42 makes a commitment as much as a distinction: "the glories of religion consist in the sweet harmony of the greater and more-real world within themselves, with one another, and with the infinite fountain and original of them."

It would be easy to see in Edwards's statement nothing but a reaffirmation of the delight in religion which had been cultivated in him, the only son of a minister, since childhood. By his own testimony this was not precisely the case. Edwards's *Personal Narrative* (c. 1740), a spiritual autobiography written some twenty years after the experiences it describes, develops very carefully a distinction between the boy who built a booth for prayer in the woods and who made religious resolutions at college, and the self that emerged from an experience he finally saw as his conversion. What Edwards said as biographer of David Brainerd he could as well have said of himself. Conversion was "the greatest moral change that ever he passed under," and left him with "that remarkable new habit and temper of mind, which he held all his life after." In the midst of a period of extraordinary intellectual energy, something had happened which radically changed his relation to the content of his consciousness, which in some sense made over that consciousness so that it felt and perceived differently. Thereafter, Edwards was necessarily a partisan, wedded to his particular experience of God, which he celebrated lyrically, but whose doctrinal implications he prosecuted with rigid determination. It is understandable that the mind which flourished at East Windsor and New Haven should prove more attractive than the man who preached awakening at Northampton and sat down to convict the race of original sin at Stockbridge. But there is no lament in Edwards that minds should descend to make choices and enter history. He argues, rather, that entirely apart from material consequences, it is a man's saving should history, the process by which the divine will was being completed, enter his mind.

II

Nothing illustrates better the changed orientation of Edwards's mind after his time at Yale than a comparison of his early and later views of nature. There is a remarkable intellectual consistency between the notes on "The Mind" and the arguments of Edwards's fully developed theology. But differences rather than similarities prevail if one considers together the series of "Things to Be Considered" among Edwards's "Notes on Natural Science" and the later set of 212 notes, compiled intermittently, which have been published as *Images or Shadows of Divine Things*. The latter work, stemming from Edwards's view of spirit as substance and matter as shadow, and from his understanding of the typological tradition of scripture interpretation, has drawn considerably more attention than the one-dimensional observations of Edwards as amateur naturalist. But the early notes contain an openness of mind and a quality of uninstructed wonder which have largely disappeared from the *Images*.

Edwards's patient observation of the spider is well known, but he appears to have devoted equal time to consideration of other phenomena, such as the "frozen fog" whose particles, he observed, were not single bubbles but "little stars, of six points, like the particles of snow, very small . . . ." More than one inspection of the stones settled into holes "in the plain flat rocks that rivers run over," would have been required to conclude: "That stone doubtless was the cause of the hole." And no mild sort of curiosity leads the divinity student's eye away from his book to observe that the sunlight "upon the leaves of the book I was reading, which crept through the crevices of the leaves of the tree, was of a reddish purplish colour," the result, he suggests, of the leaves taking up other rays of the spectrum. In the *Personal Narrative*, Edwards mentions his youthful terror of thunder, but fear must have been set aside long enough to speculate "that the rumbling among the clouds, which we hear afterwards, is only the beginning of the clap there, and that severe noise, close by us, the end of it."

From all he sees, the observer learns "who it is that sustains this noble fabrick of bodies," but his awareness of divinity remains general, and theological articulation waits its turn after the hard definitive words that register a thing just as it is perceived. Affective terms obtrude cautiously: "Red is the highest, strongest, harshest colour, . . . blue more gentle and weak." A long entry on diversification in the form of trees speaks broadly of the creator's originating role, but reverts to naturalistic explanation to describe the accidents which bring about a tree's irregular form, so that "one branch grows out here, and another there, without any order."

What theology these notes contain is buried and as yet uncultivated. The observer speaks of some branches having "advantages," though "we need not perplex ourselves to find out, what should give one a

greater advantage of growth than another," an attitude of acceptance
Edwards later developed toward the divine arbitrariness in damning
and electing. An opinion that trees now are but branches of the first
trees, "although the communication with the original branch has
ceased," bears fruit in the theory of identity with which Edwards
later supports the doctrine of inherited original sin. But as in the
most successful Transcendentalist rhetoric, spiritual implication is a
soft dew on natural things, as in this microcosmic version of the
analogies of creation, the first organic metaphor, perhaps, in our
literature: "We had as good think that branches grow out of the
ground without seeds, as that branches grow out of the trunk without
buds; for the buds are but another sort of seeds that cleave to the
tree, and the seeds are but another sort of buds, that drop into the
ground."

In *Images or Shadows of Divine Things,* however, the doctrinal
Edwards crowds nature very closely. Lightning intimates the wrath
of God, young trees are more easily bent than old trees, the pure
and pleasant but feeble color blue reflects the "holy pusilanimity" of
the saints. The actual trees whose growth patterns Edwards had
sketched in knowing detail, become now a single emblem revealing
the growth of the church. A branch "that shot forth later" is no
disconcerting accident, but the apostle Paul, who contributes, rather
asymmetrically, to "the bigger part of the future tree." The difference,
evidently, between Edwards's initial survey of the natural world and
his later catalogue of heuristic images is the change in him. He sees
sermons rather than curious deep holes in stones because he is no
longer the same viewer. In Edwards, as in Emerson and Thoreau,
nature is constituted by the eye, and the unregenerate man sees
dimly, as if stumbling through a lovely garden at night, whereas
the man infused with grace "views the garden when the sunlight
shines upon it."

While an important document in the history of American symbolism,
the *Images* promise more in their theory than Edwards's 212 entries
achieve. Convinced, as Thoreau was, that in an account of true things
the mill-dam would not appear, Edwards hopes to see the real through
material shadows. As the natural fact becomes more clear and evident,
the mind apprehends more intimately the spiritual fact for which it
is an image and inferior analogy. Refracted colors adumbrate the
spectrum of divine graces and their "consentaneity" with each other,
but to know further that colors converge in an original whiteness is
to discover something of the nature of God's essential holiness. More-

over, nature is not only ontological type but eschatological type as well. To see into the spiritual meaning of the world is to see the end for which the world was created, and which is always being accomplished in the regeneration of souls. An evangelical image, such as the heart, is the focus of both a vertical and horizontal reading: it argues the centrality of the affections in religious experience, and, appearing first in the embryo, shadows the process by which a new spiritual man is formed, indeed the process of all history, "the end of all things and the crown of all things."

Despite their objective emphasis, the *Images* also constitute a form of spiritual autobiography, as Perry Miller observed in editing them. It requires no elaborate biographical demonstration to detect in a number of entries Edwards's immersion in the turmoil of revivalism, which he both fostered and defended, and the reflection of his alternately hopeful and despairing attitudes as awakened emotions took their course. Through an extended sequence he reiterates the theme of trial: the survival of a winter crop, the burning of useless branches, the winnowing of wheat from chaff; lofty structures, he states, are the most vulnerable to thunder and lightning and topple easily. But the observer too is being tried in his own effort to find a scheme of deliverance in these shadows. Too well acquainted with corruption, he sinks to its level, finds "man's inwards full of dung and filthiness," the world "all over dirty," "all a cheat . . . nothing but death, a land of darkness, or darkness itself." When it comes, then, regeneration must be more than a private spiritual event occurring in the history of individuals. The bringing of life out of death is the dynamic of all change, shadowed by the moist and regenerative spring; "and [earth's] filthiness never so much appears as then . . . ."

No single autobiographical plot stands clear in a catalogue of so many items, but increment and cross-reference gradually advance the integration Edwards accomplishes, not simply as the world's observer, but as participant in the trial which the world shadows forth. As in Whitman's juxtaposition of grave and blade of grass, Edwards's Image 21 observes the difference between spiritual life and death, looks back at the rotting corpse of Image 1 and anticipates Image 212, the last, which finds in the vastness and beauty of the world an image of the spiritual magnificence being wrought out of it. The integrating principle of Edwards's vision, which he called grace, and to which he attributed the "wonderful alteration" that defined his experience, redeems the first image of the catalogue and partakes of the beauty of the last. Their "stupendous antagonism," to use Emerson's phrase, is carried forward in the work of Edwards's mature mind, which like Emerson's, pounds both strings to hear their harmony.

III

The success of efforts to publish a sermon that Edwards gave at Boston in 1731 no doubt confirmed his feeling that in articulating the doctrine of God's sovereignty he filled a great spiritual need in New England. Though elaborately stated, the proposition of *God Glorified in the Work of Redemption* is in itself simple and self-evident. In their regeneration, the redeemed depend on God for everything, "and are dependent on him every way." Turn where it will, the soul finds God at every door, the cause of the good which the soul enjoys in a gracious union, the medium by which it is obtained, and the good itself which has been conveyed. Or in the more technical language which Edwards went on to develop, God is both objective and inherent good for man, good in himself as well as by the saint's perceiving participation in his holiness.

Despite its publication, Edwards may have wondered whether the key doctrinal word of his sermon, the complex idea of "dependence," had really been heard and understood. In a later, related sermon, *Justification by Faith Alone* (1734*), he concludes by observing that men are "exceeding prone" to trust their own goodness and exceeding dull to apprehend any such idea as a dependent goodness. He thus restates in religious terms his philosophical assertion that derived minds have their being from un-derived mind. Those who are rational may be convinced abstractly that what they perceive is wholly of the mind, yet have great difficulty accepting an idealism which stipulates our moment-by-moment re-creation in the divine mind and our liability, on the same basis, to annihilation. Edwards did not, of course, threaten his hearers with annihilation, thinking it a form of punishment inferior to the spiritual death which the soul would suffer in eternal association with its own moral choices. But the fearsome sermons in which Edwards has always seemed so objectionable represent an alternative strategy to the rational exposition of man's dependency which he had attempted in public lecture.

Edwards's convicting art methodically troubles his hearers' existence

* Dates given for sermons are dates of delivery.

nerve by nerve, inculcating a dreadful physical knowledge of human vulnerability. The best known of these sermons, *Sinners in the Hands of an Angry God* (1741), achieves in the attentive reader a state of kinesthetic trepidation beyond anything the consciousness of a dangling spider might absorb. Conviction is also the primary strategy of such sermons as *Wicked Men Useful in Their Destruction Only* (1744), *The Justice of God in the Damnation of Sinners* (1734), and *The Future Punishment of the Wicked* (1741). The latter sermon, preached only a few months before *Sinners in the Hands of an Angry God*, isolates even more carefully the set of mind which frustrates a realization of spiritual peril. Out of his own experience, no doubt, Edwards guesses the sinner's ultimate evasion and represents it to him in dramatic form. *Evil perhaps, worthy to be punished, but no coward am I*, says the sinner; "if it shall come to that, that I must go to hell, I will bear it as well as I can." The preacher then becomes an impersonal observer in hell at the melting and vanishing of the sinner's resolution, "let a man be an infant, or a giant, it will all be one."

Edwards's convicting devices have about them the certainty of scientific demonstration. The sinner's culpability and the downward pull of gravity are indistinguishably part of the same reality, and are observed with the same coldness of tone. An evangelist rather than a moralist, Edwards finds his antagonist in the sinner's indifference rather than his sins. This is nowhere more clear than when he fastens the congregation's attention on the conditions of its own hearing. It is persons seated in the Enfield meeting house who go to hell, not nameless scriptural sinners. And to his own congregation: "You have heard such things many times: you are old soldiers, and have been too much used to the roaring of heaven's cannon, to be frighted at it." Having exhausted his resources against such hardheartedness, the preacher then leaves the sinner to his fate in the measured phrases of a final condemnation. Not the least surprising thing about the *Farewell Sermon* (1750) Edwards preached to the Northampton congregation that dismissed him is his looking forward in a last chilling phrase to "the day of infallible and of the unalterable sentence," while refusing utterly to expend energy to turn his hearers from their fate.

To praise Edwards's rhetorical skill in these sermons, while making excuses for his themes, sacrifices much to a narrow notion of the literary. His Swiftian pessimism, more pronounced than ever in a sermon of August 1750, argues convincingly that men achieve peace at the price of reflection: "It concerns him if he would keep alive his peace, to stupefy his mind and deceive himself, and to imagine things to be otherwise than as they are." As Edwards was increasingly aware, these observations applied in a special way to the developing American culture, which by Emerson's time had gained "a bad name for superficialness. Great men, great nations, have not been boasters and buffoons, but perceivers of the terror of life," said Emerson, though he was himself of more than one mind on the subject of boasting. Stephen Crane resembles Edwards more closely in the ferocity with which he exposes the mind's egocentric distortion of reality in its own favor. Crane's definition of man as metaphysical coxcomb, lurching with dumb confidence into a screaming storm, agrees in detail with Edwards's depiction of the "absurd figure . . . who, in a thunder-storm should expect a flash of lightning on his head or his breast, and should go forth sword in hand to oppose it." The charges Edwards and Crane bring against human nature are less disturbing, however, than the coldness and implacability of their rage, beyond any doctrine or conviction. In Edwards it is as if the speaker's own beatitude depended upon the congregation accepting their condemnation, some unspoken identification taking place between his convicted but always resurgent former self and the unconverted sinners seated before him.

IV

In the more abstract convicting works of his late career, Edwards develops an intellectual extension of the sermons he preached through two awakenings at Northampton. Through the late forties, the certainty had grown in him that if the "modern, prevailing notions" of those he called Arminians should ever gain dominance, the next Great Awakening, hence the next stage in history, might be pushed off beyond any man's sight. Success in maintaining the will's freedom to determine itself would give these modern divines "an impregnable castle" from which to assault all Calvinist doctrine, including original sin, and if original sin, then the doctrines associated with redemption from it. From the perspective of an Indian mission in Stockbridge, Edwards saw the enemy as no distinct doctrinal group, but as a moralistic attitude common among deists, extending high and low in the Church of England, and spreading its infection to America. Thus, while an Arminian might grant moral imperfection, agreeing that men often choose evil, he argued that such a choice was not by necessity, that man was free to choose the good, and that in this struggle lay the essence of the moral life. Praise and blame, salvation or damnation, would be rendered accordingly, and to convert this significant drama into a dark necessity was to undo the meaning of moral terms.

Edwards's position in the *Freedom of the Will* (1754) must be judged, not by his debating strategies, but in the integrity of his entire view, which proceeds from the doctrine of divine sovereignty. Theologically, Edwards is confident that God's will cannot be frustrated in either the natural or moral events of history. Philosophically, he asserts "that nothing ever comes to pass without a cause." To propose a will that determines itself is to exempt a single feature of human experience from a law that prevails everywhere else. If, as Emerson said in his account of *Fate*, "one fantastical will could prevail over the law of things, it were all one as if a child's hand could pull down the sun." If the will can have effects without having been affected, moral choices float free of any self, and moral agents bear no comparison with one another, just as no rock is "more vicious than other rocks, because rattlesnakes have happened oftener to crawl over it."

Edwards expressed his own sense of things in the sort of prose that characterizes his naturalistic observations: "The involuntary changes in the succession of our ideas, though the cause may not be observed, have as much a cause, as the changeable motions of the motes that float in the air, or the continual, infinitely various, successive changes of the unevennesses on the surfaces of the water." So far as anything has meaning, it has meaning within, not outside, these successive changes. To make a virtue of freedom from their influence is to aspire to be outside history, as Hester Prynne does, for instance, in urging her lover to be someone other than Arthur Dimmesdale. The urge to isolate a vivid experience of Now would have seemed a great delusion to Edwards.

Edwards resented charges that his arguments were all metaphysical obfuscation of plain moral sense. By the commonest sense available to him, he said, "I find that in innumerable things I can do as I will," but that, as for experiencing a will that determined itself, "I declare, I know nothing in myself, by experience, of this nature." The question evidently was, why did it please him to will in one way rather than another, since he was arguing that, barring physical hindrance, a man always satisfies his inclinations? His answer was neither entirely original nor a simple recapitulation of traditional Christian thought. The will always is "as the greatest apparent good, or as what appears most agreeable, is" said Edwards, attempting by grammatical equivalency between subject and object to indicate that apprehending something as good and inclining toward it by will are the same thing.

Despite disagreement with Locke over some details, Edwards is not reluctant to lean heavily on Locke's psychology in suggesting that the will is as the mind is. Yet the materialism and solipsism lurking in this equation can be fatal to the religious instinct, as Emerson confesses freely in his essay, *Experience*. The universe will simply wear the color of one's mood; the soul becomes a kitten chasing its own tail; and temperament "puts all divinity to route." Though he would gladly have allowed "the most to the will of man," Emerson found with Edwards that deliverance, if it came at all, came by grace. "The ardors of piety agree at last with the coldest skepticism." Melville, too, knew "Edwards on the Will," and in *Moby Dick* establishes inexorable relations between perception and willing. Ahab's fate is his idea of Moby Dick, though his speculative mind may wander to the hearth-side; and it is the resilience of Ishmael's reverent skepticism which floats him free of the *Pequod's* vortex. American writers are, of course, frequently drawn to the theme of freedom versus fate, but their fleshing out of its existential dimension would not have dismayed Edwards. He left it for others "particularly to enumerate all things pertaining to the mind's view of the objects of volition, which have influence on their appearing agreeable to the mind," and could easily have regarded *The Portrait of a Lady* as such a treatise. Isabel Archer's sense of freedom—"I was perfectly free; it was impossible to do anything more deliberate"—is precisely what Edwards allows; while the artist himself, enumerating all that pertains to the mind's view, unfolds the inevitability of Isabel's choosing Gilbert Osmond.

There are no forced marriages in hell, Edwards is saying. The will is as much wedded to the evil choices for which it is condemned as it is to the desire to spend eternity in a delightful place—both choices proceeding from the self-love of natural being. One must distinguish between Edwards's rhetorical sinner, who reeks of corruption in the convicting sermons, and the natural man of his treatises, to whom heaven will never be a true motive because he has no affective apprehension of that in which divinity consists. Evil is privative in both a philosophical and psychological sense. It is both the absence of holiness and the want of an inclination to holiness, a "moral inability." The term suggests the error of imagining Edwards's Necessity dragging sinners from defilement to defilement. Even fallen nature chooses a great many goods which, objectively considered, overlap with those chosen by the saint. But lacking a "certain divine spiritual taste," fallen man can never be motivated by "the loveliness of the moral excellency of divine things." How can a man choose love who has no idea of it? How can a man love perfectly who has not been loved perfectly?

That the possibility of perfect love existed and was being diffused through time to a final consummation in eternity was Edwards's indirect answer to the charge that he made God the author of sin. His logic could not, at the last moment, turn aside from concluding that God peopled hell by communicating his holiness arbitrarily to a portion of intelligent creation, while judging the guilt of the rest. His argument by analogy with the sun, which does not actually cause the darkness from which it is absent, limps badly. One is left at last with Edwards's unargued sense that any felt awareness of the difference between darkness and light argues the necessity of their being defined against each other. In the exclusionary habit of his mind, there lay a necessity as rigorous in its demands as the requirements of divine justice. That portion of the self which must die to accomplish the new man shares the fate of the damned, and like them, must be periodically reminded of the reasons for its sacrifice. "A sort of genie is with man," Edwards remarked in his private writings, "that accompanies him and attends him wherever he goes, so that a man has conversation with himself."

By his own standards, though not those of his opponents, Edwards leaves the sinner in possession of considerable human dignity. The god-like in man, his understanding, remains inviolate even while obeying its own gravity. And man's moral kinship with Adam is reestablished on a new basis in Edwards's defense of *The Great Christian Doctrine of Original Sin* (1758). On the other hand, Arminian talk of sincerity and man's doing "the best he can" seems to Edwards to have the opposite tendency. It negates by selective excuse-making the fallen state which all men share, and it posits an insubstantial version of human identity. Even if the mind, by being before itself, could determine which ideas would become pleasing to it, it would still lack mastery of its own identity, which consists only secondarily in the content of consciousness, however supplied. Minds persist in being one with themselves because identity is communicated to them, not because of a continuity of consciousness, whose duplicate may be imagined in another mind not one's own. For Edwards it is not created consciousness that binds its days together in a special act of self-realization. There is only the ultimately real, renewing the initial creation from instant to instant. In an ancient tree, there is perhaps "not one atom the very same" with the seedling, yet an identity of properties has always been communicated to it.

By thinking of men together out of time, God relates them in time to the guilt of the one called Adam. Hence it is not unreasonable "that men should be ashamed of things done by others, in whom they are nearly concerned." History was absurd as a congeries of moralistic anecdotes loosely strung together. More plausibly, it could be read as the narrative of a single community's guilt, even by those who never fired a shot or whipped a slave.

V

Such a theme was plain enough. The more difficult and intriguing historical questions for Edwards concerned the purposive themes which God was wresting from the world as part of the work of redemption. In essence, these questions were already answered in scripture. But even learned readers might differ about the meaning of the apocalyptic prophecies, especially concerning the thousand-year period which was to follow the defeat of the beast (the church of Rome), a millennium prior to the final judgment during which Satan would be bound and Christ would reign with his saints. Whether the millennium would take place in secular history or implied instead a spiritual reigning was a question of interpretation, as was any estimate of the distance between the present time and the beginning of those last days. Edwards's eschatology has been pointed to as a departure from Calvin's view of the spiritual nature of the thousand years and thus a harbinger of later American utopianism. It is true that Edwards looked forward to a golden age of holiness on earth, accompanied by general temporal prosperity, health, long life, and a global diffusion of learning. Yet he finally attributes spiritual meaning to the apocalyptic expression "new heavens and new earth," and observes its significance in all ages in the converting, justifying, sanctifying, and glorifying of souls. The millennial earth would be a near approach of image to spiritual reality, but in authentic conversion, one beholds the very dynamic of history. The saints "act grace." To the regenerate, the apocalypse is already essentially present in their "new sense of things."

Edwards's understanding of history has, then, multiple dimensions, rather than the single one indicated by his literal acceptance of biblical event and prophecy. To a modern historian like Peter Gay, Edwards's recitation of fundamentalist belief in his *History of the Work of Redemption* (1774) is a pathetically naive substitute for historical thinking. But through the period of the awakenings, Edwards participated in, described, and evaluated a portion of American history for which he had much better information than he received from the Bible concerning the plagues of Egypt or the fall of Jericho. In such works as *A Faithful Narrative of the Surprising Work of God* (1737) and *Some Thoughts Concerning the Present Revival of Religion in New England* (1742), Edwards contributes more than has yet been appreciated to an understanding of mass movements based on a reorganization of the emotions, that is, to a psychological understanding of history.

"I humbly conceive," said Edwards, "that the affections of the soul are not properly distinguished from the will." Long before an attempt would be made to describe the sensibility of an age or to trace a revolution or expansion of consciousness, Edwards was saying that the inclination of a period was according to its emotions, and though he did not write history in *The Distinguishing Marks of a Work of the Spirit of God* (1741) or in his *Treatise Concerning Religious Affections* (1746), he demonstrated the difficulty in any epoch of isolating its essential and durable inclination from ephemeral counterfeits. His balanced view, as judge of a reactionary formalism on one side and emotional anarchy on the other, was achieved with special difficulty, in tension with his own commitment to the movement. He half-hoped and was half-convinced, he thought it "not unlikely," that God intended present events to be "the beginning or forerunner of something vastly great." But England's capture of Cape Breton in 1745, depriving the dominions of Antichrist "of a very great part of their fish," proved not to be the faint signal of the millennium that Edwards saw in it. If Edwards was too much involved in the drama to speak of its dénouement without bias, there is, nevertheless, a remarkable steadiness of view in his treatment of the substantial issues of the Great Awakening, and it is here that his example as critic-historian of consciousness is most instructive for our own time.

As the awakening of 1740–41 accumulated its hectic momentum, promotion was less a problem than defense. Yet the appropriate grounds of defense were not immediately evident in an affair "so new that there has not been time and experience enough to give birth to rules to people's conduct, and the writings of divines do not afford rules to direct us in such a state of things." It is unlikely that rules for judgment could have been equally acceptable to friends and opposers of the movement, since those who spoke from within claimed a renovated sense of experience radically different from the view of critics. And if this difference was too subtle for outsiders, the distinction of generations was not. Edwards understood well that the work bore "an awful aspect upon those that are advanced in years." The Spirit, he said, "has taken the young people, and has cast off the old and stiff-necked generation." Edwards had in mind not only the young in whom the Spirit had so visibly brought about a "strange flexibleness" and marked concern about the things of religion. He spoke, too, as defender of those "instruments" chosen to carry on the work, "mere babes in age and standing" admittedly, whose "imprudent zeal and censorious spirit" were regrettable, but a necessary scourge when "ministers and people have sunk into a deep sleep." The Great Awakening is too complicated in its origins to be called simply a youth movement. Both Edwards and another leading revivalist, Gilbert Tennent, turned forty in 1734, and were in fact two years older than Charles Chauncy, their leading critic. But in the same year, two admiring followers of Edwards, Samuel Hopkins and David Brainerd, were nineteen and twenty-five, respectively, and leading figures in the awakening were of the same age group: Joseph Bellamy was twenty-four, Samuel Buell twenty-five, James Davenport twenty-seven, and Samuel Davies twenty. More widely known than any of these, through Edwards's promotional narrative of her spiritual experiences, was four-year-old Phebe Bartlet, as clear a demonstration as he could make that the Spirit was circumventing those old soldiers who resisted his sermons so stonily.

Looking across these divisions of age and sensibility in *Some Thoughts Concerning the Present Revival*, Edwards seems confident at first of his ability to obviate differences by reason or rhetoric or both. But his own arguments illustrate the great difficulty of the attempt. Discriminating scrupulously among words, as always, out of respect for them, he confronted the possibility that his clarity might assist no one to understand the language of the movement, which was not always verbal. "There is a language in actions," Edwards maintained, "and in some cases, much more clear and convincing than in words." The conveying of clear and distinct ideas may be inhibited rather than assisted by words. An experiencing soul speaks more effectively than "the dull narration of one which is inexperienced and insensible himself." Yet the behavior of awakened congregations was precisely what was objectionable. Read then for the spiritual sense of the action-as-word, Edwards advised, and disregard its departure from convention. The disorder on the movement's surface must be distinguished from the powerful ordering force within it, which first breaks things before making them new. "We are to consider that the end for which God pours out his Spirit, is to make men holy, and not to make them politicians." God has not bound himself, Edwards pointed out, "to increase civil prudence in proportion to the degrees of spiritual light."

The rational sensibility that Edwards addressed defined itself by its regard for decorum and was ill-prepared to comprehend history which bypasses "men of wealth and figure," is ignored by the civil government, and can best be observed in "multitudes of illiterate people." Yet this is invariably the Spirit's manner of operation, to begin "at the lower end" of things, in the "utmost, meanest, youngest and weakest part," and "in the wilderness, where nothing grows." Further, the rational attitude manifested its own unreason by attempting to confine a creative process to the standards of historical precedent. What so constricted a consciousness could not accept was the identity between the original creation, when there were "new wonders every day in the sight of the angels," and the ongoing re-creation of men in history: "While those morning-stars sang together, new scenes were opened, till the whole was finished—so it is in the progress of the new creation."

To extend awareness of possibility and inculcate the language of experience could best be accomplished by focusing history directly on the reader's mind. The core of psychological history must be the inward events of a single mind, related, ideally, by one capable of giving them names and of understanding their significance in a larger framework. Edwards combined both roles in himself in the *Personal Narrative*. In the *Faithful Narrative* he made readers present as he described the Spirit's work in the souls of Abigail Hutchinson and Phebe Bartlet. In *Some Thoughts Concerning the Present Revival*, he turned to a mature Christian, his wife Sarah, for a variant of the same process, one so powerful in its unfolding "that the soul remained in a kind of heavenly elysium, and did as it were swim in the rays of Christ's love . . . ." Aware perhaps that he had published no male experience of regeneration, Edwards took precious time after David Brainerd's death in 1747 to prepare an analytical *Account* (1749) of the young missionary's life from his autobiographical writings. That life began, Brainerd wrote, from a time when, "as I was walking in a dark thick grove, unspeakable glory seemed to open to the view and apprehension of my soul . . . . I felt myself in a new world . . . ." In all his presentations of spiritual biography as essential history, Edwards maintained the same thesis. If the reader brings together the idea conveyed by these "particular instances" of abiding faith, and the idea he has of fantastical "enthusiasm," he will find they deny each other. Or should an unscrupulous opposer care so little for words as to call faith enthusiasm, Edwards too could feign recklessness: "what cause then has the world to prize and pray for this blessed whimsicalness and these benign sort of vapours."

The *Treatise Concerning Religious Affections* removes any doubt whether Edwards entertained a clear notion of what constituted "vain, pernicious enthusiasm." A more considered view of the awakening than anything else he wrote, the treatise goes beyond the biographical presentations of his earlier reporting. It is, in a sense, a double-dimensioned and impersonal biography of the saint and his deceptive double, the hypocrite, permitting a view from one angle of the gracious affections rooted in a principle of holiness, exposing from another the varieties of self-love which frequently constitute religiosity but have nothing to do with grace.

Edwards's accumulated knowledge of ephemeral spiritual experience makes a further contribution to the history of the American consciousness. He shows that, by definition, the egocentric enthusiast is a minor historical event—"self is the first foundation of his joy"—but the type itself is perennial. Believing himself guided "by immediate direction from heaven," he is "incorrigible and impregnable in all his conduct." Alienated from the community of common faith, the enthusiast goes into "unjustifiable separations . . . under pretence of setting up a pure church." And in the separated society thus established, there prevails a distorted anticipation of that millennial state for which the forsaken community also yearns, "a kind of union and affection arising from self-love, occasioned by their agreeing in those things wherein they greatly differ from all others," one sect in particular, Edwards observes, "calling themselves the *family of love.*"

VI

The incisiveness and intelligence of Edwards's observations of history do not, of course, make him a historian. More appropriately, he bears comparison with American writers like Poe and Henry Adams, who move out from an intense and sometimes fatalistic subjectivity to construct a vast, metaphysically ambitious correlative of the soul. Personal metaphors stretch thinly, however, over the beckoning extent of space, and Edwards's vaster version of things, no less ambitious than others, has the benefit of a broad tradition of Christian apocalyptic thought, from which it inherits substance. In *The Nature of True Virtue* and its companion piece, *A Dissertation Concerning the End*

for which God Created the World, both posthumously published in
1765, and in his writings on the Trinity, Edwards attempts to plot
the complex interrelations between events in the soul and the larger
developmental process which seemed to be entering a decisive stage in
America. His question remains relevant: if, ideally, the American is a
new man, toward what end is his regeneration?

As moral philosopher, Edwards first clears the way for larger
speculation by separating the grain of true virtue from all the chaff of
self-love. The title of his treatise appears to promise a book of moral
advice, or a hymn to goodness, but it is primarily a dispassionate over-
turning of a great many eighteenth-century assertions about the in-
nately virtuous conscience and man's natural moral sensibility. Do
men reject vice out of a benevolent nature or out of some deeper vice?
Assaulted by the contempt associated with drunkenness, gluttony,
cowardice, or sloth, self-love seeks to avoid disapprobation, and perhaps ill health, by "moral" reform, achieving frequent success among
the resolute and well-educated. The morality of the white European
is thus all veneer, as the naturalists would later say, and "as any one
would be convinced, perhaps more effectually than in most other
ways, if they had opportunity of any considerable acquaintance with
American savages and their children." Does the man of sensibility
weep for others' misfortunes? "Men may pity others under exquisite
torment, when yet they would have been grieved if they had seen their
prosperity."

In true virtue, there is no such imbalance, and the beauty of its
harmonies calls for description in aesthetic terms. But as a beauty be-
longing to beings that have will as well as perception, true virtue is no
less moral than aesthetic. Edwards would have observed internal
harmony, but no virtue, in the icy collectedness of self-concern in the
"beautiful mind" of Gilbert Osmond. The moral term for beauty is, of
course, love, extended to nothing short of being in general as its object
and impelled by a motive of absolute selflessness: that something is, or
rather, by reason of everything's being. Edwards does not offer his
definition as a moral precept. Created mind cannot be instructed to
love what it cannot encompass, and for this reason *The Nature of True
Virtue,* taken by itself, is a disheartening work. It defines a standard of
virtue which only God could satisfy. Beholding himself, God is perfectly united to being in general; comprehending his own being, he
has the perfect motive to love. Hence the beauty of God's virtue and
the virtue of his being are absolute and indistinguishable.

Any such definition of deity, Edwards admits, derives at first,
crudely, from our minds, and then is revised upwards to infinity by a

denial of limits, mutability, "and other imperfections." Yet defining of this sort tends to make the absolute good static, and unknowable in any human terms. This was not the sense of things to an observer once pleased by spiders marching through seasons of time and exhilarated that the phenomenon existed to the consciousness in which he found himself. To such a mind, God would be a form of energy communicating itself. "I don't intend to explain the Trinity," Edwards said, defining the triune God, however, so as to define the dynamic of everything else.

When God views himself, has an idea of himself, his knowing differs from man's in the important respect that the idea is not simply a shadow of reality but the thing itself. Divine self-knowledge reproduces divinity, not as a lesser reflection, but as the substance again of the divine mind. Men may have children and brain-children, but only God doubles himself, and in so doing exists thirdly as a relationship; "an Infinitely holy & sacred energy arises . . . . The deity becomes all act, the divine essence itself flows out & is as it were breathed forth in Love and Joy." To say that the Spirit of God is communicated to the soul as grace is, for Edwards, to say that a created mind participates in an act of love which is the primal energy of all things, that which underlies the history of the spider as well as the history of nations.

Theoretically, God's action is complete in himself, who has no need of applause or supporting actors. But delighting in the expression of his fullness of glory, he does, in fact, express it, most appropriately to that which has perception and will. "For intelligent beings are created to be the consciousness of the universe, that they may perceive what God is and does." God's flowing forth to created consciousness is, then, the end of creation, and what God communicates out of his own nature is that propensity of heart toward all being which Edwards holds beyond the reach of natural man. True virtue is approached, perhaps, by love to larger and larger systems of being, but the natural man inhabits a closed and finished universe, whatever its size, within limits imposed by the gravity of self-love. The regenerate may not have all of being in an immediate view, but their loving is of a different sort. One is a closed system, the other has been broken open; and because open to infinity, constantly expanding. The principle of effulgence has become central to the saint, and forever seeks limits which, to his joy, do not exist.

Morally and psychologically, Edwards describes "a kind of enlargement of the mind, whereby it so extends itself so as to take others into a man's self." Metaphysically, he projects a spiritual reality for which the expanding universe is shadow. Physical imagination comes into play to set perfect union with God "at an infinite height above us." The sanctified soul, already bound into the divine energy, may be imagined approaching the perfect union between Father and Son, "rising higher and higher through that infinite duration, and that not with constantly diminishing (but perhaps an increasing) celerity; though there never will be any particular time when it can be said already to have come to such a height."

Edwards may still at this point be described as a prisoner of doctrine, but it is important in saying so to have a clear and distinct idea of doctrine. He may also be described as an early custodian of the conviction shared by a number of American writers, that the "axial lines of life," as Saul Bellow calls them, are not the exclusive property of men of figure and station. "When striving stops, there they are as a gift. . . . Truth, love, peace, bounty, usefulness, harmony!" The god-ambition can be fatal, distorting, a counterfeit, Augie March realizes, "but the man himself, finite and taped as he is, can still come where the axial lines are. He will be brought into focus." And Bellow's passive voice continues to say something of man's dependency on the lines of force that identify him.

Jonathan Edwards was certain that at the same time the saints were ascending through space, "this world shall be set on fire, and be turned into a great furnace," leaving other men to the inheritance of their own nature. In the final decades of the twentieth century, with their potential for a flowing forth of the human phenomenon or its self-destructive implosion, neither of Edwards's images is likely to lose force. If anything, they sum up our alternatives more clearly than ever, and argue the relevance of Edwards's contribution to a realistic self-knowledge and an attendant though uncertain possibility of regeneration.

BIBLIOGRAPHY

Editions

Images or Shadows of Divine Things. Edited by Perry Miller. New Haven, Conn.: Yale University Press, 1948.
"The Mind" of Jonathan Edwards: A Reconstructed Text. Edited by Leon Howard. Berkeley: University of California Press, 1964.
The Philosophy of Jonathan Edwards from His Private Notebooks. Edited by Harvey G. Townsend. University of Oregon Monographs, no. 2. Eugene, Oreg.: University of Oregon Press, 1955.

Representative Selections. Edited by Clarence H. Faust and Thomas H. Johnson. Revised ed. New York: Hill and Wang, 1962.
The Works of Jonathan Edwards. Edited by Perry Miller. 4 vols. to date. Vol. 1, *Freedom of the Will,* edited by Paul Ramsey. Vol. 2, *Religious Affections,* edited by John E. Smith. Vol. 3, *Original Sin,* edited by Clyde A. Holbrook. Vol. 4, *The Great Awakening,* edited by C. C. Goen. New Haven, Conn.: Yale University Press, 1957—.
The Works of Jonathan Edwards: With A Memoir of His Life. Edited by Sereno E. Dwight. 10 vols. New York: S. Converse, 1829–30.
The Works of President Edwards. Edited by Edward Williams and Edward Parsons. 8 vols. Leeds: Baines and Heaton, 1806–11. New edition: 8 vols., London: James Black, 1817. 2 vol. supplement: edited by Robert Ogle. Edinburgh: Ogle, Oliver, and Boyd, 1847. Reprint of the London edition and 2 vol. supplement, New York: Burt Franklin, 1968.
The Works of President Edwards. Edited by Samuel Austin. First American Edition. 8 vols. Worcester, Mass.: Isaiah Thomas, 1808–9. Reprinted "with valuable additions and a copious general index," 4 vols., New York: Leavitt and Trow, 1843. Another edition: 6 vols., including the Edinburgh supplement, New York: n.p., 1847.

Scholarship and Criticism

Aldridge, Alfred O. *Jonathan Edwards.* New York: Washington Square Press, 1964.
Anderson, Wallace E. "Immaterialism in Jonathan Edwards' Early Philosophical Notes." *Journal of the History of Ideas* 25 (1964): 181–200.
Bushman, Richard L. "Jonathan Edwards as Great Man: Identity, Conversion, and Leadership in the Great Awakening." *Soundings* 52 (1969): 15–46.
Cherry, Conrad. *The Theology of Jonathan Edwards: A Reappraisal.* Garden City, N.Y.: Doubleday, 1966.
Delattre, Roland André. *Beauty and Sensibility in the Thought of Jonathan Edwards.* New Haven, Conn.: Yale University Press, 1968.
Miller, Perry. *Jonathan Edwards.* New York: Sloane, 1949.
Winslow, Ola E. *Jonathan Edwards, 1703–1758: A Biography.* New York: Macmillan, 1940.

7

Benjamin Franklin

J. A. LEO LEMAY

BEGINNINGS: THE SILENCE DOGOOD ESSAYS

In 1722, at sixteen years of age, Benjamin Franklin wrote the first essay series in America, and showed that he was already the peer of Boston's literary men. His Silence Dogood series appeared in his brother's newspaper, *The New England Courant*. As he testifies in the *Autobiography*, and as all authorities have repeatedly pointed out, an important model for the style and content of the series was the *Spectator*. But the influence of Addison and Steele and other contemporary English writers on the young Franklin has been over-stated, whereas the influence of the members of Boston's own Hell-Fire Club (as Increase Mather dubbed the *Courant* wits), who ridiculed the religious and political establishment in the pages of America's first literary newspaper, has not been given sufficient notice. The major single influence on the content and style of Franklin's earliest writings was the prose of Nathaniel Gardner, a tanner, minor Boston politician, partner of the poet Matthew Adams, brother-in-law of the poet and wit Joseph Green, and the most prolific writer for the *New England Courant*.

Gardner's multitude of writings, under a variety of pseudonyms, confused and bewildered his opponents. In the thirty-four issues of the *Courant* that preceded Franklin's series, Gardner contributed a literary,

J. A. Leo Lemay, associate professor of English at the University of California, Los Angeles, has published a calendar of American poetry in colonial magazines and newspapers, a biography of Franklin's friend Ebenezer Kinnersley, and essays on Franklin and on the colonial poets Richard Lewis and Robert Bolling. Most recent is his work on men of letters in colonial Maryland. He was the first secretary of the Modern Language Association's Early American Literature Group, 1969–72, and has been elected to the American Antiquarian Society.

deistic essay signed "Zerubbabel Tindal"; a character of a miser; a
satire of millenarianism; a mock-advertisement; a burlesque of religious interpretations of natural phenomena; an essay on morality; a
letter in favor of inoculation, mocking the style of Increase Mather; an
attack on Cotton Mather and Samuel Penhallow, signed "Tom. Pen-
shallow"; letters under different pseudonyms in successive issues carrying on mock arguments; political essays on the rights and privileges of
men and Englishmen; a letter signed "S. B." from a husband complaining of a shrewish wife; dialogues; a spoof of the courting patterns
of young sparks; a satire on clergy and witchcraft; an essay signed
"Hortensia" by a supposedly mistreated wife; various replies to Increase Mather's attacks; a burlesque of religion signed "Johannes
Clericus"; an essay against idleness; a number of mock war-of-the-
sexes hoaxes, usually under feminine pseudonyms; and many others.
Franklin's writings, in style and content, are more similar to Gardner's
than to any other author, English or American. Moreover, these issues
of the newspaper must have been practically memorized by the young
apprentice (Benjamin Franklin), who heard the contributions discussed before they were printed, and who "after having work'd in
composing the Types and printing off the Sheets . . . was employ'd to
carry the Papers thro' the Streets to the Customers," and who eagerly
learned the public's reactions to the essays.

In the first three Silence Dogood essays, Franklin characterizes the
loquacious widow whose given name humorously reverses her ruling
passion and whose family name suggests that she is a version of Cotton Mather, Boston's most notable busy-body, and author of a popular
book, *Essays to Do Good*. Some contemporaries must have recognized
that Franklin borrowed Mather's periphrasis for a working-man, a
"Leather Apron Man," for use in the second paragraph of the first
essay. Even without recognizing that the essays mock Mather, one
sees that they ridicule the pious rhetoric and somber world-view of
the Mathers and other religious people. In the third paragraph, on the
author's birth, the archetypally humorous situation of the father's
predicament at the birth of his child and an extended series of para-
doxically witty antitheses spoof the religious clichés:

> At the time of my Birth, my Parents were on Ship-board in their
> Way from London to N. England. My Entrance into this trouble-
> some World was attended with the Death of my Father, a Mis-
> fortune, which tho' I was not then capable of knowing, I shall
> never be able to forget; for as he, poor Man, stood upon the Deck
> rejoycing at my Birth, a merciless Wave entered the Ship, and in
> one Moment carry'd him beyond Reprieve. Thus, was the *first*

Day which I saw, the *last* that was seen by my Father; and thus was my disconsolate Mother at once made both a *Parent* and a *Widow*. (1 : 9–10*)

The witty style, the clever tone, the humorous reversal (the *father* dies at the birth of the child), and the comic situation—all burlesque the ostensible tragedy (carefully called a *misfortune*) and the religious clichés. So too in the following paragraph, Franklin has Silence Dogood use the shop-worn religious phrases to say that she "past [her] Infancy and Childhood in Vanity and Idleness," but undercuts the religious rhetoric and the sentimental portrayal of the mother's hardships by using a low diction that suggests she earned a living by taking off her underclothes: "my Indigent Mother, who was put to hard Shifts for a Living." (Another punning sexual allusion occurs in the second Dogood essay, where her "Reverend Master" is described as having "made several unsuccessful fruitless Attempts on the more topping Sort of our Sex.") Franklin also introduced the perennial subject of the war of the sexes in the first essay: "Thus I past away the Time with a Mixture of Profit and Pleasure, having no affliction but what was imaginary, and created in my own Fancy; as nothing is more common with us Women, than to be grieving for nothing, when we have nothing else to grieve for." (Franklin twice used a later version of this antimetabole in *Poor Richard,* July 1741 and October 1742.)

The fourth essay directly satirizes the clergy and the abuses of college education in an allegorical dream-vision. The fifth essay, on the war of the sexes, contains a feminist defense of women; implicitly satirizes the Biblical story of Adam's fall because of Eve by alleging that "Men have not only as great a Share in those Vices as the Women, but are likewise in a great Measure the Cause of that which the Women are guilty of"; and has a straw opponent salaciously and punningly claim that "when you have once reformed the Women, you will find it a much easier Task to reform the Men, because Women are the prime Causes of a great many Male Enormities." Silence Dogood argues that women work harder than men (citing, as proof, the proverb "Woman's Work is never done"), then grants for argument's sake that men work harder—and then blames men for the idleness of women: "Who is there that can be handsomely Supported in Affluence, Ease and Pleasure by another, that will chuse rather to earn his Bread by the Sweat of his own Brows? And if a Man will be so

---

* Where possible, quotations are taken from the great Franklin edition now being published, the Leonard W. Labaree et al. edition of *The Papers of Benjamin Franklin,* hereafter cited as *Papers.*

fond and so foolish, as to labour hard himself for a Livelehood, and suffer his Wife in the mean Time to sit in Ease and Idleness, let him not blame her if she does so, for it is in a great Measure his own Fault."

The sixth essay, on pride, anticipates later sentiments in *Poor Richard* and in the *Autobiography;* comments on the foolishness of people who wear expensive clothes, "By striving to appear rich they become really poor"; and lightly ridicules women's fashions. The most famous Dogood essay is the seventh, which satirizes the New England elegy, particularly one by Dr. John Herrick on Mrs. Mehitabel Kittle. John Gay had ridiculed the pastoral elegy in "The Shepherd's Week" (1714), which Franklin probably knew. The essay concludes with a mock "Receipt to make a New England Funeral ELEGY," reflecting Pope's "Receipt to make an Epic Poem" in *Guardian* no. 78. (Franklin quoted *Guardian* no. 80 at length in the fourteenth Dogood essay.) Franklin also probably composed the accompanying mocking poem (omitted from the Labaree edition of the *Papers*) entitled "To the Sage and Immortal Doctor H[erric]k, on his Incomparable ELEGY, upon the Death of Mrs. Mehitabell Kitel, &c. A Panegyrick."

After the seventh Dogood essay appeared, James Franklin was jailed by the Massachusetts authorities for a satirical jibe at the slowness of the government's ship in setting out to pursue pirates. Franklin therefore turned his eighth number into a defense of the freedom of the press—and in order not to make his defense actionable, reprinted almost the entire essay from a recent but already classic article on freedom of speech by Trenchard and Gordon from their "Cato's Letters" in the *London Journal*. Silence Dogood no. 9 attacked religious hypocrites who became politicians. Although it was ostensibly a sketch of the detested Royalist governor Joseph Dudley (d. 1720), it slyly pointed out the ministers' influence over politicians, hinting that James Franklin was incarcerated because the ministers were angry with him, and its real subject (which no one before has noted) was Chief Justice Samuel Sewall, who was eminently religious and who had at one time considered becoming a minister. This intimation was spelled out in an accompanying note, perhaps also by Franklin, which named Sewall responsible for jailing James Franklin, reminded the judge that he had confessed his error in the Salem witchcraft trials, and asked if he could not be wrong in this case also. This Dogood essay was the most direct and vicious satire penned by the young Franklin. He may have had it in mind when he wrote in his *Autobiography*: "During my Brother's Confinement, . . . I had the Management of the Paper, and I made bold to give our Rulers some Rubs in it, which my Brother took very kindly, while others began to consider me in an unfavourable Light, as a young Genius that had a Turn for Libelling and Satyr."*

With the tenth essay, Franklin left personal satire and, quoting for the second time from Defoe's *An Essay upon Projects* (1697), proposed his first public do-good project, a society for the relief of poor widows, urging that "the Country is ripe for many such *Friendly Societies,* whereby every Man might help another, without any Disservice to himself." The next essay spoofed virgin spinsters and concluded with an amusing indirect account of how wonderful sex is to an old virgin. Dogood no. 12, a moral essay on drunkenness, with a light, sure tone, opens by paradoxically claiming: "I doubt not but *moderate Drinking* has been improv'd for the Diffusion of Knowledge among the ingenious Part of Mankind." It ends with a word catalogue of the "Vocabulary of the Tiplers," which may have been suggested, as James Parton pointed out in his nineteenth-century biography of Franklin, by Rabelais.

The penultimate essay lightly satirizes Boston's night life, expertly using the naive persona of Silence Dogood, who does not recognize as prostitutes the group of women whom she describes. He also plays with the specialized vocabulary of sailors. The fourteenth and last essay again satirizes the clergy, particularly, by paralepsis, the Reverend Samuel Johnson and the other New Haven dissenting ministers who had just proclaimed their Anglicanism. This essay, reflecting Shaftesbury's *Letter Concerning Enthusiasm* (1708), suggests that the author was already a deist, though he cleverly quotes "two Ingenious Authors of the Church of England" in order to make his argument seem palatable. When he wrote "he that propagates the Gospel among *Rakes* and *Beaus* without reforming them" is ridiculous, his contemporaries probably recognized one last jibe at Cotton Mather, whose son Increase was a well-known rake.

Although Franklin wrote other essays for his brother's newspaper, these earliest ones are of special importance for their revelation of the young Franklin's style and thought. His subjects include education, feminism, a liberal Whiggish political philosophy, pride, public do-good projects, writing itself, and, most pervasively, a satire of clergy and of religion. These subjects reappear time and again in his writings. The essays also demonstrate several characteristic techniques that remained with him throughout his life, such as his reversal of the expected, and commonplace, opinion, as in his argument that men are responsible for the vices of women. He gave an early example of this

---

* Quotations from this work are from the Leonard W. Labaree et al. edition of *The Autobiography of Benjamin Franklin.*

habit of mind when he tells how he became a religious doubter: "Some Books against Deism fell into my Hands; they were said to be the Substance of Sermons preached at Boyle's Lectures. It happened that they wrought an Effect on me quite contrary to what was intended by them: For the Arguments of the Deists which were quoted to be refuted, appeared to me much stronger than the Refutations." Another characteristic is a fondness for rhetorical feats and for logic, including patently false logic. In the *Autobiography*, Franklin mentioned his early study of the Port Royal *Logic: or the Art of Thinking* (a copy of which was in the *New England Courant* office, as was also Bernard Lamy's *Art of Speaking*), and recounted his delight in the logical processes of the Socratic method: "And soon after I procur'd Xenophon's Memorable Things of Socrates, wherein there are many Instances of the same Method. I was charm'd with it, dropt my abrupt Contradiction, and positive Argumentation, and put on the humble Enquirer and Doubter." Another characteristic technique was Franklin's clever use of personae. Since he had not previously demonstrated his literary ability, it is not surprising that his brother and daily companions, the *Courant* wits, did not guess he was the author of the Dogood series, but his exploitation of the possibilities of the persona in his earliest essays is surprising. Just as he "put on" poses in life, so in his writings he selected the most suitable persona for the desired effect.

The Dogood essays also demonstrate a wide range of tone, from the bantering quality of the war-of-the-sexes essay to the subtle, though savage, assault on Sewall. An aspect of Franklin's style is revealed in his use of aphorisms, perhaps partly resulting from his hearing sermons in which Biblical texts and occasionally proverbs are used as proofs, and perhaps partly showing a delight in rhetorical adroitness. The most characteristic technique may be his consciousness of the implications of style. He recognized and manipulated the pious and sentimental styles, and undercut them with jarring realism and vivid colloquialisms. He had earlier recognized (as the note on his copy of the *New England Courant* proves) Nathaniel Gardner's imitation of Increase Mather's jeremiad-style, and appreciated how effectively Gardner ridiculed Mather by adopting the style. During his later career, he successfully imitated a wide variety of styles of the past and present. An extraordinary grasp of the implications of syntax and diction characterize Franklin's best writings. In a satire (revealing Franklin's fundamental relativism) on religious enthusiasm, he once wrote that diction and style are tests of truth: "It is therefore much the best, considering human Imperfection, that each Party describes itself as good, and as bad, as sincerely and as insincerely as they can and will, and leave it to such as are capable, to gather as much as is possible of what is true and solid, from Peoples Stile and Expressions" (*Pennsylvania Gazette*, February 24, 1742/3; omitted from *The Papers of Benjamin Franklin*).

POOR RICHARD AND THE WAY TO WEALTH

If a colonial family had only two books, they were probably the Bible and the current almanac. The latter owed its popularity to its non-literary contents: the almanac was the colonial version of a calendar and datebook. Just as few families today are without at least one calendar, so few colonial families were without an almanac. It supplied a major source of revenue for the colonial printer, and Benjamin Franklin, soon after opening his Philadelphia printing shop, secured the profitable publishing of an almanac. The best-known American almanac of the day (Franklin advertised on October 2, 1729, that it was "far preferable to any yet published in America") was Titan Leeds' *American Almanac,* which even had the unwelcome distinction of being forged by rival printers. Franklin printed Thomas Godfrey's almanac in 1729, and both Codfrey's and Jerman's in 1730 and 1731; but in 1732 Franklin found that his main printing rival, Andrew Bradford (who published Leeds' almanac), had secured the printing of all five Philadelphia almanacs. It may seem surprising that Thomas Godfrey, a fellow member of the Junto who had lived with Franklin in 1729, would take his almanac to Bradford, but he did not do it without reason.

The origin of the most famous almanac in the world evidently goes back to Franklin's anger about the conduct of the parents of a girl he had considered marrying. In the *Autobiography,* Franklin tells of his courtship of the girl, a relative of Mrs. Godfrey. The parents of the girl encouraged him with "continual Invitations to Supper, and by leaving us together, till at length it was time to explain." Mrs. Godfrey acted as the go-between for Franklin and the parents, but they abruptly refused to meet the young printer's expectations of a customary marriage settlement, and forbade him to call again. Franklin thought that they cunningly supposed he and the girl were too much in love and "therefore that we should steal a Marriage, which would leave them at Liberty to give or withold what they pleased." Furious at their dishonesty, Franklin "went no more," though Mrs. Godfrey

later brought him "some more favourable Accounts of their Disposition." This confirmed Franklin's suspicions and he "declared absolutely
my Resolution to have nothing more to do with that Family." The up-
shot of the courtship was "resented by the Godfreys, we differ'd, and
they removed, leaving me the whole House."

This quarrel with the Godfreys probably occurred in late 1729, but
Thomas Godfrey continued to publish an almanac with Franklin for
1731 and 1732. Franklin's anger with the family found its last statement in the *Autogiography*, but it has not been noted that he described
a situation similar to his courtship in a sketch in 1732, thus publicly
embarrassing the Godfreys and the girl's family to all who knew the
history of his courtship. The account, published in the persona of
"Anthony Afterwit" said:

> when the old Gentleman saw I was pretty well engag'd, and that
> the Match was too far gone to be easily broke off; he, without any
> Reason given, grew very angry, forbid me the House, and told his
> Daughter that if she married me he would not give her a Farthing.
> However (as he foresaw) we were not to be disappointed in that
> Manner; but having stole a Wedding, I took her home to my
> House; where we were not in quite so poor a Condition as the
> Couple describ'd in the Scotch Song, who had *Neither Pot nor
> Pan, / But four bare Legs together;* for I had a House tolerably
> furnished, for an ordinary Man, before. No thanks to Dad, who I
> understand was very much pleased with his politick Management.
> And I have since learn'd that there are old Curmudgeons (*so
> called*) besides him, who have this Trick, to marry their Daughters,
> and yet keep what they might well spare, till they can keep it no
> longer. (*Papers*, 1: 238)

Franklin's own case, complete with "a House tolerably furnished," corresponded to that of Anthony Afterwit—except that Franklin did not
marry. This vicious public attack on the parents of the girl no doubt
upset Thomas Godfrey, who abandoned his former Junto friend and
gave the copy of his almanac for 1733 to Andrew Bradford.

Faced with losing a major part of his still infant printing business,
Franklin, evidently at the last minute, compiled his own almanac. Although almanacs were usually published in October, Franklin's first
Poor Richard was not printed until the last week in December. Many
almanacs were little more than calendars, but the more expensive ones
(and thus the more profitable) contained poems, useful information
(like the yearbooks of today), and short sayings. Franklin's problem
in publishing an unknown almanac was how to get a share of the
market, and, furthermore, how to get the lion's share of the market

currently taken by Titan Leeds. The preface of the first *Poor Richard's Almanac* introduces the supposed compiler, Richard Saunders, a poor, naive religious, hen-pecked astrologer, who sits gazing at the stars while his wife is "spinning in her Shift of Tow." The diffident Poor Richard explains that his wife "has threatned more than once to burn all my Books and Rattling-Traps (as she calls my Instruments) if I do not make some profitable Use of them for the good of my Family." So he has turned almanac-maker. Indeed, continues Poor Richard, he would have done this many years ago, were his desire for money not "overpower'd by my Regard for my good Friend and Fellow-Student, Mr. Titan Leeds, whose Interest I was extreamly unwilling to hurt." But poor Richard concludes sadly that "this Obstacle (I am far from speaking it with Pleasure) is soon to be removed, since inexorable Death, who was never known to respect Merit, has already prepared the mortal Dart, the fatal Sister has already extended her destroying Shears, and the ingenious Man must soon be taken from us." Then he predicts the exact hour, minute, and second of the death of the most famous American almanac-maker.

Among the many previous mock-prognostications that Franklin knew was one that Thomas Fleet, a member of the Hell-Fire Club, wrote for the *New England Courant,* February 12, 1721/2, in the persona of "Sidrophel," an "old Starmonger" with "Skill in the Art of Astrology," who predicted the death of Philip Musgrave. Franklin also knew and echoed (especially in the second and third *Poor Richard*) the most famous mock-prognostication of the early eighteenth century, Jonathan Swift's Bickerstaff hoax. Poor Richard's final characterization in the first almanac (which has been overlooked by all previous editors and commentators) occurs on the last page, after "A Catalogue of the principal Kings and Princes in Europe, with the Time of their Births and Ages," where he inserted "Poor Richard, An American Prince, without Subjects, his Wife being Viceroy over him" and gave his birth as October 23, 1684, and his age as 49.

Franklin's reputation as a "shallow optimist" and as the "quintessential ethical capitalist" is supposedly based upon the *Poor Richard* almanacs and, to a lesser degree, upon the *Autobiography.* (Actually, these ignorant and typical opinions, taken from the two most recent scholarly journals to cross my desk, are not based so much upon anything that Franklin wrote or did as upon his being *the* representative American.) Even the most hostile critic realizes that Poor Richard is a persona, but supposedly Franklin's true opinions emerge in the aphorisms concerning industry and frugality. These of course are an aspect of Franklin's common sense, but they represent only a small portion of the total number of sayings, and they were included in part because of his desire to inculcate good habits among the people who rarely read anything, and in part because they were the kind of sayings that people most wanted to read and that sold almanacs.

After publishing *Poor Richard* in the same format for fifteen years, Franklin enlarged the almanac (from 24 to 36 pages) in 1748, allowing more comment within the calendar itself, as well as more material at the beginning and ending. In the first three years of *Poor Richard Improved,* Franklin inserted within the calendar tributes to a number of his personal heroes. In 1748, on January 19, he celebrated the birth of "the famous Astronomer Copernicus," whose improvement in astronomy was explained by comparing the earth to meat and the sun to the cooking fire: "Ptolomy is compar'd to a whimsical Cook, who, instead of Turning his Meat in Roasting, would fix That, and contrive to have his whole Fire, Kitchen and all, whirling continually round it." On March 20 Franklin noted the death of "the prince of astronomers and philosophers, sir Isaac Newton" and quoted Thomson and Pope on Newton. On June 19, the anniversary of the death of "the celebrated Joseph Addison," Franklin praised the man "whose writings have contributed more to the improvement of the minds of the British nation, and polishing their manners, than those of any other English pen whatever." As befitted a Pennsylvania almanac writer, he noted the birth of William Penn on the fourteenth of October. On the 28th, he lamented the death of "the famous John Locke, Esq; the Newton of the Microcosm." And on the 29th, he defended "the famous sir Walter Rawleigh." In 1749, he singled out for praise Robert Boyle, "one of the greatest philosophers the last age produced"; Luther, "that famous reformer"; Sir Francis Bacon, "justly esteem'd the father of the modern experimental philosophy"; John Calvin; and, again, "the great Sir Isaac Newton." In 1750 he praised Algernon Sidney for "an excellent Book, intituled Discourses on Government." And throughout these three years, he attacks the great soldiers, including Caesar and Alexander, none of whom, according to Franklin, deserve reputation or fame: on February 4, 1748, he notes the birth of "Lewis the 15th, present king of France, called his *most christian* majesty. He bids fair to be as great a mischief-maker as his grandfather; or, in the language of poets and orators, a *Hero.* There are three great destroyers of mankind, *Plague, Famine,* and *Hero.* Plague and Famine destroy your persons only, and leave your goods to your Heirs; but Hero, when he comes, takes life and goods together; his business and glory it is, to destroy man and the works of man."

For twenty-six consecutive years Franklin wrote the *Poor Richard* almanacs, all but six containing an entertaining skit as a preface. The last one in the series was frequently reprinted, usually under the title *The Way to Wealth*. Twice before, Franklin had briefly gathered together a number of sayings on industry and frugality, under the headings "Hints for those that would be Rich" and "How to get Riches" (1737 and 1749 almanacs), but these were comparatively minor efforts. In the summer of 1757, as he sailed to England, he wrote the preface to his almanac for 1758. Unlike the earlier brief thoughts on riches, this preface included nearly all his former sayings relating to industry and frugality, and added others. He put them into a connected and dramatic context, and featured them in a speech by Father Abraham within a framework supplied by that vain, pompous naif, Richard Saunders.

The Way to Wealth is a tour de force, for nearly every sentence contains at least one aphorism and some contain several—yet the resulting essay is connected and unified. Poor Richard's introduction is similar to the 1750 preface, where he spoke of the almanac-maker's desire for fame and of his disappointment when the almanac was discarded at the end of the year. Indeed, the role of the philomath and particularly the value of the *Poor Richard* almanacs recur repeatedly: in addition to the 1750 almanac, the 1747 preface discussed the literary materials (especially the proverbs and poems) published annually, and praised tho productions of Jacob Taylor (a philomath, poet, and friend of Franklin), who had just died. The preface to the 1756 *Poor Richard* again examined the proverbs (as, of course, the *Autobiography* was also to do). Moreover, the substance of *The Way to Wealth* itself directly compliments the former almanacs, being, in great part, an anthology of the earlier sayings relating to industry and frugality. When he wrote *The Way to Wealth*, Franklin was fifty-one years old, the most famous writer and scientist in America. His almanacs were a major source of income and were read by thousands of barely literate people in America as well as by scientists and literati. Some of the latter despised almanac writers and jealously scorned Franklin. But Franklin was proud of his almanac. He no doubt secretly thought it (what it was) the best in the world and of great use to the poor and inexperienced. In this major effort, he subtly defended it, while mocking possible critics. Modern critics have nevertheless appeared—and have consistently demonstrated their lack of humor, their literary insensitivity, their own obvious psychological problems, and their ignorance of the eighteenth century.

Poor Richard for 1758 opens: "I have heard that nothing gives an Author so great Pleasure, as to find his Works respectfully quoted by other learned Authors." Franklin thus burlesques the naive philomath Poor Richard, for the almanac writer was despised by "learned Authors" who would not—and certainly never with respect—quote an almanac writer. But Franklin also uses and controls the attitude that condescends to the philomath.

> This Pleasure I have seldom enjoyed; for tho' I have been, if I may say it without Vanity [the reader may recall Franklin's observation in the *Autobiography:* "Indeed I scarce ever heard or saw the introductory Words, *Without Vanity I may say* &c. but some vain thing immediately follow'd"], an *eminent Author* of Almanacks annually now a full Quarter of a Century, my Brother Authors in the same Way, for what Reason I know not, have ever been very sparing in their Applauses; and no other Author has taken the least Notice of me, so that did not my Writings produce me some solid *Pudding,* the great Deficiency of *Praise* would have quite discouraged me. (*Papers,* 7 : 340)

The italics of *eminent Author* call attention to its oxymoronic quality when referring to a philomath; and the clause "for what Reason I know not," while continuing the naif pose of Poor Richard, reminds the reader that the almanac writers are jealous of one another's financial success—which is their only measuring rod of eminence and excellence, as the last part of the sentence indirectly reaffirms.

The second paragraph brings the portrait of the pompous, vain naif to a climax with the ridiculous portrayal of Poor Richard quoting himself "with great Gravity." The third paragraph introduces the speech of a "plain clean old Man, with white Locks" called "Father Abraham," who quotes a chrestomathy of Poor Richard's proverbs, frequently mentioning their source (not always accurately) in the past almanacs. The name "Father Abraham," with its solid Biblical resonance, suggests age, wisdom, and piety. It also suggests excessive literalism and fanaticism—which is borne out by the zealous repetition of a, cumulatively, comically endless series of aphorisms relating to industry and frugality, and by the oft-repeated tag "as Poor Richard says," which calls up a picture of the simple-minded philomath delightedly hearing the speech. At the end, Poor Richard is surprised to observe the people who were gathered for the sale buying extravagantly, "just as if it had been a common Sermon," but he "resolved to be the better for the Echo of it; and though I had at first determined to buy Stuff for a new Coat, I went away resolved to wear my old One a little longer."

Thus on the most obvious level the naif undercuts the majority of people in not foolishly and extravagantly spending his money. On a subtler level, Franklin undercuts the critics and "learned authors" who hold philomaths and writers of aphorisms in contempt by burlesquing their attitudes within the perfectly controlled style of the supposed philomath. In passing, Franklin also ridicules sermons, preachers, and religion; and Father Abraham's speech, as the conclusion makes clear, parodies the structure and repetitive "logical proofs" of the typical Puritan sermon. (To Father Abraham, the sayings of Poor Richard are the Bible.) The structure of the total piece complements its aphoristic content. Since sayings are usually concise gems of rhetoric as well as content, they not only can stand alone but frequently diminish their context by their rhetorical brilliance. In *The Way to Wealth* they are placed within a speech which in turn is within the framework of Poor Richard's opening and closing. Thus the sayings, which tend to diminish, dominate, and escape their contexts, are wedged, not only within the string of similar sayings, but within a speech, within still another framework. Unlike most aphorisms in prose contexts, these are absolutely controlled and precisely fixed. Since few people like to hear unpalatable truths, Franklin carefully constructed *The Way to Wealth* so that the moral spoken by Father Abraham is not addressed to the reader (except at the very end) but to those people (including that wise-fool Poor Richard) gathered at "a Vendue of Merchant Goods" who are complaining of the economy, the taxes, and their own finances and who demonstrate their own foolishness by buying "extravagantly." Of course, the main subject is industry and frugality as the surest way to wealth, a subject likely to make some critics, including myself, not only uncomfortable and unhappy, but a little neurotic.

FRANKLIN'S PERSONAL LETTERS

Franklin's letters show the man. He hated cheats, snobs, and pretentious fools. He despised greedy politicians. He scorned personal jealousies and personal vituperation. He pessimistically believed that in any absolute or ultimate sense, life was meaningless. Men were selfish and vicious animals with an ability to justify by the use of their reason whatever vain, foolish notions they fancied. But, mainly, the letters show that he loved charming women, he loved children, he loved to play, he loved jokes and humor, he loved his family and his friends, he loved Boston, Philadelphia, and America, he loved England and Scotland and France, and he loved life. He is always conscious of the three main considerations in letter writing: the characters of the writer and the recipient, the relationship between them, and the occasion. He was usually pious to pious people, though if they were his friends and peers, like Ezra Stiles, he would occasionally mock religion. But he could be blasphemous, as his letters to "that excellent Christian" (Franklin's words—Hume, of course, was an infamous atheist) David Hume show. On the other hand, he recommended, when leaving America in 1764, to his daughter Sarah that she:

> Go constantly to Church whoever preaches. The Acts of Devotion
> in the common Prayer Book, are your principal Business there; and
> if properly attended to, will do more towards mending the Heart
> than Sermons generally can do. For they were composed by Men
> of much greater Piety and Wisdom, than our common Composers
> of Sermons can pretend to be. And therefore I wish you wou'd
> never miss the Prayer Days. Yet I do not mean that you shou'd
> despise Sermons even of the Preachers you dislike, for the Dis-
> course is often much better than the Man, as sweet and clear
> Waters come to us thro' very dirty Earth. I am the more particular
> on this Head, as you seem'd to express a little before I came away
> some Inclination to leave our Church, which I wou'd not have
> you do. (*Papers*, 11 : 449–50)

Eighteenth-century writers regarded the personal letter as a major literary genre. Artful letters were treasured, copies were made by the recipient and his friends, and a copy kept by the writer, who sometimes showed it or made copies for his other friends. (Letters that were not sent to the intended recipient—like those to William Strahan and Arthur Lee mentioned below—could have circulation in the latter fashion.) But single sheets of manuscript are ephemeral, and much of Franklin's correspondence has been irretrievably lost. That his contemporaries treasured Franklin's letters is borne out by the numerous manuscript copies of some of them and by contemporary testimony. Sir Alexander Dick, a close friend of Lord Kames, the Scottish common-sense philosopher, wrote on October 28, 1766, that Kames "puts the greatest value upon a Letter from you of any of all his numerous correspondents." Franklin's letters to Kames are semiformal speculations on science, morality, and philosophy. Franklin's good friend, the great botanist John Bartram, received another kind of letter—and asked for more: "Pray my dear friend bestow A few lines upon thy ould friend such like as those sent from Woodbridge. They have A Magical power of dispeling Malancholy fumes and chearing up my spirits, they are so like thy facetious discourse in thy southern chamber when we used to be together." Elizabeth Graeme Fergusson, a poet and once the sweetheart of William Franklin, received intimate letters from her prospective father-in-law, which, she wrote, "would have been circulated thro all the anecdote writers in Europe and America under the article traits of Dr. Franklin's Domestic Character"—if she had shown them. The best testimony to the excellence and contemporary reputation of Franklin's letters is from Mather Byles, the Boston wit and poet:

> I have just been reading a beautiful Letter of yours, written Feb. 22. 1756, on the Death of your Brother, which is handed about among us in Manuscript Copies. I am charmed with the Easy and Gay Light in which you view our leaving this little Earth, as Birth among [other?] Immortals: and as setting out on a Party of Pleasure a little before our Friends are ready. The Superstition with which we size and preserve little accidental Touches of your Pen, puts one in mind of the Care of the Virtuosi to collect the Jugs and Galipots with the Paintings of Raphael. (*Papers*, 12 : 424)

Franklin's letters to his family are voluminous. Among the best to his favorite sister, Jane, is one from June 1748, answering her complaint that her apprentice son Benjamin was not being treated well by his master, Franklin's partner James Parker. His reply discusses "the nature of boys," explaining to her the probable causes and reasons for her son's irritations and demonstrating his own understanding of adolescence. On the other hand, the letter to Jane Mecom of April 19, 1757, regarding their aged half-sister Elizabeth Douse, whom Franklin supported by allowing her to live rent-free in a house which he had purchased, is a sympathetic appreciation of old age:

> As *having their own Way*, is one of the greatest Comforts of Life, to old People, I think their Friends should endeavour to accommodate them in that, as well as in any thing else. When they have long liv'd in a House, it becomes natural to them, they are almost as closely connected with it as the Tortoise with his Shell, they die if you tear them out of it. Old Folks and old Trees, if you remove them, tis ten to one that you kill them. So let our good old Sister be no more importun'd on that head. We are growing old fast ourselves, and shall expect the same kind of Indulgencies. If we give them, we shall have a Right to receive them in our Turn. (*Papers*, 7 : 190)

When his sister tried to drag him into a family quarrel and wanted him to fire a cousin as postmaster of Boston and replace him with her son, he replied, on May 30, 1757: "if my friends require of me to gratify not only their inclinations, but their resentments, they expect

too much of me." The most frequently anthologized letter to his sister
(which circulated in Philadelphia within two months of its delivery in
Boston) is of September 16, 1758, reversing the order of faith, hope,
and charity.

There are thoughtful and witty letters to his many learned American
friends: James Logan (who slighted, wrote Franklin, the Hobbesian
view, which "I imagine, is somewhat nearer the Truth than that which
makes the State of Nature a State of Love"), Governor Cadwallader
Colden, the Reverend Jared Eliot (with whom Franklin delighted to
joke), the Reverend Samuel Johnson, James Bowdoin, and Sir William
Johnson, among others. His letters to the charming young Catharine
Ray (later Greene) are affectionate and flirtatious (like a group of
later ones to the daughter of his English landlady, Mary "Polly" Steven-
son). His first letter to "Katy" tells of his last sight of her: "when I saw
you put off to Sea in that very little Skiff, toss'd by every Wave . . . I
stood on the Shore, and look'd after you, till I could no longer distinguish you, even with my Glass." Lest she misunderstand his flirtation
with her, he indirectly spoke of his love for his wife:

> I left New England slowly, and with great Reluctance: Short
> Days Journeys, and loitering Visits on the Road, for three or four
> Weeks, manifested my Unwillingness to quit a Country in which
> I drew my first Breath, spent my earliest and most pleasant Days,
> and had now received so many fresh Marks of the People's Good-
> ness and Benevolence, in the kind and affectionate Treatment I
> had every where met with. I almost forgot I had a Home; till I
> was more than half-way towards it; till I had, one by one, parted
> with all my New England Friends, and was got into the western
> Borders of Connecticut, among meer Strangers: then, like an old
> Man, who, having buried all he lov'd in this World, begins to think
> of Heaven, I begun to think of and wish for Home; and as I drew
> nearer, I found the Attraction stronger and stronger, my Diligence
> and Speed increas'd with my Impatience, I drove on violently, and
> made such long Stretches that a very few Days brought me to my
> own House, and to the Arms of my good old Wife and Children,
> where I remain, Thanks to God, at present well and happy.
> (*Papers*, 5 : 503)

A few months later, he chided her for refusing to allow him any
"Favours," showing that he, *half* in jest, asked for them—and then told
how much he enjoyed her letters: "The small news, the domestic occurrences among our friends, the natural pictures you draw of persons,
the sensible observations and reflections you make, and the easy,
chatty manner in which you express every thing, all contribute to

heighten the pleasure; and the more as they remind me of those hours and miles, that we talked away so agreeably, even in a winter journey, a wrong road, and a soaking shower."

His correspondence with his old Junto friend Hugh Roberts, is full of high spirits, puns, and pleasantries. To his Connecticut friend Jared Ingersoll, later one of the unhappy Stamp Act distributors, he could not resist satirizing Connecticut's blue laws. In Franklin's old age, his American correspondents are, for the most part, a younger generation, including the great Revolutionary heroes. His letters to William Carmichael, son-in-law of his old enemy, the poet James Sterling, are full of good anecdotes. Charles Thomson, John Paul Jones, Thomas Jefferson, John Adams, and George Washington are among the correspondents who drew out his amusing, and, by turns, serious writings. During the Revolution (echoing an analogy that he had used thirty-five years before—February 12, 1745—on the American reputation of Alexander Pope), he predicted success and fame for Washington:

> You would, on this side of the Sea, enjoy the great Reputation you have acquir'd, pure and free from those little Shades that the Jealousy and Envy of a Man's Countrymen and Contemporaries are ever endeavouring to cast over living Merit. Here you would know, and enjoy, what Posterity will say of Washington. For 1000 Leagues have nearly the same Effect with 1000 Years. The feeble Voice of those grovelling Passions cannot extend so far either in Time or Distance. At present I enjoy that Pleasure for you, as I frequently hear the old Generals of this martial Country, (who study the Maps of America, and mark upon them all your Operations,) speak with sincere Approbation and great Applause of your conduct; and join in giving you the Character of one of the greatest Captains of the Age. (pp. 401-02*)

Sainte-Beuve thought that the next paragraph in the letter, "by the sweetness of its inspiration and the breadth of its imagery, recalls the Homeric comparisons of the *Odyssey*":

> I must soon quit the Scene, but you may live to see our Country flourish, as it will amazingly and rapidly after the War is over. Like a Field of young Indian Corn, which long Fair weather and Sunshine had enfeebled and discolored, and which in that weak State, by a Thunder Gust, of violent Wind, Hail, and Rain, seem'd to be threaten'd with absolute Destruction; yet the Storm being past, it recovers fresh Verdure, shoots up with double Vigour, and

* For writings that have not yet appeared in the *Papers*, I have quoted from the convenient *Representative Selections*, edited by Chester E. Jorgenson and Frank Luther Mott.

delights the Eye, not of its Owner only, but of every observing Traveller. (*Representative Selections*, p. 422)

One of the most vicious letters Franklin ever wrote was in reply to the repeated, jealous, supercilious, suspicious letters and demands of his co-commissioner to France, the neurotic Dr. Arthur Lee. On April 3, 1778, the exasperated Franklin gave vent to his feelings:

> If I have often receiv'd and borne your Magisterial Snubbings and Rebukes without Reply, ascribe it to the right Causes, my Concern for the Honour & Success of our Mission, which would be hurt by our Quarrelling, my Love of Peace, my Respect for your good Qualities, and my Pity of your Sick Mind, which is forever tormenting itself, with its Jealousies, Suspicions & Fancies that others mean you ill, wrong you, or fail in Respect for you. — If you do not cure your self of this Temper it will end in Insanity, of which it is the Symptomatick Forerunner, as I have seen in several Instances. God preserve you from so terrible an Evil: and for his sake pray suffer me to live in quiet. (7 : 132[*])

Instead of sending this, Franklin wrote a longer letter, patiently replying to Lee's insinuations and charges, and containing at the end the substance of the first letter, which he saved.

Franklin's first major English correspondent was the influential Quaker merchant and scientist, Peter Collinson, to whom he addressed many letters on science, knowing that Collinson would read them to the Royal Society of London and that, if they were judged worthy, they would be published in the *Philosophical Transactions*. To the Reverend George Whitefield, the greatest revivalist of all time, Franklin cited the example of (not Christ, but) Confucius, in a letter of July 6, 1749. His letters to Governor William Shirley on the taxation of America and on a union of the American colonies, his political correspondence with Richard Jackson, and his correspondence with Governor Thomas Pownall all disclose the thoughts and actions of the pro-American English leaders in the pre-Revolutionary period. His richest single English correspondence was with William Strahan, part-owner of the *London Chronicle* and the *Gentleman's Magazine*, and the leading English printer of the day. Their letters range widely through the experiences and emotions of the two printers and politicians, who had so much in common. They became good friends by correspondence before they met. In a letter of June 2, 1750, two years after retiring from business, Franklin satirized the "Pursuit of Wealth

---

[*] Quoted from the ten-volume Albert Henry Smyth edition of *The Writings of Benjamin Franklin*.

to no End." When he was about to go to England, he concluded a letter to Strahan: "Look out sharp, and if a fat old Fellow should come to your Printing House and request a little Smouting, depend upon it, 'tis Your affectionate Friend and humble Servant." They saw one another frequently in England and became the best of friends. Strahan wrote to Deborah Franklin that he "never saw a man who was, in every respect, so perfectly agreeable to me. Some are amiable in one view, some in another, he in all." When Franklin was leaving England in 1762, he wrote several brief parting notes to "Straney": in one, he sent an impoverished man to the printer for work, and joked that this was his last "Legacy" to Strahan; in another, he wrote: "You have great powers of persuasion, and might easily prevail on me to do any thing; but not any longer to do nothing. I must go home." In a third brief note, he joked: "None of the Oxford people are under any other obligation to me than that of having already oblig'd me, and being oblig'd to go on as they have begun." He ends this last: "I expect to see you once more. I value myself much, on being able to resolve on doing the right thing, in opposition to your almost irresistable eloquence, secretly supported and backed by my own treacherous inclinations." The following year he wrote a facetious letter to Strahan on June 10, 1763, saying that he had nothing to say, delighting in the thought that the empty letter would cost the Scotch printer a shilling, and managing to go on about saying nothing for an entire page. A letter of just over two weeks later gave a perceptive account of Pontiac's uprising and was promptly printed in Strahan's *London Chronicle*. When Strahan despondently complained of the riots and troubles in London, Franklin wrote back a statesman-like reassurance on December 19, 1763, of the excellence of King George III—which Strahan wanted to hear. After Franklin returned to London, his printer friend asked him for an account of the debates on the repeal of the Stamp Act, and Franklin sent him a report on William Pitt's great speech of January 14, 1766, revealing his close and shrewd attention to Pitt's rhetorical method. No letter to Strahan is so famous as the shortest one. On July 5, 1775, after the battles of Concord, Lexington, and Bunker Hill, he read of Strahan's vote in Parliament and wrote: "Mr. Strahan: You are a member of Parliament, and one of that majority which has doomed my country to destruction. You have begun to burn our towns and murder our people. Look upon your hands! They are stained with the blood of your relations! You and I were long friends. You are now my enemy, and I am yours, B. Franklin." I am glad that this letter was not sent.

In 1771, after spending three weeks at the home of Jonathan Shipley, Bishop of St. Asaph, he returned to London on the same coach that took the Bishop's youngest daughter, aged 11, back to school. His letter to Mrs. Shipley, thanking her for her hospitality and telling of Kitty's safe arrival, recounts the conversation that the sixty-five-year-old scientist, politician, and philosopher had with the eleven-year-old girl, in which they settled upon the kinds of husbands that Kitty and her four sisters should marry. He later wrote several delightful letters to the Shipley girls, including one in 1772 to Georgiana Shipley lamenting the death of the American squirrel he had given her, "Alas! poor Mungo!"

The letter to Lord Howe, commander of the English fleet off the coast of America, dated July 20, 1776, combines his personal feelings of former friendship and respect, with his present sense of his own and Lord Howe's public positions: "Directing Pardons to be offered to the Colonies, who are the very Parties injured, expresses indeed that Opinion of our Ignorance, Baseness, and Insensibility, which your uninform'd and proud Nation has long been pleased to entertain of us; but it can have no other effect than that of increasing our Resentments." He says of England:

> Her Fondness for Conquest, as a warlike Nation, her lust of Dominion, as an ambitious one, and her wish for a gainful Monopoly, as a commercial One, (none of them legitimate Causes of War,) will all join to hide from her Eyes every view of her true Interests, and continually goad her on in those ruinous distant Expeditions, so destructive both of Lives and Treasure, that must prove as pernicious to her in the End, as the Crusades formerly were to most of the Nations in Europe. (*Representative Selections*, pp. 385–86)

Franklin recalls his former attempts to preserve the union of England and America in a noble metaphor: "Long did I endeavour, with unfeigned and unwearied Zeal, to preserve from breaking that fine and noble China Vase, the British Empire; for I knew, that, being once broken, the separate Parts could not retain even their Shares of Strength and Value that existed in the Whole, and that a perfect Reunion of those Parts could scarce ever be hoped for." In the latter part of the long letter, Franklin turns to Lord Howe's action in taking part in the war, concluding with an allusion to the well-known lines from Addison's *Cato*, "When vice prevails, and impious men bear sway, / The post of honour is a private station":

> I consider this War against us, therefore, as both unjust and unwise; and I am persuaded, that cool, dispassionate Posterity will condemn to Infamy those who advised it; and that even Success

will not save from some Degree of Dishonor those, who voluntarily engaged to Conduct it. I know your great motive in coming hither was the hope of being Instrumental in a Reconciliation; and I believe, when you find *that* to be impossible on any Terms given you to propose, you will relinquish so odious a Command, and return to a more honourable private Station. (*Representative Selections,* p. 387)

Writing to his physician Dr. John Fothergill on March 14, 1764, Franklin betrayed his own pessimism and nihilistic feelings, when he mockingly took the doctor to task for saving lives: "Do you please yourself with the Fancy that you are doing Good? You are mistaken. Half the Lives you save are not worth saving, as being useless; and almost the other Half ought not to be sav'd, as being mischievous." Then he chides the doctor for impiously warring "against the Plans of Providence" in his efforts to save lives. His pessimism is clearer, and unalloyed with either cleverness or humor, in a letter to his sister Jane of December 30, 1770, when he advocated the idea that "this world is the true Hell, or place of punishment for the spirits who had transgressed in a better state." And the letters to Joseph Priestley of February 8, 1780, and June 7, 1782, are even blacker. In the latter, he wrote:

> I should rejoice much, if I could once more recover the Leasure to search with you into the Works of Nature; I mean the *inanimate,* not the *animate* or moral part of them, the more I discover'd of the former, the more I admir'd them; the more I know of the latter, the more I am disgusted with them. Men I find to be a Sort of Beings very badly constructed, as they are generally more easily provok'd than reconcil'd, more disposed to do Mischief to each other than to make Reparation, much more easily deceiv'd than undeceiv'd, and having more Pride and even Pleasure in killing than in begetting one another; for without a Blush they assemble in great armies at NoonDay to destroy, and when they have kill'd as many as they can, they exaggerate the Number to augment the fancied Glory; but they creep into Corners, or cover themselves with the Darkness of night, when they mean to beget, as being asham'd of a virtuous Action. A virtuous Action it would be, and a vicious one the killing of them, if the Species were really worth producing or preserving; but of this I begin to doubt. (*Representative Selections,* pp. 443–44)

Franklin was incapable of writing an uninteresting letter, but no space remains to mention the hundreds of his letters, not even any to his French correspondents. No English letter writer—including Horace

Walpole, who, if not more prolific, has more extant letters—is greater.
No other letter-writer had so many tones and moods; practically no
other letter-writer had such a voluminous international correspondence, with such a wide variety of individuals of such disparate interests
and personalities; and no other letter-writer of the times took part in
so many historic events in America and Europe. He is the Pepys of
letter-writers. No mind is so fascinating—and so fascinated with all
that goes on around him—and no pen more artful.

THE PUBLIC WRITINGS

In only one month (January 1766) Franklin wrote nine essays and
satires which appeared in English periodicals, besides drafting a long
pamphlet against the Stamp Act. He was the most prolific American
propagandist during the pre-Revolutionary period. During the Revolution, when his time was taken up with numerous official duties, he
continued to write American propaganda; and his efforts were so distinctive and superior that contemporary English writers, like Horace
Walpole, could correctly identify as his the best pseudonymous pro-
American writings. Throughout his life, he amused himself and others
by writing satires, essays, and hoaxes—from the brief, often bawdy,
mock news items in the early issues of the *Pennsylvania Gazette* to
his vicious satire against slavery, written shortly before his death in
1790. Among the best of his pre-Revolutionary public writings are the
free-verse satire published on June 1, 1747, of an illogical speech by
the governor of Virginia concerning a fire that burned the capitol in
Williamsburg; a hoax, "Rattlesnakes for Felons," May 11, 1751, in
which he proposed sending rattlesnakes to England as "the most *suitable Returns*" for the convicts transported to America; his "Defense of
the Americans," May 9, 1759, probably the best colonial essay on the
American character (the *Papers of Benjamin Franklin* does not note
that it was twice reprinted in America: in the *Boston Evening Post* for
October 1 and 8, and in the *New American Magazine* for September
1759, pp. 607–13); his hoax "Of the Meanes of Disposing the Enemie
to Peace," August 13, 1761, supposedly reprinting an excerpt from a
treatise by a seventeenth-century Spanish priest; and his impassioned
pamphlet defending the Indians from the blood-thirsty frontiersmen,
A Narrative of the Late Massacres (1764).

Franklin's spoof of the exaggerations and absurdities of the English
newspaper accounts of America, written on May 20, 1765, uses the

tradition of the travel-burlesques to create the best tall tales of colonial America. He mocks the English fears of American wool production by writing: "The very Tails of the American Sheep are so laden with Wool, that each has a Car or Waggon on four little Wheels to support and keep it from trailing on the Ground. Would they caulk their Ships? would they fill their Beds? would they even litter their Horses with Wool, if it was not both plenty and cheap?" And he burlesques the unbelievable reports of American manufacturing and fishing:

> And yet all this is as certainly true as the Account, said to be from Quebec, in the Papers of last Week, that the Inhabitants of Canada are making Preparations for a Cod and Whale Fishery this Summer in the Upper Lakes. Ignorant People may object that the Upper Lakes are fresh, and that Cod and Whale are Salt-water Fish: But let them know, Sir, that Cod, like other Fish, when attacked by their Enemies, fly into any Water where they think they can be safest; that Whales, when they have a mind to eat Cod, pursue them wherever they fly; and that the grand Leap of the Whale in that Chace up the Fall of Niagara is esteemed by all who have seen it, as one of the finest Spectacles in Nature!
> (*Papers*, 12 : 134–35)

Like Americans before and after him, Franklin uses tall tales to burlesque the preconceptions of his audience—and to show them how ridiculous their notions are. Those who were taken in by the tall tales only demonstrated their own incredible provinciality and ignorance.

Perhaps the best known of all the pre-Revolutionary political satires is "An Edict by the King of Prussia." Franklin wrote his son, William, an account of the reception of the "Edict." During a brief summer vacation in 1773, Franklin visited the country home of Sir Francis Dashwood, Baron Le Despencer, a notorious rake and joint Post master General of England. He was there when his satire was published. When the mail arrived, Paul Whitehead, himself a poet and man of letters, who customarily scanned the papers and reported to Lord Le Despencer and his guests anything remarkable, glanced through the papers "in another room, and we were chatting in the breakfast parlour, when he came running in to us, out of breath, with the paper in his hand. Here! says he, here's news for ye! *Here's the King of Prussia, claiming a right to this kingdom!* All stared, and I as much as anybody; and he went on to read it."

The analogy for the "Edict" evidently occurred to Franklin in January 1766, while he was making notes for a pamphlet against the Stamp Act. In the fifth section, after making a series of notes against the internal taxation of America, he wrote: "They [the Americans] can sub-

sist without this Country [England] or any Trade and being too weak
to express their Resentments in any other Way it will be more strongly
express'd in this." Then, evidently searching for an analogy to drive
home the unreasonableness of internal taxes, he wrote in the margin
"Germany the Mother Country of this Nation." This inspiration contains the basic argument of the "Edict": as England is the mother
country of America, so Germany is the mother country of England;
just as America objects to being taxed by England, so England would
object to being taxed by Germany.

The "Edict" itself is contained within the framework of an impartial
persona's comment on it. The impartial observer is, significantly, a
resident of Danzig (a city with a reputation for freedom and for resistance to attempted subjugation), and the account pretends to be
reprinted from a Danzig newspaper. One reason for the introduction
is to arouse interest in the piece, since the "Edict" itself opens with a
realistic and rather dull preamble. The observer, however, begins: "We
have long wondered here at the supineness of the English nation,
under the Prussian impositions upon its trade entering our port."
(Danzig was also famous as a free port.) Calling the English "supine"
would arouse the amazement, if not the anger, of the English audience,
who no doubt believed what they constantly read of English bravery,
daring, and passion. It also obliquely reminds the audience (the concluding remarks do so directly) that the English reputation for in-
trepid action is traditionally associated with their support of freedom
and liberty. The second sentence further piques the reader's curiosity,
and reminds him of the English "sense of duty" and "principles of
equity." The third sentence directly introduces the "Edict" and first
suggests the possibility that it is a hoax.

The opening of the "Edict" itself is impersonal, formal, and realistic
(quoting a portion of the supposed original French text), thereby al-
laying any suspicion that the document is a hoax. The second paragraph, containing the precedent, cause, and first regulation, begins by
establishing the absurdly far-fetched colonial relation of England to
Prussia—thus intimating that America's colonial relation to England
is also exaggerated: "Whereas it is well known to all the world, that
the first German settlements made in the Island of Britain, were by
colonies of people, subject to our renowned ducal ancestors, and
drawn from their dominions, under the conduct of Hengist, Horsa,
Hella, Uff, Cerdicus, Ida, and others; and that the said colonies have
flourished under the protection of our august house for ages past; have
never been emancipated therefrom; and yet have hitherto yielded little
profit." Franklin here slyly burlesques the arguments that America

was settled at the expense of England and has been continuously dependent upon England throughout the century and a half of its existence, arguments that he elsewhere directly and repeatedly refuted. He also cleverly worked in the unworthy motive for the regulations—profit, a petty motive which will conclude the hoax and characterize (in opposition to their vainglorious opinion of themselves) the English.

The series of formal *whereas* clauses continues the parody of England's reasons for taxing America; and then, following the *therefore* clause, appears the first of the five regulations: the 4½% duty "paid to our officers of the *customs,* on all goods, wares, and merchandizes, and on the grain and other products of the earth, exported . . . and on all goods of whatever kind imported." The following sentence ridicules the impracticality of the duties: "that all ships or vessels bound from Great Britain to any other part of the world, or from any other part of the world to Great Britain, shall in their respective voyages touch at our port of Koningsberg, there to be unladen, searched, and charged with the said duties." It must have been at about this point that one of the company at Lord Le Despencer's broke in on Paul Whitehead's reading with "Damn his impudence, I dare say, we shall hear by next post that he is upon his march with one hundred thousand men to back this." Readers were taken in, Franklin explained to his son, partly because of the reputation of the king of Prussia. No doubt enjoying the reactions of Lord Le Despencer's party almost as much as he had the reading and comments of the *Courant* wits on his first Silence Dogood essay, Franklin remained quiet and solemn.

The next regulation dealt with the laws regarding the mining and manufacturing of iron, Franklin parodying the common argument that the colonists must have learned mining and manufacturing from England. The irony becomes savage when Franklin indirectly states what he evidently considered the proper attitude, in one of the few passages of the "Edict" that has no counterpart in the actual British law: "and the inhabitants of the said island, presuming that they had a natural right to make the best use they could of the natural [the *natural right* brings to mind the "natural rights" philosophy, and the repeated *natural* underscores the unnaturalness of the English laws] productions of their country for their own benefit, have not only built furnaces for smelting the said stone into iron, but have erected plating-forges, slitting-mills, and steel-furnaces." These are all forbidden. "But we are nevertheless graciously [royal edicts, like Parliamentary laws, have delicious ironic possibilities] pleased to permit the inhabitants . . . to transport their iron into Prussia, there to be manufactured, and to them returned; they paying our Prussian subjects for the workmanship, with all the costs of commission, freight, and risk, coming and returning." It was probably at about this point that Paul Whitehead, reading the "Edict" aloud to Lord Le Despencer's group, "began to smoke it, and looking in my face said, *I'll be hanged if this is not some of your American jokes upon us.*"

The third regulation prohibits "not only the manufacturing of woollen cloth, but also the raising of wool." Franklin parodied this and emphasized its unreasonableness by implying that it violated the Americans' sacred rights of property (on which, according to Locke, civilization is founded), by humorously cataloging the woolen goods, and by minutely specifying the ways and places that wool could not be transported:

> and that those islanders may be farther and more effectually restrained in making any advantage of their own wool in the way of manufacture, we command that none shall be carried out of one country into another; nor shall any worsted, bay, or woollen yarn, cloth, says, bays, kerseys, serges, frizes, druggets, cloth-serges, shalloons [although all these articles are listed in the original law, Franklin has changed their order to emphasize the rhymes and the incongruous awkward parechesis], or any other drapery stuffs, or woollen manufactures whatsoever, made up or mixed with wool in any of the said counties, be carried into any other county, or be waterborne even across the smallest river or creek on penalty of forfeiture of the same, together with the boats, carriages, horses, &c., that shall be employed in removing them. (*Representative Selections*, p. 361)

At the end of the regulations on wool, Franklin suddenly turns scurrilous: his purpose was not only to reveal the true outrage that Americans felt at these unjust laws, but also to show that the laws were such serious infringements of the rights of individuals and of countries that they could not ultimately be regarded with the comparatively light humor which had so far characterized the hoax. In addition, the scurrility lets the reader know that the piece is a hoax: "Nevertheless, our loving subjects there are hereby permitted (if they think proper) to use all their wool as manure for the improvement of their lands."

The fourth regulation, against "the art and mystery of making hats" is copied almost exactly from the Parliamentary statute. So ridiculous, implies Franklin, is it, that in itself it arouses humor and seems a parody. He adds that the "islanders . . . being in possession of wool, beaver and other furs, have presumptuously [this is a word that Franklin was especially sensitive to, as the second paragraph of the *Autobiography* shows, for he had repeatedly been accused of *presumption* in designing a lightning rod, which would avert the just and natural punishment of God] conceived they had a right to make some advantage thereof." This regulation ironically concludes: "But, lest the said islanders [repeatedly calling the English *islanders* is itself a form of meiosis] should suffer inconveniency by the want of hats, we are farther graciously pleased to permit them to send their beaver furs to Prussia; and we also permit hats to be made thereof to be exported from Prussia to Britain; the people thus favoured to pay all costs and charges of manufacturing, interest, commission to our merchants, insurance and freight going and returning, as in the case of iron."

The last regulation echoed Franklin's earlier satires on England's sending criminals ("thieves, highway and street robbers, house-breakers, forgerers, murderers, s–d—tes, and villains of every description") to America, "for the better [!] peopleing of that country." In the penultimate paragraph of the supposed "Edict," Franklin makes the satire inescapably clear by pointing out that these "royal regulations and commands will be thought just and reasonable by our much favoured colonists" because they are "copied from their statutes" made "for the good government of their *own colonies in Ireland and America.*"

The last paragraph, the penalty for disobedience, contains the final outrage—once again based on England's laws—that any persons suspected of disobeying these unreasonable and impractical laws "shall be transported in fetters from Britain to Prussia, there to be tried and executed [note that there is no possibility of being found innocent] according to the Prussian law." Had Franklin's satire closed after the dating and signature of the mock "Edict," it could still have been regarded as a *jeu d'esprit*, rather than as a serious protest and vicious condemnation of the petty, commercial self-interest that was depriving a people of their natural rights and even of the fundamentals of civilization. This, of course, is part of what Franklin added by ending the satire with the comment of the supposedly impartial Danzig observer:

> Some take this Edict to be merely one of the King's *Jeux d'Esprit* [for the final time, Franklin tells the reader it is a hoax—and offers one way to regard it]: others suppose it serious, and that he means a quarrel with England [just as every Englishman knew that if the Prussian king were to try to enforce such regulations, it must mean war, so too Franklin implies that these regulations against America will lead to war]; but all here think the assertion it concludes with, 'that these regulations are copied from acts of the English parliament respecting their colonies,' a very

injurious one; it being impossible to believe, that a people distinguished for their love of liberty, a nation so wise, so liberal in its
sentiments, so just and equitable towards its neighbors, should,
from mean and injudicious views of petty immediate profit, treat
its own children in a manner so arbitrary and tyrannical! (*Representative Selections,* p. 363)

Thus Franklin ends the satire by reminding the English readers
of their reputation for love of liberty and justice, by having the impartial persona refuse to believe that the English could have such blatantly
unjust regulations, by reiterating that the motive for these acts is "mean
and injudicious views of petty immediate profit," and by slyly characterizing the English as really "arbitrary and tyrannical." Although
the observer seems inconsistent, for he opened the piece by describing
the English as supine and closes it by echoing the traditional English
self-congratulatory compliments, there is (in addition to the obvious
literary reasons for the inconsistency) a level of consistency which the
sensitive English reader must appreciate: in view of the existence of
such regulations, the lovers of liberty and justice in England are
supine—and the petty, greedy, materialists hold sway.

Franklin wrote to his son: "Lord Mansfield, I hear, said of it, that it
was *very able and very artful indeed;* and would do mischief by giving
here a bad impression of the measures of government; and in the
colonies, by encouraging them in their contumacy." As George Simson
has pointed out, the "Edict" itself follows the traditional form of the
English statute: introduction (first paragraph), precedent, cause
(*whereas* clauses), regulation, and penalty (last paragraph). The impartial persona framework adds a brilliant setting and interpretation of
the satire, and the reversal in the conclusion (when the Danzig observer finds the assertion impossible to believe) is a microcosm of the
reversal that has gone on throughout the "Edict."

THE BAGATELLES

Eighteenth-century men of letters sometimes wrote *jeux d'esprit* for
their own amusement or for a select circle of friends. Many bagatelles
ultimately had a wide circulation, because the author would allow
special friends to make a copy, and they, in turn, might also give
copies. Thus Franklin gave a copy of his Biblical hoax "A Parable
against Persecution" to Ezra Stiles, and Stiles, on August 2, 1755, sent
a copy to another literary friend. Several years later, Franklin recited

it to a group of Scottish friends and was importuned for a copy by Lady Dick, which he subsequently sent; and Lord Kames asked for it in 1760, which Franklin also gave. Without asking Franklin's permission, Lord Kames promptly published it in his *Introduction to the Art of Thinking* (1761); and several years later William Strahan published a slightly different version in the *London Chronicle* for April 17, 1764, prefacing it with an amusing account of how the author, a certain North American, well-known for his "sallies of humour, in which he is a great master," would, in the middle of a conversation on the topic, get his Bible and read (that is recite from memory) this "Chapter" of Genesis. The Biblical imitation slyly burlesques Biblical morality (Abraham and his descendants will be afflicted for four hundred years because of his minor transgression), ridicules Biblical accuracy (the stranger is 198 years old), and satirizes the Scripturians who are taken in by the hoax. The parable directly recommends toleration, for if the omnipotent and omniscient creator allows various religions (and atheism) to exist, man should not object. Only six months before he died, Franklin wrote to Benjamin Vaughan of the parable: "The publishing of it by Lord Kames, without my consent, deprived me of a good deal of amusement, which I used to take in reading it by heart out of my Bible, and obtaining the remarks of the Scripturians upon it, which were sometimes very diverting; not but that it is in itself, on account of the importance of its moral, well worth being made known to all mankind."

The first of Franklin's bagatelles to be published was "The Speech of Miss Polly Baker," which mysteriously appeared in a London newspaper on April 15, 1747. It was reprinted in dozens of newspapers and magazines in England, the Continent, and America. The best text (I make this judgment for literary reasons that lack of space forbids me to spell out here) of this rhetorical tour de force appeared in the *Maryland Gazette* in the summer of 1747, from a copy in the possession of Jonas Green or some other member of Dr. Alexander Hamilton's Annapolis literary circle. This entertaining and complex hoax satirizes New England's blue laws, protests the double-standard for women, defends prostitution, ridicules traditional Christian morality, pleads for a separation of church and state, praises philo-progenitiveness, and elegantly but subtly advocates deism. In its use of the traditional Aristotelian artificial proofs (ethos, pathos, and logos), this speech stands with the rhetorical masterpieces of the eighteenth century—and is indebted to one of them, Swift's *Modest Proposal*.

The earliest of Franklin's extant bagatelles is "Old Mistresses Apologue," dated June 25, 1745, and better known under the descrip-

tive title "Reasons for Prefering an Old Mistress to a Young One."
Although several contemporary manuscript copies survive, this *jeu
d'esprit* was not popularly printed until the twentieth century. The
key reason for its extraordinary success is the amazing metamorphosis
in persona and tone: it begins with serious, almost stern advice being
given by an elderly, kind father figure, who changes (as the basic
proposition is given and the eight climactically ordered, relentless
reasons are methodically stated) to an exuberant, lecherous hedonist,
using a demonic, energetic tone, to a satyr who satiates and surfeits the
sexual desires of his partners, before subsiding in the concluding sentence back to the original persona and tone.

Other bagatelles include his letter against attacking religion, December 13, 1757; a mock petition to the House of Commons, April 1766, on
sending felons to America; the "Craven Street Gazette," September
22–26, 1770; and a great outpouring from his French period, begin-
ning with the "Model of a Letter of Recommendation," April 2, 1777.
The more famous ones are "The Flies" (propositioning Madame
Brillon); "The Elysian Fields" (proposing marriage—or at least an
affair—to Madame Helvetius); "Morals of Chess"; "The Whistle";
"Dialogue between Franklin and the Gout"; "The Handsome and the
Deformed Leg" (an archetypal story of the optimist and pessimist);
"On Wine" (burlesquing the teleological argument for the existence of
God); and the scurrilous "Letter to the Academy at Brussels" (better
known as "An Essay on Perfumes"). All of these—and others—are de-
lights, but none is more delightful than "The Ephemera."

Dated "Passy Sept. 20, 1778," "The Ephemera" begins as a letter
to a "dear Friend," recalling "that happy Day" spent "in the delightful
Garden and sweet Society of the Molin Joli."* The intimate and nostalgic recollection of past pleasures (with perhaps a suggestion of the
Edenic joys of the Garden, joys now lost) will be the dominant tone.
The second sentence indirectly introduces thoughts of death and the
brevity of life: "We had been shewn numberless Skeletons of a kind of
little Fly, called an Ephemere all whose successive Generations we
were told were bred and expired within the Day." Then Franklin
nudges the bagatelle into a childlike world of fancy, while spoofing his
own absorption in natural science: "You know I understand all the inferior Animal Tongues," and makes himself more human by mocking
his own poor French: "my too great Application to the Study of them
is the best Excuse I can give for the little Progress I have made in

---

* Quotations are from the text published by Gilbert Chinard, "Random Notes
on Two 'Bagatelles.'"

your charming Language." When he writes that a "living Company" of ephemera on a leaf were "in their national Vivacity" speaking "three or four together," he suggests that there are nations of ephemera as well as of men (thereby reinforcing the microcosm/macrocosm motif) and he lightly ridicules, while characterizing, the French. "I found, however, by some broken Expressions that I caught now & then, they were disputing warmly the Merit of two foreign Musicians, one a *Cousin,* the other a *Musketo;* in which Dispute they spent their time seemingly as regardless of the Shortness of Life, as if they had been Sure of living a Month." This sentence first clearly expresses the *tempus fugit* theme, and introduces a hint of pathos, while commenting on the vanity and shallowness of most human pursuits, including the current argument over the merits of Gluck and the German school of music versus Piccini and the Italian school (implicitly comparing them to the buzzing of two similar mosquitoes is a brilliant meiosis). The emphatic conclusion of the sentence brings home both the pathos of the shortness of life and the microcosm motif. In the remainder of the introduction to the soliloquy of the "old greyheaded" ephemera, Franklin compliments the French government, proclaims himself a devotee of the "heavenly Harmony" of Madame Brillon, and playfully calls attention to the diction by the polyptoton, *amus'd, amuse,* and *Amusements.*

The ephemera's soliloquy opens:

> It was, says he, the Opinion of learned Philosophers of our Race, who lived and flourished long before my time, that this vast World, the *Moulin Joli,* could not itself subsist more than 18 Hours; and I think there was some Foundation for that Opinion, since by the apparent Motion of the great Luminary that gives Life to all Nature, and which in my time has evidently declin'd considerably towards the Ocean at the End of our Earth, it must then finish its Course, be extinquish'd in the Waters that surround us, and leave the World in Cold and Darkness, necessarily producing universal Death and Destruction. (Chinard, p. 741)

Franklin emphasizes the macrocosm/microcosm theme by having the ephemera call the Moulin Joli, which is a small island in the river Seine, "this vast World," and by calling the river "the Ocean at the End of our Earth." The latter phrase, which suggests the ancient idea of a flat earth, is in keeping with the address to the Sun as god, for these are both characteristic beliefs of ancient men "who lived and flourished long before." The sentence says too that the universe we see reflects the limitations, the viewpoint, and the preconceptions of the observer and strongly suggests that a philosophy of relativism may be the most certain truth. Franklin mocks "the Opinion of learned Philosophers of our Race," especially those of the past, but he also implies that the present philosophers, including, of course, himself, will have their errors exposed in the future. And the sentence ridicules millenarianism.

After several brief sentences on his age and the passing generations (thus reminding the reader that time is relative), the ephemera plaintively asks "What now avails all my Toil and Labour in amassing Honey-Dew on this Leaf, which I cannot live to enjoy! What the political Struggles I have been engag'd in for the Good of my Compatriotes, Inhabitants of this Bush, or my philosophical Studies for the Benefit of our Race in general!" In comparing a bush to a nation, Franklin again employs the microcosm motif to stress relativism. The thought progresses from the selfish accumulation of wealth, to political services for the good of one's countrymen, to philosophical studies for the benefit of mankind—but none are of any help to a dying ephemera, for there is no absolute, no final system of value inherent in them. "For in Politics *what can Laws do without Morals.**" Franklin notes at the bottom of the page, "*Quid leges sine moribus. Hor." The classical reference, and especially calling the reader's attention to the fact that it is a classical allusion, affirms the cyclic, repetitive patterns of life, and indirectly argues that the "Opinion of learned Philosophers of our Race, who lived and flourished long before" are useful, at least in their art, and in their expression of the basic truths of human experiences. The ephemera continues: "our present Race of Ephemeres will in a Course of Minutes, become corrupt like those of other and older Bushes, and consequently as wretched." Here the primitivistic persona seems to reveal his American identity (his is a new country), as well as his pessimism concerning the future. The ephemera implies that nations, like individuals, go through a predetermined cycle. "And in Philosophy how small our Progress! Alas, *Art is long and Life is short!†*" Franklin footnotes "†Hippocrates," again stressing the present truth of ancient thoughts and experiences. "—My Friends would comfort me with the Idea of a Name they Say I shall leave behind me; and they tell me I have *lived long enough, to Nature and to Glory.#*" For the final time, Franklin notes the classical allusion "#Caesar." This progression represents the time-worn channel for thoughts of mortality (and possible immortality) to take. The persona logically, if nihilistically, continues "—But what will Fame be to an Ephemere who no longer exists? And what will become of all History in the 18th Hour, when the World itself, even the whole *Moulin Joli* shall come to its End, and be buried in universal Ruin?" In the return to the ephemera's opening thought, there is no longer any strong ridicule of the idea of millenarianism, which was a dominant element in the opening. Instead, the keynote is the fraility and limitations of man, who has been think-ing, feeling, fearing, and saying the same things at the thought of death since at least the flourishing of Greece and Rome. An under-current implies that man, because of the limitations of his viewpoint, cannot know the nature of death and that his ideas of it may be as fallacious as the notion that universal ruin will come with the sunset. At the same time, the sentence questions any doctrine of eschatology, for all of them but reflect the limitations of the observer. The con-cluding sentence of the soliloquy (and the bagatelle) abandons philo-sophical speculation and possible nihilistic thoughts to return to the "solid Pleasures" of reminiscence, social intercourse, flirtation, and art. "—To me, after all my eager Pursuits, no solid Pleasures now remain, but the Reflection of a long Life spent in meaning well, the sensible Conversation of a few good Lady-Ephemeres, and now and then a kind Smile and a Tune from the ever-amiable BRILLANTE."

The structure is deceptively simple: an introduction containing the setting and occasion, creating a special persona for Franklin, setting the tone, and suggesting the major themes; followed by the soliloquy, which stresses the cyclic structure, for we are reminded of the cycles of minutes and hours, of the life cycle of the ephemera (the speaker has "seen generations born, flourish, and expire"), and especially of the cycles of the sun. In the introduction, Franklin brought up, and stressed by its position, the word *month*. Units of cyclic (and relative) time are deliberately emphasized. Also, the reader is always conscious that Franklin is applying the fable to his own life and to the cycles of human life. The reference to "learned Philosophers . . . who lived and flourished long before my time," the classical allusions, and the intro-duction of the cyclical theory of the rise and fall of nations—all restate the cyclical theme. Moreover, the soliloquy in great part repeats and draws out the inferences and themes of the introduction, while the last sentence almost directly repeats Franklin's sentiments from the opening. Indeed, so strong is the tendency to view the concluding sen-tence as a return to Franklin's voice, that no present college text of "The Ephemera" prints it as part of the soliloquy, which it is.

The cyclic structure (including the two cycles of thought in the two paragraphs of the fable) subtly affirms the main theme: all life is cyclic process. The individual's participation in the process is an integral part of the whole, and possibly the individual will reappear in the cycle in the future. The structure; Franklin's persona (the friend of Madame Brillon, the lover of gardens and society, the scientist and

poor student of French, the lover of music) and that of the philos-
opher-ephemera; the reminiscent and intimate tone with its light
touch of pathos; the complexity of thought and intimation, but within
a logical and time-honored progression; the ordered syntax and simple,
yet connotative and precise diction—all make "The Ephemera" a brief
but glorious work of art. And this is what remains above relativism:
the thought of a "long Life spent in meaning well," the enjoyment of
friendships, playful flirtation, and art.

THE AUTOBIOGRAPHY

It is generally thought that the art of an autobiography arises from the
author's style, and from the selection, arrangement, and interpretation
of the facts of his life. In Franklin's case, it might be wise not to be too
certain of his facts. There is no question of the truthfulness of the major
historical facts recounted in the *Autobiography* or of the honesty of
Franklin concerning them. Nor is it of importance that he occasionally
misremembered some minor event of decades earlier, such as Sir Hans
Sloane hearing of his "aspestos" purse and coming to see Franklin,
rather than, what actually happened, his writing to Sloane about the
purse (although the slip may be said to show his vanity). There is,
however, good reason to believe that a number of passages, especially
in part I of the *Autobiography*, are deliberate fictions.

The book opens with a dateline and the salutation "Dear Son," as if
it were a letter. Of course it is no more a letter than Richardson's
Pamela is a real exchange of letters, and Franklin did not ever intend it
to be, for he immediately begins giving reasons (only two of the five
are true) for writing an autobiography. Another reason why we know
that it was not really meant to be a letter is that the audience, the
"Dear Son" for whom Franklin is supposedly writing the book, is not
his son, the successful mature man of 40 who had been the royal
governor of New Jersey for over eight years, but an adolescent or
young man, someone who may learn from Franklin's example how to
plan and conduct his own life. Besides, Franklin had three good
reasons for pretending that it was a letter. First, conduct books were
traditionally addressed to one's son, not because a number of them
were written to a son (though this was ostensibly so), but because this
made the assumptions of age and experience on the part of the writer,
and youth and inexperience on the part of the audience, more logical,
and made the roles of advisor and advised, of teacher and student,

and of father and son, more acceptable. The salutation also suggests that the book will be a conduct-book, thus preparing the reader for one aspect of its contents. Second, a familiar and intimate tone is thereby achieved, a tone suggesting that the writer and reader have shared experiences together (the reader is addressed as *you* and reminded of his travels with the writer) and implying that they love and respect one another. Third, the besetting literary sin of the genre of autobiography (a fault hilariously burlesqued by Pope, Swift, and the Scriblerians in the mock autobiography, *The Memoirs of P. P., Clerk of this Parish*, which Franklin must have read) was vanity. Franklin's modestly beginning his autobiography as a letter to his son was the first of many ways in which he grappled with this chief danger of the genre.

One of the literary building-blocks that comprises the *Autobiography* is that popular seventeenth- and eighteenth-century genre, the character. In his periodical essays, Franklin frequently used the character to illustrate a moral—and he did the same in the *Autobiography*. The most obvious character as a set piece is the portrayal of the croaker (who is even called by the generic name) Samuel Mickle, who continually warns that prices are falling, that the economy is getting worse, and that things are going to the dogs: "This Man continu'd to live in this decaying Place; and to declaim in the same Strain, refusing for many Years to buy a House, because all was going to Destruction, and at last I had the Pleasure of seeing him give five times as much for one as he might have bought it for when he first began his Croaking." Franklin's moral (as in his bagatelle "The Handsome and the Deformed Leg") is that pessimism is self-defeating and unpleasant, and that in business and in life one must persevere and act *as if* all were for the best. To make the point, Franklin deliberately misrepresented Samuel Mickle, who was a successful merchant and politician, and who frequently bought real estate.

The *Autobiography* is indebted to a major American genre of the seventeenth and eighteenth centuries, the promotion tract. By its frequent appearance in such seventeenth-century promotion tracts as John Hammond's *Leah and Rachel* (1658), the American Dream (by which I mean the rise of an individual from poverty and social impotence to a dominant position in his society) had become a characteristic American motif. In announcing in the first paragraph that he had "emerg'd from the Poverty and Obscurity in which I was born and bred, to a State of Affluence and some Degree of Reputation in the World," Franklin both borrowed from the promotion tracts and gave his own career as a testimony to the truth of the claims of promotion literature. He knew that America was already, because of the influence of promotion literature, regarded as a country where a man could become whatever he desired. America offered the possibility of metamorphosis, and America was possibility. The *Autobiography* is, among other things, a "life and times" biography, a history of eighteenth-century America, and Franklin's portrayal of himself as a representative example of the fulfillment of the American Dream and as the typical American is partially an effort to subsume himself into the history of America. The emphatic statements of faith in the individual, the belief that "one Man of tolerable Abilities may work great Changes, and accomplish great Affairs among Mankind, if he first forms a good Plan, and, cutting off all Amusements or other Employments that would divert his Attention, makes the Execution of that same Plan his sole Study and Business"—these are positions implicit in the philosophy of the promotion tracts and in their view of the meaning of America. To help make the point, Franklin gave a "character" of another man (Isaac Decow), who also fulfilled the American Dream: he "was a shrewd sagacious old Man, who told me that he began for himself when young by wheeling Clay for the Brick-makers, learnt to write after he was of Age, carry'd the Chain for Surveyors, who taught him Surveying, and he had now by his Industry acquir'd a good Estate" and had become surveyor general of New Jersey.

That the *Autobiography* is a success story and the model for success has obviously accounted for part of its popularity. But the rise from rags to riches (although Franklin had enough common-sense not to prefer rags to riches, he nevertheless scorned "the pursuit of wealth to no end") is not as important in the *Autobiography* as the rise from impotence to dominance, from dependence to independence. Although this rise is obviously true for the metamorphosis of the American colonies into the United States of America, it is even more applicable for the metamorphosis of every individual. Perhaps the enormous attraction of the idea of the American Dream in American literature may be partially explained by its archetypal recapitulation of the development of every individual. Because of the physical fact that all human beings go through a "progress" from infancy to maturity, and from nebulousness to identity, the idea of the American Dream has a certain archetypal and psychological reality, for in that development and growth from the infant's total dependence, we can all be said to conform to the basic pattern of the American Dream. It may even be that disenchantment with the traditional American Dream corresponds to learning the numerous qualifications on that (to the adolescent) seeming state of glorious adult independence. Ontogeny may not recapitulate phylogeny, but archetypally, ontogeny recapitulates both American history and the American Dream. At any rate, Franklin knew he exampled the American Dream as popularized by the promotion tracts, knew that other Americans also fulfilled this pattern, and probably believed that there were more opportunities in America than in other countries. And so the *Autobiography* was, among other things, promotional literature for America.

To fix the idea of the American Dream in the reader's mind, Franklin made his entrance into Philadelphia the dominant visual image in the book (and it is probably the most famous passage in all American literature): "I have been the more particular in this Description of my Journey, and shall be so of my first Entry into that City, that you may in your Mind compare such unlikely Beginnings with the Figure I have since made there." In a former essay I questioned the truthfulness of this account, pointing out that Franklin managed to escape from the psychological suspiciousness of his own personal testimony and secured another, supposedly impartial, witness to certify his poor, awkward, ridiculous appearance. Since I wrote that essay, Alfred Owen Aldridge has published an early memoir of Franklin that tells another version of his first entrance into Philadelphia. Because of its accuracy in other details, the 1778 account just published by Aldridge must be based upon Franklin's own testimony. But in this version, he began his career in Philadelphia when a "wealthy citizen" met him shortly after he attended church (where, in the memoir too, he fell asleep) and "made out an appointment for him in his own family." From this kindness, Franklin "progressively laid the foundation of his present exalted situation." This alternate account of his first experiences in Philadelphia illustrates one of Franklin's favorite themes, helping young persons start in life and in business. There is little doubt that he told the story, which supplies one more example (there are thousands in his various writings) of his willingness to create anecdotes, analogies, or characters to illustrate and prove whatever point he wanted to make. Some of the incidents and characters in the *Autobiography*, and parts of the description of his entrance into Philadelphia, are artful fiction.

Franklin adopts various personae in the *Autobiography*: at the opening he portrays himself as a fond, foolish, garrulous old man who loves to talk about himself and about the past and who is doing so informally, at random, without art or plan; when he tells of his return to his brother's printing shop in Boston, he portrays himself as an adolescent show-off dandy, with a "genteel new Suit from Head to foot, a Watch, and my Pockets lin'd with near Five Pounds Sterling," which he flashed about as if conducting a "Raree-Show"; when he

writes of his method for self-improvement, he portrays himself as a
naive, visionary believer in the possibility of man's attaining moral perfection—and as one who is surprised to find that he has so many faults;
and at other places he is a teacher-father-sage drawing morals and
sententia from anecdotes and characters. But these personae and many
others are all minor in comparison with Franklin's over-all interpretation and presentation of himself. His primary view of himself, the interpretation of his life and career that he set forth in the *Autobiography*,
presents the type of man whom he thought most deserving of fame.
The *amicus humani generis*, the friend of mankind, was the ideal man
whom Franklin praised throughout his life. In his earliest Philadelphia
essays, the Busy-Body series, he defined under the name Cato (who
was the greatest ancient example of the man of virtue) what he meant
by a man of virtue and concluded the "character" of Cato with a paragraph on fame. He argued that virtue is the surest path to fame, and
that men of the greatest fame are those who possessed the greatest
virtue (Franklin probably had Jesus in mind, as well as the gods of
Greece and Rome, who, according to one ancient concept, were originally men of surpassing virtue). He expressed these ideas numerous
times in his almanacs and attacked the most famous soldier-heroes,
such as Caesar and Alexander. He also maintained in his private correspondence with David Hume in 1760 and Samuel Mather in 1784
that the character of a "Doer of Good" had a "greater Value . . . than
. . . any other kind of Reputation." (One wonders if Franklin were deliberately challenging Hume when he advocated "the *Interest of Humanity*, or common Good of Mankind," for Hume had argued the more
popular opinion that legislators and founders of states most deserved
fame.) And in the character sketches in the *Autobiography*, Franklin
singled out for praise those men (lesser versions of himself) who embodied the ideal of the friend of mankind: Dr. John Fothergill, for
example, who "was among the best Men I have known, and a great
Promoter of useful Projects."

Perhaps Francis Bacon was the first person to argue that "inventors,
and authors of new arts or discoveries for the service of human life,"
men who used "the Divine gift of Reason to the use and benefit of
mankind," were more deserving of fame than the greatest "founders of
empires and commonwealths." By the eighteenth century, this was not
an uncommon opinion among intellectuals, and the literature of the
day often praised the man of virtue. This opinion was the basis for the
near deification of that trinity of eighteenth-century heroes, Bacon,
Locke, and Newton. Voltaire in the 1730s, Franklin in the 1740s, and
Jefferson at the end of the century thought them "the *three greatest*

men the world had ever produced" (Jefferson's words). Franklin wanted fame, defined the highest kind of fame when he was twenty-three, reaffirmed his belief that the man of virtue most deserved fame throughout his life, and presented himself as a man of virtue, the *amicus humani generis,* in the *Autobiography.*

BIBLIOGRAPHY

Editions

The Autobiography of Benjamin Franklin. Edited by Leonard W. Labaree et al. New Haven, Conn.: Yale University Press, 1964. [For some reservations regarding this text and the texts in the *Papers,* see my article listed below.]

Benjamin Franklin's Letters to the Press, 1758–1775. Edited by Verner W. Crane. Chapel Hill, N.C.: University of North Carolina Press, 1950.

The Papers of Benjamin Franklin. Edited by Leonard W. Labaree et al. 14 vols. to date. New Haven, Conn.,: Yale University Press, 1959–70.

Representative Selections. Edited by Chester E. Jorgenson and Frank Luther Mott. New York: Hill and Wang, 1962. [Excellent introduction and bibliography.]

The Writings of Benjamin Franklin. Edited by Albert Henry Smyth. 10 vols. New York: Macmillan, 1905–7.

Scholarship and Criticism

Adair, Douglass. "Fame and the Founding Fathers." In *Fame and the Founding Fathers,* edited by Edmund P. Willis. Bethlehem, Pa.: Moravian College, 1966.

Aldridge, Alfred Owen. *Benjamin Franklin and Nature's God.* Durham, N.C.: Duke University Press, 1967.

———. "The First Published Memoir of Benjamin Franklin." *William and Mary Quarterly,* 3d ser., 24 (1967): 624–28.

Amacher, Richard E. *Benjamin Franklin.* New York: Twayne, 1962.

Chinard, Gilbert. "Random Notes on Two 'Bagatelles.'" *Proceedings of the American Philosophical Society* 103 (1959): 727–60.

Granger, Bruce Ingham. *Benjamin Franklin: An American Man of Letters.* Ithaca, N.Y.: Cornell University Press, 1964.

Hall, Max. *Benjamin Franklin & Polly Baker.* Chapel Hill, N.C.: University of North Carolina Press, 1960.

Lemay, J. A. Leo. "Franklin and the *Autobiography:* An Essay on Recent Scholarship." *Eighteenth-Century Studies* 1 (1967–68): 185–211.

Simson, George. "Legal Sources for Franklin's 'Edict.'" *American Literature* 32 (1960–61): 152–57.

Van Doren, Carl. *Benjamin Franklin.* New York: Viking, 1938.

8

Philip Freneau

LEWIS LEARY

Philip Freneau remains inconspicuously with us, dutifully anthologized and unavoidably, though often casually, described in most
literary histories. He wrote much that was bad, hurried, or merely
useful, but he wrote also a few brief lyrics which in almost any
other country or any other situation would identify him as a poet.
The United States has not been consistently kind to its minor writers,
preferring those most massively visible who propose substantial surveys of man's confrontation with himself or nature or with demands
of a democratic society. Literary commentators among us have been
most likely to praise that which seemed to them most consistently
and substantially American: the new voice, new native insights,
comprehensive and prophetic, satisfying because suggestive of the
largeness and the newness which is America. Necessary, even inevitable, this view has shunted aside or dismissed many fine poets
who, responding to the requirements of their time, wrote more than
they should have written, hurriedly and in imitation even of themselves. The schoolroom poets of the nineteenth century have, we

Lewis Leary is William Rand Kenan, Jr., Professor of English at the University
of North Carolina, Chapel Hill, and formerly taught at Duke University and at
Columbia University, where he was chairman of the Department of English and
Comparative Literature. The author of a biography of Freneau, studies of Washington Irving, Mark Twain, Norman Douglas, and John Greenleaf Whittier, and
the editor of two volumes of Mark Twain's correspondence, he has recently completed a critical study of William Faulkner. He is Chairman of the Editorial Board
of the University of Wisconsin edition of *The Complete Works of Washington
Irving*.

   In the preparation of this chapter the author has been indebted to Charmain
Greene, and to William Andrews, Charles Bennett, Michael Collins, Carla Maz-
zina, and Donald Snook, who have re-read Freneau with him.

are accustomed to hear our friends say, had their portraits turned
to the wall, their gentility inappropriate to the commodious capacity
of a more modern world. But they are being found out now as
masters, not in many modes nor in largeness or consistent depth,
but in a few poems which time and a fresh look have rediscovered.
It is not necessary, I think, to ask how many poems a poet must
write, but whether among the mass of his work there are a dozen,
or even two, or one, which can continue to speak.

Only the most generous of readers will discover among the three
large, but incomplete, volumes of Freneau's collected verse more
than a handful to which he can respond with anything more than
patriotic or antiquarian pride. But Freneau's continuing presence
suggests that he too may be entitled to more courteous critical
attention than he has yet publicly received. Often overpraised for
what he intended or for his selfless devotion to democratic ideals,
and sometimes undervalued, often, I think, because he has been
overpraised, he has occupied a convenient place in literary history
as a somewhat stunted native talent, important to mention as attention passes from the engaging imagery of Edward Taylor to the
Wordsworthian echoes in Bryant and the deft, dark imaginings of
Poe. Harry Hayden Clark has explained in generous detail Freneau's
literary ancestry, his debt to the classics and to one or another of
the poets of eighteenth-century England, and Nelson Adkins has
explored Freneau's honest, though finally indecisive, fumblings toward explaining the "cosmic enigma" with which he was confronted.
Philip Marsh has been assiduous in the collection of Freneaueana.

But Freneau as a poet who sought to capture in words the fragile
substance of his vision has been overshadowed by attention, sometimes lingering sentimentally too long, on Freneau the patriotic poet
of the American Revolution, who laid waste his talent in defense
of political democracy or, more simply, in necessary defiant ridicule directed against people who, it seemed to him, opposed it.
His way with words and his honest anger and extraordinary talent
allowed him to overwhelm almost every opponent, but he was a
sensitive man who could not take as good as he gave, so that
his life was a series of public advances and private retreats. He
did not stand up well under the reciprocal abuse of partisan political controversy in which almost every contestant spoke with dev-
astatingly frank and sometimes scatalogical force.

I

Freneau first withdrew from public debate in 1775, when he was twenty-three, and not quite four years after he had been graduated from Nassau Hall at Princeton, with his hot-headed valedictory verses patched and expanded from a collegiate satire. He recalled his earlier literary ambitions and his one-time wish to leave America for Europe where "Poets may flourish, or, perhaps they may," but he expressed also his continuing conviction that the new world, its mountains, streams, and forests (all the "charms . . . that nature yields"), could together "conspire / To raise the poet's fancy and his fire." * Those last five words are worth pausing over, for fancy and fire became hallmarks of the young Freneau. At eighteen he had written of "The Power of Fancy" ("Ever let the fancy roam!"). Now he spoke of "the flame that in my bosom glows" as, "gall'd and slander'd," he stood alone against "foul-mouthed" opponents. "Sick of all feuds" ("wars of paper . . . wars of steel"), he would flee "the rude contest" and "to the sea with weary steps descend":

> In distant isles some happier scene I'll choose,
> And court in softer shades the unwilling Muse,
> . . . .
> Safe from the miscreants that my peace molest,
> Miscreants, with dullness and with rage opprest.
> (*Poems* [1786])

The lines rhymed, their meter was correct, but Freneau recognized these satires of 1775, which seemed to flow so easily on call, as "flighty lays," not in any sense the measure of a poet. At twenty-three, he looked confidently toward poems in "more exalted rhime, / By labour polish'd, and matur'd by time." Then during two years of retreat to the Caribbean, he continued to court the muse, but she continued to be mostly unwilling. He wrote laboriously of "The Beauties of Santa Cruz" (which I have elsewhere described

* There is no complete and textually correct edition of Freneau's poems. Fred Lewis Pattee's *Poems of Philip Freneau* is textually corrupt. Most of my quotations are taken from the periodicals in which the poems first appeared, since in that state they are most relevant to my comments. A more correct edition than Pattee's, but incomplete, is Harry Hayden Clark's *Poems of Freneau*. Unless otherwise indicated, the quotations made in this chapter may be found (sometimes in slightly different form) in one of these two sources.

as a museum piece of baroque landscape, the technique of the minia-
ture painter uneasily adapted to the gigantic canvas of the muralist),
with humorous good fun of "The Jamaica Funeral," and haltingly,
with occasional power, of "The House of Night." But soon he was
caught up in combat again, and the fire of anger was rekindled,
as during the next four years he produced his sharpest, most vit-
riolic satire. When in the early 1780s he became involved in in-
ternecine squabbles in Philadelphia, the heat of his often personal-
ized attacks drew returning fire from opponents less skilled and less
unrestrained than he, so that in 1784 he fled again to the sea and to
visions of poetry.

Much of the give and take of Freneau's wartime newspaper
quarreling can be followed in Fred Lewis Pattee's large edition of
the *Poems*. The virulence of the attacks against him, to which
Freneau finally responded by again simply withdrawing, can be
gauged by lines which Pattee in 1903 found "too vile to reproduce,"
and which may or may not record an actual but unsubstantiated,
unfortunate but unforgettable incident. After accusing Freneau of
"vile abuse, and low scurrility," an unidentified opponent in the
Independent Gazetteer of September 11, 1781, directed against
him, he said, weapons such as "you yourself have used" against
those "you've dirtily abused" by stating:

> CANNON, well pointed, may a coward hit,
> And leave him sprawling with his breeches sh—;
> Your mem'ry sure, some few years can review,
> What dire misfortune then attended you.
> A slave undaunted, laid his stripes so well,
> Your fears, how great, the consequence did tell;
> For as your hide the flagellation feels,
> The *yellow* filth came trickling to your heels.
> The people crouded, soon began to stare.
> The foremost cry'd,—Lord what a stink is there;
> It is not *Skunk*, another soon reply'd
> See how the cowskin penetrates his hide;
> At ev'ry stroke the vile *effluvia* flies,
> With stink the nose, with filth attends his eyes;
> While on the ground lay sprawling *this great wit*,
> And there we leave him, wallowing all besh—.

No wonder Freneau quit the contest in outrage, incapable, it
must be supposed, of a reply as scurrilously foul. But within more
decent limits, he was an effective satirist, as truculent and deft
as any of his generation. When he was recalled to public duty as

editor of the *National Gazette* in 1791, he resharpened old weapons
to wield them, with less recklessness, against new opponents. To
remember him, however, only as the poet of the American Revolution or—*mea culpa*—as "that rascal Freneau" is to do him injustice.
He deserves a modest but permanent place in any history of political satire in English: as a practical propagandist he knew the effec-
tiveness of the familiar in form or slogan, often adapting the manner
of other literary scolds—Horace, Pope, Churchill—so that readers
might have additional small pleasure in discovering echoes of old
favorites. As a useful, experienced veteran with a quick and willing
pen, he may indeed, as Jefferson once said, have saved the Constitu-
tion when it was galloping fast toward monarchy, but, if he did,
it was as a journalist skilled in his trade, not as a poet.

I shall say little of his writings in prose, which seem to me
workaday and somehow shoddy when examined beside the prose
of more articulate contemporaries. On public matters, Hamilton
did better, as did John Adams, James Madison, and many another;
Franklin achieved a manner of his own, homespun and plausibly
native, but Freneau's essays seldom conceal the patchwork of conventions from which they are drawn. His personae, often native in
name or residence, are clothed in tatters from transatlantic cousins
familiar to almost any reader of Addison or Goldsmith. Hezekiah
Salem does speak briefly in slapstick good humor, but he smirks
and mumbles like almost any clownish countryman from almost
any country. Priscilla Tripstreet or Christopher Clodhopper attract
more in name than in person.

The historian of what may be called the Americanization of the
essay will, however, find something instructive to say about an autoch-
thonal progression in Freneau's prose personae. Early in his newspaper career he speaks in the familiar, conventional character of a
learned hermit, a European transplant first designated as "The Pilgrim," then as "The Philosopher of the Forest"; later as the observant Creek Indian Tomo-Cheeki, native all right, but with literary relatives in France and England; and still later as the shrewd
countryman Robert Slender, whose observations on policy and custom
might have reserved for him a more respectworthy place among
native characters if he had spoken more plainly, in his own voice.
For whatever mask Freneau assumed in prose, the voice which
speaks from behind it seems to me monotonously the same and
does not carry well across the years. Some of his essays contain
passages which are usefully quotable, but I find none which in en-
tirety will stand alone, as praiseworthy rather than representative.

II

For I see Freneau as a poet, and as a poet caught between the
beckoning of his fancy and the fervor of his patriotic fire, a victim to both, neither of which he could often effectively control. He
wrote too much, too rapidly, and too long. Given a subject, he
was likely to take it in his teeth like a terrier, shaking it and worry-
ing it, then letting it drop, to slink away, neither quick nor conquered. Classic in form, his verses frequently lack classic restraint
and concision: more often than not they go on too long in round-
about repetitiveness, the focus shifting, backing away and then returning, not quite under control, inconsecutive but sometimes charming.

What certifies him as a poet is not his thought, which he shared
with many of his generation, nor his subjects, most of which were
those of almost any contemporary, but his occasional adroitness
with word or phrase, his brief insights which seem sometimes quite
aside from what he is talking about. Many of them seem to me almost Keatsian, like "Here drowsy bats enjoy a dull repose" or "So
glide ye streams in hollow chambers pent, / Forever wasting, yet
not ever spent." With Plato as persona, he can quietly advise that
"The little god within thy breast / Is weary of his mansion here."
Sometimes he packs a line with sounds which link to sense with
fearful impact as he describes the "grief in ecstasy of woe run
mad" in the chamber where death lies dying. At other times he
achieves an almost synesthetic quality in verses such as "Steep
me, steep me some poppies deep / In beechen bowl to bring on
sleep." Byron's translation a literary generation later of "Adrian's
Address to His Soul" is not more deftly musical than what Freneau
at twenty-two wrote into the margin of one of his volumes of Pope:

> Little pleasing wand'ring mind
> Guest companion soft and kind
> Now to what regions to do go
> All pale and stiff and naked too
> And jest no more as you were wont to do.

Many of these happier combinations of sound and sense appear
among his earliest poems, before his voice was coarsened by anger
or despair. And much that remains central to his thinking is found

in the early poems: life is short, death is certain, and of afterlife
no mortal mind can know. Thus at sixteen in "The History of the
Prophet Jonah" he could have Jehovah declare:

> Enjoy thy gifts while yet the seasons run
> True to their course and social with the sun;
> When to the dust my mandate bids thee fall,
> All these are lost, for death conceals them all—
> No more the sun illumes the sprightly day,
> The seasons vanish, and the stars decay:
> The trees, the flowers, no more thy sense delight,
> Death shades them all in ever-during night.

A year later in "The Pyramids of Egypt" he said much the same
again: those "piles of wonder" which were the pyramids "scorn
to bend beneath the weight of years," though the palaces and tem-
ples of Egyptian kings which once surrounded them

> all, all are gone,
> And like the phantom snows of a May morning,
> Left not a vestige to remember them!

Yet even these must vanish. Though the pride of art, they also
were erected to the pride of man as "the sleeping place of death."
Within their sturdy walls " 'Tis darkness all, with hateful silence
join'd." There "marble coffins vacant of their bones, / Shew where
the royal dead in ruin lay!" For death finally claims all, workman
and ruler, even art (this Freneau seems on the brink of saying
directly, but backs away as if in confusion), and even time which
is "but a viewless point / On the vast circle of eternity." And when
at eighteen Freneau gave himself over to "The Power of Fancy"
("Come, O come—perceiv'd by none, / You and I will walk alone"),
he asked himself,

> What is this *globe*, these *lands*, and *seas*,
> And *heat*, and *cold*, and *flowers*, and *trees*,
> And *life*, and *death*, and *beast*, and *man*,
> And *time*,—that with the sun began—
> But thoughts on reason's scale combin'd,
> Ideas of the Almighty mind.

The sources from which Freneau drew these familiar notions of
the awesome inevitability of death, the fleeting inconsequence of
man and of his creations, and the power of illusion are less important than the manner in which Freneau expressed them and
the mood of resignation to what man must endure mixed with

fitful visions of what man regenerated might become. The holding
of these two attitudes side by side was attempted in "The American
Village" and is perhaps the reason for the insertion of the tearful
tale of doomed Indian lovers into that celebration of possibilities
for excellence in a village undisturbed by the troubles which plagued
Goldsmith's degenerating Auburn. When Caffaro and Colma die, as
even lovers must, young Freneau dismisses them with wistful but
somewhat cynical agnosticism:

> FAREWELL, lamented pair, and whate'er state
> Now clasps you round, and sinks you deep in fate;
> Whether the fiery kingdom of the sun,
> Or the slow silent wave of Acheron,
> Or Christian's heaven, or planetary sphere,
> Or the third region of the cloudless air;
> Or if return'd to dread nihility,
> You'll still be happy, for you will not be.

Man's life on earth, or anywhere, is fleeting; his noblest monuments fall to ruin; time itself (that "viewless point / On the vast
circle of eternity") passes to dream existence ("Ideas of the Almighty mind"), recalled only by imperfect fancy; even death is not
immortal ("You'll . . . be happy, for you will not be"). Moving
into his twenties, Freneau attempted to share in words these elusive
certainties which had been filtered through his training in the classics,
his reading in the poets of England, and his apparently only partially directed studies in theology. They never settled to a formula,
as perhaps they never could, and as Freneau's conviction of the
elusiveness even of a poet's vision would not allow them to, but
they remained with him, providing an ambiance beyond which
his finer poetry seldom moved. As he attempted an ambitious ordering in "The House of Night," he warned:

> Poetic dreams are of a finer cast
> Than those which o'er the sober brain diffusid
> Are but a repetition . . . .

To understand its place in the story of Freneau's groping toward
expression, "The House of Night" must be read in the seventy-five
stanzas in which it first appeared in the *United States Magazine*
of August 1779. Though several seasonable stanzas may have been
added to it then, just prior to publication, this version of the poem
seems inevitably to be closer to that toward which a young Freneau
had groped two or three years before than are the 136 stanzas

into which it was expanded in the *Poems* of 1786, where it is more
rationally discursive, less subjective, and less revealing of personal
turmoil than when Freneau, ten years before, had cut his unwieldy
exploration short by exclaiming,

> Enough—when God and nature give the word
> I'll tempt the dusky shore and narrow sea:
> Content to die, just as it is decreed,
> At four score years, or now at twenty-three.

At twenty-three, rather than versifying an argument, Freneau created a nightmare vision which he did not have the skill to measure.
The elements are there: a lonely midnight ("Mist sate upon the
woods, and darkness rode, / In her black chariot, with a wild career"),
a "black ship travelling thro' the noisy gale," dim buildings seen
through darkness and surrounded by rank weeds and drooping
blossoms ("naught but unhappy plants or trees were seen; / The
yew, the willow, and the church-yard elm, / The cypress with its
melancholy green") and from these buildings the confused murmur
of voices ("Much did they talk of death, and much of life; / Of
coffins, shrouds, and horrors of the tomb"), and high above in a dim-
lit lonely chamber death lay dying ("Death, dreary death"). And dying death demanded life—"Some cordial potion or some pleasing
draught" as succor; yet he was tired also of his long continued,
quite too easy victory ("What glory can there be to vanquish those /
Who all beneath his strokes are sure to die"). With a final dramatic
gesture he

> Gave his last groans in horror and despair,
> "All hell demands me hence," he said, and threw
> The red lamp hissing thro' the midnight air.

Death's kinsmen ("Each horrid face a grizly mask conceal'd")
placed his body in a tomb, but as the poet stooped to write death's
epitaph, the light of morning came, revealing this "weary night" of
fearsome imagining to have been a dream. And as a dream, and
only a dream (though dreams "are perhaps forebodings of the
soul"), too much must not be made of it: "Stranger, whoe'er thou
art," the poet continues, "Say does thy fancy rove like mine; /
Transport thee o'er wide lands and wider seas?" "Perhaps," he said,
"in future years, / At awful distance you and I may roam." And he
seems to have explained something of what he meant when he
temporized four years later, "the rude irregularity of nature pleases
me more than the completed strokes of art." As Leslie Fiedler and

Arthur Zieger have suggested in *Brave New World,* "Freneau is finally too well-behaved and conventional to achieve full frenetic horror." But he does come close, closer than he ever would again, and as close as anyone would come for half a century.

For he never ventured so far again. These early verses reveal promise of a poet, but a poet fated never to roam at "awful distance." He was increasingly to find small relevance between what was and what should be. The world he saw was soiled by errors made by people who had gone before him. Freneau had visions of a better world, like that which had existed, perhaps in fancy only, before the cruelty and greed of man had despoiled its simple beauties. Young Freneau dreamed that in his new world there might be opportunities for riches other than of gold, for unconfused decency and individual self-reliance. Like young men everywhere, at almost any time, Freneau dreamed the good dream which subtle men call primitivist or Edenic, beyond the reach of men bewildered by progress.

Freneau did not share Joel Barlow's vision of a new world made rich by commerce and invention. Expansion of commerce, he explained in "The Rising of America," depended on the development of science. But science in turn depended on freedom for free men to work among free ideas:

> This is a land of ev'ry joyous sound
> Of liberty and life, sweet liberty!
> Without whose aid the noblest genius fails,
> And science irretrievably must die.

This "sweet haunt of peace" had been invaded by men of avarice who sought "New seas to vanquish, and new worlds to find" ("How few have sail'd in virtue's nobler plan, / How few with notions worthy of a man"). Thus at twenty in "Discovery," the most successfully compact of his early poems, Freneau affirms again the theme set forth in "The American Village," but addresses himself now to England as the miscreant who despoiled his dream, even usurping religion as a means of bending nations to her own belief:

> Ah, race to justice, truth, and honour blind,
> Are thy convictions to convert mankind—!
> . . . .
> If wealth, or war, or science bid thee roam,
> Ah, leave religion and thy laws at home,
> Leave the free native to enjoy his store,
> Nor teach destructive arts, unknown before.

III

The American Revolution allowed the young poet to focus his anger at an identifiable opponent, a nation, a force, a way of life which could be made responsible for corruption bred of mismanagement. An enemy had appeared, tangible and palpable, against which he could direct his cries of disillusionment and dissent, and reveal more plainly, without the subterfuge of poetry, his disappointing discovery of the basic irrelevance of things as they were. No longer need there be vague disquiet about mismanagement in general; a people was there to be confronted, an idea to be defended, not just talked about:

> When God from chaos gave this world to be,
> Man then he formed, and formed him to be free,
> In his own image stampt the favourite race—
> How darest thou, tyrant, the fair stamp efface!

And after he became a participant in the war and was captured and imprisoned, he vowed in "The British Prison-Ship," which has been called, though I think it is not, America's first successful long poem:

> Weak as I am, I'll try my strength to-day
> And my best arrows at these hell-hounds play,
> To future years the scene of death prolong,
> And hang them up to infamy in song.

What power his wartime verses have is the lyric power of anger or of vicious taunting as he swung with bludgeon or pierced with rapier. He became quotable because timely. His rhythms remained right, his rhymes simple, his arguments unswerving. The proper word was the effectively wrathful word, and there were few occasions for delicacy as statement subdued poetry.

Yet not always. He was to write joyfully "On the Memorable Victory Obtained by the Gallant John Paul Jones" and gleefully "On the Fall of General Earl Cornwallis," useful occasional presentations, workmanlike and appropriate. Among his battle pieces, however, only "To the Memory of the Brave Americans" survives as a poem complete, not only for such lines as

> 'Tis not the beauty of the morn
> That proves the evening shall be clear—

or the quatrain from which Walter Scott borrowed a line for *Marmion:*

> They saw their injur'd country's woes,
>   The flaming tower, the wasted field;
> They rushed to meet the insulting foe;
>   They took the spear—but left the shield,

but also for its consistent and restrained gravity in which grief balances pride as the valor of ragged Americans is told in lines which evoke classical memories. Freneau's fancy and his fire are here, and I think for the first time, effectively conjoined, producing a poem which for its time and purpose seems exactly right.

For even amid the din of party warfare in Philadelphia and the alarums of enemy activity both to north and south, poetry could fleetingly survive. During the early fall of 1781 Freneau inserted into the *Freeman's Journal,* wedged between verses of bitterness and calls for patriotic courage, a small and almost perfect poem, less distinctive in idea than in image. He called it then "A Moral Thought," though he changed the title later to "The Vanity of Existence," and it is one of the few of his writings which he did not putter over to alter for later printings. Beginning conventionally with a well-worn but well-phrased observation on what time can do to youthful vision, it calls to question, and suggests depths of unannounced meaning in, the apparently commonplace last two lines of the second stanza by the stark, controlled image with which the poem closes:

> In youth, gay scenes attract our eyes,
>   And not suspecting their decay
> Life's flowery fields before us rise,
>   Regardless of its winter day.
>
> But vain pursuits, and joys as vain,
>   Convince us life is but a dream,
> Death is to wake, to rise again
>   To that true state you best esteem.
>
> So nightly on some shallow tide,
>   Oft have I seen a splendid show;
> Reflected stars on either side,
>   And glittering moons were seen below.
>
> But when the tide had ebbed away,
>   The scene fantastic with it fled,
> A bank of mud around me lay,
>   And sea-weed on the river's bed.

But poetry was most often put aside for argument. A year later Freneau's anger and despair, never long submerged, rose again to the surface. "Curs'd be the day," he said,

> however bright it shined
> That first made kings the masters of mankind,
> And cursed the wretch who first with regal pride
> Their equal rights to equal men denied.

Freneau's critics were correct when they accused him of building a reputation on mere "newspaper verse." And Freneau recognized it for what it was: deft and timely, more polished than most, but metronymic in rhythm, repetitive in thought. Like Whittier and many another, he offered what he could of his talent in defence of what he thought, at that time and for that time, to be most important. But he seems to have been often distraught, uncertain, anxious about the vanishing of his vision: "Thou happiness! still sought but never found, / We, in a circle, chace thy shadow round."

IV

When the Revolution was over, he got away, again to the lush quiet of the West Indies and a life at sea. Was it escape from turmoil, escape to poetry, or, as Roy Harvey Pearce has suggested, a withdrawal like that of Melville's Bartleby: "I prefer not to"? Not long before in "Advice to Authors," which internal evidence suggests was another valedictory to political skirmishing, he had advised: "graft your authorship on some other calling. . . . Poets are . . . at present considered as the dregs of the community . . . lampooning each other for the amusement of the illiberal vulgar." It is, he said, "far more honourable to be a good bricklayer or a skilful weaver than an indifferent poet." And then, like Bartleby: "If fortune seems absolutely determined to starve you, . . . retire to some uninhabited island, or desert, and there, at your leisure end your life with decency."

What he wrote during the six years before 1790, during most of which time he guided coastal vessels between New York and Charleston, dropping off verse for instant publication at either port, was lighter and brighter than much that he had done before and tinged with good humor as he caricatured "The Newsmonger," "The Drunken Soldier," "The Roguish Shoemaker," and other native types chosen from among the strange but simple people who in a democracy might be supposed to have an increasingly important voice. The genre was familiar—the kind of character sketch with which Freneau would have been familiar, if not in Theophrastus, in almost any of the eighteenth-century essayists in England or America, the kind of sketch which in prose Irving, and after him Dickens and Bret Harte, would make popular. Nor was Freneau the first among his countrymen in comic caricature. Franklin, for one, had preceded him in prose, and John Trumbull in verse. But during this period Freneau did it consistently well, and as a result knew brief popularity greater than he had known before or would know again. Verses of this order were reprinted in newspapers from Boston to Savannah, bringing him affectionate renown as Captain Sinbat or Sinbat the Sailor, unpretentious, good-natured, and utterly nonpolitical.

These homely verses represented not a new departure, only a new emphasis. Even as a very young man, Freneau had an eye, if not an ear, for winsome human frailties. "The Expedition of Timothy Tauris, Astrologer," which is said to have been first printed in New York in 1775, recounts in a long, and finally tedious, burlesque narrative what seems to have been a collegiate pilgrimage to the Falls of Passaic, where, the narrator said,

> I enjoyed a regale
> Of victuals three times every day, without fail:
> There was poultry, and pyes, and a dozen things more
> That the damnable college had never in store.

There he met and described in pliant anapests a whole cast of native characters: "Here were Nellies, and Nancies, and Netties, by dozens / With their neighbors, and nephews, and nieces, and cousins." Among them was Mammon the merchant; Japhet the Jew; Slyboots the Quaker; Dullman the broker; Samuel the deacon; Nimrod the soldier, who attracted all girls; Dr. Sangrado, who "was vexed to the soul / To see so much health in this horrible hole"; a tedious lawyer named Ludwig; a belle named Miss Kitty, who has sometimes been thought to have been drawn from life; a boisterous farmer, Milhollan, who every morning "tippled three glasses of gin / With as many, at least, of three devils within"; and Pedro the Parson who "talked of his wine, and he talked of his beer, / And he talked of his texts, that were not very clear; / And many suggested he talked very queer."

The "Expedition" is jaunty good fun, buoyantly inconsequential.

Like John Trumbull's earlier "The Progress of Dullness" and Fitz-Greene Halleck's later "Fanny," it is crammed with local reference and private joking which in a more quiet time might have gained it mild applause. Freneau was fond of that kind of verse, deftly colloquial and broadly humorous, with some flick of satire in it. He was to venture it again, with more feeling, in "The New-England Sabbath-Day Chase," which poked fun at that natural enemy of any man from the middle states, through Irving and Cooper to Harold Frederic—the dour but self-filled man from Connecticut, which produced, Freneau said elsewhere, the largest pumpkins and poems and families of any state in the union. He used the humorous travel motif again in 1787 in "A Journey from Philadelphia to New York," written in the person of Robert Slender, stocking weaver. "The style," said an advertisement in the *Freeman's Journal* of 25 April 1787, "is smooth and easy, and the pleasurable air that is diffused over the whole piece will certainly render the whole poem acceptable to such as choose to read it."

Evidence does not exist that many, then or now, have chosen to read this, which Freneau later called "A Laughable Poem," to test its acceptability. In lines of lilting whimsey Freneau touched again on his distaste for city life, even in Philadelphia, that "gravest of towns on the face of the earth; / Where saints of all orders their freedom may claim, / And poets, and painters, and girls of the game":

> Our citizens think, when they sit themselves down
> In the gardens that grow on the skirts of the town,
> They think they have got in some rural retreat,
> Where nymphs of the grove, and the singing birds meet
> When only a fence shuts them out from the street;
> With the smoke of the city beclouding their eyes
> They sit in their boxes, and look very wise
> Take a sip of bad punch, or a glass of sour wine;
> Conceiting their pleasures are equal to mine.

With Robert Slender traveled William Snip, a merchant taylor, and Susanna Snipinda, his frivolous wife; bold Captain O'Keefe, a "killer of man and a lover of beef"; Touppee, a simpering French hairdresser; Billy O'Bluster, a seaman, who was "always in taverns, or always in love"; Ezekiel, a pettifogger from New England; and, not least, poor Bob, a young poet, who "Had sung for the great and rhym'd for the small, / But scarcely a shilling had got by them all." The journey to Burlington by boat was stormy, but "we

stowed away snug, / Some link'd with a lady, and some with a
jug." Proceeding then overland to Perth Amboy, the travellers' stage
tumbled off the road, was raised, and repaired, and the journey
continued, the travellers bruised and quarrelsome. A final leg was
again made by boat, and after further misadventures and much facile
rhyming the party arrived at New York as fatigued as the reader
who has followed them. Late in life, Freneau tried the long humorous
poem again in "Elijah, the New England Emigrant," in which Deacon Hezekiah Salem of that state of large pumpkins and families attempts to explain to his son-in-law the disadvantages of setting
out for western territories, telling him that

> A farm on *Alabama's* streams
> Might do in JOEL BARLOW's dreams . . .
> Such rhyming dealers in romance
> See Nature only in a trance.*

But Freneau was not good at narrative. He had a flair for
character, but not for character in action. In "The Pictures of Columbus," written, he said, in 1774, but not published until fourteen
years later (predated then, I have thought, in order to establish
precedence over Barlow's *The Vision of Columbus* [1787]), he reached
more closely toward success with a variety of meter in what may
be considered a closet-drama on his familiar theme of the new
world, once filled with "sweet sylvan scenes of innocence and ease,"
but now despoiled by greed and cruelty. The most lively of the
eighteen "Pictures," however, are not those which develop the
argument, but those which present characters in dialogue: the "Dis-
contents at Sea" and the exchange between an irascible couple
named Thomas and Susan in "A Sailor's Hut, Near the Shore" (which
was later to be presented separately as "An Irish-Town Dialogue")
in which the husband complains:

> I wish I was over the water again!
> 'Tis a pity we cannot agree;
> When I try to be merry 'tis labour in vain,
> You always are scolding at me;

to which she replies:

> If I was a maid as I now am a wife
> With a sot and a brat to maintain,

* Quoted from the Lewis Leary edition of *The Last Poems of Philip Freneau.*

I think it would be the first care of my life,
To shun such a drunkard again.

V

Other verses which Freneau wrote in the later 1780s are personal,
even plaintive, as he told of hardships and storms at sea. The rhymes
which he turned out with quick facility would not do: "Poetic
dreams are of a finer caste." New poems on death or desolation
now began to appear: "The Dying Indian" ("Vigour, and youth,
and active days are past") and "The Seasons Moralized" ("Winter,
alas! shall spring restore, / But youth returns to man no more").
He mourned "The Vicissitude of Things" and in "The Poetaster" spoke
of the folly of writing poetry. In "Verses Made at Sea in a Heavy
Gale" he dolorously complained that ruin is the lot of all, and
he marred three fine lines of showing rather than telling with a
fourth line of quizzical lamentation:

> Now to their haunts the birds retreat,
> The squirrel seeks the hollow tree,
> Wolves in their shaded caverns meet,
> All, all are blest but wretched me.

For as he moved through his thirties, Freneau's fires of enthusiasm
did not burn brightly; his fancy was walled by despondency in
"The Vernal Ague":

> Where the pheasant roosts at night,
> Lonely, drowsy, out of sight.
> Where the evening breezes sigh
> Solitary, there stray I.
>
> Close along a shaded stream,
> Source of many a youthful dream,
> Where branchy cedars dim the day
> There I muse, and there I stray.
> . . . .
> Great guardian of our feeble kind!—
> Restoring Nature, lend thine aid!
> And o'er the features of the mind
> Renew those colours, that must fade.
>> When vernal suns forbear to roll.
>> And endless winter chills the soul.

Restoring nature did come briefly to his aid when early in the summer of 1786 he came upon the Azalea Viscosa (the white, the wild, or the swamp honeysuckle) in bloom along the river banks of South Carolina: the flower was also doomed, would have its little day, and die. Moving momentarily beyond himself to observation and contemplation, in muted tones he created in "The Wild Honeysuckle" the one polished, succinct lyric meditation on which much of his reputation has depended. None certainly in the new world had done better, in restrained power or delicacy. If not a great poem, it is an almost flawless evocation of mood, deepened perhaps from its earlier expressions by realization now of opportunities lost, Freneau's own brief flowering unrecognized and wasted. As in "A Moral Thought," he discovered what Emerson would explain as a spiritual truth gained through observation of a natural fact, and Freneau wrote of that now with a simplicity which poetry in English would wait a dozen years for Wordsworth to surpass. Placed beside Bryant's "To a Fringed Gentian" or even his better "The Yellow Violet," Freneau's lines read freshly clear, graced with wonder and some awe:

> Fair flower, that doth so comely grow,
> Hid in this dreary dark retreat,
> Untouch'd thy little blossoms blow,
> Unseen thy little branches meet;
> > No roving foot shall find thee here,
> > No busy hand provoke a tear.
>
> By Nature's self in white array'd,
> She bade thee shun the vulgar eye
> And planted here the guardian shade,
> And sent soft waters murmuring by—
> > Thus quietly thy summer goes,
> > Thy life reclining to repose.
>
> Smit with these charms that must decay,
> I grieve to see thy future doom—
> (They died—nor were those flowers less gay,
> The flowers that did in Eden bloom)
> > Unpitying frosts, and autumn's power
> > Shall leave no vestige of this flower!
>
> From morning suns and evening dews
> At first thy little being came—
> If nothing once—you nothing lose,
> For when you die you are the same—

The space between is but an hour
The empty image of a flower.*

His more popular verses continued to be such things as "The Virtue of Tobacco" ("Unhappy those, whom choice or fate / Inclines to prize this bitter weed; / Perpetual source of female hate; / On which no beast but man will feed"), "The Dish of Tea" ("Let some in beer place their delight / O'er bottled porter waste the night, / Or sip the rosy wine: / A dish of tea / More pleases me; / Yields softer joys, / Provokes less noise, / And breeds no bad design"), and "The Jug of Rum" ("Within these Prison-walls repose / The seeds of many a bloody nose"). These doggerel lines, light and lilting, were reprinted, imitated, and parodied more than any of his, or any other poet's, verses of the period. Freneau was less successful when serious in "May to April," in which May dolefully reports that "Month after month must find its doom," so that, when she is gone, then "Summer dances on her tomb," creating a decently grotesque image which does not quite compensate for the stumbling lines which precede it.

Of Freneau's three poems on the American Indian written during this period—"The Dying Indian," "The Indian Student, or Force of Nature," and "Lines Occasioned by a Visit to an Old Indian Burying Ground"—I find the first, though less often anthologized, most impressive, mainly, I think, because it contains fewer lines which seem to me might better have been omitted or amended. The second is too long; it contains too many shady banks and woody wilds and dewy lawns. By what seems to be common consent, the best lines are the last when, disappointed at what Harvard cannot teach him, "to the western springs, / (His gown discharged, his money spent, / His blanket tied with yellow strings,) / The shepherd of the forest went." But, in spite of the incomparable yellow strings and the nice periodicity of that final sentence, how commonplace it is, dramatic and with a final farewell flourish which is anticipatory perhaps of Huck's lighting out for the territory, but without matter to sustain it or shimmering of suggestion to hold it in a reader's memory.

* I have used the text of the first printing in the Charleston *Columbian Herald*, July 6, 1786. When Freneau reprinted the poem in *Miscellaneous Works* (1788), the second line was changed to "Hid in this silent dull retreat," the last line of the second stanza to "Thy days declining to repose," and the last line of the fourth stanza to "The mere idea of a flower." In *Poems* (1795) the final line becomes "The frail duration of a flower." The changes seem to me significant and with alterations made in others of his poems and in his prose invite someone to take on the difficult and lengthy task of preparing a complete and annotated text of Freneau's writings.

The "Indian Burying Ground," widely admired then and now, is greatly superior, its first two stanzas and its last two stanzas as movingly effective as any which Freneau wrote. But the space between seems to me labored, and inadequate in carrying out the transition from "the soul's eternal sleep" of the first stanza to the "shadows and delusions" to which "Reason's self shall bow the knee" in the last. Here again is evidence of Freneau's lifelong adherence to the kind of Platonism ("What is this *globe,* these *lands,* and *seas*" but "Ideas of the Almighty Mind"), which was to find surer voice in Emerson half a century later. But Freneau was a poet, not a thinker: "And long shall timorous fancy see / The painted chief, and painted spear." Even if somewhat rudely forced, his familiar musings on transience, on the soul's eternal sleep, on the power of art (the "imaged birds, and painted bowls") to simulate truth, and the power of fancy to recreate what reason cannot are here set forth again, more maturely, with better economy, and less as statement than as suggestion secured by imagery: "The hunter and the deer a shade."

More diffuse, more musical, "The Dying Indian," in attempting less, achieves more. Shalum (in later versions Tomo-Cheeki) speaks in dramatic monologue as he prepares for the long, lonely journey he must make "Without a partner, and without a guide." What echoes the poem contains of other poems by other poets are good echoes. Freneau here combines his questionings of futurity with his skill in establishing a character through what the character is allowed to say. The freer rhythms of his popular verse are now seriously engaged in expression of Freneau's central concern, expressed more lightly, with memorable economy: "What mischiefs on the dead attend!"

> On yonder lake I spread the sail no more!
> Vigour, and youth, and active days are past—
> Relentless demons urge me to that shore
> On whose black forests all the dead are cast:—
> Ye solemn train, prepare the funeral song,
> For I must go to shades below,
> Where all is strange and all is new;
> Companion to the airy throng!—
>   What solitary streams,
>   In dull and dreary dreams,
> All melancholy, must I rove along!

Freneau has freed himself here from easy conventions of rhythm which makes much of his verse seem quite too facilely adept. An atmosphere of sadness surrounds this poem, of resignation and courage also, and trust that

> Nature at last these ruins may repair,
> When fate's long dream is o'er, and she forgets to weep
> Some real world once more may be assigned,
> Some new-born mansion for the immortal mind!

A pastiche perhaps of what other men had often pondered, Freneau's long musings on evanescence are here most poignantly expressed, as foreboding dramatized rather than as allegation or protest.

As he left the sea, for marriage and, he hoped, retirement to his Monmouth countryside, Freneau spoke again of quiet and seclusion. His valedictory "Stanzas Written on the Hills of Neversink" is not often reported among his more pleasing poems, but it seems to me of its kind superior. A meditation on landscape not unsimilar to Richard Lewis's lines on Patapsco or Bryant's hymns to the American forest, it speaks with simple directness as Freneau, perhaps on one of his final voyages, approaches the New Jersey highlands:

> These heights, the pride of all the coast,
> What happy genius planned,
> Aspiring o'er the distant wave,
> That sinks the neighboring land:
> These hills for solitude design'd,
> This bold and broken shore—
> These haunts impervious to the wind,
> Tall oaks, that to the tempest bend,
> Half Druid, I adore.
> . . . .
> Proud heights! with pain so often seen,
> I quit your view no more;
> And see, unmov'd, the passing sail,
> Tenacious of the shore:—
> Let those, who pant for wealth or fame
> Pursue the wat'ry road;
> Let sleep and ease—blest days and nights,
> And health attend these favourite heights,
> Retirement's blest abode.

VI

But retirement remained illusive for almost fifteen years. Drawn once more to political wars until 1793, Freneau then lived uneasily for a few years in Monmouth as a country printer, rural newspaper editor, and almanac maker, until in 1797 he ventured again to New York to edit a periodical which he hoped would be strictly literary but which turned out to be political indeed. When that failed he returned to New Jersey to fulminate, mainly in prose, against people who did not approve of Thomas Jefferson. During the first years of the nineteenth century he was again at sea, until in his mid-fifties he finally returned to his New Jersey home, to live on inconspicuously for a   quarter of a century, remembered, when remembered at all, as a gaffer more contentious and bibulous than a man of his age should have been. Experience had taught him to view his country as "a *tasteless land*," unfriendly to poets: "The home-made *nobles* of our times, / . . . Hate the bard and spurn his rhymes." Follow Washington Irving's example, he counseled: "Lo! he has kissed a monarch's—hand" and found thereby success:

> Why pause?—like IRVING, haste away.
> To England your addresses pay;
> . . . .
> In England what you write and print,
> Republished here in shop, or stall,
> Will perfectly enchant us all. *

As for himself: "My little is enough for me, / Content with mediocrity." Whether Freneau had grounds for disenchantment can be argued by others, who may find him to have been poorly repaid for years of versatile agitation. What he wrote during the last decade of the eighteenth century seems not to have been unsuccessful in stirring people to action or anger, gaining for him reputation as an American Charles Churchill, a Juvenal in smallclothes, embodying, as Henry Wells has said, the genius of a robust society in a youthful and stirring land. Launched as he was on an ocean of news and special pleading and satire, he mainly had time only for lighter verse: he wrote with a workman's precise knowledge of "The Country Printer"; he gave rhymed "Advice to Ladies Not to Neglect the Dentist"; he chuckled over graffiti found in a tavern at Log-town in the pine barrens of North Carolina. His apparently unfinished long poem on "The Rising Empire" contains occasional amusing descriptions, like that of the sturdy and strong-ribbed Dutch maiden from Long Island, unmoved by idle passions or frail ideas of romantic love, who in seeking out a prospective husband "heeds not valour, learning, wit or birth, / Minds not the swain—but asks him what he's

* Quoted from the Lewis Leary edition of *The Last Poems of Philip Freneau.*

worth," and the poem pokes fun again at Connecticut where "Bards of huge frame in every hamlet rise" and rhymes "Come rattling down on Greenfield's reverend son." All these are done with learned facility, as by a repetitive village scold, saucy with quaint fancy, but with little fire.

What may survive from Freneau's activities during these important years when a new nation was establishing itself are smaller things apparently done in days of rural relaxation. The awkward care with which he revised and reworked the verses "On a Bee Drinking from a Glass of Water" and "On a Fly Fluttering around a Candle" suggests a decline in the spontaneity of his lyric power, but "To a Caty-Did," first printed in 1815, survives with gay abandon which recalls earlier evocations to the power of fancy. Avoiding the whimsical sentimentality of Joseph Rodman Drake's "The Culprit Fay," which Poe was to find distasteful, it moves with winsome inevitability toward what Harry Hayden Clark has identified as Freneau's "indwelling master-thought," his "pensiveness on the brevity . . . of life and the certainty of death." No apology is needed for reproducing so complete a poem complete. It brings together all that had been occasionally praiseworthy in Freneau as a poet: his competence in form, his attraction to native nature, his adroitness with word or phrase, his humor, and his mood of wonder and auspicious awe; it guarantees, if no other did, his title as poet.

> In a branch of willow hid
> Sings the evening Caty-did:
> From the lofty locust bough
> Feeding on a drop of dew,
> In her suit of green array'd
> Hear her singing in the shade
>   Caty-did, Caty-did, Caty-did!
>
> While upon a leaf you tread,
> Or repose your little head,
> On your sheet of shadows laid,
> All the day you nothing said:
> Half the night your cheery tongue
> Revell'd out its little song,
>   Nothing else but Caty-did.
>
> From your lodgings on the leaf
> Did you utter joy or grief—?
> Did you only mean to say,
> *I have had my summer's day,*
> *And am passing, soon, away*

To the grave of Caty-did:—
  Poor, unhappy Caty-did!

  But you would have uttered more
Had you known of nature's power—
From the world when you retreat,
And a leaf's your winding sheet,
Long before your spirit fled,
Who can tell but nature said,
Live again, my Caty-did!
  Live, and chatter, Caty-did.

  Tell me, what did Caty do?
Did she mean to trouble you?—
Why was Caty not forbid
To trouble little Caty-did?—
Wrong, indeed at you to fling,
Hurting no one while you sing
  Caty-did! Caty-did! Caty-did!

  Why continue to complain?
Caty tells me, she again
Will not give you plague or pain:—
Caty says you may be hid
Caty will not go to bed
While you sing us Caty-did.
  Caty-did! Caty-did! Caty-did!

  But, while singing, you forgot
To tell us what did Caty not:
Caty did not think of cold,
Flocks retiring to the fold,
Winter, with his wrinkles old,
Winter, that yourself foretold
  When you gave us Caty-did.

  Stay securely in your nest;
Caty now, will do her best,
All she can, to make you blest;
But, you want no human aid—
Nature when she form'd you, said,
"Independent you are made,
My dear little Caty-did:
Soon yourself must disappear
With the verdure of the year,"—
And to go, we know not where,
  With your song of Caty-did.

It sounds almost like a lullaby, doesn't it?—soothingly sung at bed-
time to someone who is very young and very sleepy, an early nineteenth-century Christopher Robin perhaps, or Freneau's young daughter Katey, who was in her teens when the poem appeared.

More serious but less impressive are Freneau's late musings on
"Belief and Unbelief," "On the Universality and Other Attributes of the
God of Nature," "On the Uniformity and Perfection of Nature," and
"On the Religion of Nature," which fumbles toward restatement of a
familiar conviction: "All, nature made, in reason's sight / Is order all,
and *all is right.*" Deism, pantheism, and stoic faith rub shoulders here
in decent workaday stanzas when in "Science Favourable to Virtue"
Freneau reminds himself again that "The mind, though perch'd on
eagle's wings, / With pain surmounts the scum of things." During the
War of 1812 he was again a patriot poet with verses on battles and
blockades and British depredations. Weary of war and man's in-
constancy, his plaint was gentler when in "The Brook in the Valley"
he found another analogue in nature:

> The world has wrangled half an age,
> And we again in war engage,
> While this sweet, sequester'd rill
> Murmurs through the valley still.
> . . . .
> Emblem thou of restless man;
> What a sketch of nature's plan!
> Now at peace, and now at war,
> Now you murmur, now you roar;
>
> Muddy now, and limpid next,
> Now with icy shackles vext—
> What a likeness here we find!
> What a picture of mankind!

VII

Too much must not be made of Freneau. As a talented man he
responded to the impulses of his time in the voice of his time,
borrowing whatever was found useful in content or form. He
argued in verse against the cutting down of trees in cities, against
the encroachment of commercial wharves; he pled the cause of the
Negro, the American Indian, the debtor, the drunkard, and the
abused army veteran; he championed Thomas Paine as well as

Thomas Jefferson; he joined deistic societies; and he welcomed the writings of Swedenborg and, though cautiously, the advent of unitarianism. Wavering between extremes of passionate involvement and classical restraint, he has been found to be a primitivist sturdily convinced of the values of sympathy and national self-reliance, a patriot endowed with idealistic fervor and generous compassion, a brooding man dogged by personal adversity but serenely stoical in rational acceptance of his world, a humorist whose touch was not always light, a satirist of wide range and sharp-toothed striking power, but above all a lyricist haunted by a sense of the evanescence of beauty and the vacantness of death. To the historical scholar he becomes a convenient and quotable gauge. The convergence in him of familiar ideas and modes of expression render him a useful exemplar of the liberal or humane or democratic or patriotic convictions of an important time. The student of literature recognizes him as a transitional figure, grounded securely in the past and reaching tentatively toward the rewakening of sensibility called romanticism. Read carefully he may be discovered to be a poet who wrote a single poem in a variety of forms.

If Freneau did have but one effective note, and it of sadness at the frail duration of mortality, he sometimes struck that note remarkably well. His legacy may be four poems, or five, or perhaps six: each must make his own count. He was not, I think, "the father of American poetry," for in a strict sense he had no descendants. Poets who came after him looked to other models, and usually from abroad, so that it can be doubted whether the direction of literature in the United States would be in any important respect different without him. But he was there, isolated by war and his own limitations, a victim to his fancy and his fire: "To write was my sad destiny, / The worst of trades, we all agree." As a voice of his time, he shares the fate of time, but as a person who approached a mystery with wonder and stoic resignation he can survive until that mystery is explained.

BIBLIOGRAPHY

Editions

The Last Poems of Philip Freneau. Edited by Lewis Leary. New Brunswick, N.J.: Rutgers University Press, 1945. Reprinted, Westport, Conn.: Greenwood Press, 1970.

Poems of Freneau. Edited by Harry Hayden Clark. New York: Harcourt, Brace, 1929. Reprinted, New York: Hafner, 1960.

Poems of Philip Freneau. Edited by Fred Lewis Pattee. 3 vols. Princeton, N.J.: Princeton University Press, 1902–7.

The Prose Works of Philip Freneau. Edited by Philip M. Marsh. New Brunswick, N.J.: Scarecrow Press, 1955.

Scholarship and Criticism

Adkins, Nelson F. *Philip Freneau and the Cosmic Enigma: The Religious and Philosophical Speculations of an American Poet.* New York: New York University Press, 1949.

Andrews, William. "Goldsmith and Freneau in 'The American Village.'" *Early American Literature* 5 (Fall, 1970): 14–23.

Clark, Harry Hayden. "The Literary Influences of Philip Freneau." *Studies in Philology* 22 (1925): 1–33.

———. "What Made Freneau the Father of American Poetry." *Studies in Philology* 26 (1929): 1–22.

Foreman, Samuel E. "The Political Activities of Philip Freneau." *Johns Hopkins University Studies in Historical and Political Science* 20 (September-October 1902): 9–103.

Leary, Lewis. *That Rascal Freneau: A Study in Literary Failure.* New Brunswick, N.J.: Rutgers University Press, 1941. Reprinted, New York: Octagon, 1964, 1971.

Marsh, Philip M. "Jefferson and Freneau." *American Scholar* 16 (1947): 201–10.

More, Paul Elmer. "Philip Freneau." *Nation* 85 (October 10, 1903): 320–23. Reprinted in *Shelbourne Essays.* 5th ser. New York: Putnam, 1908.

9

Charles Brockden Brown

DONALD A. RINGE

Born in Philadelphia in 1771 into a Quaker family which seems to have fostered his strong intellectual bent, Charles Brockden Brown was early attracted to a literary career. Though he read for the law after first receiving his basic education at the Friends' Latin School in his native city, he did not practice this profession, but turned instead to writing. He had already published a poem and a group of essays in 1789, and, reflecting the self-conscious nationalism of the time, he had planned to write epic poems on New World subjects: the discovery of America and the conquests of Mexico and Peru. But though Brown wrote a poem called "Devotion" in 1794 and began a "Philadelphia novel" as early as 1795, it was not until the closing years of the century that the bulk of his fiction was written. His first novel, "Sky-Walk," completed in 1797, was never published, but beginning with *Wieland* in 1798, his six completed novels appeared in short order. *Ormond*, the first part of *Arthur Mervyn*, and *Edgar Huntly* followed in 1799, the second part of *Arthur Mervyn* in 1800, and two weak novels, *Clara Howard* and *Jane Talbot*, in 1801. Thereafter, Brown devoted himself to political pamphleteering and magazine editing until his death from tuberculosis early in 1810.

The burst of creative energy that Brown experienced from 1798 to 1801 is not easy to account for. Harry R. Warfel, his best modern biographer, has suggested that Brown found in writing the therapy

Donald A. Ringe is professor of English at the University of Kentucky. He has also taught at Tulane University and the University of Michigan. His writings include books on James Fenimore Cooper and Charles Brockden Brown, and, in 1971, *The Pictorial Mode: Space and Time in the Art of Bryant, Irving, and Cooper.*

he needed to overcome the spells of melancholia that letters to his friends clearly indicate he suffered, and one can even point to a passage in the second part of *Arthur Mervyn* where Brown has his narrator state that the pen can serve just such a therapeutic purpose as Warfel's hypothesis would indicate that it did for him. Another scholar has suggested, however, that the writing of fiction served an intellectual purpose for the author. According to Warner Berthoff, Brown wrote his novels to test the ideas of his times by having his characters act them out in his books. Both of these theories have their attractions, and both, of course, may be true. In either event, the writing of fiction would seem to have served its purpose, for Brown's career as a novelist ended as abruptly as it began. Apparently Brown no longer needed to write at the breathless pace of the preceding three years. He had either made peace with himself or had arrived at an intellectual position that no longer demanded the testing of ideas.

That Brown was always intellectually curious cannot be doubted. He came from a home where current books were read, even such advanced ones as William Godwin's *Enquiry Concerning Political Justice* (1793), Mary Wollstonecraft's *Historical and Moral View of the French Revolution* (1794), and Robert Bage's *Man As He Is* (1792), extracts from which were copied into his father's journal. From the evidence of his novels, moreover, we may deduce that Brown's reading was wide. Both Shakespeare and Milton are mentioned, echoed, or quoted in a number of his novels, and Cicero, Warfel informs us, was his "favorite Roman author." But if Brown was well versed in some of the classical writers, he was also conversant with what was going on in his own day. In a footnote to *Wieland,* for example, he cites Erasmus Darwin's *Zoonomia* (1794–96), and both *Arthur Mervyn* and *Jane Talbot* reveal his knowledge of and interest in Godwin's *Political Justice* and *Caleb Williams* (1794). Between these extremes of classic and contemporary, one also finds mention of such thinkers as Isaac Newton and David Hartley, who form part of Constantia Dudley's education in *Ormond*. Although no complete list can be made of Brown's reading, the evidence surely suggests that it was both wide and varied.

More important than the books themselves, however, are the ideas expressed in them. Brown's first published volume—parts I and II of *Alcuin,* a slender dialogue probably written in 1797— clearly reveals the radical thought that had influenced him up to this time, for the book defends the rights of women and suggests that they receive a sounder education and be granted political equality with men. The last two parts of this work, not published until they appeared in Dunlap's biography of Brown in 1815, are even more radical in the views they air and may even have been suppressed when the first two parts were published. They reveal the utopian schemes with which Brown was fascinated as a young man and raise at one point the question of divorce. Ideas similar to these appear in Brown's major fiction, but as his brief career as a novelist developed, the most radical views were placed in the mouths of his villains, and his final novel, *Jane Talbot*, presents the conversion of a Godwinian radical to religious faith, partly as a result of his love for the heroine of the book. Such a shifting of focus seems to imply that Brown changed his views considerably while he was writing his novels. It surely lends credence to the theory that the books themselves were the testing grounds for his ideas.

Other, more basic contemporary views are also explored in his fiction. The whole of *Wieland*, for example, turns on the problem of the conflict of appearance and reality, and questions thereby the validity of sense impressions as a reliable basis for knowledge. Most of the major characters—the rationalist Pleyel as well as the mad Wieland—are unable to penetrate the appearance of things to the truth that lies behind them. In relying on sensory evidence they invariably fall into error, a clear indication that Brown is seriously questioning the sensationalist psychology of his times. Villains like Ludloe and Ormond espouse contemporary rationalist views, project utopian societies similar to that of the Illuminati, and cause nothing but grief for those with whom they come in contact. Others, less selfish and egotistical, espouse the benevolist position and act in accordance with their own estimate of the good they may do for others. But Edgar Huntly, who assumes this position, causes serious trouble for his benefactor when he makes benevolist principles the basis for his actions. In novel after novel, contemporary ideas are taken up, tested in terms of the characters and action of the romance, and carried to a conclusion that most often suggests the need for rejecting the principle as a satisfactory guide to life.

Charles Brockden Brown may be called, therefore, a novelist of ideas, for all of his books reveal an intense intellectuality that must also have characterized the man. It is a mistake, however, to consider him closely akin to those novelists of ideas who flourished in England at the close of the eighteenth century. To a large extent, men like William Godwin, with whom Brown is often compared, were propagandists for their views, and David Lee Clark, a biographer of Brown, has made the mistake of assuming that Brown was the same.

Nothing could be further from the truth. Brown's mind was a questioning one that could not be satisfied with too simple a view of man and society. Rather, he saw the human being as a marvelously complex creature who does not always know the springs that motivate his actions, and he developed his characters in terms of symbols that reveal their inner states. For this reason, some modern critics read Brown in Freudian terms. There is no question, of course, that Brown, like Hawthorne and Melville, saw deeply into the human mind and penetrated to areas that he himself may not have fully understood. But rather than read a twentieth-century psychology back into Brown, it is better, perhaps, simply to explore what he did in terms of the fictional means he had at his disposal.

Brown, after all, is a novelist and must be judged not so much in terms of the views he holds as the literary means he employs to give them expression. As an American writing fiction at the close of the eighteenth century, he had available to him only a handful of fictional forms, and of these only three were at all suited to his artistic ends: the sentimental romance, the Gothic tale, and the novel of purpose. Brown wrote in all three forms, but in each he included some elements from the others in such a way as to make classification of his novels difficult. Thus, although *Wieland* may surely be called a Gothic romance because of the mysterious events and episodes of terror it contains, it can also be seen, as Fred Lewis Pattee suggests in the introduction to his edition of *Wieland,* as a sentimental tale of seduction in the Richardson sense. If *Ormond* is in its basic structure just such a tale of seduction, it contains as well a number of Gothic incidents and strongly resembles too the novel of purpose. This is only to say, however, that Charles Brockden Brown was an individual artist who took the materials that came to him from the contemporary literary scene and shaped them to serve his own artistic ends.

Of the three basic fictional forms he used, the sentimental romance was surely the most popular in late eighteenth-century America. William Hill Brown's *The Power of Sympathy* (1789), Susanna Haswell Rowson's *Charlotte Temple* (1791), and Hannah Foster's *The Coquette* (1797) had all appeared before Brown published his novels. But if Brown's three books in the sentimental mode—*Ormond, Clara Howard,* and *Jane Talbot*—all contain elements that relate them closely to the type, in each Brown used the form for ends not usually associated with the sentimental romance. Both *Clara Howard* and *Jane Talbot* are epistolary novels couched at times in a highly inflated style; they exploit the emotionalism inherent in the plots they recount and turn upon the question of proper marriage for the heroine. Yet even these slight books develop, it can be argued, some of the intellectual interests and themes that concern Brown in his more important fiction. Be that as it may, these novels are of little significance in the Brown canon and cannot be treated here. *Ormond,* however, is a significant book that deserves more lengthy discussion.

Many elements in *Ormond* show its kinship to the sentimental romance. Ostensibly a true story told by a woman, Sophia Westwyn Courtland, it details the undeserved sufferings and the attempted seduction of a young lady, Constantia Dudley. Faced with a series of disasters—the ruin of her father's business, his poverty and subsequent blindness, and the yellow fever epidemic that reduces them almost to the level of starvation—the virtuous Constantia shows her fortitude by bearing her miseries with patience, supporting the family with her needle, and finding expedients to keep them alive when all seems hopeless. Saved by a middle-aged gentleman from attempted rape, she refuses his offer of marriage because she cannot wed where she does not love. Constantia is eventually befriended by Ormond, a rationalist villain who tries by argument to win her to his views. When he fails in this attempt, he eventually seeks her out on a dark night and tries to attack her. Constantia, who has a penknife with her, threatens to kill herself if he will not desist, but at the final moment, she strikes desperately and at random, pierces the heart of her assailant, and faints on the spot.

But if *Ormond,* in its basic outlines, closely conforms in both subject matter and plot to the conventions of the sentimental tale, there are other elements in the book which show that Brown is using the mode for a serious intellectual purpose. The character of Ormond, for example, is obviously designed to show the fallacies of the rationalist position. In seeking to further what seems to be a utopian scheme, Ormond permits himself to use whatever means are available to advance his plans. While appearing to be open and frank, he is actually a master of duplicity who is willing to sacrifice others to his own selfish desires. He can even justify murder if the person he kills stands in the way of his plans. In the character of Ormond, therefore, Brown is using the sentimental convention of the evil seducer to develop a more general theme than one might expect to find in this kind of fiction. His villain is not simply a sensualist, such as one encounters in Belcour in *Charlotte Temple,* but the kind of intellectual egoist who elevates his desires above those of others and, regardless of human considerations, tries to enforce his will on the world.

The character of Constantia, too, has more substance than that of a heroine like Charlotte Temple. Though only a girl of sixteen when the novel opens, Constantia soon becomes a mature and capable person, largely the result of the education provided for her by her father and the experience she acquires in learning to survive in the world. At a time when the education of women was largely limited to the "sensual and ornamental"—a smattering of music and painting, Italian and French—Constantia's father had

> sought to make her, not alluring and voluptuous, but eloquent and wise. He therefore limited her studies to Latin and English. Instead of familiarizing her with the amorous effusions of Petrarch and Racine, he made her thoroughly conversant with Tacitus and Milton. Instead of making her a practical musician or pencilist, he conducted her to the school of Newton and Hartley, unveiled to her the mathematical properties of light and sound, taught her, as a metaphysician and anatomist, the structure and power of the senses, and discussed with her the principles and progress of human society. (6 : 32*)

In the character of Constantia Dudley, Brown is developing a theme on the proper education of women.

To emphasize his point, Brown creates two other female characters who are sharply contrasted with his heroine. Helena Cleves, Ormond's mistress, is adept at music and dancing, and she has developed a voice that is melodious and clear. Because of these talents, one might suspect at first that Helena Cleves is a woman of ability, but although "her understanding bore no disadvantageous comparison with that of the majority of her sex," she is far below Constantia in innate ability and education. "Endowed with every feminine and fascinating quality," Helena is simply an object of sensual pleasure, utterly incapable of taking care of herself in any practical way. At the other extreme, however, is Martinette de Beauvais, who is revealed at the end of the novel as Ormond's sister. Though her education does not appear to be "widely different from that which Constantia had received," Martinette has played a violent role in the revolutionary movements of the time, even to the point of dressing like a man and engaging in battle. Though Constantia is at first attracted to Martinette and is much affected by the story of her life, she is eventually repulsed by the acts of bloodshed and violence that her friend has performed and justified in the name of liberty.

---

* Quotations from Brown in this essay are taken from the six-volume Kennikat edition of *Charles Brockden Brown's Novels*.

Constantia occupies a moderate position between these two characters and is obviously intended to illustrate not only the kind of education that an intelligent woman should receive, but also the kind of behavior—neither too dependent nor too free—that is appropriate to her in the world. Constantia, however, lacks one element in her education. She has not been trained in religion. Though her father is himself a religious man, he did not believe that religious truth could be taught the infantile mind. As a result, Constantia regards religion "with absolute indifference," and is therefore left unguarded in precisely that area where she is in deepest peril from Ormond, the subverting of her mind to his principles. Constantia's weakness is buttressed, however, by the timely arrival of her best friend, the narrator of the story. Sophia Courtland, whose knowledge and experience abroad enable her to penetrate the duplicity of Ormond, points out to Constantia the errors of the man and wins her consent to accompany her to Europe. He, in turn, recognizing the formidable opponent Sophia is, no longer attempts to argue with Constantia, but resorts to physical force. Even the narrator, then, serves an intellectual purpose in the story, for she provides the final support needed by Constantia to resist the arguments of Ormond. All the major characters function thematically in this novel to develop some serious ideas on the conflict of rationalism and religion and the proper education of women not usually found in the sentimental tale of seduction.

Another popular fictional mode as the eighteenth century drew to a close was the Gothic tale of terror, introduced by Horace Walpole in *The Castle of Otranto* (1764) and further developed in the novels of Ann Radcliffe, the most important of which were published during the 1790s. So popular were her books in America as well as in England that in his preface to *The Algerine Captive*, first published in 1797, Royall Tyler alludes to the dairy maid and hired man who amuse themselves into a state of terror with the accounts of hobgoblins and haunted houses to be found in her works. That Brown knew the novels of Ann Radcliffe before he wrote *Wieland* seems very likely. Indeed, Fred Lewis Pattee has observed a basic similarity between Brown's treatment of Carwin, a character in that book, and the description of her villain, Schedoni, in *The Italian* (1797). England, however, was not the only source of this fiction, and Harry R. Warfel has shown that translations of both Friedrich Schiller's *Der Geisterseher* and Cajetan Tschink's novel of the same name appeared in *The New York Weekly Magazine* between 1795 and 1797. The latter work indeed, under the

English title *The Victim of Magical Delusion,* may well be a primary
source for Brown's use of sensationalist psychology in *Wieland.*

As with the sentimental romance, however, Brown used the Gothic
tale for his own artistic ends. A vehicle for arousing naive feelings
of terror in the hands of its least sophisticated practitioners, it
became with Brown—as with a number of his American successors
—a means for projecting the psychological state of his characters.
Eschewing "puerile superstition and exploded manners, Gothic castles
and chimeras" as means for presenting his themes, Brown turned to
native materials—the isolated farm, the wilderness landscape, and
Indian warfare—for the basic elements on which two of his most
important books, *Wieland* and *Edgar Huntly,* are based. In developing these novels, however, he employed a number of devices,
Gothic in their effect, which are highly appropriate to his major
purpose of showing "some important branches of the moral con-
stitution of man." Images of dark enclosure, of height and declivity,
of intricate maze-like paths are present in both these volumes.
Though all may be taken literally as objective elements in the
setting of these books or read as vehicles for inducing Gothic feelings of terror, their intimate relation with the mental states of the
distraught narrators clearly suggests that they also function as pro-
jections of their minds.

That mazy, intricate paths are to be taken figuratively in these
books is suggested by the epigraph to the first edition of *Wieland,*
where the straightforward journey represents the path of virtue "and
mazy paths but lead to ill." Though the image is a trite one, it is
worthy of mention simply because the figure of the maze recurs
so constantly in Brown's books. In "The Memoirs of Carwin, the
Biloquist," a fragment that recounts the adventures of this character
before the action of *Wieland,* Carwin tells how he followed a circuitous road, became entangled in a maze, and followed a steep,
narrow path "overshadowed by rocks" on the day he discovered
his talent for ventriloquism. In a similar fashion, the elder Wieland,
in the opening chapter of the novel itself, spends his time in London
"pent up in a gloomy apartment, or traversing narrow and crowded
streets"—effective images of isolation and mental wandering—before
he chances upon the Albigensian book that turns his mind to the
strange beliefs that he soon acquires. Details like these, of course,
are only of minor significance in the books in which they appear,
and too much, it may be objected, is made of them when they are
analyzed in these terms.

Their significance becomes clear, however, when we turn to

Edgar Huntly, where the maze-like path is one of the major figures through which the mind of the protagonist is revealed. Indeed, whenever he goes on a journey, Huntly's progress is so closely related to his mental state as to suggest that it functions as the objective projection of his mind. The book has hardly begun when the first of these journeys occurs. While he is walking home to Solesbury one night, Huntly's mind begins to turn to the recent murder of his friend Waldegrave, who was found mortally wounded beneath an enormous elm tree. Though the road he has been traveling leads a different way, the mental process that Huntly has begun diverts his mind and his steps from their originally intended purpose. He knows his journey will be protracted by returning to the tree, where he has already searched for clues "a hundred times," but a strange compulsion leads him there once more. The way is "trackless and intricate," as indeed is his mental process, but he is thoroughly familiar with it, and he goes "with undeviating aim" to "the craggy and obscure path" that will lead him yet again to the scene of the murder.

From this point on, the attentive reader is aware that Huntly's mental and physical journeys are one. Beneath the elm tree he finds a strange person digging in the earth, a man eventually identified as Clithero Edny, a hired man at one of the houses in the vicinity. As the story develops, it becomes increasingly clear that Clithero is in some sense a double for Edgar Huntly. Both are sleepwalkers, both keep some important papers in an intricate box or cabinet, both hide the papers in strange places while walking in their sleep, and both, by their mental obsessions, cause serious trouble for Sarsefield and Mrs. Lorimer, people who have befriended them. It is not at all far-fetched, therefore, to see Clithero Edny as a part of Huntly's mind, one he obsessively seeks in his highly symbolic mental journeys. These journeys take them into a wilderness region, Norwalk, as Huntly attempts to penetrate, as he himself suggests, "into the recesses of [Clithero's] soul." Walking in his sleep, Clithero, whom Huntly suspects of Waldegrave's murder, leads his pursuer down "an obscure path" into a wood and makes "his way, seemingly at random, through a most perplexing undergrowth of bushes and briers." He perpetually changes direction, leads Huntly along a precipice, plunges into the deepest thickets, and eventually disappears into the mouth of a cavern. Into "the windings of the grotto," Huntly dares not follow him.

Edgar Huntly extricates himself from the wilderness by going forward in one direction in a straight line. But on a second night he pursues Clithero again, traversing another "maze, oblique, circuitous, upward and downward." He plunges after his double through "the darkest cavities" and up "the most difficult heights," surmounting obstacles which "in a different state of mind, and with a different object of pursuit," he would have feared to attempt. When he does finally confront Clithero in the daytime and reveals his suspicions that he is guilty of the death of Waldegrave, the two retreat into Norwalk to hear Clithero's story. "We lighted on a recess," Huntly observes, "to which my companion appeared to be familiar, and which had all the advantages of solitude, and was suitable to rest." Here Clithero tells the story of his past, especially the major incident of his life in which a strange mental process overpowered him, and, penetrating a maze of rooms, he almost killed his benefactress. He had justified the deed in his mind as an act of benevolence. By this murder, he thought, he would spare her the sorrow she must feel on learning that Clithero has in self-defense shot and killed her brother.

Deeply affected by Clithero's revelation, Edgar Huntly becomes much disturbed when Clithero disappears, for Huntly begins to fear that he may destroy himself. Once again he sets out in pursuit, following him into the physical and mental maze that is Norwalk. His description of the way is highly significant.

> A sort of continued vale, winding and abrupt, leads into the midst of this region and through it. This vale serves the purpose of a road. It is a tedious maze and perpetual declivity, and requires, from the passenger, a cautious and sure foot. Openings and ascents, occasionally present themselves on each side, which seem to promise you access to the interior region, but always terminate, sooner or later, in insuperable difficulties, at the verge of a precipice or the bottom of a steep. (4 : 92)

Working his way through these intricate passages, Huntly finds again the steep declivity that leads to the cavern, and although he fears that he might become "involved in a maze, and should be disabled from returning," he enters the cavern for the first time and eventually makes his way through its winding passages.

Huntly comes out of the cave by another entrance to find himself on a high hill whose sides are so steep as to make the summit inaccessible from below. A perpetual mist rises from the torrent that dashes at the foot of the cliffs, and Huntly is overawed by "the consciousness of absolute and utter loneliness" that he feels. He confronts his double on an opposite peak but is separated from him by a deep and gloomy abyss. Although he eventually cuts a tree to bridge the gulf, he does not retrieve the solitary Clithero, and he almost perishes himself when a storm destroys his bridge just after he has come back across it. Taken literally, the novel up to this point is a Gothic tale of mystery, developed in an American wilderness setting that is not very realistically drawn. But if we take the book symbolically, we may read this wilderness as a mental landscape. On the high and lonely peak, Huntly arrives at a part of his mind he has never reached before, one he must find by leaving his normal path and plunging after his second self through the tortured intricacies of a savage wilderness and the dark maze of the cave.

The remainder of the book amply confirms this interpretation. His mind deeply disturbed by the events of the recent past, Huntly begins to walk in his sleep and to behave in the same manner as Clithero. At the end of one of these sleeping journeys, he awakes in the cave, thoroughly disoriented, and unable to account for his presence there. His return to Solesbury is described in a series of images that suggest the intricate maze he must penetrate in order to return to sanity. Huntly performs deeds he would hardly be capable of under different circumstances, killing both a savage panther and five Indians, even though he has a strong aversion to bloodshed. He endures severe physical and mental hardship, including three symbolic deaths and rebirths, as he threads the maze that leads him home. At the end of this experience, Huntly believes that he has now acquired a knowledge of self he did not possess before, that enlightenment has at last burst upon him. He still retains, however, his interest in Clithero, and he clings to his belief that he can help him. His attempts to do so, however, lead to further disasters when the obviously mad Clithero attempts to kill Mrs. Lorimer, who loses the child she is carrying on hearing of Clithero's approach. Clithero, in turn, is drowned after his capture when he leaps from a boat on which he is being transported to a mental hospital.

Brown gives us no indication of what will happen to Huntly after Clithero's death. Aware at last that Clithero is indeed mad and himself relieved from the compulsive mental journey he has made throughout the book, Huntly is presumably brought back to sanity with the recognition of Clithero's madness and his death in the sea. But however we interpret the end, one thing is clear. Charles Brockden Brown has transformed the unsophisticated Gothic tale into a vehicle for expressing an important psychological theme.

By projecting the mental state of his protagonist into the external landscape, he has managed to maintain the suspense and terror one expects to find in the Gothic romance, but he is able at the same time to transcend the puerilities of the form. His theme is a serious one that engages the interest of the reader even today, and his method of developing it through the images of intricate mazes and dark enclosures is admirably suited to the presentation of the material.

The same may be said of *Wieland*. Though mazes are not so central to this novel as they are to *Edgar Huntly*, images of isolation and enclosure are of the greatest importance to the development of the theme. Consider the hill on which the elder Wieland builds his temple. With its steep, rugged sides "encumbered with dwarf cedars and stony asperities," it is the precise counterpart of the rugged peak to which Huntly penetrates by his trip through the cavern. Both are symbols of isolation, and both reveal much of the mind of the man who is found there. Huntly's peak is misty, chaotic, and wild, a fit image of his intellectual state. The elder Wieland's hill is narrow and severe. "Without seat, table, or ornament of any kind," it is a suitable emblem of the old man's personal belief—that he must avoid social worship and "retire into solitude" to pray alone. The temple, of course, undergoes a change after the father's death, for the son converts it into a place of social pleasure. By adding the bust of Cicero and the harpsichord, by singing, talking, reading, and even banqueting there, the younger Wielands reveal how far they seem to have been removed from the strange predilection of their father. Though it remains an image of isolation no less than it was before, the isolation is no longer that of the single individual, but rather that of the Wieland family from their neighbors, an isolation that is further reinforced by the position of the Wieland farm.

To a certain extent, too, the temple may be seen as an even more specific symbol of mind. Not only does it reveal the mental bent of its successive owners, but it is also there that they undergo the experiences that have so great an effect on the subsequent events of the story. The temple is the scene of the elder Wieland's bizarre end, a fate that is linked by some of the other characters to "the condition of his thoughts." The temple, too—or its near vicinity— is the place where the younger Wieland and Pleyel first hear the mysterious voice, that, although generated by Carwin, penetrates the minds of the characters and predisposes Wieland to hear the imaginary one that eventually commands him to murder his wife and children. The temple, of course, is not the major symbol in the book, any more than the Wieland men and Pleyel are the major characters. But it is the image that first introduces us to the idea that an isolated, enclosed space may be read as a mind symbol. Hence, it prepares us for the more important ones that are to ensue, the summerhouse and the dwelling of Clara Wieland, the central character in the book.

That the summerhouse serves as a symbol of Clara's mind is obvious enough. Isolated in a recess of a declivity in the river bank, it can be reached—like Huntly's cave—only by a "rugged and intricate" path. It is here, moreover, that Clara falls asleep and dreams the strange dream that her brother is beckoning her forward to a gulf that lies in her path, in which, if she continues, she will be destroyed. Prevented from falling in her dream by a voice crying "Hold! hold!" Clara awakes—like Huntly in his cave—thoroughly disoriented. Unable for the moment to distinguish between sleep and waking, she is not aware that the voice in her dream is objectively real, since it was generated by Carwin, nor does she recognize that the warning of her dream—that she should fear her brother—is to be heeded. The real and the mental worlds are so closely associated in this scene that Clara cannot distinguish between them. For the reader, however, the episode is a clear intimation that the summerhouse experience projects the state of Clara's mind.

An even more important symbol of mind, however, is to be found in Clara's dwelling. Like the temple and the summerhouse, it is separated from the main buildings of the farm, standing three quarters of a mile from her brother's house. It is here that she remains apart from company on a stormy day and indulges in mournful thoughts of her brother and his children, an anxiety that she cannot throw off and which fills her mind when she tries to sleep with "vivid but confused images." It is here, too, that she retires to give herself over to reflection when Pleyel fails to appear for the promised reading of a new German play. Yet if isolation and reflection are associated with Clara's dwelling, certain parts of her second-floor apartment are of particular importance as a symbol of mind. Adjoining her room is a closet that appears to represent an inner part of her mind. Since the window is small and the door opens only to her chamber, the closet is particularly private. Here she keeps her important books and papers under lock and key while she is away, and here, most significantly, she keeps her father's manuscript, which she treasures above all other books in her possession.

Like Wieland's and Pleyel's, moreover, Clara's mind is penetrated by the mysterious voices that Carwin generates in that chamber. On the first occurrence, Clara believes that they come from her closet, and she flees the room to faint on her brother's doorstep. This experience, however, and the one in the summerhouse cause her mind to associate a whole cluster of strange ideas, including the thought, revealed in her dream, that she must beware of Wieland. When she is at home alone on a subsequent night, all of these ideas come together at once in the sudden conviction she has that some evil thing is hiding in her closet. But instead of fleeing in terror as she had done before, she ignores a shriek of warning and turns to the closet to open it, even though she fears that Wieland lurks within and intends to kill her. Though the man in the closet turns out to be Carwin, Brown has projected some important information about the deep recesses of Clara's mind. Confused by the sensations she has received and amazed by the strange workings she has detected in her mind, the increasingly distraught Clara is prepared for a mental journey no less frightening than that of Edgar Huntly.

From this point on, Clara's room becomes increasingly associated with madness, and her removal from it with sanity. It is in her room that she finds the body of her murdered sister-in-law and confronts for the first time the now totally insane Wieland. Clara has resisted the idea that she has anything to fear from her brother, and, utterly misconstruing his mental state, she does not realize the danger she is in. Only the chance arrival of some people prevents her murder. At this moment, Clara's hold on sanity is very tenuous indeed, and when she learns of the death of the Wieland children and a serving girl, she becomes temporarily mad. Removed to the city by some friends and placed under her uncle's care, Clara has to be held under physical restraint. She gradually recovers, however, and eventually learns the truth: that her brother has murdered his family. Clara once more briefly relapses into madness, and, unwilling to accept the fact of her brother's guilt, she now blames Carwin for instigating the murders. Her uncle, in the meantime, has planned to take her to Europe, but before she goes, Clara resolves to return to her room to retrieve and destroy a manuscript she has left in her closet.

On the symbolic level, of course, such an act must be seen as a kind of introspection. Clara turns inward at this point and even contemplates suicide when she finds herself alone in the darkened chamber that had been her bedroom. Interrupted first by Carwin, who tries to explain what has really happened, and then by Wieland, who has escaped his captors to seek her life, Clara is forced to face up to the truth: that Carwin's imposture was rash, but essentially innocent, and that Wieland's diseased mind has induced him to imagine the voice that has prompted him to kill. Though she is saved from death by the agency of Carwin, the experience is too much for Clara, who retreats completely from the outside world. Neither force nor persuasion will lure her from the house. Her "soul," she writes, "prizes too dearly this little roof to endure to be bereaved of it," and nothing anyone can do will persuade her to leave. Her repugnance to do so "gave birth to ferociousness and frenzy when force was employed, and they were obliged to consent to [her] return." A prisoner of her own mind, Clara has withdrawn to its inner recesses, where no rational argument can reach her.

Clara remains some time in this state before an unusual circumstance at last frees her. "One night," she writes, "after some hours of restlessness and pain," she falls into a deep sleep, but her tranquillity does not last.

> My fancy became suddenly distempered, and my brain was turned into a theatre of uproar and confusion. It would not be easy to describe the wild and fantastical incongruities that pestered me. My uncle, Wieland, Pleyel, and Carwin were successively and momently discerned amidst the storm. Sometimes I was swallowed up by whirlpools, or caught up in the air by half-seen and gigantic forms, and thrown upon pointed rocks or cast among the billows. Sometimes gleams of light were shot into a dark abyss, on the verge of which I was standing, and enabled me to discover, for a moment, its enormous depth and hideous precipices. Anon, I was transported to some ridge of Etna, and made a terrified spectator of its fiery torrents and its pillars of smoke. (1 : 255)

The worlds of reality and dream merge in Clara's mind, as they had in the summerhouse, for even during this dream, she is conscious of her real situation. Her struggle is useless, however, until someone at her bedside wakens her, and she opens her eyes to find her house on fire. This incident marks the final turning point in Clara's career, for once her anguish of mind has been purged by the flames that destroy her dwelling, she recovers her health and travels with her uncle to Europe, where a new and happier life awaits her.

Like *Edgar Huntly*, then, *Wieland* describes the mental progress of its major character, a progress that Brown depicts through his skillful handling of the Gothic mode. The shadowy paths, gloomy recesses, and darkened enclosures that figure so largely as sources of external terror in the Gothic romance have been used by the American novelist to project most convincingly the psychological terrors that beset his protagonists. Each loses his hold on the world of objective reality and eventually becomes lost in the dark enclosure of his mind. Since each tells his own story, moreover, and is never fully conscious of his mental aberration, his psychological state is projected into the external world of the romance, where it assumes the symbolic value we have examined here. Brown's achievement in these novels, then, is a major one. It is one, moreover, that has had far-reaching consequences in the development of American fiction. Beyond him lie Poe and Hawthorne and Henry James, all of whom use the same Gothic devices in the development of their own psychological themes.

The third of the fictional forms that came to Brown from the contemporary literary scene—the novel of purpose—provided him with yet another model for his fiction, but one that he also used in a rather unusual way. As critic after critic has observed, William Godwin's *Caleb Williams* was the obvious source for *Arthur Mervyn*. The Falkland-Williams relation in Godwin's novel is closely paralleled by the Welbeck-Mervyn one in Brown's, and the problem of penetrating the appearance of things to the reality that lies behind them is an important one in both books. Yet *Arthur Mervyn* can hardly be called a novel of purpose in the same sense as Godwin's work. *Caleb Williams* was first entitled *Things As They Are*, and William Godwin had the obvious intent in his novel of making a significant commentary on the structure of English society at the close of the eighteenth century. No such fundamental purpose informs the American's book. To be sure, Brown includes some scenes that reveal the conditions to be found in contemporary American prisons, and he presents as well a memorable episode in his description of the plague in which the horrors of contemporary hospitals are vividly portrayed. Such incidents, however, are by no means so central to the meaning of the book as the prison scene in *Caleb Williams* and cannot be taken as illustrations of the book's major theme.

Indeed, even those aspects of *Arthur Mervyn* which can be read in terms of social purpose are developed with an ambiguity that is absent from Godwin's novel. One does not read far in *Arthur Mervyn* before he is aware that Brown is developing what seems to be an important contrast between countryside and city. As several critics have suggested, Arthur Mervyn can be seen as a prototype of the American innocent, departing "the Jeffersonian hinterland" of agrarian virtue to confront the evils of the city. On his first evening in Philadelphia, the innocent Arthur, fresh from the country, is deeply impressed by the lights on Market Street, and he feels as if he has been "transported to the hall 'pendent with many a row of starry lamps and blazing crescents fed by naphtha and asphaltos.'" These lines, slightly misquoted from Book I of *Paradise Lost* (lines 727–29), relate the scene to Pandemonium and suggest that the city itself is a kind of hell. Small wonder, then, that Arthur soon becomes the dupe of a prankster, loses most of his possessions on his first night in town, and quickly falls under the spell of Thomas Welbeck, whose fine external appearance conceals the villain that he actually is.

Arthur Mervyn, however, has ambivalent feelings about Philadelphia. Though he clearly recognizes the evils he has been led to expect in city life, he is very much taken with "the lofty edifices, the splendid furniture, and the copious accommodations of the rich,"—objects that excite his "admiration and . . . envy." He is willing to serve Welbeck without question in return for a job and a fine suit of clothes, and it is only when he is forced to leave the city, after Welbeck's flight and apparent suicide, that Arthur seriously reconsiders the advantages of rural life. He attaches himself to a Quaker family, the Hadwins, who own a farm many miles from the city, and he soon concludes that the rural scenes, so sharply contrasted with those he had recently left "were congenial with every dictate of [his] understanding and every sentiment that glowed in [his] heart." Thus, although Brown seems to be drawing the typical late eighteenth-century contrast between rural virtue and urban vice, the question is complicated by Arthur Mervyn's willingness to accept whatever environment will provide him with comfort and, as we soon come to suspect, with the means for material improvement. Since Mervyn is the narrator of his own story and shifts his views as his environment changes, the philosophic question raised in the book cannot be easily resolved.

The handling of point of view marks out precisely a major difference between Brown's and Godwin's novels. There is never a question in *Caleb Williams* of where Godwin stands on the social issues of his time. Though the tale is narrated by Williams himself, Godwin finds means to make his social doctrine apparent to the reader. This is not true of *Arthur Mervyn.* Unlike Caleb Williams, who is clearly a reliable narrator, Arthur Mervyn, who narrates most of the book, tells so ambiguous a story and acts so consistently in his own interest that we cannot be sure that a given statement on the value of rural or urban society is to be accepted as Brown's own view. Mervyn has hardly established himself on the Hadwin farm before he is deeply attracted to Eliza Hadwin and sees as the major obstacle to their love, not the religious differences between them, but the fact that the farm cannot support two families, if, on Hadwin's death, it should be divided between his daughters. When the deaths of Eliza's father and sister remove this economic problem, Mervyn again considers the prospect of marriage, recognizing quite frankly that his own self-interest recommends the idea.

Several things happen, however, to influence his decision. By the time of Hadwin's death, Mervyn has already made his second journey to town and has been befriended by Doctor Stevens. This man not only takes him into his house when he is sick with the yellow fever, but accepts without question his profession of innocence in his dealings with Welbeck, and even offers to teach him to become a doctor. With two opportunities open to him, Mervyn must now estimate for himself the relative value of each mode of life. Though he still prizes highly the many advantages farm life can give him, he thinks he can appreciate them more fully if he mixes first with the world and develops his mind before settling into a rural retreat. He determines, therefore, to suppress the tenderness he has felt for Eliza Hadwin. In a sense, however, the final decision is made for him. Eliza does not inherit the farm. Her uncle, Peter Hadwin, holds a mortgage on the property and takes possession of it. From this point on, Mervyn says nothing of the advantages of rural life, and it is only a question of time before he is no longer thinking seriously of Eliza as a potential wife. Instead, Mervyn moves to the city where he further improves his position by marrying a rich widow!

Thus, as the novel progresses, city and countryside are reversed as places of significant value. By the end of the book, the city no longer appears to be the seat of vice, and the final view we receive of the countryside is the picture of Peter Hadwin as Mervyn describes him. He is said to be a selfish and obdurate person, a man who curses and swears and makes his life a perpetual brawl— hardly the type one expects to find in the pastoral scene! To be sure, one may argue that the change in Mervyn's views is a reasonable one, that as he matures he comes to understand more clearly the relative advantages and limitations of both city and country.

Seen in this way, his final decision would then represent a considered opinion that might well be viewed as resolving the contrast that Brown has presented in the book. But since Arthur Mervyn has a personal interest in each of the episodes he recounts and stands to gain or lose by the way they turn out, his opinions are always suspect. Faced with a choice, he invariably decides in terms of personal profit. The point of view of the novel precludes, therefore, our reading the book in any simple terms.

Brown's purpose in *Arthur Mervyn* is something much more subtle than the propagandistic one in Godwin's *Caleb Williams*. Whatever Brown's original intent may have been in this book—and one of his letters clearly shows that he at first intended to write a simple tale of the rewards of virtue—he changed the course of the narrative while he was writing and created a hero who surpasses Caleb Williams in complexity of character. Indeed, one suspects that as Brown wrote, the possibilities of Mervyn's character became increasingly clear to him, and rather than force his story in the preconceived direction indicated by his letter, he allowed the protagonist to develop in ways he had himself not foreseen when he began to write. Yet there is no wrench in the story, no place where one can say that here the novel takes a new direction. The book proceeds smoothly and logically to arrive at a conclusion perfectly consistent with the development of Mervyn's character from the opening pages. The result is a fascinating novel whose purpose, as in most of Brown's major fiction, is fundamentally psychological.

The book is sharply focused on Mervyn's character throughout. Blessed with an innocent face and voluble tongue, Arthur Mervyn can smooth away whatever serious charges of moral laxity others may level against him. The story he tells is never shown to be true, nor are the charges against him disproved. Yet Arthur is able to win the support of influential men like Doctor Stevens who can benefit him in life. He survives whatever adversity afflicts him, and, indeed, even moves up in the world. He attaches himself to a series of men—Welbeck, Hadwin, and Doctor Stevens—each of whom can help him in one way or another, and he repeatedly sees the opportunity to improve himself through marriage—with Clemenza Lodi, whose social position seems superior to his, with Eliza Hadwin, and finally with Achsa Fielding, the rich Jewess he eventually marries. His career, however, cannot be described as deliberately self-seeking. All the professions of innocence and benevolence he makes could conceivably be true, and there is no evidence that Arthur Mervyn is a conscious sharper. Yet his only defense of even his most suspicious actions is his innocent appearance and plausible story in a book where a fine appearance (like Welbeck's) is shown to conceal a vicious character, and a plausible story (like Welbeck's tale of the counterfeit notes) is revealed as a lie.

What makes the book so fascinating, then, is the reader's inability to label Mervyn either opportunist or innocent. In a sense, the terms simply do not apply to him. Both tough and pliant, as he describes himself at one point, Mervyn is able to place all of his actions in the most favorable light and enjoys thereby a self-esteem that is perfectly invulnerable. Mervyn, however, seems totally unaware of what he is doing and probably does not understand his own motivations. He simply becomes what others want him to be, accepts their gifts as if he were conferring a benefit upon them, and acquires in the process the material wealth and position that elude the more consciously mercenary Welbeck. From this point of view, *Arthur Mervyn* may be seen as a prototype of the American success story, and the hero himself as an early example of, in Warner Berthoff's words in his introduction to the novel, a "native American moral type." Only in this frame of reference can *Arthur Mervyn* be called a novel of purpose, though the term may well be too strong to describe a tale, the most obvious purpose of which is not the social comment, but the subtle psychological development of its major character.

Arthur Mervyn is thus a truly remarkable achievement. In this book, Charles Brockden Brown has transformed the novel of purpose into a kind of fiction that cannot really be called by the same name. His success in *Arthur Mervyn*, however, is essentially no different from what he achieved in his other major novels. In all of them he managed to turn some rather limited contemporary forms to his own artistic ends and created in the process a body of fiction that still deserves to be read for its literary value. Not that his books are flawless. By any reasonable standards, one must object to the lapses in plotting and style so very apparent in even the best of his novels, and the twentieth-century reader unwilling to pass over these flaws in silence will find much to object to in his fiction. But to stress these faults unduly is to miss the historical and artistic importance of his four best books—novels that are significant for the fine characterizations that a number of them contain and for the truly skillful way that Brown could turn some unpromising literary forms into vehicles for expressing themes that can still engage the intelligent reader today.

Of least significance, perhaps, is Brown's use of the sentimental mode. Although all of his novels in this form have their points of interest, one doubts that Brown would survive as more than a literary curiosity if all we had from his pen were *Ormond, Clara Howard,* and *Jane Talbot.* Better, of course, was his use of the novel of purpose, for he took the form as he found it in *Caleb Williams,* developed the point of view with considerable subtlety, and created in *Arthur Mervyn* what is surely the most modern and most novelistic of his major works. His greatest success, however, was in the Gothic romance. Although this particular mode might seem to be among the least appropriate for developing themes arising out of the American experience, Brown turned this essentially limited form into a vehicle for significant art. That American writers from Poe to Faulkner have followed Brown's lead gives us some indication of what he achieved in *Wieland* and *Edgar Huntly.* For these two books alone, he would deserve an important place in the history of the American novel. With them, he established a kind of American fiction that some of our ablest writers have used with unquestioned success.

BIBLIOGRAPHY

Editions

Charles Brockden Brown's Novels. 6 vols. Philadelphia: McKay, 1887. Reprinted, Port Washington, N.Y.: Kennikat, 1963.

Scholarship and Criticism

Bernard, Kenneth. "Charles Brockden Brown and the Sublime." *The Personalist* 45 (1964): 235–49.
Berthoff, W. B. "Adventures of the Young Man: An Approach to Charles Brockden Brown." *American Quarterly* 9 (1957): 421–34.
————. "Introduction." *Arthur Mervyn; or Memoirs of the Year 1793,* by Charles Brockden Brown. New York: Holt, Rinehart and Winston, 1962.
————. " 'A Lesson on Concealment': Brockden Brown's Method in Fiction." *Philological Quarterly* 37 (1958): 45–57.
Brancaccio, Patrick. "Studied Ambiguities: *Arthur Mervyn* and the Problem of the Unreliable Narrator." *American Literature* 42 (1970): 18–27.
Clark, David Lee. *Charles Brockden Brown: Pioneer Voice of America.* Durham, N.C.: Duke University Press, 1952. [To be used with caution.]
Dunlap, William. *The Life of Charles Brockden Brown: together with*

Selections from the Rarest of His Printed Works, from His Original Letters, and from His Manuscripts Before Unpublished. Philadelphia: James P. Parke, 1815.

Kimball, Arthur. *Rational Fictions: A Study of Charles Brockden Brown.* McMinnville, Oreg.: Linfield Research Institute, 1968.

Pattee, Fred Lewis. "Introduction." *Wieland; or, the Transformation, together with Memoirs of Carwin, the Biloquist, a Fragment,* by Charles Brockden Brown. New York: Harcourt, Brace, 1926.

Ringe, Donald A. *Charles Brockden Brown.* New York: Twayne, 1966.

Warfel, Harry R. *Charles Brockden Brown: American Gothic Novelist.* Gainesville, Fla.: University of Florida Press, 1949. [The most reliable biography.]

Witherington, Paul. "Image and Idea in *Wieland* and *Edgar Huntly.*" *The Serif* 3 (1966): 19–26.

Ziff, Larzer. "A Reading of *Wieland.*" *PMLA* 77 (1962): 51–57.

Index